KU-024-728

Cambridge Studies in Biological and Evolutionary Anthropology

Series Editors

HUMAN ECOLOGY
C. G. Nicholas Mascie-Taylor, University of Cambridge
Michael A. Little, State University of New York, Binghamton
GENETICS
Kenneth M. Weiss, Pennsylvania State University
HUMAN EVOLUTION
Robert A. Foley, University of Cambridge
Nina G. Jablonski, California Academy of Science
PRIMATOLOGY
Karen B. Strier, University of Wisconsin, Madison

Consulting Editors
Emeritus Professor Derek F. Roberts
Emeritus Professor Gabriel W. Lasker

Cambridge Studies in Biological and Evolutionary Anthropology 26

Human paleobiology

Human Paleobiology provides a unifying framework for the study of human populations, both past and present, in a range of changing environments. It integrates evidence from studies of human adaptability, comparative primatology, and molecular genetics to document consistent measures of genetic distance between subspecies, species, and other taxonomic groupings. These findings support the interpretation of the biology of humans in terms of a smaller number of populations characterized by higher levels of genetic continuity than previously hypothesized. Using this as a basis, Robert Eckhardt goes on to analyze problems in human paleobiology including phenotypic differentiation, patterns of species range expansion and phyletic succession in terms of the patterns and processes still observable in extant populations. This book will be a challenging and stimulating read for students and researchers interested in human paleobiology or evolutionary anthropology.

ROBERT B. ECKHARDT is Professor of Developmental Genetics and Evolutionary Morphology in the Department of Kinesiology at the Pennsylvania State University. His previous books include *The Study of Human Evolution* (1979) and *Population Studies on Human Adaptation and Evolution in the Peruvian Andes*, with Terry W. Melton (1992).

Human paleobiology

ROBERT B. ECKHARDT

Pennsylvania State University

CAMBRIDGE
UNIVERSITY PRESS

PUBLISHED BY THE PRESS SYNDICATE OF THE UNIVERSITY OF CAMBRIDGE
The Pitt Building, Trumpington Street, Cambridge, United Kingdom

CAMBRIDGE UNIVERSITY PRESS
The Edinburgh Building, Cambridge CB2 2RU,UK
40 West 20th Street, New York, NY 10011–4211, USA
10 Stamford Road, Oakleigh, VIC 3166, Australia
Ruiz de Alarcón 13, 28014 Madrid, Spain
Dock Houe, The Waterfront, Cape Town 8001, South Africa
http://www.cambridge.org

First published 2000

Printed in the United Kingdom at the University Press, Cambridge

Typeset in Times 10/12.5pt [vn]

A catalogue record for this book is available from the British Library

ISBN 0 521 45160 4 hardback

OWEN GLENDOWER: I can call spirits from the vasty deep.

HOTSPUR [HENRY PERCY]: Why, so can I, or so can any man;
But will they come when you do call for them?

William Shakespeare, *King Henry IV*

Contents

Preface

The face of human evolutionary studies that outsiders most commonly see is a nomenclatural thicket pruned by recurrent extinctions. Hypothetical rounds of species succession are so characteristic of paleoanthropology that they often are echoed in novels that use the evolutionary past as settings. Thus William Golding's *The Inheritors* represents Neanderthals while they are being exterminated by anatomically modern humans, as do Jean Auel's *Clan of the Cave Bear* (plus its imaginative sequels) and Björn Kurtén's *Dance of the Tiger*. Works of this sort add a lot of local color and speculative detail to conceptions of phylogeny that date back over a century.

As a result of these works, professional and popular, many nonspecialists believe that the central activity in paleoanthropology consists of argumentation about how many species existed, how many of them lived simultaneously during various time periods, and which ones emerged as survivors while their contemporaries passed into the oblivion of extinction.

These recurrent disagreements make the field appear to be so forbiddingly complex that even scientists in closely allied specialties can feel overwhelmed. This comment is based on my own experience over a period of years with a respected colleague, Paul T. Baker, who now has retired from his position as Professor of Anthropology at the Pennsylvania State University. Paul's area of specialization is the biology of human adaptability. In this realm he has been recognized internationally with various honors, including the Huxley Memorial Medal of the Royal Anthropological Institute. This recognition came because he helped to provide insights into the mechanisms by which human populations have adapted to a variety of environmental challenges: desert heat; high altitude hypoxia; and rapid acculturation to new food sources and activity patterns.

During the 15 years that we were colleagues in the same Anthropology Department at Penn State, Paul and I had a continuing dialogue that was reopened by each new announcement of a fossil hominid discovery. In this recurrent collegial conversation he would take the position, as ever more discoveries of fossil hominids were made, that it was becoming increasingly difficult to make any sense of the overall course of human evolution. In this viewpoint, Paul is in respectable company. Regarding interpretation of the rapidly expanding hominid fossil record, it has been stressed by some workers, such as Ian Tattersall in *Evolutionary Biology at the Crossroads*, that with each new fossil the picture has tended to become more confused, or at least more complex, and phylogenies have regularly needed substantial readjustment to accommodate such new finds (Tattersall, 1989a: 140). A similar argument was made by Fleagle (1995). Even more recently, paleoanthropologists have been warned that with regard to a cranium discovered in 1989 at Sterkfontein (Stw 505): another new specimen . . . is about to wreak havoc on our view of hominid evolution (Falk 1998:1714).

As a scientist, my steadfast response to Paul Baker, as well as to others, has been that additional data points should make a pattern easier to discern, not harder – as long as a field has an adequate theoretical structure. Paul Baker had, in fact, taken a short but important step toward building such a structure in the Huxley Memorial Lecture that he delivered to the Royal Anthropological Institute in 1982. Published the following year in the *New Scientist*, that paper sketched in the inductive and deductive arguments for a fundamentally important concept: the need to establish connections between the biology of extant populations and their predecessors of the past.

This book builds on those ideas. It is not a beginning, because it relies heavily on important work by many other scientists who have carried out the studies on which I have drawn for examples and perspectives; nor is it an end, because I have provided only a modest introduction to the many ways in which studies on living populations can be used to provide a perspective for studies of those that lived before. Much more remains to be done.

Acknowledgments

An author's debt to a publisher, commonly large, is especially so here. Without Alan Crowden the task would not have been started, and without Tracey Sanderson it might never have been finished. Rita Owen ensured that what had been written also was readable. From conception, through constructively critical readings, to location of essential references, valuable assistance has been given by several editorial board members of the Cambridge Studies in Biological and Evolutionary Anthropology: Nina Jablonski, Robert Foley, Gabriel Lasker, and Derek Roberts.

The writing has been done in a setting that betters Joseph's dream recorded in Genesis: I am now enjoying the seventh good year after as many lean ones. For this a double dose of gratitude accrues to my valued colleague Gerry McClearn, former Dean of the College of Health and Human Development at the Pennsylvania State University – first, for bringing me into this congenial environment, and second, for recruiting my current Department Head, Karl Newell, who nurtues accomplishment by exceptional example.

Throughout I have endeavored to give credit for the concepts synthesized here, whether discussed critically or approvingly. In providing the necessary documentation I have been assisted by many librarians abroad and at home, particularly those in the Radcliffe Science Library at Oxford and the Life Sciences Library of the Pennsylvania State University. The graphs in Chapter 11 showing morphological continuity between Neanderthals and extant humans represent the work of my friend Bill Dean; all other figures were executed by Rick Sharbaugh. I thank Derek Pearsall for providing a context showing that the dismissive epithet 'sparse and fragmentary evidence' (Chapter 12) tells more about limitations of interpretation than of evidence.

Many researchers will find their work incorporated here. In particular, Roscoe Stanyon helped guide me through the current literature on genomic evolution, while his colleague Stephen O'Brien took time to vet my inferences about probable molecular relationships among past hominid populations. Among legions of others cited in the text, Dave Frayer, Phil Gingerich, Clifford Jolly, Maciej Henneberg and Alan Templeton merit special recognition; while appreciative of their contributions, I accept responsibility for the interpretations made.

I join Alan Fix (author of another book in this series) in acknowledging a profound intellectual debt to Frank Livingstone, who has long been a wellspring of ideas for so many of us.

Last, Carey, my wife and constant companion of 36 years, remains the one who makes all conceivable things not only possible, but worthwhile.

1 Paleobiology: present perspectives on the past

Paleobiology has been referred to variously as a science, a discipline, and a paradigm. These terms all sound rather dauntingly formal for what might be characterized more modestly as an attitude toward the past. Logically, paleobiology is a subdivision of paleontology, since it derives its most direct evidence from the fossil record. But although paleontological evidence is itself static, comprising fossilized skeletal parts and associated remains for the most part, the paleobiological approach to this evidence is dynamic. Paleobiologists endeavor to reconstruct credible impressions of past populations and their members as they were in life: feeding; mating; giving birth to offspring and caring for them; avoiding predators; and enduring vagaries of weather, parasites, and diseases. The author of one paleobiological study covering an extinct group of tetrapods commonly referred to as 'mammal-like reptiles' noted that her aim was 'to present the "hard facts" about dicynodonts and then go on to interpret these facts in physiological, behavioural and ecological terms . . .' thereby 'turning mere piles of bones into entities more approaching living animals' (King, 1990).

Reviewing King's work, Rowe (1991) remarked that paleobiology is no longer the central paradigm that it had been in the 1960s and 1970s; instead other issues, particularly the reconstruction of phylogenies and the related question of evolutionary rates, have replaced paleobiology at the forefront of paleontological research and debate. Perhaps. Nonetheless, paleontological monographs dealing with fossil hominid remains continue to appear (e.g. Trinkaus, 1983; Rightmire, 1990; Madre-Dupouy, 1992; Höpfel, Platzer & Spindler, 1998) and many of these include valuable data that are pertinent to paleobiological reconstructions (Tobias, 1967, 1991). Walker & Leakey (1993) edited a publication on the Nariokotome skeletal remains which combines descriptive morphology with functional biology, and explores the implications of these and other diverse types of evidence for resolving questions about phylogeny and evolutionary dynamics.

The Nariokotome monograph and others like it reinforce the belief that in the study of hominid evolution, the several perspectives noted by Rowe – paleobiology, phylogeny, and velocity of character change – operationally are all but inseparable. Each fossil displays features that can be observed, but moving from characteristics of specimens to parameters of populations requires knowledge about allometric changes with age, influences of climate, and nutrition on the development of body size and proportions, variations in population-specific patterns of sexual dimorphism, and the like. Reconstructions of hominid phenotypes should be based on as many specimens as possible; yet increasing the numbers of individuals included in a reference sample raises the possibility that the group might become heterogeneous, and include multiple taxa. Consequently, paleobiological and phylogenetic inferences also are intertwined. Furthermore, if stratigraphy cannot be strictly controlled, morphological differences among specimens might be due to change through time within a single evolving lineage (as well as to differences in age, sex, and other within-population influences), rather than to sampling from two contemporaneous taxa. Thus matters of phylogeny and evolutionary rate are also intertwined, not only with each other but also with interpretation of the basic paleobiological data.

These complications heighten the challenge encountered in addressing several interrelated issues of central importance in the study of human biology past and present, chiefly the extent, distribution, and causes of variation within and between populations. Because we are interested not only in living human populations but also their hominid ancestors who endured through successive lineages over hundreds of thousands of generations past, much of the variation discussed here will concern morphological features that continue to mark fossil bones and teeth thousands of years after death. Attention to skeletal anatomy is not an end in itself, however, but the means to a more challenging objective: reconstruction of earlier humans as living members of populations, adapted to particular ecological niches, as real in every respect as the various animal species that are our contemporaries, or as real as ourselves. In a similar vein, Larsen (1997:4) urged that 'We must seek to envision past populations as though they were alive today and then ask what information drawn from the study of skeletal tissues would provide understanding of them as functioning, living human beings and members of populations.'

The daunting nature of the task posed by reconstructing our ancestors and their ways of life through long stretches of the paleontological past was brought home to me recently as I was reading a minor classic of historical writing, William Seymour's (1975) *Battles in Britain*. In his Preface, Seymour noted that 'In the 700 years of military history covered by . . . this book there were many changes in weapons and tactics, but all the battles were fought by men like ourselves, who experienced the same emotions of fear, boredom, weariness, despair (and sometimes defiance) in defeat and exhilaration in victory, for basically the deep springs of human action have remained fairly constant down the ages.' By contrast, during the seven million or so years explored in later chapters here, the elements of material culture increased from twigs, stones, shards of bone, and other nearly indistinguishable bits of the natural environment to controlled use of fire, tools made from composite materials, clothing tailored from animal skins, and well-constructed dwellings. The artificers of these cultural revolutions were varied beings who must have experienced some of the same physiological and emotional states familiar to us – for after all, hunger, fear, sexual arousal, and parental solicitude are found among all mammals. Yet the earliest bipedal hominids whose remains are preserved in the fossil record appear so much more similar to chimpanzees than to extant humans that clues to their emotional states and behavioral patterns are far more likely to be found in works such as Fritz de Waal's *Chimpanzee Politics* than in William Shakespeare's *Macbeth*. Even within the last few hundred thousand years, which were peopled by the Neanderthal predecessors of anatomically modern humans, the weight of evidence suggests that some aspects of their behavior still remained very different from patterns that would seem familiar to us.

Although in some ways the skeletal and cultural remains of the hominid populations evolving through time increasingly resemble those of hunter–gatherers known from the historical present or very recent archeological past, such similarities often have led to confusion about causality. For example, we commonly encounter statements that earlier hominid populations were 'evolving in an increasingly human direction.' However unintentional, such formulations hint at the existence of some pre-ordained orthogenic trajectory that simply reveals itself over time. Yet orthogenesis, the idea that there is an intrinsic force in nature that leads evolutionary lines to increasing perfection, is in direct conflict with a view of the world in which order and pattern are believed to be provided by naturalistic processes, such as adaptation and natural selection, acting on genetically encoded information that exists in staggering amounts in every human genome and is augmented each generation.

Rather than orthogenesis, human evolution is marked by the interplay of stochastic and deterministic processes – metaphorically, by chance and necessity. These dual influences are detectable on at least three planes. First, at the genetic level that underlies all evolutionary phenomena, mutation can generate novel alleles at any locus or position in the genome, and processes such as recombination and independent assortment reshuffle in each generation genes from past inheritance as well as recent origin. In addition to the prodigious variation that can be generated by these long-known mechanisms alone, recent decades have seen the discovery of additional phenomena that operate more sporadically. Included here are duplications of partial or even entire genomes (Ohno, 1970; Li & Graur, 1991:137) and horizontal gene transfer, the incorporation of genetic information from one species into the genome of another via transposable elements (Benveniste, 1985; Li & Graur, 1991:198).

Second, at the population level, further factors come into play. Included here are additional stochastic elements such as random genetic drift, and more systematic influences such as gene flow among populations of a given species and natural selection. The deterministic nature of selection arises from the differential reproduction of genetically distinct genotypes in a population, arising from individual differences in longevity, fertility, mating success, the viability of offspring, and so on. Although they sometimes are treated in rather abstract terms, differences in fertility and mortality are shaped or determined by real-world interactions between organisms and their surroundings. In every generation, new ecological challenges and opportunities confront populations whose gene pools have been shaped by past interactions with the physical and biotic environment.

Third, at the level of human action and cognition, discoveries of new evidence (specimen AL 288–1, KNM-WT 15000) and new theories (particulate inheritance, natural selection) occur at points in history when they will be interpreted within a particular climate of thought. The combined result of these phenomena at all levels is a world in which directionality exists and is perceived to exist, without necessarily being foreordained.

Two ideas help to make sense, in a non-teleological framework, of the increasing hominization that we know, in retrospect, really did occur. These concepts might be termed ecological specificity and retrospective contingency.

Ecological specificity means, simply, that over the course of millennia earlier prehuman and human populations had their gene pools shaped by daily interaction with whatever environment was at hand, as their genetic and behavioral heritage from the past was constantly reshaped by the immediacy of the present. Members of previous hominid populations were not consciously or intentionally doing anything to evolve in an increasingly human direction (or any other direction, for that matter). Yet, in each ecological setting, certain traits in their anatomy and physiology, and certain patterns of behavior, would have increased the probabilities of survival and reproduction of their individual possessors.

Our ability to state these outcomes and probabilities in an explicitly evolutionary framework does not imply that our long-distant ancestors ever perceived their actions in such terms. Early hominids were just doing their best to make it through another day, while enjoying whatever material and social rewards were available. They would have tried to get enough to eat, rest without being harassed or preyed upon, mate without interference, care adequately for their offspring, and survive each of life's events until the cycle was interdicted by death.

Over several millennia, as hominid populations increased in numbers and expanded their range, they would have come to occupy an increasing variety of environments. From their beginnings on tropical savannas, hominids eventually spread into temperate woodlands and boreal forests, scorching deserts and frigid arctic tundras. These settings presented divergent demands and opportunities. In responding to these challenges, various combinations of chance events and adaptive processes must have interacted to produce a diversity of biological, behavioral and, increasingly, cultural solutions to basic needs and desires. Possible outcomes were manifold but not infinitely varied. The potential for adaptation always was to some extent entailed by the antecedent biological responses accrued in ancestral populations, which together represent what sometimes are called characters of heritage; these characters in turn shaped each population's repertoire of responses to its present environment, sometimes referred to as its habitus. In turn, the interaction of heritage and habitus produced new spectra of responses that would be available to their descendants.

Some of the specific adaptive responses suited populations to a restricted subset of environments. One example of a highly environmental-specific response is the level of melanin production in the skin. Higher levels of melanin are produced in tropical areas, inhibiting tissue damage from ultraviolet radiation; lower levels of melanin are produced in higher latitudes where UV radiation is less. Other responses, probably equally specific at first (such as cognitive-based abilities to modify twigs and other natural materials into objects useful in obtaining food and water), now enable humans from any climatic zone to survive in any other zone by fabricating clothing, shelters, and chemical sunscreens that make differing degrees of skin pigmentation relatively unimportant. The more narrowly gene-based responses such as differences in levels of pigmentation are examples of ecological specificity that remained specific (although their adaptive optima differ from population to population as a result of natural selection). In contrast, although the cognitive-based adaptations must have originated as responses to specific ecological conditions, in time they led to a system of more open-ended behavioral responses that can be recognized as a new mode of adaptation – that of human culture.

By retrospective contingency I mean the process that has produced some particular evolutionary outcome that may now seem to have been inevitable, even though it was only one of several alternatives at some previous period in our ancestry. For example, in our lower jaws the first of the two premolar teeth on each side has two cusps, which is why dentists often refer to it as a bicuspid. But among the hominids recovered from deposits dated to 3.5 million years ago (Ma) at Hadar and Laetoli, only some individuals had bicuspid premolars, while others had single cusped teeth that were more like the norm in extant chimpanzees. Technically, the Hadar and Laetoli hominids displayed a polymorphism for the crown structure of this tooth, while later hominids (including modern humans) became virtually monomorphic for this character.

As another example, most modern humans have five lumbar vertebrae. But it is easy to imagine that our modal number might have been six instead, because numbers of lumbar vertebrae varied in earlier hominid populations – just as they do in hominoid populations now. Complete or nearly complete vertebral columns rarely fossilize; however, among the few specimens of this sort known – STS 14, which was a small-brained early Pleistocene hominid from South Africa and KNMWT-15000, a later and larger-brained hominid from East Africa – each possessed six lumbar vertebrae. If these specimens were representative of the populations from which they were sampled, and if populations with these modal numbers of vertebrae contributed to our ancestry, the higher number might have continued to predominate. At this point we simply know that it did not, though we do not yet know for certain why. In both cases, bicuspid premolars and the reduced number of lumbar vertebrae, it is possible to formulate *post hoc* hypotheses to account for what has become the norm. One continuing challenge in human paleobiology will be to develop meaningful tests of such hypotheses. We know much of what has happened over our evolutionary past, but for particular characters often we still do not know the relative roles played by accident and adaptation – again, by chance and necessity.

Nevertheless, the pattern of multiple possibilities at one time-level narrowing to a fixed outcome subsequently is in itself no more difficult to understand than the course of any day's weather. In the morning we might hear a prediction that there is a 30 percent probability of showers. By midnight that probability will have been converted into certainty for one or the other alternative – rain will either have fallen or not. If it did rain, a few seeds might sprout that otherwise would have withered. The resultant plants, in turn, could later serve as fodder for a hungry herbivore, with further ramifications up the food chain. Absence of rain would preclude all of the contingent events just enumerated – yet result in other happenings no less definite. The natural world is full of such possibilities, only some of which will translate into reality – yet whatever actual alternative becomes established will not only be likely, it will be certain.

In the same spirit, it seems that we have become human animals with a given set of biological and cultural attributes not because these outcomes were inevitable from the first, but rather because each successive alternative outcome along a particular trajectory proved to be viable, and probably better than some of the others. Consequently, any impression that the present state of our species was inevitable is illusory. It is far more enlightening, instead, to think about human evolution in reverse: antecedent populations of hominids did not become more similar to us – since we did not yet exist as models or goals and therefore could not have had any influence on events. Instead, we came into existence through the sequences of biological and – increasingly in later phases of human evolution – cultural contingencies that shaped our ancestors, who in turn have shaped us. Apes that were ancestral to the earliest hominids held their bodies upright as they moved through the trees, suspended beneath branches or standing on them as they clung to other branches overhead. There were multiple anatomical correlates of this type of postural and locomotor behavior, including the evolution of forelimbs that were markedly longer than hindlimbs. Thus when our ancestors adapted to life on the ground, given the asymmetry of the limbs a shift to bipedal posture while walking and running was more likely than a reversion to quadrupedal locomotion. In contrast, during the same time period when apes were giving rise to a human lineage, the baboons are descended from quadrupedal monkeys that could adapt to terrestrial niches simply by shifting from running and jumping on branches to performing the same activities on the ground (Aiello, 1981; Foley, 1987, 1995; Fleagle, 1988). Interacting with evolving upright posture in early hominid populations, other elements in the extensive roster of successive contingencies included giving birth to neonates that were relatively helpless, the use of tools, the ability to manage complex social interactions within and between groups, language, and so on.

In attempts to reconstruct ways of life through the past, studies of any group of organisms can be based on comparisons with living taxa or fossil evidence. In the best of circumstances, both sources of evidence are used to complement each other. The study of our own evolution is unusual in that there is only a single extant human species. Our closest living relatives are the African apes, particularly chimpanzees, which are very similar to us molecularly but strikingly different in form and behavior. Fortunately, however, the human fossil record is relatively rich and is supplemented by an even larger body of material remains (tools, shelters, hearths, and so on). Each of these domains of evidence has its own advantages and limitations.

It is particularly fortunate that the skeletal evidence that serves as one important basis for reconstructing human evolution is increasing steadily in abundance. The *Catalogue of Fossil Hominids* first issued in parts from 1967 through 1975 by Oakley & Campbell listed a total of approximately 570 fossil hominid sites, of which more than 500 were located in Africa, Europe and Asia, and hence directly pertinent to the evolution of anatomically modern humans. Though the numbers vary widely from region to region, these sites contained an average of about two specimens each, for a total set of about 1000 individuals. Due to numerous advances, including technological (satellite mapping of geological formations), theoretical (taphonomic prediction and evaluation of specimen distributions) and cultural (opening of the borders in many developing nations, allowing increasing levels of scientific cooperation), the period from 1975 through the present has witnessed a sharp expansion in both the numbers of known hominid fossil sites and the numbers of specimens recovered from each site. For example, the 1971 *Catalogue of Fossil Hominids* listed a total of 34 sites discovered in Italy up to 1971. By 1988, Orban's update for Italy listed an additional 26 sites, for a gain of over 76 percent in 17 years. There has been an even greater increase in the numbers of hominid fossil specimens per site, particularly in parts of Africa. For Kenya, the 1967 volume of the *Catalogue of Fossil Hominids* records 19 specimens from 12 sites, for an average of just under two specimens per site. Only 11 years later (Leakey & Leakey, 1978), the Koobi Fora site alone had yielded 129 specimens, a sixtyfold multiple. Even if no other sites had been discovered in that country, addition of the Koobi Fora material alone increases the average number of specimens at this one site approximately tenfold. If all of these numerical gains in the hominid fossil record are taken into account, including the many sites at which materials remain uncatalogued at this time, the total Eurasian and African sample may have increased to perhaps 8000 or so. This is a very crude estimate, but even if it is halved, it marks an impressive increase over just a few decades.

If there are about 4000 specimens distributed over the four million or so years of securely documented hominid evolution, that is on average one fossil hominid specimen for every 1000 years. Of course, the numbers are not evenly distributed, but if they were, we would have one fossil hominid for every 50 generations of 20 years each. Whatever its quantitative and qualitative limits, the hominid fossil record no longer can be dismissed as sparse and fragmentary, as it has been by some molecular anthropologists (e.g. Merriwether *et al.*, 1991; Vigilant *et al.*, 1991).

Criticisms of the value of the fossil record also have been raised by some specialists in cladistics, although in his establishment of that field, Hennig

(1950, 1966) introduced a method that he believed could be applied to living organisms alone, to fossils, or to both groups combined. Furthermore, he noted that fossils might be of particular value in assessing the direction of evolution in characters and in identifying cases of convergence, although he also realized that the incompleteness of fossil remains could limit their utility. Subsequently, serious reservations have been expressed about the ability of cladists to discover ancestral species (Wiley, 1981; Rowe, 1988) or to detect trends in character change (Eldredge & Cracraft, 1980; Stevens, 1980). It has even been asserted that in practice, fossils have had little influence in helping to establish relationships among extant groups (Patterson, 1981). In their consideration of the importance of fossils for the reconstruction of phylogeny, however, Donoghue *et al.* (1989) demonstrated that fossils are particularly important if there are large gaps in a cladogram based only on extant groups. In such situations, fossils can present combinations of characters not found among extant groups, to the extent that in some cases a true phylogeny cannot be obtained at all in the absence of fossil evidence. As we will see in Chapter 3, fossils have played a critical role in documenting the mosaic pattern of human evolution.

In a very particular sense, then, using the fossil evidence adds a critical dimension to our reconstruction of the past. The title of the British polymath J. B. S. Haldane's influential collection of scientific essays, *Everything Has a History* (Haldane, 1951), stresses this point. Human biology is no exception to this maxim. The evolution of our species has a basis in external reality; it comprised a sequence of real populations and particular environments. Our knowledge of that vast web of relationships over several million years across several continents can never be complete, but this sobering realization does not free us from the obligation of making the best of all the data available to use. Because in the paleobiological approach the primary emphasis is placed on earlier humans as living organisms, in this book the skeletal anatomy that can be inferred from fossils will be interpreted as far as possible in the broader contexts of physiology, biochemistry, genetics, and behavior of the individuals and populations represented by material remains.

In this process of interpretation, it must be realized that there is a difference between what happened in prehistory and our understanding of that complex reality. The initial awareness that there *was* a hominid fossil record emerged within a particular historical milieu. Consequently, the sequence of discoveries was interpreted in the context of a body of paleontological and biological theories that also were evolving. In early studies of human evolution, Linnaean taxonomy had a major influence in structuring the interpretations of fossil material. That taxonomic system, devised in conformity with a worldview that was static and typological, eventually proved unsuited to comprehending a natural world now known to have been shaped by the dynamic processes that generate evolutionary change.

Continued use of the Linnaean system also perpetuates nomenclatural conventions that can be misleading for a variety of reasons. For one thing, assignment of one specimen to a particular species and another specimen to a different species on the basis of morphological differences also implies to many investigators that their populations were discontinuous reproductively, even when we do not have any independent evidence for that assumption. For another thing, the use of formal taxonomic names can obscure the nature of a particular problem being studied. Paleoanthropologists sometimes seem to be making inferences about evolution (that is, events that occur at the population level) but instead may merely be comparing individual fossil specimens. The problem is exacerbated by taxonomic conventions. When a specimen is found, it is given an identification number (AL 288–1 for 'Lucy' from Hadar, OH 62 for 'Lucy's daughter' from Olduvai Gorge). Then the specimen is referred to a taxon bearing a Latin binomial, reflecting its assignment to an existing species or establishing it as the holotype of a new species. Thus AL 288–1 is assigned to *Australopithecus afarensis*, and OH 62 is assigned to *Homo habilis*. Other specimens may be assigned to either or both of these taxa. Subsequently, discussions of similarities or differences, phylogenetic inferences, and other generalizations commonly are phrased in terms of comparisons between the species *Australopithecus afarensis* and the species *Homo habilis*. In such cases the compositions of the reference samples, however, are not always clear. Is the taxon represented by one specimen? Or several, and if so which ones? If several specimens are included in the sample, were they from the same site or different sites, and were the sites close in time and space or widely separated? If the sample comprises a single specimen, do we have a basis for believing that it was sampled from near the mean of its population, or is its degree of representativeness just assumed? For such reasons, the use of specimen numbers often fosters greater clarity than use of formal binomials. It has the additional value of focusing attention on the limited extent of many samples that are studied.

In the study of human paleobiology it is critical to think of individuals not as the embodiment of character states but as samples from underlying populations in which these character states commonly must have been variable (for continuous traits) and polymorphic (for discontinuous traits). Suitable models for such patterns of inference are found not only in various disciplines of population biology (such as ecology and genetics) but also in established realms of physical science. Chemists who study gases summarize the observed behavior of this state of matter in terms of certain laws, and account for the observations with a corresponding set of theories. However, these physical scientists accept that their generalizations hold for volumes of gases comprising at the very least billions of molecules – that is, for gas molecule populations. Researchers in chemistry normally do not attempt to describe or explain the attributes of individual molecules in terms of position, velocity, or past history of collisions with other individual molecules. It is difficult to imagine a chemist urging abandonment of Boyle's Law following observations on a particular gas molecule. But as noted in the Preface, some paleoanthropologists do make statements such as 'Either we must discard this fossil or we must discard all previous theories of human evolution'. It is worth pondering the state of a field in which all of the previous theories might be overturned by one data point.

Some individual fossil specimens are of greater value than others, but it usually is because their characteristics shed light on general evolutionary phenomena. For example, KNMWT-15000 is distinguished from hundreds of other hominid fossils by the specimen's rather high degree of completeness at its time of discovery. While we may only guess how this adolescent male died, from his relatively intact skull and numerous post-cranial skeletal parts, experts really can make reasonable inferences about how he *lived* (Ruff & Walker, 1993). For example, the limb proportions of WT-15000 were strikingly similar to those of Africans found in the same climatic zone today. To a paleobiologist, this observation suggests several intriguing possibilities. One inference is that adaptation to heat stress has been a factor shaping hominid adaptation in East Africa for 1.5 million years; another is that populations living in the same region today could have ancestry that reaches back continuously to the boy's contemporaries. The material remains of KNMWT-15000 and direct implications from them comprise what one of my colleagues has referred to as 'the drama of information' (Rubinstein, 1983). This sort of drama conveys an intellectual excitement all its own, as recognized earlier by the British essayist G. K. Chesterton (1908): 'when we are young children we do not need fairy tales: we need only tales. Mere life is interesting enough. A child of seven is excited by being told that Tommy opened a door and saw a dragon. But a child of three is excited by being told that Tommy opened a door.' Hominid fossils do open a door, figuratively a portal to the past. My own feeling is that this opening to understanding our ancestry – and through it, ourselves – is so inherently exciting that no speculative elaboration is necessary.

Human paleobiology has a place as part of modern population biology, which emphasizes causation over categorization and populations over individuals and their unique attributes. There is no scientific necessity for paleobiologists to provide a particular causal explanation for every feature that distinguishes an individual fossil from all others. Anyone who really is familiar with wild or domestic animals, as Charles Darwin took pains to be, knows that there is immense variation within any given species, even without allowing for the further variation introduced by evolutionary change over time. Natural interbreeding groups of sexually-reproducing animals never are uniform, even within a single generation. The rules that generate the magnitude, distribution, and patterning of this variation are general biological principles, chiefly those of population and developmental genetics. Human biologists carrying out research on human adaptability have built upon these principles to great effect, often showing in impressive detail how extant populations in our species meet the challenges of the environments in which they live.

Some of the adaptive responses now known as a result of this research are genetic, and lead to changes in allele frequencies of populations over many generations. Others include developmental plasticity, in which phenotypic potentials are molded by environmental influences within a single generation. Still further, behavioral and physiological adjustments can be accomplished in hours, minutes or seconds. A very clear statement of these adaptive responses had been discussed by Lasker (1969) at the beginning of the International Biological Program, which focused attention on the interaction of human populations with various ecosystems. As we will see in Chapter 5, the resultant comprehensive perspective continues to be valuable for organizing thought about human variation because, as had been stressed previously by Harrison (1966), the human adaptability approach is concerned with the totality of the human response – at the level of both the individual and the population – to the totality of the environment (see Figure 1.1).

The known array of explicit and experimentally distinguishable adaptive responses gives the human adaptability framework great potential. This framework can encompass the perspective, evolutionary in theory and largely morphological in observation, of hominid paleontologists – and go beyond it in some rather important ways. For instance, a fundamental and necessary operating assumption of paleontology has been that the morphological features visible in fossils (hominids or any others) are heritable; their variations reflect directly the expressions of underlying inherited instruction sets encoded in the genomes of individuals and the gene pools of populations.

Although traits are assumed to be inherited, the extent of heritability rarely is estimated in the context of hominid paleontology, although there is some basis for doing so in theory and in fact. We know that in living

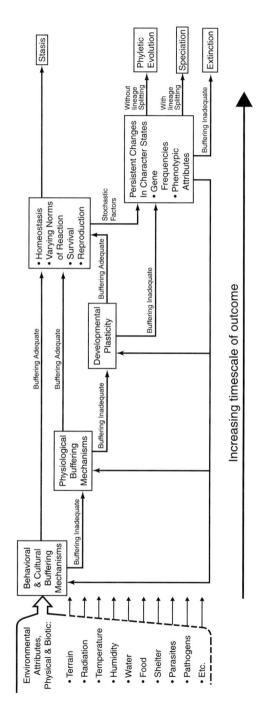

Figure 1.1. A simplified model of environmental influences and population responses over time.

organisms, different traits are inherited to different extents. Among extant humans, for example, there have been numerous studies of the modes of inheritance and heritabilities of numerous cranial traits (e.g. Hauser & DeStefano, 1989), demonstrating that some are simply inherited while others are far more complex in their mode of transmission. These studies on living populations can help to provide an explicit basis for exploring relationships among representatives of past populations. But beyond such inherited differences in character states, human biologists concerned with human adaptability also are used to dealing formally and operationally with the effects of developmental plasticity and physiological as well as cultural accommodations to environmental challenges.

There are at least two respects in which a human adaptability framework goes beyond some of the alternative interpretive contexts employed in paleoanthropology. The first is highly detailed and quantitative documentation of the extensive intrapopulation and interpopulation variation within our species as it exists today. The second is the awareness that although much of this variation is heritable, some of it arises via developmental plasticity and physiological as well as cultural accommodations to environmental challenges.

The framework proposed in this book is straightforward. The characteristics of extant humans are accepted as having resulted from biological evolution, in which those chance variations that conferred advantages in survival and reproduction have been preserved and multiplied by natural selection operating in a succession of particular environments over several million years. Over these millennia, evolution expanded the capacity for certain types of response that are based on genetic capacities, but are facultative in their expression. Included here are a variety of physiological, behavioral, and cultural characteristics (shivering, sweating, fashioning tools, building shelters, making fires, speaking a particular language). When such a framework is applied to the paleontological record, it encourages explicit consideration of the possibility that not all features of a given fossil bone necessarily represent the direct expression of genes, but rather may have been shaped by variations in activity or nutrition during development. In numerous ways and to varying extents these genetically based but facultatively expressed adaptive mechanisms help to buffer human populations against a host of particular selective agents, lessening the need for numerous biological adaptations keyed to particular environments. With facultative cultural support, a modern person can live one year on the Alaskan tundra, the next on the steppes of Uzbekistan.

At this point we encounter a paradox. If hominid evolution has been characterized by increasing non-genetic adaptation that lessened the need for morphological adaptations to environmental zones, why are so many species of hominids recognized in the scientific literature? Many paleoanthropologists would answer: because they were there. My own response to this 'Everest' answer is (as intimated earlier): history. Hominid fossils have been discovered over the course of nearly two centuries, while the body of biological theory and data pertinent to understanding their biology, adaptation, and evolution is much more recent, with much of it concentrated during the last half of the twentieth century. For example, over the last several decades, genetic research has documented the extremely close kinship of all humans to extant African apes, while enlarging the overall framework for understanding changes within and between populations. During the same timespan that the hominid fossil record has grown from a modest number of debated fragments to thousands of specimens, the scientific world has witnessed several revolutions. The rise of evolutionary biology has been a central development. In addition, thanks to advances in geology, especially geochemistry, the timescale known to have been available for human evolution has expanded about tenfold (Chapter 2).

All of these advances have reshaped the framework within which hominid fossil material is interpreted (Chapter 3). The corresponding theoretical development of the field is explored in Chapter 4; this historical background material may be skipped by readers who already are familiar with the study of human evolution. Chapter 5 outlines the human adaptability framework that holds the potential for expanding our understanding of earlier hominid populations. Chapter 6 surveys the biology and behavior of several extant primates, principally the papionines (macaques and baboons) and chimpanzees. The former predominantly terrestrial, quadrupedal monkeys became widely distributed over Africa and Eurasia, adapting to life on the ground at about the same time and for much the same reasons as did our apelike ancestors. Unlike the hominid evolutionary pattern, however, which has left a single surviving species, the papionines are subdivided by many primatologists into a variety of taxa in recognition of their biological diversity. The chimpanzees add important comparative data on the extant primates that genetically are our nearest relatives.

Chapter 7 suggests that we now have independent methods for estimating the number of hominid species that ever existed, and argues that this number may be less than now is accepted by many scholars. Paradoxically, however, there does not seem to be any objective criterion for deciding *which* of the currently numerous recognized species are invalid. Although the precise number of hominid species probably is very important for some purposes, it appears unknowable from the current state of our data, and may be ultimately unknowable in a philosophical sense as well.

In compensation, as I hope to show, there are many aspects of human paleobiology that are not only well documented, but fascinating.

Chapters 8 through 10 use human adaptability concepts derived from studies of extant human populations to reframe some paleobiological problems. These applications represent an attempt to meet the challenge for colleagues and students that was set forth in outline by Paul Baker's *New Scientist* essay (Baker, 1983). Similar ideas already have been explored in two books with the intriguing titles *Another Unique Species* and *Humans Before Humanity*. The author of those two works, my British colleague Robert Foley, wrote in the second volume about two dichotomous paths that researchers commonly take. In one tradition, he notes, the authors provide countless details about hominid fossils, documenting a path of change but providing little in the way of explanatory mechanisms – 'all bones and no flesh.' In the other tradition, writers concentrate on the evident contrasts between apes and humans and the various sequences of cause and effect that could have led intervening populations to traverse the gap that now exists, but give little detail of when and where the processes actually happened – 'all flesh and no bones in a timeless past.'

My own view is that in the reconstruction of human paleobiology, the past is not timeless. Chronology figures prominently, as it is the necessary setting for gene-based evolutionary change. Bones and teeth document this change and preserve fascinating details of some individual lives in the past. We now have sufficient knowledge of behavioral, physiological, developmental, and evolutionary mechanisms to flesh out the bones and animate the bodies of at least some of our ancestors.

2   *Constancy and change: taxonomic uncertainty in a probabilistic world*

Introduction

This chapter starts with a view of the world as short in duration and long on certainty, and concludes with a world long in duration and short on certainty. Explaining how this transition in outlook came about requires some background to trace how the conceptual framework of human evolution came into being, how some of its present limitations came to be built in, and the ways in which it must be changed. In this brief survey, time – chiefly geological time, including perceptions about the age of the earth and life on it – is part of the inquiry. However, the major focus is on the ways in which ideas about constancy and change (which are embedded in temporal contexts) have shaped the perceptions that scientists have about the extent of variation within populations and the nature of relationships between populations.

Several sets of readers may wish to skip this chapter entirely. The first group comprises those who believe that paleoanthropology is in a period of 'normal science,' and that its practitioners should just get on with the pragmatic tasks of description, comparison, and classification. The second group is more theoretically inclined, but content with some of today's *avant garde* ideas (such as characterizing species as individuals) which provide justification for working assumptions about low levels of intraspecific variation and punctuational shifts among species. The third group is made up of people who share my concerns about what seem to be large inherent contradictions in representing continuous (but not necessarily gradual) processes in terms of discrete categories, and who do not need to be reminded again of the details.

To a considerable degree, the historical material has been included here partially out of a feeling of obligation to newcomers to the field, who may wish to know the reasons why certain archaic and complex conventions (such as using Latin binomials to refer to specimens and populations) are followed. But even more, the review is offered out of a feeling of respect for colleagues who are not only familiar with these conventions but comfortable with their use. To this last group in particular, this chapter is intended as an extended explanation for why standard taxonomic conventions are avoided in this book as far as possible – because they reflect a worldview that seems to me to be substantially at variance with the biological continuities among present and past populations.

What are species? Do these populations comprise closed categories of near-identical units, like cans of peas and diced carrots on a shelf in Jehovah's Grocery, or do they more closely resemble amorphous cheese-cloth bags holding different spices suspended in Gaia's long-simmering stewpot? These images provide some contrasting metaphors for biological questions about the relationships among human populations during our evolutionary past. The preferred answers to these questions, however, appear to have changed over several thousand years of thought because of influences coming in good part from other scientific disciplines, chiefly geology and physics.

The first of these, geology, has enormously expanded estimates of the duration of the earth and life on it. The second, physics, has provided some independent corroboration of geology's timescale, but only after a period of confusion arising from over-confidence in the reliability of physical constants. Physics also has contributed a stochastic perspective that has influenced other areas of science in ways both pragmatic and profound. In paleoanthropology, for example, the ability to measure rates of radiometric decay has yielded several important techniques for dating materials associated with hominid fossils. These techniques, in turn, have led to discoveries that challenge paleoanthropology's epistemological framework, raising questions about limits to the certainty that we can have about inferences drawn from individual fossil finds. As for certainty, a remark by Albert Einstein captures the spirit central to this book: 'Opinions about the obvious are to a certain extent a function of time.' What is obvious at one point in time may seem shocking at another. Questions are raised here about the seemingly obvious complexity of human evolution, and a foundation is laid for an alternative, less particularistic, framework that nonetheless is entirely in accord with current bodies of evidence drawn from present as well as past populations of humans, other primates, and mammals in general.

The objective of paleobiology, as explained in Chapter 1, is to reconstruct the lifeways of past hominid populations – their biological characteristics, the environments in which they lived, their behavioral interfaces with environmental opportunities and constraints – and overall to gain as much insight into their ecological niches as possible. While much of the direct evidence for this knowledge comes to us through hominid fossil remains, this book is designed to augment the limitations of the fossil evidence with the abundant evidence available from studies of living organisms, chiefly molecular data.

The impact of molecular biology

We are living in an era in which the biological sciences are dominated, appropriately, by the marvels of molecular biology. The first electrophoretic studies documented an unexpected wealth of variation in natural populations (Lewontin, 1991). Then (especially during the 1990s) gene sequence data have become sufficiently abundant to enable scientists to trace patterns of relationships using various loci in the nuclear and mitochondrial genomes. Even more important, we now have detailed comparative studies of the homeobox genes that regulate developmental processes in multicellular plants and animals.

Many evolutionary biologists now feel that the reconstruction of our own lineage is better accomplished by applying molecular methods to large samples from living populations, rather than studying remains scattered through the geological strata of several continents. Against the dynamic discoveries in molecular biology now occupying center stage, attempts to reconstruct the appearances and ways of life of earlier populations whose remains are preserved as fossils seem archaic. Why persist in bothering with these puzzle bits from the past? After all, comparisons of whole organisms in terms of their external phenotypes, skeletal morphologies, and various other organ systems have been made for at least 2000 years. Further, at least cursory notice has been taken of fossils since antiquity; and vigorous, organized studies of invertebrate and vertebrate paleontology have been pursued for over a century. Aside from detailed descriptions of new discoveries and their temporal contexts, what is left to be done?

The answer is – a lot. As recounted in the previous chapter, quantitatively the hominid fossil record already is large, numbering many thousands of specimens. This body of evidence is also growing rapidly, thanks primarily to burgeoning technology. Satellite mapping of remote regions helps to locate promising geological deposits, and affordable air travel makes it possible for scientists from any part of the world to reach distant countries where there are geological strata of appropriate ages that might hold hominid fossils. There they often join forces with other experts, with the combined team using helicopters and all-terrain vehicles to provide transport into hitherto all but inaccessible areas. Laboratory breakthroughs, including various isotopic dating techniques, electron microscopy and computer imaging, all make it possible to extract more information from fossils than ever before. There have been sharp qualitative gains also in the specimens recovered. From early in the nineteenth century, the hominid fossil record began to be built up largely through accidental discoveries of bits and pieces of bones and teeth here and there. In contrast, the fossil remains recovered over the last quarter of the twentieth century include many specimens – such as CLl-18000, AL 288–1 and KNM-WT 15000 – represented by major portions of their skeletons.

These breakthroughs have been accompanied by underlying philosophical shifts as well. Following a confrontational phase of 'genes versus fossils' in the 1960s and 1970s, genetic and morphological data are increasingly seen as complementary rather than contradictory. Of course, the phylogenies based on both kinds of data must be in accord – their congruence is a philosophical necessity. Logically, all biological data are sampled from an interrelated web of populations, past and present. From a more empirical perspective, philosophy soon may be ratified by technology, as it proves increasingly practicable to extract and analyze meaningful sequences of DNA from fossil hominid remains. This potential was realized several years ago with organisms even more ancient than hominids, and tantalizingly short fragments already have been sequenced from a Neanderthal predecessor of anatomically modern humans (see Chapter 11). Constraints now are in the realm of technical details rather than theoretical boundaries. Ultimately, consideration of all available data should make it possible for us to integrate discoveries that have been accumulating for several decades.

Fossils provide tangible links with the past

Within this increasingly synergistic perspective, fossils still continue to provide the most compelling direct evidence about the ways in which the past differed from the present – because, except in the relatively rare chance events that preserve organic molecules, the mineralized teeth and bones of fossils are what usually remain to be compared with the corresponding parts of surviving organisms. Skeletal parts also provide principal clues for our understanding of the dynamic aspects of past lives: how members of ancestral populations moved, fed, fought, and gave birth. Still further, the geological strata in which fossils are found hold some of the clues needed to arrange past forms of life into networks of relationships and lineages of succession.

Against this background the molecular data, which until recently have chiefly been used to carry out a kind of ultra-reductionist comparative biology, must be seen as having larger and more complex implications. The necessity for this broader perspective became clear over 30 years ago, when Vincent Sarich and Alan Wilson calibrated a molecular 'clock' from changes in albumin molecules, and used it to cut the estimated time of hominid origins by more than half – initially, from about 14 or 15 million years ago to approximately 5 million years ago (Sarich & Wilson, 1967). A pongid–hominid split on this order of magnitude seemed reasonable to some researchers who were familiar with both the genetic and fossil evidence (Eckhardt, 1971, 1972), but wider acceptance of a truncated chronology for hominid evolution did not come about until a decade later. This delay was influenced by numerous factors, but in large part can be attributed to the belief by many paleoanthropologists that a short chronology for hominid origins was contradicted by the existence of several jaw fragments found in India early in this century (Lewis, 1934) and believed on morphological grounds to represent ancient hominids.

When more extensive finds in the 1980s clearly showed these earlier fossils to have represented apes rather than hominids, the revised and shortened molecular chronology became broadly accepted, but its full implications still remain to be realized. The required revisions to the evolutionary picture are profound. All of the behavioral and anatomical changes required to transform an ape into an early hominid must now be telescoped into a fraction of the time that had been thought to be available by most anthropologists working in the 1960s. Structural reorganizations also must have taken place much faster than had been believed. There are other dimensions to the dynamism interjected by molecular biologists into the study of fossil and extant skeletal remains. It now is possible to extend measurement of adaptive processes to the molecular level (Gillespie, 1991) and to see how these processes may have interacted with structural adaptations in the same populations (Wilson *et al.*, 1974). Integrating the molecular and morphological perspectives now is essential. So far, molecular data have been used more for studies of phylogeny than of function. The integration of structure and function, at whatever level, is an area in which organismic biologists may be able to provide leadership.

Ferment in physics

As has already proved to be the case with modern physics, structures of thought that have served well in the past can become so constraining that they impede further progress until they are modified sharply or even discarded. At the end of the nineteenth century, the British physicist Lord

Kelvin is said to have advised his best students to avoid careers in physics because all of the interesting work had been done. So typical was this attitude that it was echoed in Albert A. Michelson's (1905) book *Light Waves and Their Uses*: 'The more important fundamental laws and facts of physical science have all been discovered and these are now so firmly established that the possibility of their ever being supplanted in consequence of new discoveries is exceedingly remote.' All that remained was to tidy up a few 'apparent exceptions to most of these laws . . . in most cases due to the increasing order of accuracy made possible by improvements in measuring instruments . . . that will suffice to justify the statement that our future discoveries must be looked for in the sixth place of decimals.'

One of these small but nettlesome exceptions or anomalies had arisen from the attempts of Michelson himself, and his colleague Edward Morley, to measure the velocity of the earth as it traveled through the universal ether, within which all solid bodies were believed to be suspended. Another small dilemma concerned the need to decide between two alternative possibilities, whether electrons traveled as waves or as moving particles. The general feeling among physicists was that both of these problems would be resolved with, of course, further experiments and more precise measurements. Reality proved otherwise. Results from the Michelson–Morley experiment stimulated Albert Einstein not to collect more data but instead to formulate his theory of relativity, which has propelled us into a world unimagined in the early days of physics.

Newton's clockwork universe has become a gambling casino where deterministic calculations have given way to a universal roulette wheel, sort of a computerized rolling of dice and calculation of odds, with the bettor influencing the bet. While the older physics described a universe of separate parts bound to each other by rigid laws of cause and effect, in the newer view quantum events are probabilities, with some only more likely to occur than others. Given a large enough set of observations, scientists can predict only that the outcome will follow certain patterns.

Within this indeterminate universe, the wave/particle dualism contemplated by Einstein was resolved by the work of other physicists, including Louis de Broglie, Niels Bohr and Erwin Schrödinger. Bohr articulated the 'principle of complementarity,' which proposed that whether light or electrons were waves or moving particles depended on the specific properties which were being investigated, and the way we studied the phenomena. Schrödinger developed equations for wave mechanics that made the dualism at least mathematically plausible. His equation describes for the wave function all possible observations of a quantum system, now and into the future, but it really is just a set of odds of the kind that a bookmaker makes on a football pool. There rarely is anything usefully determinate that can be said about a single quantum event (Marshall & Zohar, 1997:201). Following Schrödinger, it seemed that 'science had run up not only against "common sense," which already was suspect when it began to deal with events in the subatomic world, but against rational logic. For could anything be one thing and its opposite at the same time?' (Clark, 1971:336). What is more, Schrödinger showed that by observing a quantum-mechanical effect such as the emission of a photon from an atom, the observation itself unavoidably affects events, so that the observer is part of the outcome – as if in weighing out meat, the butcher always rests a thumb on the scale, but with varying and unpredictable force.

In the preceding brief sketch of the transition from classical to quantum physics, there are three crucial components: the probabilistic outcome of observations; dualism in the properties of the units studied; and the significant effect of the investigator on the observations. All of these phenomena have their counterparts in the reconstruction of hominid evolution.

Paleoanthropology has its own set of contradictions that might be resolved by acceptance of a more probabilistic attitude toward data points. As noted in the preceding chapter, our sample of hominid fossils now numbers in the thousands. With few exceptions, as with certain extremely fragmentary specimens, each of these has been assigned to a particular genus and species. In the tradition of the field that has existed from its outset, however, the taxonomic allocation of many complete, well known specimens is disputed. The Taung specimen discovered in 1924 provides a familiar example that will be explored in more detail in Chapter 3, although its nomenclature is pertinent here. Despite establishing it as the type specimen of *Australopithecus africanus* (southern ape of Africa), Raymond Dart (1925) believed that the fossil represented a human ancestor, though most anatomists and physical anthropologists placed it in a 'juvenile ape' category, where it had nothing to do with human ancestry. Then an entirely different fossil hominid found at Piltdown in England was exposed as fraudulent, opening the way for Taung to be reinterpreted as an early member of our lineage for the following two decades. Subsequently suggestions have been made that Taung might more appropriately be viewed as belonging to an extinct lineage of robust early hominids (Tobias, 1973; Falk *et al.*, 1995), and hence would again exit our narrowly-construed line of ancestry. Of these alternative taxonomic boxes, in which did Taung 'belong'? Was it a robust hominid relative aside from our ancestry, or a gracile hominid ancestral to us? Neither? Or, following Schrödinger's lead into the quantum realm of indeterminate simultaneities, somehow both at once?

In a period of science that no longer deals with absolutes, these questions are more than rhetorical. Similar disputes exist with regard to the Laetoli and Hadar specimens (Chapter 8), all of which originally were assigned to the single taxon *Australopithecus afarensis*, but have been subdivided into multiple taxa by several other investigators. Yet despite disagreements about the taxonomic allocation of particular specimens (Taung) and sites (Laetoli, Hadar), most paleoanthropologists would agree broadly on many patterns, trends, and sequences – the pervasiveness of mosaic evolution, with structural modifications of the hindlimb for upright posture and bipedal locomotion evolving early and, even given the spottiness of the early finds, appearing episodic; brain expansion, commencing later but compounding more steadily (Chapter 9); hominids existing in Africa long before populating Eurasia. Thanks to Schrödinger, 'quantum mechanics taught that a particle was not a particle but a smudge, a traveling cloud of probabilities, like a wave that in the essence was spread out. The wave equation made it possible to compute with smudges and accommodate the probability that a feature of interest might appear anywhere within a certain range' (Gleick, 1992:89). Since general trends and patterns are more widely agreed upon than taxonomic assignments of particular specimens, is it possible that paleoanthropology already is tracking a traveling cloud of probabilities even while debating vigorously over the correct names for its subpopulational particles?

As for dualism, or more broadly the simultaneity of multiple properties, it is widely acknowledged among systematists (e.g. Mayr, 1997) and paleoanthropologists (e.g. Jolly, 1993) that the species category combines phenomena at several levels: morphological (the features variously referred to as character states or structural adaptations); genetic (the developmental integration of the genotype, the cohesion of gene pools containing at certain loci more alleles than can be included in any single genome, other population level phenomena such as balanced polymorphisms); and behavioral (mate recognition and other pre- and post-zygotic isolating mechanisms). These properties demonstrably are not coeval in many extant taxa, and may not have coincided in populations of the past. Just as subatomic particles may propagate as waves or particles depending on observational methods, paleobiological units may fragment or combine according to studies of either their morphologies or of the genes inferred to underlie the phenotypes.

The phenomenon of observer effect, well-known in primate paleobiology, can be illustrated by the changing taxonomic status of one hominoid primate mandible (M 14086) from the East African Miocene site of Koru. This fossil was assigned by its discoverer, A. T. Hopwood (1933), to

Proconsul africanus. The same specimen was subsequently transferred by Le Gros Clark & Leakey (1951) to *Proconsul nyanzae*, and then still later to *Dryopithecus* (subgenus *Proconsul*) *major* by Pilbeam (1969). At the time, all three taxa generally were considered to be closely-related species of the same hominoid primate genus or subgenus, so this shifting among categories could be written off as a modest taxonomic revision while more knowledge of the group accrued. The problem with that resolution of the matter arises when we think of fossils as they once were, living members of animal populations, not as remnant bearers of taxonomic labels. The taxonomic names are associated with diagnoses and descriptions that are supposed to correspond to real differences in body size, with significant ecological implications. For instance, *Dryopithecus (Proconsul) africanus* commonly is referred to as a gibbon-sized species of ape, while *D. (P.) nyanzae* often is likened to a chimpanzee and *D. (P.) major* supposedly is gorilla-sized (Pilbeam, 1969). Either M 14086 has grown considerably after death, or the taxonomic names of fossil primates sometimes convey less (or less ecologically meaningful) information than we would consider acceptable for living primate populations. No one would now confuse a gibbon with a gorilla. The dietary and other behavioral correlates of the anatomical distinctions between the extant taxa are profound.

Whether we are studying entire extant organisms, their parts preserved as fossils, or gene sequences extracted from either source, modern biologists of all disciplines work with data derived from limited samples and think in terms of populations – or at least should do so, since evolution is about the fates of populations and their gene pools. Because extrapolation from small samples to larger groups is necessary, the familiar processes of reasoning that are involved mask some daunting logical challenges. For example, in paleoanthropology the discovery of an incomplete, isolated fossil is the rule, as opposed to the recovery of a large array of relatively complete skeletons more closely approximating a population. The usual assumption is that the individual fossil is sampled from around the mean of its population, and inferences about taxonomy and phylogeny are made accordingly. But given the fact that the hominid fossil record now comprises many thousands of specimens, how likely is it that all are sampled from their population means? Certainly it is a paradox that an assumption that may be reasonable for each fossil taken separately is unlikely for all of them taken together. We will return to this problem later in a specific context (Chapter 9), but for now let us acknowledge that some of the uncertainties that exist in paleoanthropology cannot be resolved by declaring them as certainties – without distancing the field from the rest of the natural sciences.

The revolution that supplied new explanations from quantum mechanics for problems that were intractable in Newtonian terms might hold a lesson for us here: old disciplines that some scientists suggest are being superseded (as Michelson once opined about physics) can be revitalized by creating new frameworks for thought. Paleoanthropology, against a background of much 'normal science,' the everyday work that reflects routine thinking, has seen several such creative salients in recent decades. A stream of initiatives has come steadily, for instance, from Phillip Tobias. In the highly canonical setting of his monograph on OH5, he offered two related comments. The first was that 'the overall resemblances between the australopithecines in the two gracile and robust lineages are so great as to suggest that they belonged to the same evolutionary *grade*, not by parallelism but by homology or real genetic relationship. In fact, the evidence seems to indicate that (1) it is unlikely they were genetically isolated from each other throughout the Lower and Middle Pleistocene; and/or (2) they had a not very remote common ancestry.' His second related observation was, 'It is not outside the bounds of possibility that crossing [between gracile and robust early hominids] may have led to 'gracilisation' of *A. boisei* into the later and somewhat toned down *A. robustus*' (Tobias, 1967:244). These statements signal a willingness to think outside the boxes of formal taxonomic categories (Figure 2.1).

Other anthropologists (Clark, 1988; Willermet & Clark, 1995) have been even more explicit about the need to scrutinize some taxonomic practices that have become widely adopted. Questions of this sort are not incidental or peripheral to the study of hominid paleobiology; they are central even when raised sporadically and tentatively. We might consider this background to provide a new context for Shakespeare's classic rhetorical question, 'What's in a name?'

Taxonomy as a conceptual framework

Naming objects and arranging them into categories is a fundamental and universal aspect of human mental activity. Some of the specific forms of names for organisms, and the systems used to frame discussions of relationships among populations represented by human fossils (as well as all other things now or once alive), trace back at least to the time of ancient Greek civilization. An identifiable early figure who shaped this line of thought was Plato (429–347 BCE – Before the Christian Era), a disciple of Socrates. As noted by Nordenskiöld (1928), Plato combined a liking for the conclusive deductions of mathematics with a strong inclination toward the mystic. A

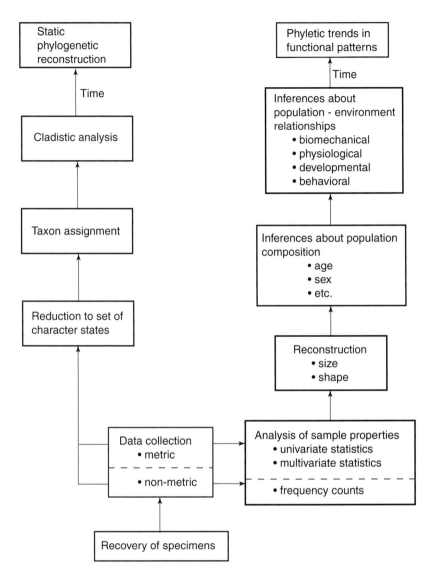

Figure 2.1. Different pathways in the use of fossils in order to understand evolutionary phenomena. It is commonly stated that taxonomic assignment of a fossil is a necessary prerequisite for inferences about evolutionary patterns. A counter example is provided by the Bouri Hata postcrania. Not yet allocated to a given species, these fossils nevertheless clarify important temporal trends in the evolution of hominid locomotion (Asfaw *et al.*, 1999). Adapted from Hartwig & Sadler (1993).

principal legacy, well-known in Western philosophy, was his belief that what humans perceive via the senses can only approximate the eternal ideal; every individual dog is but an imperfect image of an eternal and perfect 'idea dog' that generalizes the attributes of its kind. Preference for the abstract ideal over the imperfect dog (or tulip or human) at hand has given rise to one lasting conception of the species, which is a category of pervasively similar organisms, among whom any differences are relatively trivial.

It is upon the species that all higher and more abstract taxonomic categories (genera, families, orders and so on) are based. The Platonic conception has had enormous influence on biological thought down to the present day. In a paradox that is all too easily overlooked, elements of Platonic philosophy may be even more important in our own increasingly ahistoric times than they were in previous generations, although ever fewer students have any firsthand familiarity with Plato's writings and the idealized conceptions that they embody. In another context Lord Keynes (1936) remarked, 'Practical men, who believe themselves to be quite exempt from any intellectual influences, are usually the slaves of some defunct economist.' We should be alert to the possibility that his comments about the sources of ideas in economics might apply to the philosophical core of biological theory as well.

The intellectual legacy of Plato comes to us chiefly through the work of his pupil Aristotle (384–322 BCE), who has left his mark on many fields of science. In the realm of classification, Aristotle realized that the study of plants and animals could be simplified greatly by arranging them according to their similarities and differences. Aristotle's system of classification was based on four different types of information: appearance; actions; habits; and way of life. This operational empiricism has helped to mask Plato's influence on the ideal image that still was central to Aristotle's system – each separate kind of living thing was placed in a unique *eidos*, a term which translates in modern biology as the species. Several similar forms of an *eidos* were combined in a single *genos*, which is the linguistic and logical antecedent of the modern category of genus.

Plato's ideas about the groupings of organisms were preserved and elaborated, first through Aristotle, then by a series of scholars who perpetuated and transmitted the philosophical underpinnings of current taxonomic practice. As one example, the Roman scholar Pliny, who was born in 23 CE (Christian Era) and died in 79 CE while investigating the first historically documented eruption of Vesuvius, compiled a volume titled *Natural History*. This work was an encyclopedic summation of the biological knowledge accumulated to his time, uncritically presented, particularly where his information had not been acquired firsthand. Pliny's descriptions and comparisons tended to be superficial. When comparing the horns of oxen, snails, and certain snakes, he represented these structures as similarities indicative of relationship, rather than as unrelated convergences. In this tendency he departed from the standard attained previously by Aristotle, who had attempted to understand the origins and relationships among structures found in different animals. Nevertheless, imperfect as Pliny's contributions now seem, they were among the more widely available works of natural history in Europe through the fifteenth century.

During the European Renaissance, descriptive taxonomy was represented by ambitious but derivative publications by many workers such as Zürich's Konrad Gesner (1516–1565) and Oxford's Edward Wotton (1492–1555). Gesner's scholarship produced some 3500 pages, divided among four huge folio volumes. These were illustrated by the best technology then current, as in the rhinoceros depicted in a woodcut executed by the distinguished German artist Albrecht Dürer. Gesner's contributions were marked more by attention to technical details of design and production than by original contributions to systematic logic. To the extent that his books still included accounts of fabulous animals, they represented derivative scholarship rather than empirical scientific work founded on observation. A heavy reliance on predecessors such as Aristotle also marked Wotton's publication, *De differentiis animalium*. This work generally avoided the inclusion of mythical creatures, though it also failed to include much about animal specimens introduced to Europe by explorers of distant regions.

Wotton's principal successor among English taxonomists was John Ray (1627–1705). Ray used a system of nomenclature that was clumsier than Aristotle's, denoting each species with a long phrase rather than a single name. His system also lacked common corresponding units for both plants and animals. On the empirical side, some of Ray's categories were based on resemblances as superficial as those used by Pliny 15 centuries earlier. For example, Ray grouped whales with fish and bats with birds, though Aristotle had realized that both whales and bats are mammals. However, Ray did progress beyond Aristotle in organizational terms, realizing that if various plant and animal species resembled one another to differing extents, they could be arranged into a hierarchy of taxonomic categories.

Between Wotton and Ray lived Francis Bacon (1561–1626). Like his contemporary in the physical sciences, Galileo (1564–1642), Bacon saw Aristotle and other classical authorities as unacceptably credulous, and subjected their ideas to criticism and ridicule. In place of received wisdom, Bacon championed experience as the sole acceptable foundation for knowledge, with observation and experiment as the tools by which scientific inquiry must proceed. Although not himself a taxonomist, except perhaps by way of his having systematized the abstract laws of nature, through his insistent empiricism Bacon exerted considerable influence on the whole body of natural science. However, any effect that he had on the tracing of relationships among organisms was only indirect and long delayed. Over two centuries later, the Danish biologist Wilhelm Johanssen would cite Bacon as the source of the experimental principles that guided his investigations of heredity. In the meantime, Bacon's scepticism toward the philosophical heritage from the ancients was lost on his more immediate successors such as Linnaeus, who collected abundant data but interpreted them within a framework still shaped by Platonic essentialism and bounded by Aristotelean categories.

The Swedish botanist Carl von Linné, or Linnaeus (1707–1778), generally is referred to as the founder of modern taxonomy because of his influence on taxonomic practice, which has lasted to the present time. His system represents the epitome of two thousand years of classical learning, augmented by a prodigious amount of original empirical and theoretical research. The scientific career of Linnaeus manifests some identifiable influences of the Baconian attitude, though not Bacon's scepticism. With support granted from public funds, Linnaeus undertook journeys to explore Lapland and the Dalecarelia region of central Sweden, and in general made many observations of plants and animals in their natural states. His experimental work was more limited, as has been the case for many a gifted field naturalist, but he did discover the common developmental sequence leading to leaves and flower petals in plants (a discovery more commonly attributed to Goethe). Linnaeus greatly streamlined taxonomy by reestablishing a system of binary nomenclature, similar to that employed by Aristotle, but using predominantly Latin terms and forms. The key feature of this system was that, once recognized and described, every living creature had its place in a clear and comprehensive hierarchy. The system's utility was quickly demonstrated as Linnaeus classified Europe's known fauna and flora. Moreover, the Linnaean system proved capable of integrating new organisms, though not entirely in the manner expected. For instance, one intention of Linnaeus was that anyone who had become familiar with his system would be able to place a new plant from anywhere in the world in its correct class and order, if not genus. A critical test of this scheme came in 1749, when the naturalist Michael Adanson, posted to Senegal by the Compagnie des Indies, attempted to apply the universal Linnaean system to the tropical forest flora and fauna (Heywood, 1985: 8). In Adanson's own judgment, this endeavor failed, and badly enough that he felt impelled to develop a new system, one that differed in approach by being phenetic (based on appearance) and multivariate (using multiple characters). Adanson received scientific recognition, including membership in the French Académie and foreign membership in the Royal Society of London, but his methods were not widely adopted. The Linnaean system continued to be extended, in much the same manner that it originally had been crafted, by pragmatic adjustments within a codified framework that could accommodate new data, however uneasily.

Just as the Linnaean system was challenged by the many novel plants and animals that Europeans found in regions of the world that were new to them, other hitherto unknown realms of life were being opened even in Europe – through microscopes. Linnaeus addressed the newly magnified cosmos with microscopical research of his own, as he described in his book *Mundus invisibilis* (1767), parts of which sound distinctly modern, with suggestions that some microscopic creatures might be 'living disease carriers' and might belong to a new kingdom apart from those of plants and animals. One name suggested for the new kingdom, *Regnum chaoticum* presages the concept of protista (Broberg, 1980: 168).

From the vantage point provided by this historical foundation, we can now examine the key features of the Linnaean binomial system that appeared to be so broadly useful in its time, but now are recognized as serious constraints.

According to Linnaeus, the correct scientific designation of our own species is *Homo sapiens*. Both parts of the scientific label are significant. Linnaean binomials can convey everyday meaning as well as unique identity; thus *Felis domesticus* denotes the domestic cat, while *Felis nebulosa* serves as an appropriately descriptive tag for the clouded leopard of Asia. Sometimes a scientific name highlights a highly diagnostic feature, as in the case of *Tarsius spectrum*. *Tarsius* is a tiny prosimian primate capable of prodigious leaps, and its generic designation refers to the greatly elongated tarsal segment of its foot. On the other hand, some Linnaean binomials communicate information that, while once believed to be true, has been disproved by subsequent evidence – *Adapis* is the name originally coined for a genus of mammals believed to be on the line of evolution leading to ungulates (*ad* meaning 'toward' and *Apis* referring in Egyptian mythology to the sacred bull of Memphis), but *Adapis* now is recognized as a lemur-like prosimian primate. To help ensure the stability of nomenclature, in cases of this sort the taxonomic names have not been changed.

In a second way Linnaeus's system of Latin binomials, intended primarily to clarify discussions about the relationships among particular animal groups, can convey information that is false and misleading, insofar as it unduly emphasizes separateness. A good instance of this concerns the nomenclature for domestic dogs, usually referred to as *Canis familiaris*, and for wolves, *Canis lupus*. Despite this species distinction, dogs and wolves interbreed readily on contact, in the wild as well as in captivity, and their offspring are viable and fertile. In such a situation, of which there are numerous other examples, the formal species names signal the existence of a genetic isolation that is partial at best. Though often glossed over, this is an important point, since the Linnaean system of classification was based originally on the assumption that species were reproductively isolated. In fact, since at the time of Linnaeus different kinds of plants and animals were widely believed to represent separate acts of creation, continuity among kinds was not to be expected. In the case of the canines, the species names do not even correspond clearly to similarities and differences in appearance. There is much more resemblance between a wolf and either a Siberian husky or a German shepherd, for example, than there is between either of those breeds and a dachshund or a chihuahua. This kind of problem represents a critical flaw in the Linnaean scheme, but although beautiful ideas can be killed by ugly facts, the demise often is very slow.

Linnaeus, while surpassing his predecessors empirically, thus pursued a taxonomy whose inherent logic remained that of dichotomization. An organism is either one thing, or it is another – cat or mouse, dog or wolf, ape or human – and by extension, *Homo habilis* or *H. rudolfensis*. There is no middle ground. To Linnaeus, as to those on whose writings he had built, the biological realm was a world of fixed types, species, and races, each believed to have been created separately by a supreme being as part of a world that had endured for only a few thousand years.

In the interests of fairness, a caveat should be interjected here. The picture just given is incomplete. Linnaeus commonly is represented in starkly black and white terms, as either the hero of systematists or an object of scornful criticism by those who are more interested in the dynamics of living systems. Reality is more complex. It is true that he once wrote, 'We count as many species today as were created in the beginning' (Linnaeus, 1736). However, during the next decade Linnaeus altered his views on the fixity of species, elaborating a rather complicated scheme permitting superficial changes in organisms, some development of new species from crossing of others, and even the creation of new species not by God directly but by the action of natural laws. Apparently Linnaeus was trying to harmonize a Genesis account with recent discoveries in natural history by adhering to central dogmas with a bit of compromise around the edges. As noted by Broberg (1980), Linnaeus evidently believed that there was no real contradiction between science and Genesis.

Despite a few modest attempts at accommodation to complexity in the natural world, however, the classifications of Linnaeus must be seen in the context of fixity of types. His taxonomic work was evidently superior in quantity and quality to that of all systematists who had come before. Yet if his contributions represent a peak, then we might be better using this point, metaphorically, not as a platform on which to build, but as a fulcrum to lever off future advances. Having met several challenges of expanded biological diversity, first from a tropical diversity of fauna and flora, then from the microscopic realm, the Linnaean system would ultimately be strained beyond its conceptual limits by another category of evidence that long had been known, but not recognized as the source of a serious philosophical challenge – fossils.

Taxonomy encounters fossils

Fossils are naturally preserved portions or imprints of organisms that lived in geological periods prior to our own time. These remnants come in various forms as bones or teeth in which the original organic matter has been replaced by minerals from water percolating through the ground in which they were buried; as hardened impressions made in sediments by leaves or other parts of plants or animals; or as natural casts of those impressions; and so on. This characterization of fossils is modern. Originally the word fossil, from Latin *fossa*, trench, simply referred to things that had been dug from the earth. The term was first used by the German geologist, Georg Bauer, better known by his literary name of Agricola (1494–1555).

Even in the modern and more restricted sense of organic remains, fossils had been known long before Bauer's time – at least since the beginning of recorded history. For most of that period, however, opinion was divided on whether fossils represented natural phenomena, or misleading illusions attributed variously to a creator, malign spirits, or plain accident. A naturalistic perspective existed at least as early as the fifth century BCE, when Xenophanes, a pupil of Anaximander, composed a long narrative poem, fragments of which survive. These contain an account similar to his master's work *On Nature*. In one part Xenophanes recounted how fossilized marine animals, embedded in sediments at high elevations, proved that the mountains once had been under the sea. Aristotle and his school considered fossilization to be '*lusus naturae*,' a game of nature (though here a nature unnaturally personified), a belief that persisted for some two thousand years in Europe. In the early modern period, naturalistic explanations again were asserted, as by Leonardo da Vinci (1452–1519). Others holding similar views to those of Leonardo included another Italian scholar, Girolamo Fracastoro (1483–1553), and the Dane, Niels Stensen (1638–1686), who held church offices in Italy. All three men had extensive experience in anatomy, and when they encountered fossils in the course of other work, simply accepted them as the remains of ordinary organisms that had lived and died in earlier times, evidently without much consideration of what they might imply about a greater time depth for the earth.

In the Linnaean system, taxonomists did not deal with fossils as portions of plants or animals that once had been alive, but saw them as part of a third realm on a par with plants and animals – a mineral kingdom. This third kingdom was modeled analogically on patterns seen in the preceding two, even to the idea of minerals growing, seedlike. An Aristotelian progression toward perfection was suggested by the phrase '*lapides crescunt, vegetabilia crescunt & vivunt, animalis crescunt, vivunt & sentiunt*' (stones grow, plants grow and live, animals grow, live and feel). Of course some stones do 'grow' in the sense that crystals expand in solutions of certain concentrations, and concretions can form around certain bodies. Similarly, the mimosa and Venus fly trap, both known to Linnaeus, could be cited as plants that 'move'. Other aspects of the Linnaean treatment of fossils also demonstrate that the realities of the natural world commonly were subordinated to organizational imperatives. Any fossil shell could end up in any of three places – in the mineral kingdom; in the Vermes class under *Testacea* or *Mollusca*, based on the superficial appearance of the shell alone; or as part of a natural classification of the animal that built the shell, as explored in Linnaeus's uncompleted treatise *Fundamenta testaceologiae*. Most important for our purposes, to Linnaeus fossils presented no major challenge to the timescale of life's existence. In a manner similar to his views on the relative, rather than absolute, fixity of species, he was willing to concede that the earth was older than about 6000 years, perhaps as much as 30000 or even 75000 years old (Broberg 1980:37). Without much conceptual strain, Linnaeus could have fossils and Genesis too. Just a century later, most scientists would feel compelled to choose between the two.

It sometimes is impossible to pinpoint the shift in a climate of thought because it does not occur at an identifiable moment, but rather as a trend over time. Like a newly-arisen recessive mutation, an idea can come into existence at a given instant, but for a long time be effectively invisible due to the dominance in expression of alternatives and predominance in their distribution. So it was with beliefs about the age of the earth. For Linnaeus, the 6000 years estimated for Genesis could be adjusted to five or ten times that duration by simple expedients. If each minute really lasted an hour, and each hour a day, then a week would stretch into a period long enough for the necessary events to have taken place under the watchful eye of a creator who just might give things a nudge now and again as needed – for Linnaeus saw all creatures as living under God's constant guidance. Such a blend of the naturalistic and the supernaturalistic should have passed the scrutiny of all but the most literal-minded religious authorities of the age.

Fossils imply time

Between Linnaeus and his contemporaries on the one hand, and Cuvier (1769–1832), commonly referred to as the 'Father of Paleontology,' on the other, came the beginnings of a transformation in estimates of the age of the earth, the duration of life on it, and beliefs about what had happened to organisms over that timespan, however short or long it was. Contributing to this reinterpretation of the geological timescale and its consequences was the lifework of the great French naturalist, Count Georges le Clerc Buffon (1707–1788). Buffon and Linnaeus were almost exact contemporaries; both were born in the same year, though Buffon outlived the Swedish taxonomist by a decade. Yet these two scientists were polar opposites in scientific outlook. Categorizing separate taxa comprised the lifework of Linnaeus, who styled himself as the modern Adam responsible for naming all living creatures as they became known to him. Buffon, in contrast, saw pervasive evidence of continuity throughout the natural world.

In 1778, the year in which Linnaeus died, Buffon published his influential book *Les époques de la nature* (*The Epochs of Nature*). In this work the French naturalist documented a great but unquantified depth of earth history, which he divided into seven successive periods. His scheme neatly paralleled the seven days of creation, even to the extent of having humans appear only in the very last epoch, but he immensely lengthened the timespan. Buffon's work was received by a large international readership avid to learn more about the history of the earth in its earlier periods. Its impact was further heightened by Herder's *Ideen zur Philosophie der Geschichte der Menschheit*, which was published subsequently in four volumes over the period from 1784 to 1891 (Collingwood, 1946). These works helped bring about what in retrospect was a clear and powerful shift from a static view of natural history to a temporalized one (Rupke, 1983:4).

These early contributions to the foundation of historical geology largely bypassed England. Beginning with the second decade of the nineteenth century, however, a group of scholars centered at Oxford became interested in learning what details geology could supply to augment Biblical history. In that setting they were well shielded from the increasingly secular philosophy of history being propagated on the continent by French and German scholars. The investigations begun by the Oxford group were shaped from the outset by strong Anglican tradition, in which natural and revealed religion were blended, in Rupke's (1983: 5) terms, with 'the form and substance of science'.

As the English school of historical geology grew, it came to include important scholars from Cambridge, such as Adam Sedgwick and William Whewell, as well as prominent Oxford academics such as William Daniel Conybeare. A combination of ambition, energy and intellect soon established William Buckland as the circle's central figure. In the 1820s, when he was 36 years old, Buckland attained prominence through explorations of what were then referred to as 'antediluvial' dens of hyenas. These studies were carried out in a larger framework of knowledge, one in which the Biblical deluge was accepted as a reality.

Although to most of us the ingredients would seem incompatible, the combination of historical geology and literal interpretation of the scriptures was unexceptionable to Buckland and his associates (Rupke, 1983). Religious commitment was common among scholars, and orthodoxy was an integral element in Oxford's curriculum. The patronage of that institution, in turn, was needed to establish historical geology as a scientific discipline and to advance Buckland's academic position both in the field as well as in the university. The combination worked for several decades, during which Buckland accomplished much by the standards and traditions of the times, carrying out investigations in the field and publishing prolifically (Buckland, 1820, 1823, 1824).

As often happens, success in these endeavors became self-limiting. The early historical geologists pursuing support for the Biblical deluge found plenty of evidence of submerged lands and buried beasts. Too much evidence. The accumulation of more and better geological data inexorably exposed the flaws in the diluvial system. Documentation of more and more strata in increasingly orderly succession, along with the varied assemblages of fossils contained within these layers, required adherents of the diluvial theory to postulate ever more deluges. If the timescale were finite and fixed at just 6000 years ago, catastrophes would have had to recur with a frequency that strained credulity. Eventually even Buckland (1836) had to abandon diluvial geology in his *Bridgewater Treatise*. Ironically, one of the geologists prominent in showing the way out of this interpretive straitjacket was Charles Lyell, who had been one of Buckland's students before coming increasingly under the influence of his own Scots countryman, James Hutton.

Huttonian uniformitarianism was conceived in a different mold than that of either Cuvierian continental historical geology or its British counterpart practiced by Buckland and his school. For one thing, Hutton and Lyell argued that earth history and the Bible should be kept apart. Geology required open inquiry in the spirit of what we would recognize as modern science, which they felt was not germane to moral and religious questions. For another thing, the uniformitarian vision was that of a 'permanent present' (Rupke, 1983:5).

In the uniformitarian framework, observations on everyday phenomena (ice fracturing rocks, rain eroding banks, rivers carrying sediments into lakes, waves pounding away at seacoasts) were believed to hold the key to understanding the past. To uniformitarians, infinitesimal but inexorable processes operated iteratively over time, replacing the episodic cataclysms, such as the flood, required by catastrophists. The uniformitarian viewpoint had a corollary – if the changes in any one year, or even over an entire human lifetime, were slight, then vast geological transformations such as the excavation of valleys by glaciers or the elevation of mountain ranges by tectonic activity must have required eons.

Time and change undermine taxonomic categorization

As we have seen, taxonomy, at least in the European tradition, had started with Plato's conception of an abstract ideal of the species. His concept of our perception of real organisms as imperfect, flickering shadows on the wall of a cave, mere reflections of an abstract and more perfect reality, was nurtured from antiquity, through the Middle Ages and the Renaissance. This vision was later multiplied by Linnaeus into thousands of taxa that were for the most part discrete, plus a very few fossils – all of which were packed into just the few thousand years permitted by Biblical chronology. Historical geology with reluctance, and its uniformitarian rival with gusto, greatly increased the known expanse of geological time. As this geological record was being pieced together, the earth's strata yielded enormous numbers of fossils, not all of which could be kept compartmentalized; some undeniably sampled populations that were intermediate in appearance as well as stratigraphic location. We now know of numerous cases in which lineages of invertebrate (Sheldon, 1987) and vertebrate fossils (Gingerich, 1979) are so rich and continuous that the horizontal segmentation of lineages into species must be arbitrary.

As we will see in Chapter 4, Darwin's *Origin* instituted a system of classification based on a combination of two components, common descent and degree of resemblance. His system was designed to accommodate explicitly the complications that arise when a taxonomic system designed for living species (the extant tips of branches representing lineages evolving from the past) is adapted to encompass past populations represented by fossils. Although some past taxa themselves are the tips of lineages that ended in extinction, others must represent segments of continuous and evolving lineages (branch sections, not tips). The term phyletic species has been coined more recently for these non-terminal taxa; however, this terminology introduces the potential for confusion, since the extant species that comprise our most common standards of reference originated by splitting. The proportion of known fossils representing past taxa that have arisen by gradual lineage transformation, versus population splitting, has not been established empirically for all groups of organisms, and the problem has been exacerbated by some formulations that have tended to obscure the relationship between microevolutionary and macroevolutionary processes. If one were to take an extreme view, it might be tempting to observe that Plato's vision and the Linnaean system based on it, even with recent modifications, have become as useful in representing evolutionary dynamics as Newtonian mechanics in the pursuit of quarks.

Beyond binomials: plural and pragmatic species concepts

Some of the inherent contradictions in taxonomy, as outlined here in their historical context, have been noted by practicing systematists as well (Hull, 1964, 1965; Løvtrup, 1979; De Quieroz, 1988). Among these, Michael Donoghue and his colleagues have been prominent. Mishler & Donoghue (1992) argued for pluralism in species concepts on the grounds, noted previously here, that discontinuities of various kinds (such as morphology, breeding behavior, and ecological tolerances) often delimit different sets of organisms. Not all morphotypes behave as species in terms of reproductive behavior. Their solution to the theoretical and practical problems represented by these discontinuities was to adopt a pluralistic approach in general, recognizing that the species concept refers to several different kinds of units. In particular, they recommended that the species as a basic *taxonomic* unit be decoupled from notions of its role as a basic *evolutionary* unit. In groups where the actual interbreeding units are small relative to morphologically delimited units, species would be like higher taxa such as genera or families; that is, they would be assemblages of populations united by descent, among which there would exist the potential for reticulation (that is, gene exchange through hybridization). Of particular interest is their adoption of some of the language of physics, as in the suggestion that 'there are many reasons why species should not be treated as particles or quanta.' In the context of this chapter, perhaps the best reason is that our words frame our thoughts, and just now the species concept carries different meanings for different investigators.

3   A century of fossils

Introduction

Paleoanthropology is a challenging subject in modern science, not just because any day can witness the announcement of an important new fossil hominid specimen, but because well over a century of such finds has increased the data base of the field about a thousandfold while leaving many conclusions, ostensibly based on the enlarged body of evidence, relatively unchanged and still in need of reconsideration. Here are a few questions that might be considered of broad interest to anyone interested in evolution. Prior to the divergence of the lineages that led to present day apes and humans, what did our common ancestors look like? When, and under what circumstances, did upright posture evolve? How far back in time did material culture become an integral part of our adaptive repertoire? Is there any way of estimating, in the absence of preserved soft tissues, when diversity in skin, hair, and eye colors arose? When did humans first evolve brains so much larger than would be predicted for primates of our body size?

All of these inquiries about the biology of early humans – human paleobiology – are influenced to some extent by judgments about taxonomic diversity during the evolution of our ancestors over the past five or six million years. However, the debates about taxonomy and phylogeny often loom so large in the field that considerations of more dynamic biological questions are overshadowed. In one relatively recent example, the editors of a symposium volume on species and species concepts in primate evolution concluded that '*How should nature be carved up into entities called species*' was 'arguably the most fundamental operational problem in evolutionary biology' (Kimbel & Martin, 1993). Building on this premise, they held that 'knowledge of the origins and extinctions of species (historical events) and of the phylogenetic patterns of species diversity (the cumulative results) is logically prior to the formulation of specific hypotheses regarding process (adaptation, competition, dispersal, and the transformation of morphology over time).' This is an interesting viewpoint, but one that is contradicted by widely-known occurrences. For example, the 1972 discovery of the relatively large-brained early hominid KNM-ER 1470 in East Africa attracted great scientific and popular attention despite the attribution of this specimen to an undetermined species of the genus *Homo*, a status that remained unresolved for sixteen years (Alexeev, 1986) and still is debated today. Popular interest in this specimen has been consistently high from the first announcement of its discovery through the present day. Nonspecialists are intrigued, for example, because this specimen is relatively complete (while its high degree of fragmentation when found possibly added to the appeal of a puzzle) and seemed morphologically advanced for the geological age initially assigned to it (but see Chapter 9 for an update and analysis).

To understand this curious situation in some kinds of paleoanthropological research, in which questions about function and adaptation are subordinated to concerns about taxonomy, it is essential to have a perspective that is rooted in the origin of the field. As a matter of historical fact, many of the taxonomic questions still being grappled with as central concerns of many authorities – for example, are most of these fossils and the taxa that they represent to be counted among our ancestors or only a few of them? – were first posed by investigators who traveled by horse-drawn carriages to the various field sites and wrote out their reports of their finds in longhand, using pen and ink, by gas light before despatching them to colleagues weeks or months away by post. Now similar problems concern workers who fly to sites around the world and compose their thoughts on personal computers powered by solar batteries and linked by satellites orbiting the earth and fibre-optic cables buried beneath its surface. This situation of relative conceptual stasis against a background of incredible technological advance, a contrast which must seem more puzzling to intelligent outsiders than to many experts who have become habituated to it since their student days, has been conditioned in part by the sequence of past discoveries, with all of the attendant vagaries and chance occurrences.

These stochastic events in the intellectual realm began as antiquarians across Europe unearthed some important hominid fossils at least several decades before naturalists had formulated any of the key theoretical components of the modern evolutionary theory that now forms the interpretive framework of our current scientific perspective on the world. These accidents of circumstance created a situation in which antiquarians and naturalists – later more formally educated in a variety of disciplines and called anatomists, archeologists, geologists, and paleontologists as they diversified into various specializations – had to begin building a bridge, one mineralized bone at a time, over a temporal void so deep that its bottom could neither be seen nor imagined. The fossils were key structural elements in an arch of scholarship that was held up by empirical inference, intellectual creativity and courage of conviction, against the ever-present awesome counterweight of tradition. These empiricists who brought human fossils to public notice commonly lived at the uncertain margins of social acceptability, risking reputation and position as they worked along an uncertain edge to which they clung with the force of reason even as they peered over it in curiosity.

Anatomically modern humans

In the early days of this scientific enterprise, discoveries that many paleoanthropologists now consider to represent the major categories of fossil hominids were made in a historical sequence that was the reverse of the evolutionary sequence of earlier human populations. Consequently, specialists who scarcely had come to terms with one set of hitherto unknown ancestors were challenged yet again by another set, even more different – then again, and again, and again. Specifically, skeletal parts of early anatomically modern humans were first recognized as fossils in 1823, followed by Neanderthals in 1857, then pithecanthropines in 1890, and more recently still, the first australopithecines in 1924.

Some specialists (e.g. Groves, 1989) have argued that the preceding brief summary of the order in which hominid fossils were recognized as our ancestors makes a complex situation far too simple. Human remains of apparent antiquity had generated curiosity and comment now and again well before the nineteenth century. For example, during the sixteenth century the Italian Michèle Mercati concluded that the shaped stones called *ceraunia* (thunderbolts) were instead stone tools fashioned prior to the discovery of metallurgy (Oakley, 1964). However, the modest level of public interest in this subject can be gauged from the fact that although Mercati died in 1593, his book *Metallotheca* was not published until 1717. Those who wonder at the reason for the long delay might take into account that in the interval between Mercati's research and its publication, a work by the Frenchman Isaac de la Peyrè, claiming that the ceraunia were the work of a pre-Adamite race of humans, was publicly burnt in Paris in 1655.

As another example of the confused intellectual atmosphere that lasted for a few centuries, a hominid skull fragment from the site of Cannstadt, near Würtemberg in Germany, was discovered about 1700. Although of questionable context and uncertain date – as might be expected for a discovery considered to be ancient at a time when the accepted duration of the earth itself was no more than about 6000 years or so – this specimen later was resurrected by Quatrefages & Hamy (1882) as the prototype of their 'early fossil race,' a catch-all category that later came to include some Neanderthal material as well. Potentially more important was the skull of a child recovered along with Mousterian chipped flint implements and Pleistocene fauna from Engis Cave in Belgium by Schmerling (1833). Ultimately this hominid fossil also came to be accepted as a Neanderthal, but not until more than a century later (Fraipont, 1936). Hindsight can bring order to scattered observations, but it should not be used to reshape the sequence of events as they unfolded at the time; history may be rewritten but, absent a time machine, not remade.

In attempting to understand the early antiquarian investigations and the contemporaneous reports that were published about them, it is critical to avoid having in retrospect an attitude of superiority rooted in our current levels of knowledge. If anything, the primary scientific literature from a century and more ago should arouse in us feelings of admiration. The early publications on human prehistory record a wealth of original insight, fierce enthusiasm, vigorous effort, strong disagreement, and much honest uncertainty.

It is difficult, in fact, to capture fairly, in a few pages, the spirit shown by pioneering scientific investigators of more than a century ago. These were scholars who had to devise not only techniques of excavation but rules for interpreting the evidence that they recovered– what mattered and what did not – as they went along. They carried out these physical and intellectual labors in a cultural milieu characterized by public attitudes that began with amusement at adults grubbing about for fragments of bone and stone, then hardened into opposition to the investigators' increasingly strong insistence that their carefully excavated bits and pieces comprised evidence of a world far older than that sanctioned by any authority. Religious orthodoxy was rooted in a literal reading of the Bible, which militated against the very idea of great antiquity. Conditioned by clerical traditions, the popular mind could comprehend fossil bones with unfamiliar shapes only by considering them to be remains of antediluvian beings, the term often used for those humans who had lived before the time of Noah's flood as recorded in the Bible. It was difficult even for scientists of the time to accept the existence of peoples and cultures so different from their own. During the superficially orderly and progressive times leading into the Victorian era, it was disturbing for members of educated classes to realize that their earlier European ancestors must have lived as savages equipped only with chipped stone tools, and used these crude implements to hunt beasts as strange and forbidding as any that might be encountered in the far-distant tropical colonies. General acceptance of these heresies against conventional religious and social thought came tentatively, and only over the course of decades. Although the nascent archeologists and paleoanthropologists didn't always get things right, they did manage to make a start toward effectively recreating the past for generations of the future, including our own. As a result, we can now see more clearly the shattered mosaics of lost ages that the antiquarians had only begun to piece back together. If ever there were a bootstrap operation to change a worldview, this was it. And it succeeded spectacularly, however slowly and haltingly at first.

After realizing, of course, that there *was* a hominid fossil record, it is not so difficult to see that making sense of this fossil record required the integration of information from several sources of evidence that usually were not all found together. These included ancient tools or other cultural remains of stone or bone, the hominid remains themselves, skeletal parts of prehistoric animals; and geological evidence that all of the other elements had been contemporaneous during the life of the hominids long ago.

Why did people bother with these problems? Simple curiosity played a large role. Additionally, as still is the case today, so did a desire for attention, reputation, position, and financial reward. During the period when the early antiquarians were starting to sort things out, some of the European finds genuinely were exotic, or at least were made to seem so by the journalistic touches of the day.

Much excitement was generated by the discovery in 1822 of the so-called 'Red Lady' of Paviland from Wales, who was diagnosed erroneously as female on the basis of its accompanying ornaments. The discovery was made by a small party under the direction of the Reverend William Buckland, Professor of Geology at Oxford and who later became Dean of Westminster. The skeleton, found in a cave with the decidedly unromantic name of Goat Hole, exhibited features such as large articular heads on the arm and leg bones which, along with a narrow sciatic notch in the pelvis, are male characteristics. It had belonged to a tall, anatomically modern young man whose partial skeleton was stained with iron oxide pigment that had been spread over the body at the time of interment, and accompanied by an ivory ring, pendant, and other decorative items, as well as several hundred flint implements. Chiefly bones of the left side were recovered. To account for the missing parts it has been suggested (Molleson, 1976) that the skull, along with many bones of the right side, had been washed away by waves breaking into the cave before tectonic movements distanced the entire cliff face from the present level of the sea.

The faunal remains accompanying the Paviland hominid included bones of the woolly rhinoceros and elephant as well as wolves, hyenas, wild horses and cattle. Overall these are consistent with a cold, dry, later Pleistocene climate. The archeological context suggests that the corpse had been placed on top of earlier, reworked deposits containing tools similar to those from another site, Ilsen Höhle, previously dated to 27 000–29 000 BCE (McBurney, 1965). Oakley (1968) arranged for a ^{14}C date on collagen extracted from the left femur and two tibias; the age of this material was determined by Barker *et al.* (1969) to be 18 640 + 340 BP, or approximately 16 510 BCE. The Paviland Lady, or lad, evidently lived and died at the height of the last glaciation, during a climatic phase in which the surrounding environment was tundra, with the nearest glacier only 6 km to the north. Average annual temperatures were below freezing, so the body may have been covered with only about 15 cm of pigment-sprinkled soil rather than having actually been buried in hard, frozen ground.

Buckland's own overall interpretation of the Paviland find represents, to a modern reader, an odd attempt to reconcile a Biblical account of the world with the more objective geological explanatory frameworks now familiar to us. This relatively enlightened cleric believed for much of his life in a universal deluge, but he also held that bones found in many deposits, such as the Paviland Cave, were those of animals that had lived in Britain before the flood. Still further, although he accepted without cavil the existence of what then were termed 'antediluvial' animals in Britain, he could not accept that equally antediluvial humans were their contemporaries. In Buckland's view, therefore, the Paviland human skeletal remains must have been introduced into the cave at a later date, for which his guess was Romano-British times. The Dean's intellectual balancing act was sufficiently plausible and persuasive in its time that his book treating the subject, *Reliquiae Diluvianae* (Buckland, 1823), sold well to an enthusiastic readership. The work found a ready market among optimistic people who wanted to reconcile the results of current scientific investigations with already familiar interpretations of the Biblical account of creation and human history.

His letters indicate that Buckland had hoped to publish a second edition of his work, but the climate of opinion shifted. Toward the end of his life, under the influence of a new generation of geologists who were amassing an increasingly disturbing body of evidence, Buckland gradually gave up the belief in deluges of the Biblical sort, but not before attacking the inferences of another cleric, the Reverend J. MacEnery, who had the insight and courage to state publicly his conclusion that humans and extinct mammals had lived contemporaneously in antediluvian England (Keith, 1925a).

In 1825, MacEnery had found stone and bone tools apparently of human manufacture mixed with bones of Pleistocene mammals similar to those at Paviland, beneath a stalagmitic crust covering the floor of Kent's Cavern near Torquay along the Devonshire coast in Britain. Evidently out of deference to Buckland's views, MacEnery refrained from publishing his findings. Thus Buckland's contribution to the shaping of our current view of the past, while influential, was neither conclusive nor unblemished. Nevertheless on balance, as noted by Boule & Vallois (1921), to the explorer of Paviland falls the credit of having exhumed and placed in a museum the first fossil remains of an anatomically modern human skeleton.

Among the other influences that contributed to an acceptance of a greater human antiquity was a widely-read account by Edouard Lartet (1862). The paper titled 'New researches respecting the co-existence of man with the great fossil mammals, . . .' which Lartet regarded as characteristic of the latest geological period, recounted the significant find at Aurignac, France, made accidentally by a laborer, J. B. Bonnemaison. Further digging revealed a cache of human bones that excited local interest, which was judged annoying by the local mayor. To end controversy over the source of the skeletons, this public official had the bones reinterred in the parish cemetery. Fortunately, in the course of the burial the mayor had a tally kept of distinctive parts of the skeletons; this indicated the presence of 17 individuals. Lartet, who learned of the find by accident, conducted an excavation that demonstrated that the human remains had been accompanied by the faunal elements now familiar from Buckland's inventory – reindeer, aurochs, horse, rhino, cave bear, and hyena. Additional cultural remains reinforced Lartet's conclusion that 'the sepulchre of Aurignac should be referred . . . to an epoch *anterior* to the *diluvium* properly so termed . . . Regarding the subject archeologically, we perceive, in the absence of any kind of metal, and the common employment of implements and weapons of flint and bone, sufficient indications that the station of Aurignac should be referred to that ancient period of prehistoric times, denominated by antiquaries of the present day – the *Age of Stone*. Palaeontologically, the human race of Aurignac belongs to the remotest antiquity . . . evidently contemporary with . . . mammals, generally regarded as characteristic of the last geological period.'

Lartet's words carried weight, but not finality. Discoveries of anatomically modern humans in a fossil context continued to be made and at least some authorities continued to misunderstand them. Such was the case when Louis Lartet, son of the already eminent Edouard, discovered the remains at Cro-Magnon in France, the site that is now virtually synonymous with Upper Paleolithic hominids. The five skeletons clearly were purposeful burials conducted with attention to ritual details such as accompaniments of red ochre and strings of *Littorina* sea shells. The layer that contained them revealed a continuous series of hearths. Nevertheless, Boyd Dawkins (1880), one of England's leading authorities on cave sites, misrepresented the remains of Cro-Magnon as occurring in deposits that were 'later than the Paleolithic.' In science, cherished ideas die hard.

Eventually the controversies over the existence of hominids as fossils in antediluvian contexts were resolved, at least to the satisfaction of most scientists familiar with the evidence. A turning point came in late 1858 and early 1859, largely through British intervention on the side of a most persistent French researcher. The English paleontologist Hugh Falconer and geologist Joseph Prestwich concurred in accepting as genuine and of ancient human manufacture the shaped stones that the Boucher de Perthes, Controller of Customs at Abbéville, had been recovering for decades from the gravels of the Somme. At the same meeting of the Royal Society on May 26, 1859 where Prestwich gave his paper on the subject, William Pengelly confirmed the reliability of MacEnery's unpublished reports from Kent's Cavern, showing that flint tools were being found regularly with the bones of extinct mammals beneath stalagmitic deposits. Lyell, also present at the meeting, endorsed these views on the spot, and his views appeared in print during 1863, the same year as Huxley's essay on *Man's Place in Nature*. Watered by these steady streams of opinion, the ground had been prepared sufficiently for the next step backward in human ancestry. Yet opinion is never unanimous where the human fossil record is concerned. In the same volume as Prestwich's report, it was noted (Anon., 1859) that M. Isidore Geoffroy St. Hilaire, a respected anatomist, argued that 'mankind should be regarded as a distinct kingdom of nature, the 'Regne humain,' equal in rank to the mineral, the vegetable, or the animal kingdom – a proposal which, singularly enough, appears to have originated with the great scoffer, Voltaire.'

Neanderthals

The next tentative – and difficult, for the time – step backwards from the familiar features of humanity took place more than three decades later in Germany, near the locality of Hochdal. The evolutionary significance of the find there was controversial from the moment that it was made, and remains no less so today. The setting was picturesque. Above a small stream, the Düssel, rises a high, narrow valley called the Neander (*Neander Thal* in Old German). In 1857, workers about to begin quarrying limestone were clearing mud from a cave piercing the ravine's southern face when they found most parts of a rather robust skeleton. Not realizing its potential importance, they discarded all but a skullcap and a few of the larger postcranial bones. Just as at Aurignac, accidental discovery was followed by inadvertent destruction of evidence for human evolution. Fortunately at least some of the bones were saved when they came to the attention of Dr. C. Fuhlrott, a local physician, who transferred them to Professor H. Schaaffhausen of Bonn.

Schaaffhausen's description of the robust skeleton attracted wide attention in Germany when it was published in *Müller's Archiv* in 1858, as did the English translation of his paper published by English geologist Busk in 1861. His inferences, set out plainly as a series of numbered propositions, represent clear advances beyond Buckland's odd (at least to us) combination of empiricism and orthodoxy. Schaafhausen concluded that: (1) the form of the Neanderthal skull was normal rather than pathological, although of a form not known 'even in the most barbarous races'; (2) that these human remains 'belonged to a period antecedent to the time of the Celts and Germans' and probably derived from 'one of the wild races of Northwestern Europe, spoken of by Latin writers; and which were encountered as autochthones by the German immigrants'; and (3) that the human bones were contemporaneous with the 'latest animals of the diluvium.' Most of Schaaffhausen's paper was a comparison of the Neanderthal skullcap with those of present humans from various regions. However great the differences from these later samples, he could not as yet fathom the great span of time that would have separated a Neanderthal population from groups that had been living during the times recorded in historical sources. Neither, for that matter, could Busk.

In his brief comments on Schaaffhausen's paper, Busk did make an explicit comparison between the Neanderthal find and one that had been made three decades earlier by Schmerling at the Engis site (as Lubbock also did later, in 1864) terming it 'the most interesting relic of early humanity in existence'. It would appear that, in Schaafhausen and Busk, as well as Buckland and other predecessors, powers of observation simply were not equaled by comparable levels of imagination. They could not foresee that these first two Neanderthals known, manifestly akin to each other and even then distinguishable from modern human samples, would ultimately prove to be ten to twenty *times* older than had been allowed for in the chronologies then current.

From these earliest reports onward, response to the Neanderthal find was intense and diverse, though the balance of opinion generally was against a position ancestral to modern humans. One exception was Thomas Huxley (1863). Demonstrating the judicious phrasing that in time made him an influential statesman of science, he pronounced that although the Neanderthal fossil was the most apelike human skull he had ever seen, it was merely an extreme variant of modern humans rather than a separate species. A decisively opposite view was taken by William King, Professor at Queen's University in Belfast (Northern Ireland) and Queen's College, Galway, Ireland. In a paper read at the 1863 meeting of the British Association, King advocated designating the fossil as a new species of human, *Homo neanderthalensis*. Then, in a paper published the following year, he amended this position to one favoring an even greater distinctiveness from extant humans (King, 1864). Since these conclusions still are echoed by some recent scholars in the field, it is worth summarizing the process by which they were first reached.

King devoted about seven of the nine pages of his 1863 paper largely to anatomical characterization of the Neanderthal specimen, giving descriptions of the sort that would not differ strikingly from many papers that appear in anthropological journals today. However, this routine description is combined with statements of comparison that are now astonishing, 'The ribs, which have a singularly rounded shape, and an abrupt curvature, more closely resemble the corresponding bones of a carnivorous animal, than those of man' and 'so closely does the fossil cranium resemble that of the Chimpanzee as to lead one to doubt the propriety of *generically* placing it with Man.' Lastly, one reads that 'considering that the Neanderthal skull is eminently simial, both in its general and particular characters, I feel myself constrained to believe that the thoughts and desires which once dwelt within it never soared above those of the brute.'

On the evidence of his own words, William King, the first scientist to place a Neanderthal fossil into a taxonomic category separate from our own, manifestly did so by grossly exaggerating its morphological differences from anatomically modern humans. To him, the temporal separation of the population represented by the find was not an issue, since the age of the specimen was but poorly known and estimated to be on the order of a few thousand years at most. The argument that Neanderthals were too different *in relation to the time available for their evolution* into modern humans would come later, notably in the work of Sir Arthur Keith. That eminent, later, anatomist saw in finds such as Combe Capelle 'men of the modern type who, if not actually the contemporaries of Neanderthal man, were so closely his successors in point of time that it became impossible to believe that Neanderthal man represented a stage in the evolution of modern man' (Keith, 1925a: 710–11; see also pages 221–3).

King's negative reaction to the concept of the Neanderthal as a human ancestor was largely, if not exclusively, impressionistic. He gave no measurements, made no estimates of cranial capacity, or directed any other efforts toward the objective assessment of similarities or differences. Throughout his paper one can sense great strength of conviction about our distance from the Neanderthal specimen, in phrases ranging from 'I now feel strongly inclined to believe that it is not only specifically but generically distinct from Man,' to 'there are considerations of another kind which powerfully induce the belief that a wider gap than a mere generic one separates the human species from the Neanderthal fossil.' Nonetheless, the firmness of King's conclusion was not matched by corresponding strength of evidence. Numerous subsequent finds of Neanderthal fossils would undercut every particular of his subjective inferences. Ribs characterized by robust cross-sections are found in present humans with powerfully-developed thoracic muscles (as in fact had been realized by Schaaffhausen). The 'simian' crania of Neanderthals have proved to be more capacious on average than those of many extant humans, and evidence from other sites shows that these 'brutes' apparently supported their handicapped and elderly, and then buried them after death with what reasonably have been interpreted as offerings of food and flowers (e.g. Solecki, 1971).

Reading the early reactions to the Neanderthal find lends strength to the point that the study of past scholarship serves the understanding of present science. In King's work, far stronger in emotion than evidence, yet published in the day's very respected *Quarterly Journal of Science*, it is possible to see the first instance in which Neanderthals were dismissed by authorities as brutish creatures outside our ancestry. It would not be easy to account for the persistence of this position into our own time, except in light of the historical sequence reviewed here.

Fortunately, other workers of King's era took more quantified and otherwise objective approaches than he did, and left judgments that have withstood the passage of time, probably having had lasting effects even when the specific references have been forgotten. Thus in 1864, William Turner, Senior Demonstrator of Anatomy at Edinburgh, Scotland, reported measurements on the incomplete Neanderthal skullcap that (correctly) placed its cranial capacity in the range of modern German crania.

In response to the papers by Turner, King, and several others, Thomas Huxley weighed in again. Huxley's 1864 paper in the *Natural History Review* showered blows on mistaken scientists in several camps and countries. Professor Mayer of Bonn, Germany (who had hypothesized that the Neanderthal bones were those of a ricketty Mongolian Cossack belonging to one of the hordes driven by the Russians through Germany and into France in 1814) was dismissed with appropriately frank derision, and in devastating detail. In his critique, Huxley noted that Mayer's strained interpretation was occasioned by the German's reluctance to admit 'that the skeleton may possibly be thousands of years old . . . that anything is better than admitting the antiquity of the Neanderthal skull!'

While accepting its possession of some primitive characteristics, Huxley relied entirely on morphological grounds to reaffirm the position that he had outlined the previous year in his essay on *Man's Place in Nature*. The Neanderthal man was in no sense intermediate between men and apes. Its skull could be connected to a series of graded forms found among recent humans, so there was no basis for generic or even specific separation from extant *Homo sapiens*. Its anatomy could not justify any conclusion as to the age to which it belonged. While this analysis cannot be termed the final word on the phylogenetic status of the fossil hominids that have come collectively to be called Neanderthals – since the controversy swirls on, unabated even now – Huxley spoke with assurance on the position of Neanderthals in human ancestry, as well as on the larger issue that there had been an extended period of human antiquity. Even making allowances for the confident personality of the man who would go down in history as 'Darwin's bulldog,' we might still wonder – what was the basis on which Huxley's assurance rested in this case?

A good part of the answer would be found in the emergence of a new authoritative tome to replace the chronological traditions of the Bible. Between Buckland's work at Paviland and the discoveries at Neanderthal in Germany had come the publication of Lyell's *Principles of Geology* (several editions, in fact, beginning in 1830–1833). This work summarized an immense body of observations that established the foundations of uniformitarianism – the principle that processes in the physical world are so constant in all times and places that the present can be taken as a reliable key to the past. Oakley (1964) made a convincing case for the view that in the climate of opinion that Lyell's *Principles* helped so much to create, hominid fossil finds gained a whole new context. No longer were they isolated, unrelated observations; instead they could be related to each other and to a larger framework of knowledge. There was not yet a comprehensive theory of biological evolution, but the building blocks were piling up for its empirical foundation.

Pithecanthropines

At this point in the expansion of the hominid paleontological record the pattern changes, with the fossil evidence beginning to attract enough attention that anticipation was even running a bit ahead of the evidence.

For instance, in his work *The Evolution of Man*, the German naturalist Ernst Haeckel (1879) went so far as to coin a name, *Pithecanthropus alalus*, for a fossil yet to be discovered. As events developed, however, he didn't have to wait long for his expectations to be realized. Inspired by the writings of the German authority as well as those of Darwin and Huxley, a young Dutch scientist named Eugene Dubois determined to find more ancient hominids in the tropics of Asia. At the time, many specialists in the field were predicting that Asia was sure to hold earlier fossil human ancestors than those known already from Europe. Dubois first tried to persuade the Dutch government to finance an expedition with him as its leader – unsurprisingly, he was not successful. Delayed but not deterred, he resigned from his university position, secured a job in the Dutch colonial service as an army surgeon and in 1887 managed to get posted to the Dutch East Indies.

Once in Java, the determination that had driven Dubois to begin his quest carried him into energetic searches of ancient river gravels. His first success came at Kedung Brubus in central Java on November 24, 1890, with the discovery of one side of a fossilized human lower jaw lacking all teeth except for a canine root – the sort of thing that is intrinsically uninformative, but nevertheless encouraging. The following year in the valley of the Great Solo River near the village of Trinil, in Java, close to the foot of the two-mile (*c.* 3 km) high Lawu-Kukusan volcano, his excavations into a bone-bearing layer produced an upper molar tooth that Dubois attributed to a chimpanzee. This was a plausible call at the time, since fossil ape teeth previously had been found in the Siwalik hills of India, and Dubois believed that the two regions belonged to the same faunal province. In the next month further searches produced a cranial fragment representing the same portion as the Neanderthal skullcap, but lower in volume and much more constricted behind the very prominent brow ridges. His diagnosis again was chimpanzee. A year after his first find at Trinil came another tooth, this time a premolar that still made no problem for the running diagnosis being pursued by Dubois. Then came a femur, the large bone that forms the upper half of the leg, that very definitely did break with the expected pattern for a large ape.

The new femoral shaft was so straight that it simply had to belong to a being that walked upright. This was seen as a problem not only by Dubois but also by others. In fact, as late as 1925 the eminent British anatomist and physical anthropologist Sir Arthur Keith would write, 'The thigh bone is less ape-like in its general form, and in its individual features, than the thigh bone of Neanderthal man.' Yet all of the remains had been found close enough to each other that it was reasonable to believe that all came from a single species, if not the same individual. At least that was the opinion expressed by a large number of anatomists who commented on the Trinil find over the next several years, though as always there were dissenters (e.g. Ramström, 1921). But what sort of individual was it? Chimpanzee? Human? An upright ape of a sort not previously known? At the time all of these were plausible alternatives, even the last not being beyond consideration, since the preceding decades already had seen the expected range of ancestors expanded into entirely unexpected forms.

Dubois set out to arrive at a resolution using the framework of research in comparative anatomy, for which he was equipped through his training as a surgeon. From a series of cranial measurements he estimated that the capacity of the whole skull represented by the calvaria he had found would have been in the range of 900 cm^3. (Actually, in a bit of misguided precision he calculated the value as exactly 908cm^3.) The average for modern humans is about half again as large. Although the modern range is very wide, from roughly 1000 to 2000 cm^3, with the extremely high and low values encountered infrequently, Dubois' fossil was nearly 100 cm^3 below the expected modern range. Dubois also compared the teeth with known ape and human specimens, made endocranial casts to show the impressions left by convolutions of the brain within the skullcap, and so on. Overall he did a very creditable job of analysis and description, and reported his results in a series of papers beginning in 1894.

As might be expected, the overview provided by Dubois generated much discussion and controversy. It was not unreasonable that questions would be raised about whether the geological epoch represented by the Trinil deposits was Pliocene or Pleistocene. It was expected that there would be doubts about the degree of association between the cranial and postcranial parts. And there surely would be an attempt to sort out the phylogenetic position of what Oakley (1964) aptly characterized as 'a skull more human than that of any known ape, and more ape-like than that of any known man.' But at this point, in many accounts of the story of Dubois and his Javan fossils, the story takes a turn that is odd even in the annals of paleoanthropology. It often is noted (e.g. Williams, 1973:152) that toward the end of his life, Dubois became angered by the response of other scholars, and in consequence hid the fossils away from view for over two decades. It is also said that Dubois again shifted his interpretation, accepting the association between the ape-like skullcap and the modern-appearing femur, but explaining these mosaic characters by the suggestion that *Pithecanthropus* was not a hominid at all, but a large ape – a giant gibbon of some sort.

Neither of these parts of the legend describing a distant, or even demented, Dubois is correct. In fact, an abstract describing work done by Dubois on the brain-cast of *Pithecanthropus erectus* was read at a general meeting of the Fourth International Congress of Zoology in Cambridge, England, on the 26th of August, 1898. At the end of the meeting a resolution was read by Professor Macalister and seconded by Professor O. C. Marsh, two respected scientists.

'That, in the opinion of this meeting of the members of the Fourth International Congress of Zoology, the Dutch Indian Government, by ordering the exploration of Trinil, Java, leading to that most remarkable discovery of *Pithecanthropus erectus*, have laid the zoological world under a most weighty obligation, and that the aforesaid members of the Fourth International Congress of Zoology hereby desire to express their fervent hope that these investigations may be continued in the future with the same thoroughness as in the past.' (Macalister, 1898: 276)

The above paragraph is not the sort of endorsement made either commonly or casually by scientific societies, and it certainly would not have been done in recognition of a position propounded by a scientific crank. What is more, the massive bound tomes from the 1920s and 1930s of the *Koninklijke Akademie van Wetenschappen te Amsterdam* (the Dutch equivalent of the British *Proceedings of the Royal Society*, or *Proceedings of the National Academy of Sciences of the United States*) include many papers by Eugene Dubois. Among these are: descriptions of the Javan *Pithecanthropus* material in 1924, 1926, and twice in 1932; figures of the calvarium; of later discoveries describing more recent hominid fossils from Wadjak, another Javan site, in 1920; hypotheses concerning the cranial capacity of Neanderthals, also in 1920; and numerous papers documenting the extensive research conducted by Dubois on the evolution of the mammalian brain in 1924 and 1928. This was not the behavior of a man who had dropped out of the mainstream of science for several decades. Such a record of research and publication is inconsistent with the allegation that Dubois was a recluse.

It is never easy to track down the source of a rumor, and the passage of over half a century does not make the task any lighter. However, the following line does appear in the widely-read book *Up From the Ape* by E. A. Hooton (1946:297): 'Strangely enough, in his old age, when the important subsequent discoveries of von Koenigswald had conclusively established the primitive human status of Pithecanthropus, Dubois, the original finder, swung over to a view favored by a number of anthropologists; that the Java fossil was only a gigantic ape allied to the gibbon.' Dubois did discuss attributes of the Javan material in connection with characteristics of gibbons, but in a much more interesting and complex context, as has been noted by Gould (1990).

While Dubois did not advocate excluding his hominid finds from human ancestry, others certainly did. For example, Keith (1925a: 436, 437) ruled pithecanthropines out of the ancestry of modern humans not by evidence or compelling logic but by analogy; 'the gorilla of today is not a human ancestor, but retains, we suppose, in a much higher degree than man does, the structural features of the stock from which both arose. It is in this light I would interpret Pithecanthropus; a true survival, into late Pliocene or early Pleistocene times, of an early stage in human evolution.'

Why were these fossils a problem for Keith, similar enough that if relatively unchanged they represent survival of an ancestral stock, but in themselves too late to be actual ancestors? Keith's own words reveal an interesting thought pattern. 'How difficult it is to fix the exact position of Pithecanthropus in the common family tree of man and ape becomes manifest when we consider the structural characters of the thigh bone, the teeth, and the skull. The thigh bone is less ape-like in its general form, and in its individual features, than the thigh bone of Neanderthal man. The human thigh is moulded to suit the needs of a body balanced perfectly on the lower extremities' (Keith, 1925a: 425).

We can infer that for Keith, the evolution of our own direct ancestors was a unilinear progression of forms, not a sequence of populations made up of members adapting to the situations in which they found themselves, suited more or less well, and thus subject to the operation of evolutionary forces that could produce mosaic patterns of morphology.

There are numerous and diverse perspectives to be gained from the discovery, description, and phylogenetic diagnosis of the Javan pithecanthropine material. Among these is the realization that finding a fossil does not necessarily establish that the discoverer is the one best suited to diagnose the taxonomic position and phylogenetic significance of the find. Dubois, it will be remembered, initially thought that he had found a chimpanzee. In this regard, current developments in the field of paleoanthropology hold some promise for improvements in the future. No longer is one person expected to be an expert in all aspects of the research. Geologists and geophysicists using the various technologically sophisticated tools of our time are able to predict likely areas for discovery of fossils; anatomists using medical marvels such as computerized tomography are able to see inside matrix-encrusted fossils; and population biologists are able to use quantitative genetic theory derived from agricultural research to calculate rates of evolution that would have been beyond the ken of Keith and his contemporaries. Although it has become fashionable to bemoan the expansion of specialization in our time, it is evident that teamwork in research makes it possible to gain more information, not to mention the possibility of a more balanced perspective, on the past.

Australopithecines

By now the course of events in which a fossil hominid is discovered, advocated as an ancestor, shunted to a side branch, then ultimately (though never unanimously) accepted into the sequence of hominid phylogeny, is a familiar pattern. Another curious repetition also can be pointed out. Beginning with the Paviland discovery in 1822, the interval between a major discovery used to recognize one new grade of hominid evolution (such as anatomically modern humans) and the one subsequently discovered but geologically earlier (such as Neanderthals in the mid-1850s) averaged about three decades. This pattern, with all of the appearance of chance, was repeated again in 1924. The series of events that unfolded in this case – one chance happening after another – has been summarized authoritatively by Tobias (1985a).

Raymond Dart was an Australian by birth but had been trained as an anatomist in Britain. After finishing his education he took an appointment as professor of anatomy at the University of Witwatersrand in Johannesburg, South Africa. That country was known then, as now, for its incredibly rich mineral resources. These include not only gold, platinum and other precious metals, but also base metals. There also was an abundance of stone that could be quarried for building; although it was interspersed with pockets of less desirable material called breccia, the limestone in particular was generally of very high quality. The limestone deposits were also of interest to paleontologists, who knew that they contained fossils of many periods. Fortunately the commercial and scientific interests were reasonably compatible. The fossils, concentrated particularly in the least economically desirable breccias, consisted of mineralized bone fragments interspersed with pink sand, the entire mass being cemented together by the lime that made up the bulk of the surrounding stone. Aware of this situation, Dart asked his students to help him acquire specimens to build a museum collection. They did, thereby linking him into a series of events already underway.

In about the middle of 1924, E. G. Izod, one of the directors of the Northern Lime Company that was supplying building stone for the expanding construction of Johannesburg, visited the Buxton quarry in the vicinity of Taung. In the office of A. C. Spiers he saw a fossil baboon skull, and secured it for use as a paperweight. In his own office in Johannesburg this curiosity was seen by his son, Pat, a student at the University, who mentioned the baboon fossil to Josephine Salmons, another student working on a science course in the Wits Anatomy Department. She showed the specimen to Dart, who discussed it with Robert Burns Young, the Professor of Geology at the University. Young in his turn contacted the general manager of the Northern Lime Company, A. F. Campbell. Campbell promised to alert Dart to other finds, and instructed quarry workers to be on the alert for fossils that might be of interest.

There wasn't long to wait. Late in 1924, after blasting in a pocket of breccia, the quarry worker M. de Bruyn found a piece of stone that appeared to show the impressions from inside a skull; because this natural endocast was larger than the usual ones from baboons, he saved it and the surrounding fragments. These sat in Spiers' office for an indefinite period of up to several weeks, then were given to Young when he visited the quarry. Young then took the fragments to Dart. On opening the crate containing them, the young anatomist could see that the endocast fit into a cavity at the back of one breccia block. Realizing that the anterior part of the skull and perhaps the face might be imbedded in the breccia, Dart began at once to chip it out. He removed the matrix with a hammer and chisel, supplemented with a sharpened knitting needle for the more painstaking work. What emerged was the anterior portion from the skull of an immature hominoid primate. In addition to the endocast, it comprised a face from forehead through chin, including both an upper and lower jaw. Nearly all of the teeth were of the first set, or deciduous dentition, with the addition of first permanent molars that would erupt at about the age of five or six years in a modern human child. Nothing like the Taung child had been seen before by a trained scientist.

Dart's quick assessment of the specimen's potential significance can be gauged from the pace at which he conducted the work. The endocast and breccia block came into his hands on November 28, 1924. From that point he had to devise his tools, free the face and jaw from the matrix, describe and measure the specimen, compare it with other primate materials, then write and type his report. He did all of this in just 40 days (and, one suspects, at least a few long nights). That would be a very rapid pace even now for a laboratory team equipped with imaging instruments, power drills, and selective chemical solvents. For one person working alone with relatively rudimentary resources it was almost unbelievably expeditious.

As soon as his study was completed, Dart despatched the manuscript, on 6 January 1925, to the respected British journal *Nature*, which published the report on February 7, 1925. The paper deserves to be read today as a model of clear scientific description combined with bold inference, all done in a very lively style. The article began with a brief account of the history and setting of the find. Then followed an anatomical description of the skull, dentition, jaw, and endocast. Even allowing for the young age of the specimen, the face and dentition were, to use Dart's term, humanoid. Evidence for this point was the absence of a diastema or gap between the mandibular canines and the premolar teeth behind them in the dental arcade. Proceeding from this basis in careful anatomical observation, he was able to build a structure of reasoning about various aspects of the behavior of the group represented by the individual fossil that had come into his hands. For example, the placement of the foramen magnum, the large hole through which the spinal cord passes to meet the brain, was rather far forward, implying that 'greater reliance was being placed by this group upon the feet as organs of progression, and that the hands were being freed from their more primitive function of accessory organs of locomotion.' Dart acknowledged that use of the hands by early humans to manipulate tools and weapons had been suggested as a logical possibility by Darwin (1871) in the *Descent of Man* before finding its tangible support in features of the Taung child's skull and dentition. Dart's anatomically-based behavioral reconstructions then were placed into a plausible reconstruction of the environmental setting that had existed during the lifetime of the ancestors represented by the Taung find. Again acknowledging Darwin's inference that Africa would prove to be 'the cradle of mankind,' Dart stressed that the Taung child had lived in 'a more open veldt country where competition was keener between swiftness and stealth, and where adroitness of thinking and movement played a preponderating role in the preservation of the species . . . Southern Africa, by providing a vast open country with occasional wooded belts and a relative scarcity of water, together with a fierce and bitter mammalian competition, furnished a laboratory such as was essential to this penultimate phase of human evolution.'

In all, it is amazing that Dart's detailed evidence and close reasoning was accomplished in 40 days, and summarized in just a little over four printed pages. This was a feat that stands in the scientific literature as a monument to outstanding energy as well as intellectual courage. Yet the readers who chose to respond in print at the time were not so enthusiastic in their judgments. One of the more blunt critics (Bather, 1925) remarked in the June 20 number of *Nature* that 'Prof. Dart does not yet realize the many-sidedness of his offences.' Just what were these supposed transgressions?

Dart was accused of serious scientific failings on the basis of evidence that in retrospect seems rather trivial. For example, the Latin binomial *Australopithecus africanus* was held technically to be 'barbarous' because it combined Latin and Greek linguistic elements (Woodward, 1925). Similarly, Bather (1925) pointed out that the family name Homo-simiadae, coined by Dart to signify his belief in the transitional position of the australopithecines between apes and humans, violated the international rules of zoological nomenclature (which, based on Linnaean taxonomy, are inherently dichotomizing). Of course there were some more substantive objections, with many specialists (Duckworth, Keith, Smith) dismissing Taung as representative of no more than a new variety of ape that had developed a few characters in parallel with humans; but this was opinion rather than fact, and in time an overwhelming body of evidence would support Dart on point after point.

One has the impression that the critics' opposition was strongly expressed but weakly supported.

At the time of his paper in *Nature* (Dart, 1925), the superficial caveats expressed may have been based on older and stronger reasons for opposition to the position advanced by Dart. From his student days there lingered about him a reputation for brashness and incaution – the perjorative terms sometimes applied to people with great independence of mind. Certainly a less confident scholar might have sent the Taung skull back to the British Museum for analysis, description, and diagnosis, and it is part of the apocrypha of paleoanthropology that Dart had risked his reputation by not doing this.

There is evidence that the folk history of the field could be correct in this instance. In the autumn of 1924, at just about the same time that the Taung skull came into Dart's hands, a skull was found at the site of Kent's Cavern. The cranial fragments were sent by the Curator of the Torquay Natural History Society's Museum to the Royal College of Surgeons in order that a reconstruction might be effected and a report made on the characters of the skull by Sir Arthur Keith, a leader in the field of anatomical research. This was the expected course of action. Dart, in not following what appears to have been common procedure, instead pursuing his solitary, rapid research on the specimen, had only reinforced the impression of his storied 'rashness.' Though the comment by Bather focused particularly on nomenclature, his admonition to Dart could have been taken far more broadly – 'if you want to join in a game, you must first learn the rules.'

We might now say that Dart, more in the tradition of, say, Thomas Huxley, was more interested in the game of nature than the game of nomenclature. And if it seemed that Dart was wrong in the latter contest, it was because the game was, in a sense, rigged. In 1925, to most experts occupying influential positions in the fields of anatomy and anthropology, *Australopithecus* presented a pattern that contradicted both the dominant

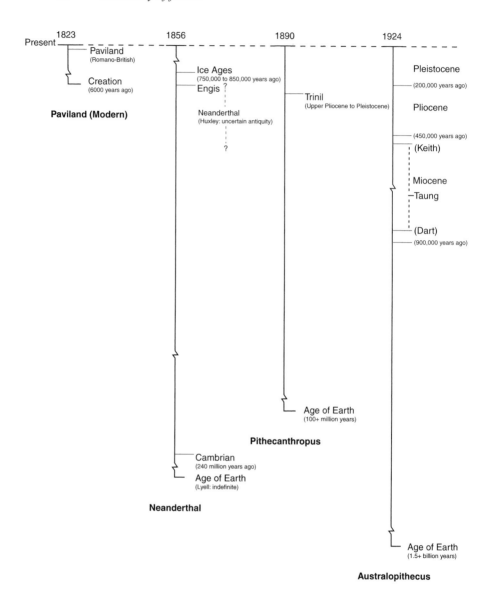

Figure 3.1. Cultural contexts of several key early hominid fossil finds. Over the course of a century, discoveries representing successively more ancient human populations occurred against a background in which the evolutionary timescale itself expanded irregularly to vastly greater durations. Data from Huxley (1893), Keith (1916, 1925a,b, 1931), Oakley (1964), and Burchfield (1975).

theory of the time, which was Sir Arthur Keith's view that the brain had led the way in human evolution, and the fossil evidence that supported this theory so perfectly that it could have been made to order. That evidence had been found at Piltdown, and in fact it had indeed been made to fit – a realization, however, that would not be established beyond doubt until nearly three decades had passed. Eventually Dart's views would emerge triumphant, but in a scientific world that would be almost unrecognizably different from the one in which the Taung child had first emerged. In the intervening period the evolutionary record would be documented as enormously longer than believed at the time of the first fossil hominid discoveries, chiefly by the use of techniques borrowed from chemistry and physics. Time itself would be the field on which evolutionary processes could operate; processes that only later would be brought together in a powerful synthesis unknown to the discoverers whose contributions have been described so far (Figure 3.1).

Paleoanthropology: the end of the beginning

By the end of the period summarized here, researchers working on human evolution had seen it all – lucky breaks, mistakes, and fakes; triumphs and errors. Before it had the name, paleoanthropology had the fame. It was a highly undisciplined discipline, one in which an ounce of evidence could be worth a pound of reputation, and as Buckland learned, a reputation founded on a fragmentary discovery might last for decades before itself falling to pieces.

4   *About a century of theory*

Introduction

The preceding chapter covered the mid-1820s to the mid-1920s, the period in which representatives of the major stages or grades of hominid evolution were discovered. Now we turn our attention to the events of the twentieth century. These events, however, in reality began with the publication of *The Origin of Species* by Charles Darwin in 1859 and which in many areas of paleontology, continue through to the present. Research in areas as diverse as developmental biology and field ecology were stimulated strongly by Darwin's publication.

Work along these many lines, and more, continues at a high rate. However, what might be considered an interim status report was provided by the publication in 1942 of *Evolution, the Modern Synthesis*. Janus-like, this volume by Julian Huxley surveyed the great strides that had been made since Darwin's work, and looked forward to the nascent expansion in fields such as ecological and biochemical genetics as well as the integration of studies on past and present populations.

Huxley's synthesis did not present a new theory of his own creation, nor did it mark an end to theory building in evolutionary biology. Instead, it described the logical superstructure of evidence and theory that had been built up from many elements – experiments and insights, controversies, and reconciliations. Many more gains in evolutionary theory and evidence would come, continuing powerfully to restructure the life sciences into their present forms. As already shown in the last chapter, the realm of research that later would become known as paleoanthropology had come into existence principally through the raw empiricism of fieldwork. Its first important discoveries having come from a depth of time that seemed always to be at the outer limits of the barely imaginable. The same depth of time – awareness of which came to anthropology as a joint legacy chiefly from geology and physics – made possible a formulation of the first workable mechanism, Darwin's, to explain generational change through time.

This chapter will begin with an overview of Darwin's key biological breakthrough, then follow that with a similar survey of Mendel's different but equally essential insight for studies of evolution. Next will come a summary of the long and contentious, but ultimately productive, efforts to reconcile what seemed at first to be inherent contradictions between the Darwinian and Mendelian perspectives on the maintenance of hereditary variants and changes in their frequencies through time.

Because of apparent contradictions between Darwinism and Mendelism, evolutionary biology went through a period of scientific strife that lasted for about three-quarters of a century. Within that timespan, three phases can be distinguished. During the first period there was no workable theory of heredity, a situation (even with the publication of *The Origin of Species* in 1859) that lasted through to 1900, when Mendel's work became widely known in biology. Second, from 1900 until 1918, came a period of conflict between two groups usually referred to as Mendelians and biometricians. Mendelians focused on the study of contrasting characters that appeared to be inherited as distinct units. Biometricians studied characters that were essentially continuous in their distributions, many of which had been documented by breeders and naturalists. Most biologists of the time agreed that these contrasting views could not be reconciled. Their pessimism was unjustified substantively – it is now known that the same laws of genetics regulate the transmission of genes, whatever the magnitude of their phenotypic expression. Nonetheless, the intellectual heritage of this conflict persists today in several continuing controversies. These include the fundamental question of whether macroevolution can be explained in terms of microevolution, as well as related issues concerning punctuated equilibrium, species selection, and the modifiability of developmental programs (Levinton, 1988).

Third, after 1918, when it was demonstrated that continuously distributed phenotypes could be explained in terms of numerous discrete genes individually having small phenotypic effects, there followed a phase of several more decades, during which other influences on gene frequencies (mutation, gene flow, genetic drift) were documented and their interrelationships explored. The outcome of all of these developments gave rise directly to the branch of modern biology known as population genetics, which in turn was a major component of what became known as the synthetic theory of evolution. Following an overview of evolutionary synthesis this chapter will conclude with a brief summary of some of the major subsequent theoretical developments in evolutionary biology that continue to shape the study of human paleobiology.

Darwin and natural selection

Darwin's breakthrough in biology came along a path smoothed by major advances in other natural sciences such as physics and geology. As discussed in Chapter 1, the Scottish geologists Hutton and Lyell gave to Charles Darwin 'the gift of time,' millennia beyond easy measure, and certainly outside of ready comprehension (Eiseley, 1954). During these vast reaches of geological time, evolutionary changes could accumulate over many millions of generations, eventually bringing about remarkable transformations in the characteristics of organisms. The mechanism that Darwin used to explain these changes was natural selection, and its enduring place in the history of ideas was established by publication of the *Origin of Species* in 1859. Darwin's epochal book followed closely upon the much briefer joint presentation of abstracts authored by Darwin and the independent co-discoverer of the concept, Alfred Russell Wallace (Irvine, 1959: 81).

It is a truism that natural selection is a simple idea; superficially it is so easy to grasp that to many people it appears disappointingly obvious. Even Thomas Huxley, who became Darwin's staunchest defender, remarked 'How extremely stupid not to have thought of that!' (L. Huxley, 1901: 183). At the core of Darwin's theory was the proposition that in every generation, the numerous members of each species compete with each other for the resources that determine their own survival and access to mates, as well as the survival of their offspring. In this contest, the classic 'struggle for existence,' those who possess the most advantageous hereditary characteristics persist and, through their differential production of offspring in numbers above the average, multiply the representation of their inherited characteristics in subsequent generations.

Evolution by means of natural selection is a concept that rests on several empirical observations. First, in every animal and plant species, parents produce offspring in numbers substantially greater than their own. Second, despite the large numbers of individuals born, the total number of adults in any given species tends to remain approximately constant from generation to generation. Third, no two individuals are precisely alike, so that among individuals within populations, and among populations within species, there is abundant variation. Fourth, much of this natural variation is heritable, supplying the raw material for evolutionary change.

The first two observations taken together have the inevitable consequence that there must be competition among the members of each new generation for survival and reproduction. The third and fourth observations indicate how the competition could produce evolutionary change –

those inherited variations giving their possessors an advantage over others would make it possible for them to survive longer and produce more offspring. These more numerous offspring would multiply the advantageous characteristics of the parents in the population. Through a combination of matings that would spread the beneficial features, coupled with death or displacement of less favored competitors, the advantageous inherited variations would come to predominate among the members of subsequent generations. Competition, inherited advantage, and differential outcome – joined together, these ingredients provided the logical basis for a mechanism that could explain evolutionary change. That idea has transformed our view of the world.

Darwin's insight commonly is attributed to the broad experience that he had gained as a naturalist accompanying the H.M.S. *Beagle*. He may in fact have been stimulated initially by the intensity of his experiences as a young field naturalist in South America and the Galapagos Islands. However, the things that he saw during his journey were seen by many other naturalists. Indeed, similar observations must have been made casually and piecemeal by many people, and the same patterns still can be seen today. However he came upon his insight, though, unlike most of his contemporaries, Darwin persisted in collecting and systematizing additional data over the course of decades. Ultimately he built up the body of evidence that eventually would convince other scientists that the patterns he saw compelled inescapable inferences – no matter how disturbing their consequences.

Whatever its genesis and however long its gestation, at the core of the Darwinian conception of evolutionary change was an intuitive realization of the immense power of compounding. Familiarity with the effects of compound interest may have been fostered by Darwin's experience as a rather astute and successful rentier whose reinvested gains transformed his family from a household of comfortable but modest means at the time of his marriage to one that was distinctly wealthy by the time of his death at age 73. Darwin's conceptually sound but largely unquantified grasp of evolutionary dynamics later would be put into more precise numerical terms by J. B. S. Haldane in works such as *The Causes of Evolution* (1932). Chapter 9 explores the implications of compounding through geological time for some interpretations of hominid evolution.

As has been realized by many others (e.g. Levinton, 1988; Dennett, 1995: 290), in our own time Darwin has been represented through selective citation as the archetypal gradualist, but this characterization is neither balanced nor accurate. Darwin's argument for evolutionary change, as noted previously, was structured logically as an 'even if' approach. *Even if* the gain in each generation were exceedingly slight in any characteristic, then after the passage of many generations, if selection were directional and recurrent (not necessarily constant) the overall gain could be prodigious.

In adopting his 'even if' approach, therefore, Darwin really was bending over backwards, creating the largest possible stumbling block for natural selection as a hypothesis. He realized that no matter how small a change might take place in any given generation, the sufficiently large number of generations documented by Hutton, Lyell, and others would make nearly any biological change that had occurred easily explicable. Phenotypic differences were givens, visible among populations of living organisms and in the fossil record. The magnitudes of these differences were measurable, and in many cases the span of time over which they had accrued could be estimated. The causal mechanism – natural selection – had been hypothesized. These factors could be put together and from them rates of evolution could be estimated. Gradualism, if that is the term that is applied to such reasoning, was not an essential part of Darwin's theory, but algorithmic compounding was. Betting on compounding was his way of handicapping a sure thing.

Darwin's explications of evolutionary patterns were diverse because his grasp of natural history was broad and deep. He knew from firsthand experience bodies of data as diverse as the fossil record of South American megafauna and the natural history of numerous continental and island species. He also carried out extensive correspondence with animal breeders, thereby gaining a grasp of the extent of intraspecific variation and evolution. This empirical base enabled him not only to understand the consequences of long-term change, but also to recognize readily and to integrate into his overall theory other phenomena such as extinction, or enduring phenotypic stability resulting in taxa that have persisted for millennia as living fossils (a term that Darwin coined). Nonetheless, Darwin did seek explanations for transformations in the structure of the eye and many other complex organs. Although in our day some of these have been worked out convincingly, stage by stage (with recent research summarized cogently by Dawkins, 1996), awe has remained even though much of the mystery has disappeared.

To Darwin, then, gradualism was not a pat, abstract explanatory mechanism. Differences in fossil assemblages from one geological stratum to another were observed regularly, and constituted the central challenges to be met by his theory. Persistent incremental change was the strong inference that he made in response. The challenge posed by the fossil record, moreover, was far greater in his own time than it is today. This is because when Darwin lived, the duration of the earth generally was considered to be only a fraction of current estimates of three to four billion years, and hence the number of generations available for evolutionary compounding were far fewer than we now know to have elapsed.

If the geological record provided the tapestry through which natural selection and other forces wove lasting patterns, then variation provided the diverse threads from which the images were incorporated by natural selection and other forces of evolution. How this variation was maintained and transmitted constituted a central problem for Darwin's theory. He grappled through all of the editions of the *Origin of Species* without ever coming up with a satisfactory explanation of how genetic material was inherited or its variants were perpetuated. Through familiarity with empirical research, Darwin was aware of the abundant variation that was a basic property of populations. He also knew this firsthand from his own field studies, reinforced by the extensive correspondence with breeders and other naturalists. Like other observers, he also considered variation to sort into two categories: infrequently-occurring discontinuous variations of large phenotypic effect, often termed 'sports'; and the far more common continuous variations of minor degree.

Sports were exploited by breeders, using artificial selection to create commercial stocks of animals and plants, and could be concentrated by a variety of techniques – inbreeding, back-crossing and the like – that would keep them from disappearing. But it was generally doubted that such protection would exist in species populations not under human control. It was believed that in the wild, blending inheritance would act constantly to dilute the impact of favorable variants, major as well as minor. This dilution posed a serious theoretical problem, one for which Darwin had no single good answer. Instead, over the years he offered several poor ones: the production of abundant heritable variation in each successive generation (comparable, in modern terms, to a high mutation rate) and even a form of the inheritance of acquired characteristics that he referred to as a 'Provisional Hypothesis of Pangenesis' (Darwin, 1868).

Darwin's cousin, Francis Galton, differed from him on this point, believing that evolution was discontinuous and that only large mutations could serve as a permanent basis for evolutionary change (Provine, 1971: 19–24). Galton's position would later serve as the focus of strong, lasting debate, following the rediscovery, decades later, of Mendel's experimental work on plant breeding, which might have given Darwin the missing piece that he needed to account for the persistence of variation.

Mendel and particulate inheritance

Entirely unknown to Charles Darwin, a mechanism that could explain conservation of variation in the face of selection, and without blending or dilution, already had been supplied by Gregor Mendel (1822–1884), an Augustinian monk who lived in Brü, Austria (now Brno in the Czech Republic). Mendel's name and the general nature of his scientific contributions are widely familiar. Although many people today are aware of Mendel's fame, few appreciate fully the nature of his work or its significance. This is not surprising. Growing plants quietly in a monastery garden seems such an anachronistic and dull enterprise, and peas are almost archetypally mundane – even their Latin binomial denotes the plant as the *common* pea. Perhaps for these reasons, among others, Mendel's results were ignored for a quarter of a century, then rediscovered – only to be misunderstood and misinterpreted for nearly as long again. It is critical to understand why these scientific problems occurred.

Like many botanists of his time, Mendel was interested in problems of plant hybridization as well as other aspects of inheritance. In pursuit of these interests, he began the research project in which he used garden peas (*Pisum sativum*) as experimental organisms. This was a fortunate choice, because there were available many pure varieties that differed clearly in numerous readily observable phenotypic characteristics such as seed color, seed shape, and height of mature plants. Each of the pure varieties was known to breed true to form in its characteristics – after planting, seeds from tall plants predictably produced tall plants which in turn produced more seed that would perpetuate this tall phenotype into future generations. The same was true for seed color, and so on.

Mendel's experimental design involved making crosses between different pairs of these true-breeding lines by transferring pollen from the male parts of flowers produced by short plants to the female parts of flowers from tall plants, as well as the reverse cross. Then, in a feature that evidently distinguished his research from much similar work carried out by predecessors and contemporaries, Mendel and his assistants kept extremely careful numerical records of the experimental results over three generations (the original parents plus the subsequent two generations of progeny). In each generation, the resultant phenotypes and their numbers were recorded.

A repeating pattern was observed. In the first generation of offspring (technically abbreviated as the F_1 generation), one member of each pair of phenotypic characteristics disappeared, leaving no visible trace. That is, when tall and short plants were chosen as the respective parents, members of the F_1 generation were all tall. In the next step of the experiment, members of the F_1 generation were self-fertilized (this is the genetic equivalent in plants of crossing opposite-sex members of the F_1 generation in animals). The resultant F_2 offspring showed both phenotypes that had been present in the parental varieties, short as well as tall. That is, the phenotypic characteristic that had marked one of the parents (short plant height), although missing in the second generation, had reappeared in the third generation.

These results differed in two ways from those that would have been anticipated on the assumption of blending inheritance. First, on the blending hypothesis, plants of the second (F_1) generation should have been intermediate in height between the two parents; they were not. Instead, something that had been introduced into the F_1 offspring from one parent masked the expression of whatever had been received from the other parent. Second, if the blending hypothesis had been correct, all of the plants in the third generation (F_2) also should have been intermediate in appearance, since a blending of inherited materials already would have been accomplished in the second generation. But again, they weren't. Instead, the parental traits had reappeared – not blended, but sorted out into the same two phenotypic categories that had existed at the start.

From the outcome of his experiments, Mendel inferred that characteristics such as tallness and shortness are determined by factors, or stable particles, originally contributed by the parents and not affected by being in contact with each other while in the offspring. This concept, i.e., that stable particles constitute the basis for the inheritance of biological characteristics, is the core of Mendel's principles. These particles have been called genes since Gregory Bateson's suggestion in 1906, although as early as 1819 the German phrase *genetische Gesetze* was used by Festetics to refer to regular patterns of biological inheritance in animal breeding. The alternative forms of any particular gene are referred to as alleles. Most commonly these exhibit small-scale differences in their chemical structures that have arisen through past mutations. A cell or zygote that contains two copies of the same gene is said to be homozygous, while one that contains two different alleles is termed heterozygous.

Sometimes the central importance of Mendel's discovery of particulate inheritance is obscured by attention to what is merely a peripheral feature of gene expression – the phenomena of dominance and recessiveness. In the example just considered, when the two alternative alleles influencing plant height were together in the F_1 generation, the externally visible phenotype of the mature plant was tall. But in the nucleus within each of the plant's cells resided two alternative genes for plant height. In the heterozygote the allele for tallness masked the expression of its alternative allele for short plant height. The allele that is phenotypically expressed is said to be dominant, while the allele that has its expression masked is said to be recessive.

If dominance and recessiveness were all there had been to Mendel's discovery, its importance would have been superseded entirely in the modern era, when more powerful techniques of analysis, such as electron microscopy and electrophoresis, make it increasingly easier to distinguish between the products of alternative alleles. Now that it has become possible to sequence entire genes, the detectable phenotype converges on the genotype and very literally the medium becomes the message. Consequently, much of the earlier terminology used to describe gene expression has become obsolete. We now know that dominance and recessiveness are not intrinsic properties of genes as much as they reflect a limited ability to detect the variation that is present. The real significance of Mendel's work arises from the fact that his methods and inferences were statistical, with frequency ratios among the offspring holding the key to his inferences about the regular transmission patterns of unit characters. These frequencies are the well-known Mendelian ratios, such as 3:1 and related permutations.

Mendel's major contribution to the advancement of evolutionary theory was the statistical demonstration of particulate inheritance, and the details of his discoveries are formalized into what usually are referred to as Mendel's laws of segregation and independent assortment. Segregation refers to the behavior of the two members of a single pair of alleles. When the gametes are formed by adults of the F_1 generation, the members of a pair of alleles separate or segregate from each other, so that each sperm or egg gets just one allele of the pair. Independent assortment deals with the results of gene transmission when more than one pair of genes is considered. Segregation occurs for each allelic pair independently of every other pair. Strictly speaking this occurs only as long as the gene pairs are carried on different pairs of chromosomes, which is not always the case. For example, peas have only seven pairs of chromosomes, while human beings have many thousands more loci borne on their 23 chromosome pairs. However, Mendel appears fortunate enough at the beginning of his research to have chosen phenotypic features that were scattered widely enough through the genome of his plants that their gene pairs did segregate independently.

The addition of Mendel's laws to Darwin's mechanism for evolutionary change produced a powerful explanatory combination. No longer was it necessary to think only in terms of one entire species of organism replacing a previous species. Instead, populations can attain new optima generation after generation, since new combinations are assembled anew every time that gametes are formed. Whenever the reshuffling produced an improved combination, selection could bring about increases in frequency, with the rate of increase being roughly proportionate to the selective advantage. Under these circumstances, genes coding for other features might remain little changed in frequency, since independent assortment generates new combinations with each generation. The predictable result would not be the replacement of an entirely uniform group of organisms – one 'type' in the terminology of the day – by another type. Rather, the effect of allelic substitution would appear as the emergence of numerous new phenotypic blends within existing populations, as the advantageous genes increased within the milieu of various genomic backgrounds.

The awesome ability of genetic reshuffling to generate novel allelic combinations on which selection can operate to bring about evolutionary change seems evident only in retrospect. Historically, the abstract rules of genetic transmission that Mendel discovered were formulated and published in 1866, but had little or no discernible impact on discussions of heredity until they were rediscovered around the turn of the nineteenth century. At that point their importance was seen, but many of their implications were misunderstood. Certainly no general grasp of the utility of the combined explanatory package (inheritance in the form of unit characters unaffected by blending, plus selection operating to change the frequencies of the units) for resolving long-standing problems occurred immediately when Mendel's laws were rediscovered, or in fact even for several decades afterwards.

Part of the reason why Darwinism and Mendelism were seen as contradictory rather than complementary elements in formulations of evolution had to do with some important accidents in the history of science. One of the three European biologists who rediscovered Mendel's work on plant hybridization in 1900 was Hugo de Vries, who in the same year published the first volume of his own *Mutationstheorie*. In this influential work he argued that selection simply was insufficient for the genesis of new species, which instead arose through large-scale mutations. This viewpoint was seen as flatly contradictory to much of the work on inheritance of continuous characters by most biometricians.

Large gene effects or small? Mendelians vs. biometricians

Far from facilitating the acceptance of natural selection by removing the problem posed by blending inheritance, the rediscovery of Mendel's laws actually retarded the acceptance of Darwin's theory by calling into question the outcome of selection acting on small continuous variations. Ammunition was thereby given to partisans of large discontinuous phenotypic effects then referred to as 'sports' – or so the Mendelians thought (Provine, 1971). Because the interchange of viewpoints involved some influential and colorful scientific personalities, its detailed history is interesting and pertinent to the argument here. Especially important to us is the timing of the debate and how it may have influenced the interpretation of hominid evolution.

The controversy surrounding the resurfacing of Mendel's discoveries had begun some time earlier. Biometric work on a considerable scale was begun by Francis Galton, first cousin of Charles Darwin and a serious researcher in his own right. Galton focused his attention on the inheritance of human phenotypic features such as eye color, artistic ability, temperament, and perhaps most notably, stature. During these investigations he became aware of the phenomenon of regression, the tendency for progeny of various crosses to converge on (or revert to) the group mean. Galton devoted much energy to the mathematical derivation of regression coefficients. Although these proved to be of little lasting value in themselves, they did lead to the regular statistical analysis of correlations. As a result, Galton's book *Natural Inheritance* (1889) has been considered by many to mark the beginning of biometry, a discipline with empirical applications that continue to have important applications to the study of morphometric skeletal variation (Howells, 1973; Lahr, 1996).

Like Darwin, Galton made a distinction between sports and smaller scale variations; unlike Darwin, he considered that larger-scale differences provided the only significant, enduring source of hereditary variation. Because of his emphasis on large-scale gene effects as the basis of evolution, Galton subsequently was seen by the Mendelians as their progenitor. At the same time, because of the methods that he had developed for the study of continuous variation, Galton was also considered to be a mentor by later biometricians. Aside from this common intellectual predecessor, for about the first three decades of the twentieth century all that was shared by the Mendelians and the biometricians was their mutual engagement in intense scientific conflict. If the Mendelians had worked with – rather than against – the biometricians, the synthesis of Mendelian inheritance and Darwinian selection into a coherent mathematical structure (as was accomplished later by population genetics) might have occurred much sooner.

Biometricians logically supported Darwinian evolution, with its central emphasis on small-scale, gradual changes that could compound into measurable trends under the cumulative influence of natural selection. The

Mendelians advocated saltational changes (nongradual leaps) as causes of evolution, a position affirmed by the sort of discontinuities that they could see arising spontaneously in their laboratory stocks. Powerful personalities were arrayed on both sides of the conflict. The biometricians included Karl Pearson and W. F. R. Weldon, while the leading Mendelian was William Bateson. Collaboration between the two camps was impossible because of the intensity of disagreement generated by strong personal antagonisms.

Pearson began his scientific career in mathematics, though his intellectual diversity led him into many other endeavors. Beginning in 1891, with the arrival of the biologist W. H. R. Weldon at University College (London, UK), however, Pearson's work came to concentrate on the joint study of heredity, evolution, and statistics. Weldon was a morphologist by training, but had come to realize that comparative anatomy and embryology were limited by their intrinsically descriptive approaches to structure. He saw the potential for a new approach to the study of variation through Galton's work, from which Weldon derived the fundamental principles of a biometrical approach to the study of evolution. With Pearson and others he was instrumental in forming a special committee of the Royal Society for 'Conducting Statistical Inquiries into the Measurable Characteristics of Plants and Animals.' But serious problems arose when these biometricians, inspired by Galton's principles and methods, found themselves in conflict with Galton himself, who believed that regression was so powerful that the selection of small-scale variations underlying continuous phenotype distributions could have but limited effects. Only large jumps, in his opinion, would support lasting evolutionary change.

Eventually Bateson also came around to this position. His viewpoint on the subject was attributable to the outcome of various investigations that he had carried out to show the relationship between environmental and morphological changes. These failed to accomplish their intended objective, quite possibly because the observations were guided more by vague hopes than by tight experimental design. Nevertheless, Bateson turned increasing attention to discontinuous variations of a particular sort – what now often are referred to as meristic traits: serially repeated structures such as fingers and teeth. His attempts to find explicable changes in continuous characters were frustrated. He accepted the common argument (which still is made today by some morphologists) that continuous variants would confer selective differentials so small as to render natural selection ineffective.

Bateson's theoretical break with Darwinism was also accompanied by a complete separation from Weldon. The tombstone of this relationship's end was the publication of Bateson's (1894) *Materials for the Study of Variation*, a major work in which he presented nearly 900 examples of discontinuous variation. Galton (1889) was pleased, as was Thomas Huxley. Weldon was not, and made his views plain through a review in *Nature*. With this publication, a battle was joined between Pearson and Weldon that was to last over a dozen years until Weldon's death. The conflict drew in dozens of intellectual combatants, who marshalled armies of dark words across the paper plains of scientific journals.

Throughout this long period, confusion reigned among biologists about the mechanisms of heredity and evolution. Much of the problem was attributable to the continuing influence of Galton, who formulated and reformulated his 'Law of Ancestral Heredity,' expressing it in several mathematically contradictory forms (e.g. Galton, 1897). The next year Pearson published yet another revision, but to no practical purpose. As pointed out by Provine (1971: 54) 'The confusion surrounding Galton's law was so complete that biologists never straightened it out. The rise of population genetics showed that Galton's law was irrelevant and it simply dropped from sight.' Although Galton's contributions clearly were influential, they had been directed toward a set of problems that were intractable for reasons now obvious – environmental influences such as nutrition and health status can obscure genetic contributions to the phenotype, experimental matings cannot be arranged because of ethical grounds, and so on. Despite these handicaps, and in part to overcome them, Galton and other biometricians developed highly sophisticated mathematical approaches to describe continuous quantitative variation, and some of these tools retain enduring value.

The Mendelians, for their part, were obtaining some results that diminished the gap between their position and that of the biometricians. The research responsible for this transformation in viewpoint included T. H. Morgan's (1916) work with *Drosophila*, which showed that mutations on a very minor scale could follow Mendel's laws of transmission. Morgan's results were reinforced by William Castle's demonstration that the selection of continuous coat color variants in rats could change phenotypic expression in a population to a new stable level beyond the original limits of variation. But perhaps preeminent among these related research findings were the demonstrations, by H. Nilsson-Ehle (1909) in Sweden and Edward East (1910a,b) in the United States, that Mendelian inheritance could explain certain continuous variations that appeared to be subject to blending.

The basis for Nilsson-Ehle's work actually had been laid by some of Mendel's lesser-known results – with the bean *Phaseolus*. Crosses between one stock that had white flowers and another with purple produced first generation hybrids, all with purple flowers. But crosses among members of this offspring generation produced a second generation with flowers ranging from white through pale violet to a dark reddish purple. Mendel (reprint 1958 in Provine, 1971: 58) realized that these results could be explained in terms of several independently inherited factors. Had the biologists who rediscovered Mendel's work and debated about its compatibility with Darwinism come to the same realization, years of bitter controversy might have been avoided.

Nilsson-Ehle knew of Mendel's experiments with *Phaseolus*. Thus, when some of his crosses with cereal grains such as oats and wheat produced ratios other than the common 3:1 in the F_2 generation, he was able to interpret some of his results correctly as resulting from two-factor and three-factor crosses. He even had one case that suggested, though not definitively, that he was dealing with four independent factors. Nilsson-Ehle was able to extrapolate from these experimental results that 10 independent factors exhibiting incomplete dominance could produce nearly 60 000 different phenotypes, each with a different genotype.

Two of Nilsson-Ehle's further inferences were exceedingly powerful in their significance for Darwinian evolution. The first was that certain variations which many biologists had been calling mutations really were not altered alleles at all, but merely uncommon gene combinations formed by recombination. This realization yielded a ready explanation for the occurrence of atavisms, reversions to phenotypes seen in ancestors, that had greatly puzzled Darwin and others. The second realization was that sexual reproduction was a prodigious generator of these new genotypes. These clarifications clearly supported Darwinian evolution, since they established not only that blending was a phenotypic artifact or illusion rather than the result of fundamental genetic alteration, but also that variation was exceedingly abundant in populations of sexually reproducing organisms. At one stroke the problems of the depletion of variation in general, and dilution or swamping of advantageous genes, were practically solved.

Certainly, and unfortunately, most biologists of the time did not immediately grasp the full implications of these results. Edward M. East (1910b), who was familiar with Nilsson-Ehle's paper and had done similar research with maize, initially concluded that all selection had done was to have isolated 'sub-races . . . intermingled by hybridization'. Only later did he realize, as Nilsson-Ehle had, that selection could be effective in moving a character beyond its original limits of variation.

Helping to remove the last impediment to joining Mendelism with Darwinism as foundation stones in explaining evolutionary change were the breeding experiments of W. E. Castle with hooded rats. In 1911, he reported that after 13 generations of selection, he and his colleagues had been able to establish degrees of expression that were beyond the original limits of variation in the population. This inference was basically similar to the results reported by Nilsson-Ehle and East. However, Castle believed that he had been selecting variations in the Mendelian trait itself – that is, modifications of the basic allele.

Other geneticists disagreed with this explanation, and their reservations pushed Castle and his co-workers, including Sewall Wright, to further levels of experimental demonstration (Castle & Wright, 1916). Eventually it became clear, particularly after the criticisms of Sturtevant (1918) arising from the extensive work done by him and others with *Drosophila*, that selection actually was acting on modifier genes at other loci. As late as 1916, Castle had been attempting to defend a compromise position by suggesting that there were two categories of hereditary characters, those following Mendel's laws and another set of hereditary factors that are modified in the zygote and blended gradually over the course of several generations. This interesting attempt at compromise simply did not stand up in the light of later work.

Several years later Castle (1919) retracted his previous stand on the modifiability of Mendelian factors. He not only made an honest acknowledgment of error but also furnished a classic example fitting the pattern of thesis and antithesis followed by synthesis. As a result, objections to early experiments were met with ever more cogent responses until an outcome was reached that could be accepted by all partisans. By the end of this sequence, it had been established that Darwinism and Mendelism were complementary central ingredients of a workable theory of evolution. This theory remained to be completed by additional necessary discoveries that would be made over another two decades, but the key elements of both approaches had been joined.

From the Mendelian side, it had been demonstrated that inheritance was particulate at the level of the genotype, so that blending was an impression at the level of the phenotype only, and occurred most convincingly when multiple genetic loci influenced any particular character. Prodigious numbers of genotype combinations, numbering into the tens of thousands, could be generated by independent assortment among the relatively few loci contributing to the phenotype of a quantitative character, such as flower color in a plant or coat pattern in a mammal. From the Darwinian side, selection could be considered as a creative agent of change – as certain gene combinations were favored, population frequencies could shift markedly over the course of generations, making rare gene combinations more common, and entirely new gene combinations possible. Phenotypic distributions could change not only in terms of population means, but also in terms of extremes, some of which should produce novel character states.

These conceptual advances were important to plant and animal breeders. Some of these breeders used the new knowledge to generate substantial economic returns, as in the industry that created hybrid seed corn (or maize – *Zea mays*), which gained substantially increased yields over the previous random-bred varieties. This hybrid grain, fed to farm animals also improved by selection, resulted in yields of meat, milk and eggs so great that surplus production became a serious economic problem. The same discoveries had a comparable potential, though intellectual rather than economic, to revolutionize paleobiological interpretations of the fossil record.

Genes and chromosomes

Important as the basic discoveries were, there is more to evolutionary theory than Darwin's mechanism to account for directional change and Mendel's empirical demonstration that inheritance is based on the orderly reshuffling of relatively stable hereditary particles rather than the irreversible blending of contributions made by parents to their offspring. The other ingredients came swiftly in biology's intellectual ferment at the beginning of the twentieth century.

As early as 1902, Mendel's hypothetical particles were shown to have a very tangible reality, as a result of two independent discoveries. W. S. Sutton, then a graduate student at Columbia University (New York, USA), and Theodore Boveri, a well-known German cytologist, both realized that the transmission of Mendel's particles matched the regular distribution of chromosomes during cell division. Independently the American and the European scientists reasoned that unit characters are transmitted from parents to offspring in the ratios observed by Mendel because the genes are located on chromosomes and the chromosomes are passed on in regular patterns during cell division. This insight came to be known as the chromosome theory of inheritance.

The nature of gene mutations, and hence of genes themselves, was for a very long time lost in a terminological tangle. Biologists initially associated the term mutation with large-scale alterations in appearance – 'sports' – as opposed to more continuous phenotypic variants. This association was confirmed strongly through the publication by Hugo De Vries in 1900 of his *Mutationstheorie*, which, as mentioned, championed the idea that large-scale changes were necessary ingredients in the genesis of new species. This idea arose largely from his work with *Oenothera lamarckiana*, the evening primrose. Only after much experimental work carried out by B. M. Davies from 1909 through 1916, and summarized in the incisive publications by Castle (1916) and H. J. Muller (1918), was it realized that *Oenothera* was a permanent hybrid in which the regular appearance of 'mutants' was due to the operation of a complex system of balanced lethal genes. In the interim, fortunately, work with *Drosophila* had established the existence of numerous 'definite mutations.' This was the term introduced by Morgan and his co-workers (1916) at Columbia for stable changes of very small scale that followed regular patterns of Mendelian transmission. Later H. J. Muller would receive a Nobel prize in 1946 for his demonstration that such changes could be induced by ionizing radiation.

Predicting and measuring evolutionary change

Early in the twentieth century it was widely believed that new mutations, once they had occurred, would spread automatically through a population. This point was made explicitly by Udny Yule in the discussion following a lecture on 'Mendelian Heredity in Man' delivered by R. C. Punnett at the Royal Society of Medicine in London (UK) in 1908 (Provine, 1971: 134). Yule suggested that a new dominant gene would increase in frequency until it reached stability at 50 percent. Punnett took up this point with a friend of his, the mathematician G. H. Hardy, who immediately saw that Yule's suggestion was fallacious. In a letter to *Science* in 1908, Hardy established the mathematical conditions for the stability of gene frequencies in a Mendelian population. The German physician Wilhelm Weinberg had delivered a paper about six months earlier making the same point, and published it later in 1908 in a German journal with a narrower distribution than *Science*. Together, these publications were significant in that they showed how to establish a definite quantitative baseline from which changes in gene frequency could be measured. This known starting point was an essential prerequisite for the quantitative study of evolutionary change. Very swiftly it was put to practical use in studies of microevolution.

By 1916, Morgan had incorporated into his lectures the concepts of the chance fixation of a mutation and an increase in its frequency through selection. Even before this time, more precise work had been underway in England. In response to a request from Punnett, the Cambridge mathematician H. T. J. Norton prepared a table that showed what the effects on gene frequency change would be with various levels of selection intensity. The table was included in Punnett's book on *Mimicry in Butterflies*, published in 1915. The results were striking. With a selective disadvantage of only 0.01, a recessive gene could be reduced in frequency from 44 percent to under 3 percent in about 700 generations. With a disadvantage of 0.10, the time dropped to roughly 70 generations. Evidently under some circumstances, natural selection could be an extremely potent factor in bringing about evolutionary change.

Substantial debate existed on the boundary conditions under which selection could operate. Many geneticists and naturalists, including Bateson, Punnett and de Vries among others, asserted that allelic substitutions that produced only small phenotypic differences should have no effect on fitness. This argument did not follow from empirical data but rather from unexamined anthropocentrism – if humans could not see much of a difference, how could blind nature discern any? The mathematical geneticist Ronald Fisher disagreed, arguing for a near linearity of effect across the phenotypic scale – if a change of 1 mm has selective value, then a change of 0.1 mm could be expected to have a selective value approximately one-tenth as great (Fisher, 1930: 15). This position was in many ways an important contribution to the synthesis of Darwinism and Mendelism. Just two years later, J. B. S. Haldane published his own complementary work, *The Causes of Evolution* (1932), which brought together principles that quantified the theory of natural selection.

Sewall Wright was less deterministic in his approach to evolutionary change, believing that random genetic drift in small populations was very important, since it could bring about new combinations of genes. In a review of Fisher's book *The Genetical Theory of Natural Selection* (Fisher, 1930), Wright offered his own perspective, holding that in populations of intermediate size there could be a 'kaleidoscopic shifting of the prevailing gene combinations' (Wright, 1930: 354–5). These shifts could bring into existence new adaptive combinations that never would be reached by a direct process of selection. Wright's belief in the importance of interaction among systems of genes, or gene complexes, was rooted in part in some of his early work using guinea pigs as experimental organisms. Guinea pigs usually have four toes on each front foot and three on each hind foot, but Wright detected a mutant that increased toe numbers. Breeding from animals carrying this allele, he eventually was able to restore a condition that mimicked the ancestral mammalian phenotype of pentadactyly, though the underlying genes very likely differed from the original alleles. Wright interpreted his results conservatively in terms of the evolution of modifier and suppressor genes, but this position should not have prevented paleontologists from grasping the broader implications of the work – that discontinuous character states, with visible counterparts in the fossil record, could be altered markedly over the course of just a few generations.

From broad experience, applied and theoretical, Wright developed not so much an alternative to the approaches of Fisher and Haldane, but rather an added dimension to the understanding of evolutionary mechanisms. It was Wright's work, in particular, that directed the attention of many biologists to the importance of population structure. He also examined the evolutionary consequences of populations that were influenced by various levels of internal subdivision and external gene exchange, or gene flow.

The very brief summary of population genetics theory provided here, from the work of Darwin (1859) through the more comprehensive and formally mathematical treatments first by Galton (1889) and Pearson (1894), then Fisher (1930), Wright (1931) and Haldane (1932). Such an overview must almost of necessity leave an erroneous impression of contentious but relatively steady theoretical progress that made the synthesis of ideas all but inevitable. That is only a retrospective impression.

The evolutionary synthesis: a midterm report between the *Origin* and the present

The elements of particulate inheritance, mutation, natural selection, gene flow, and drift constitute the principal factors that interact in the course of evolution. This much had been established by about 1930 in a wealth of publications in scientific journals, with many of the broader implications brought together in the important books published by Fisher and Haldane in the early 1930s. Explication of the interrelationships among forces of evolution, with consideration of population structures and attention to environmental changes over time, formed the basis of Julian Huxley's work *Evolution: The Modern Synthesis*, first published in 1942. Other important discoveries remained to be made in the future, particularly the bodies of work that comprise ecology, ethology, and molecular biology. By the early 1940s, however, the major elements of evolutionary biology had been articulated. At this point we can turn briefly to consideration of the extent to which these insights influenced the study of human evolution.

Genetic theory and the interpretation of human evolution

In 1924, the same year that Raymond Dart began his study of the Taung fossil (his findings were published in *Nature* 1925), R. A. Fisher summarized in the *Eugenics Review* two lectures that he had delivered that same year at the London School of Economics (Fisher, 1924). Fisher was able to make the strong inference that quantitative characters of humans and other organisms are transmitted by Mendelian factors and that selection is likely to have exerted appreciable influence on the evolution of such characters. The coincidence of these two events in 1924 is just one particular instance of a point already made in Chapter 2, that there was a lag in the application of evolutionary theory to the data being generated by human paleontology. Alternatively, it could be said that all of the abstractions referred to as major stages or grades (in the terminology of Thomas Huxley) of fossil hominids – anatomically modern humans, Neanderthals, pithecanthropines, australopithecines – had been discovered prior to the forging of the evolutionary synthesis.

For the most part, hominid fossils were discovered in a period that can be described, from the standpoint of evolutionary mechanisms, as nearly a theoretical vacuum through which a few misleading impressions drifted about inconclusively. Examples abound. The first fossil remains of anatomically modern humans, discovered in 1823, were received in a cultural setting in which the very idea of evolution was implausible to most biological and physical scientists. The first Neanderthal remains (found in 1856) antedated by several years the publication of *The Origin of Species*. The Javan *Homo erectus* fossils (found in 1890) were discovered and debated in a scientific world still ignorant of Mendel's laws. To return to Taung, that first fossil of an australopithecine was freed from its matrix at a time (i.e., 1924) when in journals of human heredity, Lamarckian inheritance was still discussed as a viable alternative or useful adjunct to Darwinism, and when a geneticist could write that 'a species is a group of organisms that . . . tends to become pure for one genotype' (Hagedoorn, 1924). Thus, by the time evolutionary synthesis had taken place, all of the major categories of fossil hominids already had been discovered, discussed, and debated. And nearly all of them already had been dismissed as having any relevance to the ancestry of modern humans.

In the scientific traditions of the times, paleoanthropologists would naturally have been among the last of the groups grappling with evolutionary problems to have realized the utility of selection acting on combinations of genes that were reshuffled anew each generation. Long before the time of the evolutionary synthesis, human paleontologists were accustomed to working within a temporal framework that was believed to have been of rather short duration. Given that constraint, which we know in retrospect to have been artificial, the central problem of explaining morphological differences among fossil specimens almost inevitably implied an answer in terms of population replacement. Consequently, paleoan-thropologists became accustomed to explaining how one species or type replaced another. At the same time, geneticists were working out mechanisms of gene expression and gene frequency change that could explain how evolutionary change could take place *within* populations. Theoretical developments in population genetics not only dealt with the restructuring of gene pools, but they also provided a basis for comprehending phenotypic transformations, as demonstrated by experimental findings as diverse as those of Nilsson-Ehle and Sewall Wright. Paleoanthropologists had abundant company, including eminent scientists with impeccable credentials in other areas of biological research.

Microevolutionary transformation and discontinuous human types

It remains to ask whether this is merely an interesting minor observation about a brief passing phase in the history of interpretations of human evolution, or whether the heritage has been more pervasive. Did the historical sequence of events – with discoveries of hominid fossil material preceding the development of a coherent theoretical framework – have any effect on how the fossil material was interpreted?

One fortuitous juxtaposition of journal papers provides a useful insight into this question. In 1933, the *Eugenics Review* published two articles, both of which could be considered in the general realm of opinion pieces, as perspectives on developments in the broad purview of human heredity. One, titled 'Evolution by selection,' summarized the implications of Floyd Winter's long-term work on selection in maize. Its author was 'Student,' the chosen publishing pseudonym of the Cambridge mathematician W. S. Gossett. This paper (Gossett, 1933) was followed, in the same issue, by an article by Solly Zuckerman on 'Sinanthropus and other fossil men,' in fewer than 10 pages.

Gossett's paper reviewed the implications of the long-continued selection experiment on maize conducted by Floyd Winter (1929). The work had begun in 1896, well before the rediscovery of Mendel's laws, and had continued until 1924. Since maize produces a crop each year, the time spanned 28 generations of mass selection for two characters (oil and protein content) in two directions (high and low). The results were striking. From the starting point, through continuous mass selection, Winter was able to produce one line that had, in absolute amounts, more than twice the oil content of the starting strain, while the other had less than one-third of the original oil content. In statistical terms, the average in the high-oil line was *12 times* the standard deviation in the original population, while in the low-oil line the average was about *7 times* below the original population average, for a total divergence between the descendant lines of nearly 20 times the original population average. Despite the magnitude of the total divergence, the two lines remained interfertile with each other and with the original parent stock. Somewhat less dramatic but generally similar results were obtained with respect to protein content.

Gossett was able to use Winter's published data to estimate the minimum numbers of genes that permitted such an impressive response to selection, and found that this was in the range of at least 100 to 300 loci. Moreover, since there was little indication that selection had yet reached its limit, he felt that it was possible that the numbers of genes affecting the characters might run up to thousands. This inference was considered by Gossett to be significant, because '. . . if we have thousands of genes, continuous selection in one direction may, in fact must, result in progress almost without limit . . . for although the selection will reduce the number of genes there will be time for fresh mutations to occur to keep up the possibility of further selection' (Gossett, 1933: 296). While considering the possibility of gains through various types of genetic systems and levels of selection, Gossett made an explicit connection of Winter's experimental results with Darwin's theory: making gains under some sets of conditions might be 'tedious work – but for the Origin of Species there is now plenty of time' (Gossett, 1933: 293).

Zuckerman's paper dealt chiefly with some of the logical issues underlying human taxonomy, in his words 'the trying issue of the correct classification of the zoological family to which modern man belongs' (Zuckerman, 1933: 273). Part of his argument was an explicit response to criticisms leveled by Lancelot Hogben in his work *Genetic Principles in Medicine and Social Science* (Hogben, 1931). Hogben, an articulate and influential British popularizer of science, suggested that physical anthropology had been pursuing its course 'with a serenity unimpaired by the results of experimental investigation,' so that physical anthropologists were ignorant of the advances made in genetics.

On substantive grounds, Zuckerman set forth his objections to Davidson Black's (1927) creation of a new hominid genus and species, *Sinanthropus pekinensis*, for the fossil remains recently discovered in China, implying that reference to an existing taxon such as *Pithecanthropus* might be in order. Using data compiled by Morant (1927), Zuckerman noted the anomalous fact that intra-specific differences in linear dimensions of the skull among extant humans often are greater than generic ones in then-current classifications of the Family Hominidae. However, rather than simply concluding from this modest empirical base that the two Far Eastern populations of fossil hominids should be placed at least in the same genus, if not the same species, he effectively inverted the argument, noting that 'on the grounds of special morphological characters it would seem that Neanderthal man as much merits generic distinction from *Homo* as *Sinanthropus* does from *Pithecanthropus*, (Zuckerman, 1933: 281). Zuckerman (1933: 284) concluded by arguing that a 'rational classification' would divide the Hominidae into two subfamilies, the first of which would include 'archaic types like *Sinanthropus* and Neanderthal man, the second modern man and men of the Upper Palaeolithic'.

Conspicuous by their absence in Zuckerman's paper were details of the sort that might have refuted Hogben's criticism, or at least have responded to it substantively – quantified use of at least the data that did exist; estimates of the numbers of generations that might be spanned in portions of the geological record that contained the hominid fossils; and so on. In short, use of just the approaches from evidence and reasoning employed also by Gossett. It might be argued that Zuckerman was not representative of physical anthropologists working in the century following Darwin's devising of a mechanism that could produce enormous evolutionary changes, given sufficient time. In one sense such an objection would be correct. Zuckerman, however, was one of the *more* quantitatively oriented physical anthropologists of his time, often framing hypotheses about fossil material that could be tested objectively. Yet his verbal descriptions of categorical distinctions between hominid fossils do not take into account the precisely contemporaneous knowledge of how great changes can be wrought by iterative generational increments. Nonetheless, within decades, biological anthropology would be transformed by scientific advances.

Beyond the synthesis

By the accidents of history, the period following publication of Julian Huxley's (1942) *Evolution, the Modern Synthesis* coincided with the emotional, intellectual, and technological aftermath of the Second World War.

As will be developed in greater detail in Chapter 5, beginning around 1910 anthropologists carried out many studies of human migrant populations and developed research strategies by which they were able to assess quantitatively the extent of direct environmental influences (diet, climate, and so on) on body size, composition, and proportions. Many of the measured effects were of substantial magnitude. For example, Shapiro

(1939) documented a change of 2.6 points (equivalent to six-tenths of a standard deviation in the measurement) in the cephalic index between parents and their children. This and other studies documented similarly large changes in stature and other dimensions that reflected dimensions of the underlying skeleton. These findings called into question an entire domain of research that had been pursued extensively for over a century, and on the basis of which many inferences had been drawn about relationships among human populations, past and present.

Over about the same time period, studies of human blood groups and other serological characteristics had proliferated, and were yielding results that, in contrast, appeared to be impervious to direct environmental influences. The juxtaposition in perceived reliability of inferences about evolutionary relationships between the two domains (often referred to colloquially as 'bones vs. blood') led to a shift in attention (as well as resources and, to a certain extent, prestige) from anthropometry to serology. Effectively, this marked a change in focus from continuous to discontinuous variation – although there are, of course, important discontinuous variants in the skeleton (Hauser & DeStefano, 1989).

It should be emphasized that studies of human anthropometric and osteometric characters did not cease. Indeed, in addition to much empirical research on skeletal remains there also was steady, and increasingly sophisticated, attention devoted to multivariate analytical techniques that could be applied to the study of continuous variation in present and past human populations. As noted by Howells (see Lahr, 1996: xiii) such leading mathematical and statistical luminaries as Pearson, Hogben, Fisher, Mahalanobis, and Rao made lasting conceptual and operational contributions in this area. The use of the resultant methods in studies of biological distance among human populations has been reviewed by Buikstra *et al.* (1990). In the context here (i.e. this volume), it is interesting to note that they have detected a shift from the use of skeletal data to measure relationship, and toward the use of skeletal materials for studies of population–environment interactions that reflect influences of factors such as diet and disease.

Within the domain of paleoanthropology, studies of fossil remains long tended to emphasize comparisons that were descriptive and qualitative over more quantitative, population-oriented studies. A major explanation for this research pattern was that, until relatively recently, large samples were unknown or at least relatively inaccessible. That situation has changed markedly over the last several decades, and there now are abundant studies of fossil material. Although some of these (such as Tattersall, 1993) focus on discontinuous features (character states, in cladistic terminology), others use metric data as a basis for multivariate analysis (e.g. Albrecht & Miller, 1993).

Discontinuous genetic traits: empirical results and paradigm shifts

During the half century or so when geneticists and other biologists were limited in their observations to visible phenotypic characteristics, a consensus developed about the organization of genomes in populations of eukaryotic organisms (Lewontin, 1974: 24; Dobzhansky, 1995). The result was what generally is referred to as the 'classical' theory of population structure. Translated into a physical model of the genome, classical theory assumes that at nearly every locus, all members of a given population are homozygous for a 'wild type' (for which read 'normal' or 'typical') gene. At the same time, each individual has a scattering of rare, deleterious genes; if homozygous these would be deleterious or fatal, but in heterozygotes their expression is masked by the alternative 'wild type' allele. Differences between individuals, then, are manifested chiefly in their different sets of deleterious mutant genes. In contrast, populations differ in the nature of their 'wild type' alleles (they may also differ in their stock of deleterious recessives, though this is of relatively minor consequence). From these assumptions about the extent and distribution of diversity, individuals sampled from within a given population would be relatively uniform, while most genetic and phenotypic differences would exist between populations.

The contrasting 'balance model' assumes that a high proportion of genetic loci in all individuals are heterozygous, with each locus potentially being occupied by selections from a large set of alternative alleles (the sets sometimes being referred to as mutiple allelic series). From the properties of this model, it follows that any two individuals sampled from a population would differ at a very high proportion of their loci. This picture yields the prediction that variation within populations should be high in proportion to differences between populations, which therefore are less significant (Figure 4.1).

As noted by Lewontin (1974: 26), Platonic notions of type show a propensity to extend from one domain of thought to another. Here, the classical model is consistent with a typological conception of phenotypic variation, while the balance model decidedly is not. In its historical context, it should be noted that the balance model was formulated only long after representatives of all of the major categories of fossil hominids were discovered (Chapter 3).

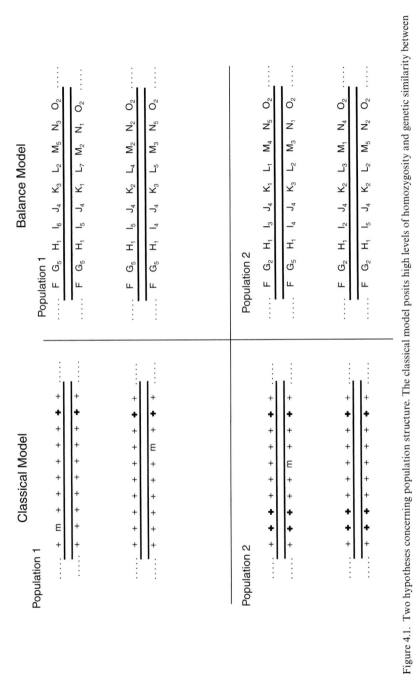

Figure 4.1. Two hypotheses concerning population structure. The classical model posits high levels of homozygosity and genetic similarity between individuals in the same population; most genetic differences are seen as occurring between populations. In the balance model, it is believed that there are comparable levels of genetic variation within and between populations; many loci are polymorphic in most populations, with some loci fixed for the same allele in all populations and a few loci fixed for a given allele in some populations but not others. The classical model, now abandoned, was conceptually compatible with typological views of the species and dichotomizing approaches to relationships among taxa.

Following the development of multiple techniques (electrophoresis, DNA hybridization, gene sequencing, etc.) for detecting formerly 'invisible' molecular variants, predictions of the balance model have been amply borne out (Lewontin, 1972, 1991). In humans, the amount of intrapopulation is high, and on a par with interpopulation variation for comparable traits (Templeton, 1998). This discovery has profound implications for the interpretation of variation in human populations throughout their existence.

From present human populations to those of the past

For obvious reasons, we have much more data, quantitatively and qualitatively, from populations of living humans than from those long dead. It follows, lamentably but unavoidably, that the amount that we ever can know about the appearances and ways of life in earlier hominid populations must be less than what we can learn about our contemporaries.

With that limitation acknowledged, a more positive prospect follows. The study of past hominid populations should not occur in an interpretive vacuum. Our structures of inference must build upon the hard evidence provided by fossil remains, but not ignore that these limited pieces of primary evidence were once parts of functioning organisms with biological and behavioral characteristics that can be inferred from collateral sources of evidence.

Chapter 5 explores the basis for realizing that there are multiple pathways from genotypes to phenotypes in extant humans. Chapter 6 establishes that there are highly comparable patterns demonstrated by nonhuman primate species, including the papionines (macaques and baboons) as well as hominoids (including chimpanzees, recently the focus of much genetic research). Since these primate groups bracket fossil hominid populations, it is a reasonable inference that the latter, during their periods of existence, manifested broadly comparable patterns of genomic organization, population structure, and phenotypic variation.

In proceeding from this structure of inference, and its possibilities as well as limitations, we may never be able to know what the frequency of an ABO blood group allele was in South African Plio-Pleistocene hominids; but we know for a certainty that the earlier hominid populations displayed such polymorphisms. We may never find fossilized skin from an archaic East African hominid of half a million years ago, but we can reasonably infer that its depth of pigmentation matched that of present inhabitants of the region. We have no reasonable basis whatever for assuming that the skeletal parts of some past hominid population should have been highly uniform and sharply different from a neighboring group hypothetically clustered about some other norm. In short, *due to theoretical advances alone*, aside from the dramatic gains in the primary basis in fossil evidence, our analytical tools and predictive capacities, though limited, are far more powerful than generally realized.

5 *Human adaptability present and past*

Introduction

The challenge of paleobiology is to explain the forms, the functions, and the behaviors of past populations – here, those of our hominid ancestors. Toward this end it is desirable to consider our antecedents on the same terms as members of present populations: as organisms functioning, at least adequately if not always optimally, in a variety of particular environmental settings.

Since the time of Darwin, the fit between organism and environment has been believed by many biologists to be the result of adaptation. A century after the idea of evolution by means of natural selection was outlined, Colin Pittendrigh (1958) stressed that 'the study of adaptation is not an optional preoccupation with fascinating fragments of natural history, it is the core of biological study.' In studies of living populations, this core concept is based on repeated observations of the pervasive relationship between features (or in the terminology of cladistics, character states) and functions. When the temperature drops below a given threshhold, we shiver; when the temperature rises above a given level, we sweat. Children born and raised during a prolonged famine tend to be shorter and lighter at maturity than the generation of their parents. If, however, there is a marked improvement in nutritional conditions, the offspring still can become as tall and as massive as their parents and grandparents. Members of populations that have lived for hundreds of generations under hypoxic conditions at high altitude in the Andean (South America) region exhibit chests that are large relative to stature, with the absolute thoracic dimensions changing little in the next generation even among descendants who migrate to sea level (Eckhardt, 1992a). Human biologists studying extant populations of our species carry out research programs that have among their objectives the clarification of the mechanisms by which such responses operate, and the ways these responses contribute to the fit of human populations to their environments.

Some paleoanthropologists, particularly those whose own research has a basis in ecology or other dynamic areas of population biology, accept the possibility that there was a similar adaptive fit between earlier hominids and their respective environments. For example, Foley (1995) considered explicitly the adaptive strategies pursued by human ancestors, and outlined persuasively how these strategies could have shaped basic human biological features such as upright walking and large brains. However, many other paleoanthropologists treat these and other characters more as markers for species identification in phylogenetic reconstruction than as functional attributes that were influenced by adaptation, selection, and other evolutionary processes, placing them at variance with the mainstream of modern biology.

Mammalogists, for example, over a century ago already had formulated the principles commonly referred to as Gloger's rule (1833), Bergmann's Rule (1847), and Allen's Rule (1906). Inductively based, these generalizations described widely observed patterns of variation among warm-blooded vertebrates distributed over extensive geographic regions. Bergmann's rule holds that in species of mammals and birds, the body sizes of polytypic populations generally increase with a decreasing mean annual temperature of the habitat. Allen's rule formulates a correlation of body form with temperature as well, stating that in warm-blooded species, the relative sizes of anatomical parts projecting from the body (limbs, tail, ears) decrease with declining annual temperatures. Bergmann's and Allen's rules describe different aspects of a common pattern in which, among homeothermic animals, the body surface area relative to enclosed body volume tends to decrease in proportion to ambient temperatures. Gloger's rule refers to pigmentation levels in warm-blooded species. As usually stated in its simplest form, this rule holds that the intensity of melanin pigmentation tends to decrease with mean temperature. However, there are related influences of light and humidity. Levels of black eumelanins are elevated more in association with high humidity and temperature, while high temperature in conjunction with greater aridity increases the levels of reddish-brown phaeomelanins.

Early adaptability studies in human biology

Confirmation that the patterns inferred by Bergmann and Allen held for humans as well as other mammals was not provided in anthropology until the pioneering work of Derek Roberts (1952, 1953), who showed that worldwide variations in human body weight and basal metabolism were distributed in accordance with climatic rules. Weiner (1954) documented similar relationships between climate and nose form, suggesting that environmental variables could influence not only overall body size, but also details of skeletal morphology. At first these climatic rules were generally assumed to be under direct genetic control (Huxley, 1942). Later, however, Harrison and his colleagues (1964) demonstrated experimentally that tail length in mice increased in proportion to the temperature under which the animals were raised; this work provided support, under controlled laboratory conditions, for some measure of direct environmental influence on skeletal development during the lifespan.

Harrison's demonstrations of direct environmental shaping of the phenotype were in accord with other observations that had been accumulating for many years, as summarized by Roberts (1995). Gould (1869) reviewed the military records of over a million men inducted into the Union Army during the US Civil War and showed that American recruits were taller than those born in Europe, perhaps reflecting greater nutritional adequacy. Subsequently Baxter (1875) reanalyzed these data, eliminating all records of stature that were self-reported or not taken under standardized conditions by Army medical personnel. In the carefully revised and edited data set, the outcome remained unchanged. Bowditch (1879) showed that working class children in Boston, USA, were shorter than children from families of higher occupational status. It was reasonable to suspect that different levels of nutrition were among the influences at work in such cases, with dramatic confirmation being provided by studies of the impact of famine in Russia (Ivanovski, 1925). Repeated measurements on the same set of subjects documented marked decreases in body mass, as was expected in times of famine. More surprising were reductions in stature, head length and breadth, face height and breadth, and numerous other dimensions thought to be determined more by hard than by soft tissues.

Migration places genotypes against new environmental backgrounds

Attention turned from phenotypic change *in situ* to human groups that had moved from one environment to another. Fishberg (1905) carried out a study of both stature and cephalic index, comparing Jews in the US and in Europe. The US sample on average was taller and longer-headed. Taken together, early studies of this sort provided presumptive evidence that some aspect of the US environment was directly influencing the physical growth of migrants to its shores. Capitalizing on one of America's recurrent xenophobic phases, the eminent anthropologist Franz

Boas (himself an immigrant from Westphalia, a former province of the Prussian region of Germany) perceived a way of tapping the public's concerns (and purse) to support the collection of scientific data pertinent to understanding human adaptation to new environments. He persuaded the US Congress to fund extensive studies of immigrants in New York City. Data collection took place from 1908 through 1910, and the results were published two years later (1910, 1912). Boas and his co-workers demonstrated that children born in the US to immigrant parents differed in head shape and other aspects of body form from foreign-born controls. What is more, the divergences tended to be greater in proportion to the length of residence in the US. The physical changes were attributed to direct influences of the new environments in which growth and development had taken place.

The conclusions reached by Boas were confirmed in even more rigorous form by the work of Harry L. Shapiro. In his classic work, *Migration and Environment* (1939), Shapiro described his comparisons of three groups: Japanese who had emigrated to Hawaii; their relatives who had stayed in Japan (termed 'sedentes'); and the emigrants' children who grew up in Hawaii. Shapiro, like Boas before him, found generational differences. Measurements and proportions of the head differed between the Japanese-born parents and their Hawaiian-born children. Males born in Hawaii developed heads that were shorter from front to back and broader from side to side than those of immigrant males. Other body features that had been believed to be stable across generations, and hence to function as reliable indicators of 'racial' (i.e., population) relationships, had changed as well. In comparison with sedentes, both the immigrant Japanese and their Hawaiian-born descendants developed noses that were narrower and longer (consequently with lower nasal indices). Sitting height, a good measure of thoracic development, increased significantly in the Hawaiian-born over their parents or Japanese sedentes. The inference was that the environment in Hawaii had directly modified the expression of genes influencing morphological development.

The studies of Boas and Shapiro, along with further work by, for example, Goldstein (1943), Lasker (1952, 1954), and Hulse (1957a) along similar lines, demonstrated convincingly the developmental lability of anthropometric features. What is more, these studies helped to shape the reception of other findings in which environmental influences had been known to extend beyond overall size and proportions to details of skeletal morphology. Earlier, Walcher (1905, 1911) had demonstrated that infants placed so that they habitually slept on their backs, with the weight of the head concentrated on the occipital region of the skull, develop broader heads than babies allowed to sleep on their sides. Traditional cradling against a wooden headboard also produces much the same result externally as well (Ehrich & Coon 1947), along with an increased probability of Wormian bone formation. An explanatory mechanism along developmental lines was offered by Oppenheim (1907), who suggested that increased sutural complexity may be associated with delayed obliteration at these junctures (this was later confirmed by Ossenberg, 1970).

Among the other researchers on human migration was Gabriel Ward Lasker. In two early field studies (1952, 1954) he compared Mexican immigrants to the US at various ages with their counterparts who had remained at home, finding no evidence for self-selection in size or related characteristics among the migrants (later confirmed by Malina *et al.*, 1982). Beyond his empirical contributions, Lasker generally is accorded major credit for outlining the theoretical framework within which human adaptability studies subsequently would proceed. An essential element of this framework was the concept of plasticity. As noted by Roberts (1995) this was yet another idea that had been brought to the attention of many biologists by Huxley's *Modern Synthesis* (1942), where it had been used in several senses, all connoting broadly related facets of genetically based variability. Later, Dobzhansky (1957) sharpened the term in the context of evolutionary biology by noting that species of higher organisms become adapted in two manners: by direct modifications in their gene pools; and by homeostatic adjustments to phenotypes using mechanisms of gene expression accumulated through past evolutionary change.

Lasker's classification of adaptive levels

Lasker (1969) expanded Dobzhansky's dualistic approach into a tripartite array of adaptive levels available to humans: (1) short-term behavioral and physiological responses, commonly referred to as acclimatization; (2) developmental plasticity; and (3) genetic changes, as from natural selection. The differing durations of these responses can be characterized metaphorically. Acclimatization can be likened to a tree 'bending in the wind'; the organism responds to the forces impinging on it, then returns to its original condition when the pressures cease. The defining feature of plasticity is captured by the phrase 'as the twig is bent, so grows the tree'. During growth, an organism's genes express themselves in a particular environment that gives a lifelong set to its phenotype. Adaptive genetic changes occur as if in response to a hypothetical injunction to 'be fruitful and multiply'. Genotypes favored in a given environment increase relative to others in the gene pool, with their spread enhancing the fit between population and environment.

These modes or types of adaptation occur on rather different timescales. Acclimatization involves behavioral or physiological adjustments that can take anywhere from seconds to weeks, and encompasses processes ranging from sweating and shivering through changes in levels of enzymes, hormones, and skin pigmentation. All of these adjustments are reversible over similarly limited timescales. Developmental plasticity can be thought of as a molding and remodeling process that occupies not only the growing period but continues through adulthood and into senescence, influencing characteristics from overall body size, through body proportions (including the head, trunk, limbs, and limb segments), down to details of tissue restructuring. Genetic changes take place between successive generations and are virtually certain to have a permanent effect on the population and its members.

Genetic changes endure for several reasons – these include fixation, interaction, and selection. Fixation is said to occur whenever a gene attains a frequency of 100 percent, reflecting the displacement of all its alternative alleles at the particular locus. Prior to fixation, the existence of multiple alternative alleles at a given locus (by convention each having a frequency above one percent) constitutes a genetic polymorphism. Polymorphisms were known first in morphological and other phenotypic traits, where they commonly – though not invariably – have a genetic basis. When the distinction is not clear from context, confusion can be avoided by distinguishing between genetic (almost invariably single locus, by common usage) polymorphisms and structural or morphological polymorphisms (for which the basis commonly is polygenic). Between the origin of a new allele through mutation and its subsequent replacement of its predecessor at the same locus, the situation that exists is referred to as a transient polymorphism. However, not all polymorphisms are transient, many have persisted for millions of years, as in the cases of alleles coding for blood group antigens and the major histocompatibility system. Along with other sources of variation, polymorphisms are important evolutionary phenomena, however problematic they may be for specialists interested in constructing phylogenetic arrays from limited data sets.

Interaction is a concept that summarizes the diverse and complex influences that genes can exert within and between loci. This idea reflects the formal recognition by students of heredity that evolution is far more complex than could be treated adequately by the heuristically useful but extreme simplifying assumptions of 'bean bag genetics.' Dominance is one sort of interaction, in which a gene masks the expression of its alternative allele at the same locus. Epistasis is the term for a similar masking or modifying effect, but by genes at one locus on those at another locus elsewhere in the genome. A gene with major developmental impact often will be influenced in its expression by the buildup of modifier genes of lesser effect. As genes interact during development, they shape the phenotype and thereby should be expected also to influence the individual's fitness. Consequently, a gene frequency change at any locus is likely to modify frequencies at numerous other loci, leaving a vanishingly small likelihood that the gene pool will ever revert exactly to any prior state. Because of gene interactions, although in theory changes in allele frequency are reversible as long as fixation or loss has not occurred, in practice this situation obtains only as long as our attention is limited to just one locus. This intrinsic genotypic complexity helps to explain why Dollo's Law in paleontology, concerning the irreversibility of evolution at the morphological level, holds over longer timescales.

Selection results from what was perceived originally by Darwin to be a causal relationship between the population and its surroundings. Because certain genotypes convey advantages for their possessors in a given environment, their constituent genes should increase in frequency in the population, countering whatever stochastic effects might occasion fluctuations in gene frequency.

Aside from relative timescales and degree of permanence, genetic changes differ from behavioral, physiological, and developmental changes in another important way – allocation of cost. Acclimatization and plasticity help to buffer individuals in their interactions with the world around them; the common outcome is homeostasis. Selection occurs at the boundary where homeostasis fails, leaving individuals of certain genotypes unable to reproduce or, in more extreme cases, even to survive. Theoretically, genetic adaptation results when non-genetic adaptation fails (at least in some cases; extinction of populations can occur when the capacity for genetic adaptation also is overwhelmed). Reality is more complex, of course. Much of the time, individuals and populations are responding to multiple challenges by the simultaneous action and interaction of several adaptive responses at multiple levels. In the forced migration of a population across a desert, the stresses of heat, water shortage, and fatigue all interact. For example, some individuals may survive because they have a more linear body build and can maintain body temperature with less water loss through sweating. Others may live because they carried a supply of water sufficient for their needs.

Complexities: norm of reaction and genetic assimilation

Two additional concepts are of help in understanding the overall complexity of adaptation – norm of reaction and genetic assimilation. Norm of reaction is the range of phenotypic expression that can be exhibited by a given genotype in different environmental settings. The underlying potential for variation differs markedly from trait to trait. Skin color will darken in response to increased levels of ultraviolet radiation, with the extent of pigmentation being reversible under different light levels. The norm of reaction is substantial and its expression reversible. Identical twins reared apart can differ permanently in adult stature by several inches if their inherent plasticity was molded by differences in nutrition and other factors. Again, the norm of reaction is measurable, though in this instance it is determinate rather than reversible. Blood group antigens are established directly by heredity; the norm of reaction is effectively zero, with the character state remaining virtually invariant as long as life can be sustained.

Genetic assimilation is a term sometimes used to account for another way in which gene expression can vary in response to environmental influences, one in which an extreme environment can lead to the manifestation of developmental potentials that remain unexpressed under more usual conditions. Genetic assimilation sometimes is referred to as the 'Baldwin effect,' in recognition of a paper published by J.M. Baldwin in 1896 proposing this process as a 'new factor in evolution' that offered an alternative to natural selection. The first experimental data that seemed to be in accord with Baldwin's idea were published by Waddington (1942, 1953a,b, 1957). Larvae of *Drosophila melanogaster* were subjected to a temperature shock, after which about 40 percent of the flies that matured expressed a phenotype called 'crossveinless.' When crossveinless flies produced in this manner were bred for several successive generations, eventually they produced the crossveinless phenotype even in offspring that had not been subjected to the temperature shock.

Although many discussions of this and similar occurrences have been said to represent an integration of neo-Lamarckian and neo-Darwinian ideas, genetic assimilation is entirely consistent with what we know about the operation of selection on quantitative genetic systems (Mayr, 1963). In these terms, we are dealing with a polygenic system in which genes capable of producing a given phenotype are present at relatively low frequencies. It is only the flies who respond to the environmental extreme (heat shock at a given larval stage) by producing a given phenotype (crossveinless) that have a sufficient number of genes to cross some critical developmental threshold. What the extreme environment has done is principally to reveal this subset of genotypes, which are the only ones allowed to reproduce. This, in turn, makes it possible for selection to increase the frequency of relevant polygenes in the next generation. We do not have to assume that the environment has acted in some mysterious way to transform non-genetic variation into genetic variation. Instead, an unusual environmental factor has acted to amplify the action of uncommon genes that are capable of producing a phenotype that usually remains unexpressed. When expressed under atypical circumstances, this phenotype and its underlying genes can be increased in the population by selection. As stressed by Roberts (1995) the value of the idea of genetic assimilation is that it provides an explanation in terms of current genetic theory (Waddington, 1957, 1966; Pritchard, 1986) for the capacity of species to develop unusual morphologies and functions rapidly in response to the demands of particular habits and habitats.

Extension of an adaptability focus in human paleobiology

Despite the manifest utility of the adaptability framework in studies of living populations, it has found relatively little direct application in human paleobiology until recently (e.g., Ruff, 1988) . There are historical reasons for this dissociation. They are far too complex to explore fully here, although the studies discussed earlier in this chapter document that by the late 1940s and early 1950s, human biologists studying extant populations were demonstrating that skeletal characters manifested developmental plasticity in response to functional demands during the lifespan, as well as being able to change over multiple generations in response to forces of evolution such as natural selection.

While the resultant insights into human adaptability and plasticity held the promise that the study of skeletal characteristics could be integrated into a more dynamic population biology, they simultaneously showed that skeletal traits could not be used formulaically as uncomplicated indicators of population affinity. This shift in awareness concerning the type of biological information preserved in skeletal traits coincided with dramatic technological advances in serology. Thus investigators who were interested in human anatomy and physiology not because of what their study revealed about biological function or process, but rather for their perceived value as indicators of population affinity, turned to biochemistry for 'markers.' Coincidentally, because blood groups and other biochemical traits were largely unaffected by direct environmental influence, and had not yet been shown definitively to respond to selection and other forces of evolution, these single locus traits were declared to be the new nonfunctional, neutral indicators of affinity.

In his work on *Genetics and the Races of Man*, Boyd stressed explicitly the importance of using nonfunctional traits to trace relationships: 'The sort of character we shall be led to choose as being relatively non-adaptive will probably be the characters for which we cannot imagine any survival value. (Of course the fact that we cannot imagine any usefulness in evolution of a character does not prove that such usefulness does not exist, but such characters are at any rate to be preferred to those which obviously have high survival value.) The bony structures obviously have high survival value, and we shall hardly select the more important features of them. Among the racial characters which we would be tempted to pick out at the present time as non-adaptive, there are certain serological features of the blood, such as the genes O, A, B, M, N, etc.; many other characters, such as the direction of hair whorls, general body hairiness, (probably) tooth cusp patterns, fingerprint patterns, etc., might be considered' (Boyd, 1950:26–7).

It was at about the same time that Sherwood Washburn outlined his views for a 'new' physical anthropology (Washburn, 1951), which was envisioned precisely as a dynamic combination of behavioral, functional, and populational approaches which, blended together, would help to elucidate human biocultural history as a 'history of genetic systems' underlying a 'sequence of more effective behavior systems' (Bowler, 1997). The scientific impact of Washburn, his students, and the others influenced by his work has been significant, but the outcome that they envisioned remains to be fully realized.

Application to the hominid fossil record of a human adaptability framework designed to elucidate the extent and causes of variation may not be analytically simple or resolve all problems to everyone's satisfaction, but it is conceptually logical and should serve to focus appropriate attention on the dynamics of past populations whose members once were as alive as we are today.

Skeletal biology: a bridge from the present to the past

Present human populations exhibit diversity not only in body size and proportions (usually recorded via anthropometric measurements) that reflect the underlying skeletal framework, but also in virtually every system of tissues and organs that can be examined by direct observation (anthroposcopically) or numerous sophisticated instruments for imaging, sampling, and analysis. As a result, human biologists can discern abundant variations in everything from skin color, through patterns of adipose tissue deposition and muscle conformation, to blood group antigens, serum protein composition, and even polypeptide and nucleic acid sequences in the nuclear and mitochondrial genomes.

On turning to populations of the far distant or even the relatively recent past, we immediately confront a sharp diminution in the extent of data available. Except in extremely unusual circumstances, biological remains are limited to hard tissues – bones and teeth. Fortunately for archeologists and paleontologists, however, skeletal and dental tissues preserve much information about the lifeways of past populations. As a result, it is possible to reconstruct patterns of interaction between gene pools and environments across periods encompassing millennia. In his book *Bioarchaeology*, Larsen (1997:4) has made a strong case for using the information encoded in hard tissues to understand members of past generations as functioning members of biological populations.

This bioarcheological perspective serves as a bridge between research agendas carried out by human biologists studying living populations, and paleobiological reconstructions of the lifeways of hominid populations from the far distant past. Though not necessarily in theory, in practice bioarcheology most commonly deals with populations of anatomically modern humans from the relatively recent past. The principal difference between human biological studies of living populations and bioarcheological research on past groups is that in the latter case, material remains are limited largely to the skeleton and dentition, while in studies of living populations, as already noted, greater ranges of tissues are available.

Bioarcheology's nearly exclusive focus on hard tissue remains is shared, in turn, by paleobiology, which must reconstruct phenotypes and behaviors chiefly from material remains of fossil hominid populations. Of course, paleobiological studies must proceed with greater caution in the face of unknown or disputed phylogenetic relationships among populations represented by smaller samples of more fragmentary material, and whose temporal dimensions may have error terms of tens or even hundreds of thousands of years.

These three disciplinary foci – human adaptability, bioarcheology, and human paleobiology – are united, however, by their emphasis on populations as units of study. As we move from the present to the far distant past, bones and teeth, however limited or fragmentary, become the beginning points for reconstructing ways of life, not just artifacts preserving 'markers' of taxonomic discontinuity or affinity.

Although Larsen (1997) was careful to stress that his volume was not a critical review of techniques used in studying the biological component of the archeological record, he did succeed in compiling a comprehensive overview of the kinds of evidence and types of reasoning that can be used to make an extraordinarily great range of behavioral inferences from hard tissue remains. Included here are assessments of nutritional adequacy, other aspects of physiological stress, exposure to pathogenic agents, patterns of injury and violence, levels of physical activity, dietary and other influences on the face and jaws, and population history.

Skeletal evidence of adaptation

Within the human adaptability framework, the three levels of response – short term acclimatization, developmental plasticity, and genetic change – all can be documented with numerous examples drawn from bioarcheological studies. By the nature of the material remains, of course, developmental phenomena predominate, because differences in nutrition, physical activity, and many other processes are recognizable primarily from remodeling of various skeletal parts. However, the observable features of skeletal and dental remains provide an informative basis for making inferences about phenomena of human adaptation on timescales that range from immediate antemortem events, through protracted developmental processes, to multigenerational shifts in genomic patterning.

Skeletal and dental evidence of short-term adaptation

Dental microwear

Behavioral and physiological responses of the sort that human biologists working with living populations would group under the heading of acclimatization can be documented abundantly from hard tissues. For example, very high power microscopic analyses, particularly scanning electron microscopy of wear on the occlusal surfaces of teeth can provide very detailed information on non-dietary tool use as well as characteristic dietary adaptations within and between species (Teaford, 1991). In fact, one of the more notable practical limitations to interpretation of microwear patterns is its temporal immediacy – the possibility that dental occlusal surface features such as scratches and pits may record masticatory behavior only for the timespan very shortly before death, producing the aptly-termed 'Last Supper' phenomenon (Grine, 1986). In practice this potential limitation can be overcome in living populations by experimental studies that measure the rapidity of wear pattern obliteration following altered dietary regimens (Teaford, 1991; Teaford & Lytle, 1996). However, in more ancient hominid populations known only from the archeological or pale-ontological records, the degree of commonality in microwear seen among specimens from different seasonal samples and sites could be used as a measure of the extent to which a given configuration of surface wear represents a consistent adaptive pattern rather than an unusual occurrence. The chief point made here is not that analyses of microwear are limited in the extent of information that they preserve. Rather, it is that hard tissues, even in populations known only from the past, hold the potential for documenting events on timescales that in some cases can be exceedingly brief, giving paleobiologists the ability to observe traces of events long ago that spanned mere days or weeks.

Of course, the same microscopic and micrographic procedures can be used to infer the existence of more enduring trends as well. As noted by Larsen (1997), there have been numerous studies of dental microwear in temporal series of populations that are known from independent sources (such as artifacts and carbon isotope ratios) to have lived during periods of dietary transition. As just one instance, in comparison with their prede-cessors, some later Neolithic human populations show smaller diameters of occlusal surface pits, along with a decline in overall feature density. This has been interpreted as having resulted from a shift to softer diets that were the product of increased meat consumption and cooking of grain in ceramic vessels. Furthermore, it has been suggested that softer foods permitted earlier weaning and more closely spaced births, which both could have contributed to the striking demographic phenomena of rising birth rates and increasing population sizes (Buikstra *et al.*, 1986). Evidently, observations of even minute details of hard tissue change can enhance our under-standing of behavioral phenomena that underlie large scale adaptive shifts.

Enamel defects

The crown mass of a tooth, as well as its surface, can record a great range of physiological perturbations, some of which have been demonstrated to be event specific. Some teeth have been shown to preserve a clearcut 'neonatal line' on the deciduous teeth and first permanent molars that were being formed at the time of birth (Schour, 1936; Whittaker & Richards, 1978; Eli *et al.*, 1989). Such lines are particular cases of histological features called

Wilson bands. These are microstructural disruptions in the formation of the tooth's enamel matrix, which is built up in layers termed striae of Retzius. Wilson bands are legitimately thought of as phenomena on the timescale of acclimatization, since they record fleeting periods of stress that last from about one to five days.

More enduring periods of stress can produce macroscopic flaws in the enamel surface that are visible to the naked eye. Over a decade ago a system was developed (FDI, 1982) for classifying defects of enamel that could be used as an international epidemiological index. The resultant scale comprises six categories: type 1 included enamel opacities that are white or cream in color; type 2, covers yellow or brown opacities of the enamel; type 3 encompasses hypoplastic defects that are expressed as pits; type 4 defects are horizontal grooves of the sort that are referred to as linear enamel hypoplasias or transverse enamel hypoplasias; type 5 defects are vertical grooves; and type 6 defects are those in which the enamel is entirely absent. These categories commonly are discussed in shorthand form, with changes in enamel color or opacity being referred to as hypocalcifications and variations in enamel thickness referred to as hypoplasias; however, there really is a continuum of expression from milder to more severe defects.

Although hypoplasias can result from inherited syndromes or specific incidents of trauma, the overwhelming majority of instances in living populations reflect systemic metabolic stress lasting from weeks to months, and a similar pattern probably is preserved as well in archeological and paleontological samples of teeth. Because of the longer timescale, it is possible to think of macrodefects such as hypocalcification and hypoplasia as conventional developmental phenomena, in contrast to the microdefects which record events on the briefer timespans appropriate to acclimatization. Again, however, there is as much a continuum in time as there is in expression. Regardless of the duration of the process recorded or the strength of the signal that is preserved as an enamel defect, it is important to bear in mind that these various defects form permanent records because dental enamel is not metabolically remodeled later in life. Larsen (1997) provides an extensive recent review of the nature and causes of these defects and their usefulness in reconstructing numerous aspects of adaptation in recent human populations.

Harris lines

Skeletal as well as dental elements can record relatively short-term environmental effects. Transverse striations, commonly referred to as Harris lines after the physician (Harris, 1931, 1933) who was an early explorer of their biological significance, comprise a category of effects that now are relatively well understood. These features appear in radiographs as dense bone horizons that range from under 1 mm to over 1 cm in thickness, most commonly in regions of the skeleton that normally would be foci of rapid growth. Repeated observations on extant animal and human populations confirm that these lines can be generated following a wide variety of influences that perturb the metabolic processes involved in bone forma- tion. The dense bone perceivable as radiopaque lines results when mineral deposition occurs without simultaneous proliferation of epiphyseal carti- lage at the growth plate (Garn et al., 1968). Since normal bone growth and its defects are effectively bounded in development by epiphyseal union, Harris lines serve primarily as markers of early childhood stress, appearing as early as the middle of the first year of life and peaking within the first five years.

Harris lines are nonspecific stress indicators. In addition to factors likely to be encountered only in extant populations, such as immunizations (Garn et al., 1968), are those that are likely to have impacted human populations and those of their nonhuman primate relatives over millennia into the past. Other influences include nutritional insufficiencies (Wegner, 1874; Harris, 1931, 1933; Park & Richter, 1953; Dreizen et al., 1956, 1964; Stewart & Platt, 1958; Platt & Stewart, 1962; Garn et al., 1968; Blanco et al., 1974; Martin et al., 1985), infectious diseases (Harris, 1931, 1933; Acheson, 1959), fractures (Ferrozo et al., 1990), weaning (Clarke & Gind- hart, 1981), and probably many other causally specific but effectively systemic stresses that remain to be identified. It is useful to consider Harris lines in the context of acclimatization as well as development, because in some cases events of rather brief duration (reactions to immunization or brief but intense bouts of infectious disease) can leave traces that endure for decades.

Several unresolved problems limit the usefulness of Harris lines as entirely straightforward correlates of systemic stress during the years of childhood development. For one thing, when some patients' X-rays are compared with their corresponding medical histories, there are many instances of observable Harris lines that cannot be matched with episodes of disease or exposure to other particular stressors (Garn et al., 1968), and in the other direction, some children who are below age-specific weight norms show relatively few Harris lines (Walimbe & Gambhir, 1994).

Another problem in the use of Harris lines as indicators of the stress that has acted on past populations is that the processes of bone remodeling that continue throughout life can cause thinning and even disappearance of the dense bone horizons (Garn & Schwager, 1967; Garn *et al.*, 1968; Hummert & van Gerven, 1985). Consequently, as noted by Larsen (1997), although transverse lines that are present in the bones of adults can be taken as relatively reliable indicators of past metabolic stress, the absence of such lines could indicate either the absence of growth disruption or merely the secondary resorption of the horizons of dense mineralization. The reliability of Harris lines as records of stress history must, therefore, diminish with each passing year of adult life. This obliteration of Harris lines with age may be an even greater problem in paleobiological interpretations of earlier hominid remains than in bioarcheological contexts because ages at death generally must be reconstructed from skeletal features (presence or absence of epiphyseal union in long bones, degree of surface detail at the pubic symphysis, osteoarthritic degenerative changes on joint surfaces, etc.). In cases where remains are highly fragmentary, clues from such sources may not be available. Even when they are available, the information that they record reflects developmental age, itself perhaps stress related, more directly than chronological age.

These cautions, fortunately, are likely to be lessened as greater insights are provided by further research on extant populations. Among other possibilities, it may become possible to understand variations in Harris line patterns in terms of interactions among different categories of stressors or perhaps being influenced by genetic differences among various populations.

Developmental effects visible from hard tissues

In addition to some instances of enamel defects and Harris lines, the skeleton records numerous other markers of important developmental phenomena. In fact, although analysis of skeletal parts sometimes have been undertaken in an interpretive framework that appears to incorporate the assumption that bones are static structures that reliably record phylogenetic relationship, bone is a living tissue that is remodeled throughout life. Moreover, the dynamic nature of bone has been known for over a century. In 1892, the German anatomist Julius Wolff set forth his 'law of bone remodelling.' The principal tenets of Wolff's Law hold that every component of bone remains active throughout life, and that the elements of bone tissue orient themselves in the directions of functional demand.

Initial skeletal growth during infancy and early childhood is achieved principally by the activity of the cells that comprise functional units called primary osteons. Beginning in early childhood and continuing throughout life, a remodeling process ensues, involving complex tissue elements that make up the Haversian system. At the center of this system are the Haversian canals, which are vascularized channels formed as the osteoclasts burrow through existing bone. Subsequently, bone is deposited in thin layers on inner canal surfaces by secondary osteons, producing concentric lamellae. While remodeling is an integral part of skeletal growth through early adulthood, the rates at which it occurs can be influenced by various stresses, including dietary problems and disease experience, as well as differential loading of different skeletal parts caused by activity patterns.

Bone remodeling with age

Skeletal elements commonly are categorized as long bones (femur, humerus, digits, etc.), flat bones (scapula, innominate), and irregular bones (such as vertebrae). Long bones increase in length by growth of the elongated central shaft or diaphysis through early adulthood. In humans there are two peaks of velocity, one in infancy and the other during adolescence. In addition, the Haversian system is involved in the increases in bone circumference or mass that take place through deposition of remodeled bone onto the subperiosteal and endosteal surfaces into the fourth decade of life. After about age 40 bone deposition continues periosteal deposition but is resorbed endosteally. These counterpoised processes have primary consequences in terms of both bone mass and bone form. As a general rule, bone mass peaks at about 35 years of age. Afterward not only does bone mass usually decrease, but this reduction in mass is accompanied by changes in shape, which can be seen in cross-section. In present human populations as well as many known from the relatively recent archeological record there is a pattern of diaphyseal expansion (increase in shaft circumference) during adulthood. It has been hypothesized that the observed expansion is a response to bone loss along the endosteal surface (Smith & Walker, 1964; Garn et al., 1967; Ruff & Hayes, 1982; Martin & Burr, 1989). This suggestion is logical in mechanical terms, since for many aspects of stress loading a thinner tube of larger diameter can exhibit resistance comparable to a smaller diameter tube with thicker walls. Moreover, numerous empirical studies (Ruff & Hayes, 1982, 1983) have demonstrated that periosteal expansion with age in the bones of adults maintains the mechanical integrity of long bones even as bone mass declines (for a more extensive review see Larsen, 1997).

Bone remodeling in response to activity patterns

In addition to various influences on bone mass that can have generalized outcomes such as osteoporosis (Stini, 1990, 1995; Smith & Walker, 1964; Heaney, 1993; Anderson & Pollitzer, 1994; Anderson, 1995), there are numerous documented examples of bone hypertrophy in response to localized patterns of use. Resultant bone remodeling has been shown to increase diaphyseal diameters, modify articular surfaces, and to alter the bone surface at points of attachment for tendons and ligaments.

One of the larger-scale examples of bone hypertrophy in response to specific physical exercise was documented in professional tennis players, among whom males exhibit up to a 35 percent increase in cortical area at the level of the distal humerus of the racquet-wielding arm, while female professional athletes in the same sport show a 29 percent differential (Jones *et al.*, 1977). Buskirk *et al.* (1956) also documented a significant increase in the lengths of the radius and ulna in tennis players. Similarly, baseball pitchers show substantial diaphyseal hypertrophy of the long bones along the dominant throwing side. More symmetrical but nevertheless high levels of long bone shaft hypertrophy have been documented in rodeo cowboys (Claussen, 1982) and to lesser but measurable degrees in people who perform regular, vigorous physical exercise (Watson, 1973; McMurray, 1995).

Alterations to articular surfaces can occur in response to types and extents of activity and rest; however, despite some earlier claims (Charles, 1893), many of these modifications are difficult to link to particular behaviors. For example, after reviewing numerous features of the femur, tibia, talus, and calcaneus, Trinkaus (1975) concluded that none of the postulated modifications could be taken as unambiguously diagnostic of a squatting posture rather than as general correlates of very high levels of overall physical activity. However, there are a few instances in which particular activity patterns leave characteristic marks on articular joints. One such case takes the form of extended or supplementary facets on the superior surface of the bone near the distal ends of the metatarsals. These appear to result from habitual dorsiflexion at the metatarsal–phalangeal joints during extended periods of kneeling during various activities including grinding of maize (Ubelaker, 1979) or other cereals (Molleson, 1989), as well as canoeing (Lai & Lovell, 1992; Lovell & Lai, 1994). Population frequencies of these supplementary facets range from less than 2 percent up to approximately 20 percent, with some cases accompanied by osteoarthritic degeneration (Larsen, 1997).

Many human populations exhibit surface modifications of bone at sites for attachment of muscles, tendons, and ligaments. In the case of muscle attachments, various depressions commonly are referred to as cortical defects, but they really represent functional responses to chronically elevated mechanical stress. Both the distribution of skeletal parts that are usually affected (i.e., femur, tibia, and metatarsals in the lower limb; humerus, radius, and metacarpals in the upper limb; phalanges) and bilateral asymmetry attributable to right-side dominance are highly suggestive of the relationship of these modifications to various patterns of heightened activity. Similarly, various surface irregularities and bone projections, at the sites of attachment for tendons and ligaments are termed enthesopathic lesions, but they also represent developmental responses to habitual activities of various sorts. Specific activities associated with particular skeletal modifications observed in various populations include carrying heavy loads (Dutour, 1986), unusually high levels of walking or running (Dutour, 1986), frequent use of missile weapons (Kennedy, 1983), and kayaking (Hawkey & Street, 1992; Hawkey & Merbs, 1995). These and other examples are incorporated in the extensive review by Larsen (1997).

Bone remodeling in response to other systemic stresses

Stress from diverse influences is recorded in bone density. To begin with, there are the age-related decreases seen in both sexes, as well as sex-specific factors that progress with age, such as reductions in estrogen levels following menopause in females (Stini, 1995). Also important is nutritional balance (Schaafsma *et al.*, 1987), taking into account not only dietary intakes of raw materials such as calcium (Arnaud & Sanchez, 1990; Bales & Anderson, 1995) and protein (Stini, 1995), but also losses due to lactation and high levels of physical activity (McMurray, 1995). For some dietary components, overnutrition can pose risks at least as serious as undernutrition. Diseases comprise yet another category of stress that can influence bone development, but far more often than not, effects of this sort are intertwined with other social disruptions (e.g., Owsley, 1991).

Genetic adaptations in skeletal features

The bony framework of the human body is part of an adaptive complex (the musculoskeletal system) that traces its origins to ancient chordates that lived hundreds of millions of years ago. From then until now this system has been modified repeatedly by evolutionary processes that have adjusted the characteristics of populations to the environments that they have occupied successively through time.

Human paleobiology is concerned only with the last several million years of these dynamic interactions that have shaped our species and its more immediate antecedents. Our knowledge, both of the patterns that have existed through the past, and of the mechanisms that have enabled populations to undergo the transitions among various adaptive plateaus, have been gained chiefly from studies of living populations and those in the more immediate past explored by bioarcheology. The picture that is emerging from intensive research remains uneven, but clearly has become one of unexpected complexity.

The foreword to another volume in this series opened with the wry comment (by Howells, in Lahr, 1996: xiii) 'When Anders Retzius, a century and a half ago, invented the cranial index, he gave us an answer for which there was no question.' But pertinent questions were in the air, first about the relationships among extant human populations, and a short time later about where human fossil remains fit into various systems of relationship. In confronting these questions, anthropologists have added to the cranial index numerous other anthropometric and osteometric measures, along with diverse systems for observing and scoring osteometric traits. Yet disagreements remained. To resolve these, vast amounts of additional data were gathered, and improved statistical methods for analyses were devised. Nevertheless, despite some very impressive efforts at data collection, synthesis, and analysis (e.g. Howells, 1973; Lahr, 1996), major questions still remain unresolved. Why?

Part of the answer is that as prodigious amounts of time and effort – over a century of work by thousands of investigators – were devoted to studies of anthropometric, osteometric, and odontometric data, a new element entered the picture – a vastly better understanding of skeletal biology. The effect of this impressive new domain of knowledge has become comparable to the situation, described briefly in Chapter 1, at the end of the nineteenth century in physics. In physics, more abundant and detailed data were expected to resolve such lingering questions as whether light traveled in waves or particles. Instead, more and better observations documented problems that were cognitive rather than empirical in nature, and the answers devised to resolve them required new frameworks for thought that ultimately swept away the interpretive framework of Newtonian physics and replaced it with quantum mechanics.

In the parallel case of skeletal biology, the cranial index devised by Retzius has been supplemented by hundreds of anthropometric and osteometric diameters, angles, arcs, and indices, several dozen of which are in common use (Buikstra & Ubelaker, 1994). Over 200 nonmetric cranial traits have been documented in great detail for humans (Hauser & DeStefano, 1989). In addition to all the dental measurements that can be taken for various purposes, some 30 nonmetric dental traits commonly are employed in studies of biological distances among human populations (Scott & Turner, 1997). But as noted briefly in preceding sections of this chapter, while amassing this impressive battery of observational approaches, human biologists have learned ever more about the dynamic responsiveness of bone to specific (and sometimes brief) life history events, the tendency of the skeleton to record developmentally the various stresses experienced throughout life, and the responsiveness of genetic systems to restructure altered norms of reaction when the limits of intragenerational buffering mechanisms are challenged.

A complementary effect of this enhanced understanding of the adaptability inherent in a major biological complex has been to make it clear *why* phylogenies based on dental and skeletal traits continue to yield divergent answers. For example, to the extent that attainment of a given stature is dependent not only upon a given genetic potential but also particular regimens of nutrition and disease, then similarities or differences in body size are less sure indicators of relatedness than they are of particular life history experiences. To the degree that skeletal gracility or robusticity reflect combinations of diet and activity rather than direct expressions of genes, then the similarities or differences become diminished as markers of biological relatedness even as they are enhanced in their informativeness about the lifeways of the populations being compared. The attendant interpretive complexities ramify in several further directions. Since proportions commonly are allometric correlates of size, then shape becomes less reliable as an indicator of relationship and more meaningful as yet another dimension of the interactions between form and function. Not even skeletal nonmetric traits are independent of environmentally-mediated developmental influences. Larsen (1997) notes that the humeral septal aperture, a variant frequently used in biodistance analysis, exhibits a high degree of association with robusticity.

The emerging pattern of knowledge about skeletal biology built up by anatomists, archeologists, human biologists, and physical anthropologists has created an evident paradox in paleoanthropology – skeletal plasticity (a dimension of adaptability) and stability (a desirable basis for assessing biological relatedness) are juxtaposed. The more stable the features or character states of bones and teeth, the more readily and reliably that they can be used to trace phylogenetic relationships. Yet it is beyond question that dimensions and details of skeletal parts can change within generations (due to developmental plasticity and even shorter term influences) as well as between generations (due to processes involved in genetic adaptation). Both Wolff's Law and Darwin's theory of evolution by means of natural selection – and the thousands of research papers that have followed from each of these scientific insights – have established the extent to which skeletal characteristics are dynamic rather than static entities.

From the standpoint of being able to use skeletal characters to assess biological relatedness, it is somewhat ironic that the realm about which we would like to know the most – the genetic information encoded in skeletal characters – we have learned perhaps the least. Overall, detailed knowledge of the roles played by genes in the expression of skeletal features remains rather limited. The relatively secure areas of knowledge that we do have, however, establish that the relationships between most genes and most skeletal and dental traits are complex. Only in the rarest of instances does it appear that there is anything approaching a one-to-one correspondence between gene and character, though this situation may be approached in some discontinuous skeletal and dental features (see Hauser & DeStefano, 1989 and Turner *et al.*, 1991 for respective reviews). The general pattern, instead, is one in which most skeletal characters are multifactorial, with their visible expressions determined by interactions between particular environmental settings and the genotypes that develop in these settings. Aside from complexities introduced by environmental sources of variation, many skeletal and dental traits are polygenic, their development being influenced by the joint action of multiple independent loci, each of which may be occupied by pairwise combinations of numerous alternative alleles. Consequently, any given skeletal or dental feature may be produced by numerous alternative genotypes developing in multiple common or alternative environments. For example, over the world the phenotypic sample of all people who are exactly two meters tall expresses a highly diverse set of genotypes that has led to the development of this stature. Conversely, two identical twins who have inherited the same complement of genes may differ in stature by several centimeters. Such differences arise because skeletal characteristics, particularly metric traits (but also nonmetric features such as those affecting joint articular surfaces, as already discussed), can be altered in their expression by different regimens of physical activity or nutrition.

For all of the preceding reasons, even when certain phenotypes or character states characterize populations in given regions or timespans, there is no assurance that the underlying genotypes are shared in the same sense that nucleotide sequences sampled from two different individuals can be shown to be identical. These cautions should be borne in mind whenever skeletal and dental features are used as indicators of biological affinity among populations, or when differences in such features are used to argue against relationship. As noted previously, in the early days of physical anthropology the constraints detailed above were not well understood. As a result, the attempts to use skeletal and dental features to assess relationships among specimens and populations were less systematic and more subjective than superficially similar but scientifically more sophisticated studies that have been carried out in recent years. Over the last several decades, however, very considerable attention has been devoted to appropriate theoretical and methodological concerns (Larsen, 1997).

In bioarcheology as well as human biology, the degree of resemblance among groups is commonly expressed in terms of biological distance, which is estimated from a variety of alternative multivariate methods. The observations from which these distances are inferred comprise continuous and discontinuous traits in the skeleton and dentition. Continuous traits include measurable features such as diameters, circumferences, mass, and various indices derived from such values. Discontinuous traits, in theory, are those that can be characterized as present or absent – a suture or foramen is either in a particular anatomical location or it is not. In practice, however, skeletal and dental variations do not conform to such straightforward categorizations. In the skeleton, sutures may be either open or closed, but they also may be fused for only a portion of their length. A foramen may be absent or present, but it also may be represented by multiple openings that differ in size and even may be scattered around the expected location at varying distances. In the dentition, shoveling may be present to such varying degrees in a population that it approaches being a continuous variate. Supernumerary teeth (such as fourth molars) may be present, either bilaterally or unilaterally, and in either the upper or lower dental arch, or both, and vary considerably in size whatever their locations, as would be expected for structures that express an underlying distribution of genes influencing development. Hominoid third lower premolars may be either unicuspid or bicuspid, and where bicuspid, the two cusps may be similar in size or greatly disparate. Traits of the sort noted here commonly differ in expression within populations as well as between them. These factors are important because they add to the complexity of scoring skeletal and dental traits. They are even more important because they suggest that morphological similarity as well as diversity rests on a base of genetic polymorphism (Eckhardt, 1992b).

Temporal dimensions shaping the dynamics of skeletal change

The rates at which skeletal traits change through time may be temporally constrained (there are limits to demands placed on adaptive systems which, if exceeded, lead to extinction) but are not proportionate to chronology alone. From the preceding material in this chapter it is evident that skeletal characters respond adaptively to forces that act within and between generations to varying extents, producing changes that occur at varying rates. Variability in rates of change pose further problems. An analogy can be drawn with attempts to measure objects using a ruler that is inaccurate. If the discrepancy is one part in ten, then one's perception will be off by one millimeter in every centimeter – up to ten centimeters in every meter, and one hundred meters in every kilometer. That is, the longer the absolute span, the greater is the extent that observation will diverge from expectation. The problem is further compounded if the degree of inaccuracy is inconstant, as might be the case with some estimates of biological distance from skeletal data. Skeletal characters not only change over time, but change at rates that differ from one period to another, as if in our analogy the ruler had a variable degree of elasticity along its length.

The practical challenges posed by this conceptual conundrum are different for workers in the several domains of human population biology. Because it is generally believed that skeletal characteristics do not evolve at very high rates, the paradox may be less problematical over relatively brief periods, while it becomes increasingly serious over longer stretches of time.

The availability of alternative research strategies also has some effect on the problem. In studies of the biological relationships among living human groups, adaptive genetic changes probably produce only modest distortions. Nonetheless, skeletal characters and the anthropometric dimensions that reflect them have largely been supplanted by electrophoretic and nucleotide sequence data. For bioarcheologists, data from hard tissues continue to provide valuable evidence for assessment of the differing degrees of relationship among populations (though even here molecular approaches are beginning to be used). Also in bioarcheological contexts, efforts sometimes are made to base distance studies on dental traits, which tend to have relatively high heritabilities and substantial (although far from complete) developmental stability in the face of environmental perturbations.

Perhaps most important, the great majority of bioarcheological studies using hard tissue data to infer genetic relationships among populations have been in the post-Pleistocene period. This period encompasses less than 0.2 percent of the human evolutionary record, i.e. approximately

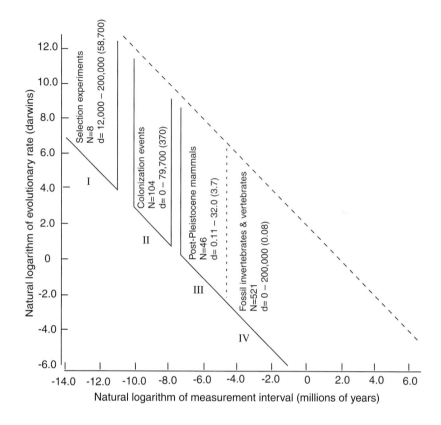

Figure 5.1. Relationship between rates of morphological evolution and time periods over which the changes accrued. There is a pronounced inverse relationship between the calculated evolutionary rate (in darwins, d) and the time interval encompassing the change. The highest rates are observed in selection experiments, and the lowest rates in the fossil record where episodes of change and stasis may be conflated. A darwin (d) is defined as change by a factor of *e* per million years, where *e* is the base of the natural logarithm. Values of d in parentheses are geometric means. Redrawn from Gingerich (1983).

10000 years out of over 5000000, or about the last 500 generations against a total exceeding over a quarter of a million lifetimes. During this period of time there have been measurable evolutionary changes in the skeleton and dentition, including some at rather high rates (Frayer, 1997; see Chapter 11), although the relatively few generations that have passed through that evolutionary change have had less scope to obliterate traces of relationship.

Human paleobiology deals with vastly longer timescales that encompass major transformations of brain size, body size, and limb proportions, as well as structural reorganizations for altered posture and locomotion. Some of the changes appear so great – either absolutely or relative to the time available – that the possibility of an ancestral–descendant relationship appears to be precluded. However, Gingerich (1983) has provided a classic paper that furnishes a comprehensive framework for comparing rates of change in morphological characteristics among extant and fossil populations (Figure 5.1). It is noteworthy that some of the highest evolutionary rates have been measured in selection experiments on living populations of mammals, followed by changes estimated for post-Pleistocene mammals. Evolutionary modifications documented in both categories (regardless of whether the rates at which they occurred were approximately constant or highly uneven) exceed by many orders of magnitude most changes in the vertebrate fossil record. Even at the genetic level, skeletal and dental characters appear to have more potential for change than had previously been believed, as demonstrated in Chapters 9 through 11.

For all of the reasons explored above, in the fossil record, methods used in the study of biological distance are rather blunt tools. But this interpretive constraint carries with it the compensation of a greatly increased scope for paleobiological inferences through the past hominid fossil record. The possibilities of making such inferences should be enhanced by exploring the extent to which adaptive mechanisms can be observed directly in populations not only in extant humans, where culture bulks large as a buffering mechanism, but also in populations of nonhuman primates, where such influences are far more modest, and perhaps more representative of the situation among our earlier hominid predecessors.

6 *Primate patterns of diversity and adaptation*

Introduction

The previous chapter presented the broad framework developed by human biologists for the interpretation of variation in living populations of our species. This chapter examines the comparative perspective provided by studies of some nonhuman primate populations. Its major objective is to demonstrate that the same interpretive framework that has proven to be so powerful in understanding patterns of variation in living humans also can be extended to extant primate taxa.

Our taxonomic order, which includes apes, monkeys and prosimians as well as humans, is unusual among existing mammals in its remarkable biological diversity. Primates are among the most ancient group of placental mammals to have evolved, with some early members having contributed to the mammalian adaptive radiation about 100 million years ago. Over this enormous timespan, primate populations have become so anatomically and behaviorally differentiated that it is difficult to find many characteristics that all share in common. For the most part, however, the earliest and latest species to appear are linked by common trends – for example, reduction of the apparatus of smell, elaboration of the visual system, and progressive expansion of the brain – running through a series of intermediate forms. Perceiving this pattern over a century ago, Thomas Huxley remarked (1863:98), 'Perhaps no order of mammals presents us with so extraordinary a series of gradations as this – leading us insensibly from the crown and summit of the animal creation down to creatures, from which there is but a step, as it seems, to the lowest, smallest, and least intelligent of the placental Mammalia.' As suggested by their anatomical distinctions, primates also are adaptively diverse. The Order Primates includes species that range from mouse lemurs weighing a few grams to gorillas exceeding a quarter of a tonne, and from small-brained nocturnal prosimians that hop about on elongated legs to relatively large-brained anthropoids that swing and clamber about in what is functionally a four-handed manner. The overall array provides a rich source of comparative data.

116

Foley (1987) has outlined three basic approaches to the use of nonhuman primates to provide a context for studies of early hominids. He refers to the first of these as a 'species model approach.' In studies of this sort, one or another primate species is taken as a model for early hominids, usually on the basis of phylogenetic proximity (e.g., chimpanzees) or inferred environmental similarity (e.g., savanna baboons), and sometimes both (e.g., chimpanzee populations that live in savannas). Because no two species are identical, allowance must be made for differences as well as similarities.

The second approach referred to by Foley is 'attribute analysis.' Human characters or attributes are listed and their counterparts are sought in various nonhuman primates. The finding of attributes (maternal care, meat eating, nongenetic transmission of behavioral elements) that are shared in common with nonhuman primates can establish a broader context for understanding their function in early hominids. In contrast, the absence of a particular attribute among nonhuman primates could suggest that it held the key to understanding the distinction between humans and other primates. Foley notes that some behavioral 'Rubicons' – tool use, hunting, language– once thought to be uniquely human, are sometimes crossed, perhaps most commonly by chimpanzees. These trends in the breaching of supposed behavioral barriers reinforce earlier exercises in which anatomical distinctions once attributed exclusively to humans (possession of an intermaxillary bone, endocranial volume above 750 cm^3, and so on) also have disappeared.

The third approach might be termed 'pattern recognition and extrapolation.' Also comparative, this research agenda screens attributes of nonhuman primates to detect more general trait configurations, which are then applied to hominids through some other variable. Thus, building on earlier work by Milton & May (1975) on the relationship between body mass and home range size in primates, Foley was able to estimate home range sizes for early hominids and compare them with estimates arrived at independently from other data. Approaches of this last sort are particularly powerful because they can lead to the discovery of general rules governing behavior, which are potentially more useful than extrapolations from particular shared attributes.

Against the broad background of adaptive diversity and the existence of multiple strategies for utilizing the abundant available data, this chapter focuses on two groups, the papionines (in particular baboons) and the hominoids (particularly chimpanzees), because of the perspectives that they provide for understanding aspects of the paleobiology of earlier hominids.

Papionine primates

Papionine primates form an evolutionary clade that includes the semi-terrestrial and terrestrial macaques and baboons, along with the closely-related drills, mandrills, and mangabeys. Although there are considerable anatomical, behavioral, and ecological differences within and between these populations, they form a distinct evolutionary subset among the Old World higher primates, characterized by numerous shared features such as a karyotype comprising 42 diploid chromosomes. This group provides a basis for exploring the broad patterns that relate geographic dispersal into diverse ecological settings with related morphological distinctions and patterns of genetic relationship inferred from molecular and behavioral data.

Systematics

Like any group of organisms long known to humans, the macaques and baboons have been the objects of numerous taxonomic revisions. Consequently, the names for taxa – scientific as well as common – can mean different things to different authorities. For example, Barbary macaques were known to Linnaeus, but under the name *Simia sylvanus*; now they are formally designated by the binomial *Macaca sylvanus*. Comparable shifts in nomenclature could be elaborated extensively for baboons, mangabeys, and other taxa.

To provide a brief systematic overview for this group, the strategy followed here was to choose one authority who has worked on the systematics of all of these taxa, thereby making it possible to achieve the kind of consistency that comes from a common perspective. Over the course of several decades, W. C. Osman Hill produced a series of encyclopedic volumes on all of the primates except the hominoids, work on which remained to be completed at the time of his death. Two of the completed volumes (1970, 1974) covered all of the macaques, baboons, and their near relatives in what Hill referred to as the subfamily Cynopithecinae. These genera and species of living animals are listed in Table 6.1.

Hill's totals for the extant genera and species in the subfamily are 6 and 29, respectively. These numbers do not include further species of the same genera known only from fossil material. Adding the species included in genera that are known only from fossils of Pliocene and Pleistocene age would augment the total by another 6 genera with 11 included species. Pre-Pliocene fossil remains recognized by Hill raise the number by an additional 20 taxa. His grand total for all of these monkeys therefore

Table 6.1. *Papionine classification*

Genus: *Cercocebus*
  species: *atys, torquatus, galeritus, albigena, aterrimus*

Genus: *Macaca*
  species: *irus, mulatta, cyclopis, fuscata, sylvanus, silenus, nemestrina, radiata, sinica, assamensis, arctoides, thibetana, maurus*

Genus: *Cynopithecus*
  species: *tonkeanus, hecki, niger*

Genus: *Papio*
  species: *cynocephalus, anubis, ursinus, papio, hamadryas*

Genus: *Mandrillus*
  species: *leucophaeus, sphinx*

Genus: *Theropithecus*
  species: *gelada*

Hill (1970, 1974).

comprises about 60 separate genera and species, illustrating the extensive array of papionine taxa that sometimes are recognized in a conventional Linnaean taxonomic framework.

A more recent classification of the papionine primates has been provided by Groves (1989), whose system includes 8 genera with 30 species, and differs in a number of particulars from Hill's. For example, Groves recognized an additional genus, *Lophocebus*, as separate from *Cercocebus*. In addition, he considers the *Papioninae* to include a central group of genera (*Papio, Theropithecus, Mandrillus, Cercocebus,* and *Lophocebus*) plus up to three other genera which 'lack some of the synapomorphies of the central group. These are *Miopithecus, . . . Allenopithecus,* and . . . *Macaca.*' However, on grounds of genetic biology, particularly karyotypic patterns, *Allenopithecus* and *Miopithecus* are more closely allied with the *Cercopithecus group* (Eckhardt, 1979; Lernould, 1988). In the other direction, the celebes black 'ape,' for which the separate genus *Cynopithecus* was recognized by Hill, was more logically placed in the *sylvanus-silenus* species group of macaques by Groves, following Fooden (1976).

Human biologists and primatologists concerned chiefly with problems of adaptation among living populations might be tempted to disregard differences among systematists of the sort noted briefly here. However, there long have been challenges to papionine systematics on a larger scale. Several decades ago, Buettner-Janusch (1966) called attention to 'A problem in evolutionary systematics: nomenclature and classification of baboons.' Buettner-Janusch's paper pointed out anomalies of many sorts. In the morphological realm, he cited Gregory's (1951) demonstration of the continuum into which papionine skulls could be arranged, with an Asian macaque at one end of the array and a mandrill at the other. Of equal interest was his complementary documentation of the occurrence of not only interspecific, but also numerous intergeneric hybrids. His most minor, yet disturbing, observation was that some taxonomic nomina commonly used in the scientific literature were of dubious validity because 'The same animal was often used as the basis for several names.'

Formal taxonomic designations remain a general problem in primates, despite the fact that one of the reasons commonly given for using the Linnaean-based system of taxonomy in general and Latin binomials in particular is freedom from confusion. Paradoxically, however, among papionines common names are the most stable. In recognition of the problem with the formal nomenclature of the papionines, Jolly (1993:74) noted that 'vernacular names . . . are taxonomically neutral and also, in this case, often less ambiguous than a formal bi (or tri-) nomial.' Following Jolly's lead, wherever possible here, these monkeys are referred to simply as macaques and baboons or, where appropriate, with differentiating vernacular modifiers such as 'rhesus macaque' or 'chacma baboon.'

The comparative context provided by papionine primates

Two major factors endow the papionine primates with particular value for enhancing our understanding of the earlier hominid populations that will be treated in subsequent chapters. The first is their spatial distribution, and the second is their temporal distribution. Spatially, among extant primates the geographic range of the papionine group is second only to that of modern humans, which have expanded their range to the arctic and antarctic regions chiefly through elaborate cultural adaptations. Temporally, papionines evolved on a timescale (sometime within the last ten million years) comparable to the one that encompassed the divergence of hominids from hominoid primates similar to chimpanzees, and for much the same reason, the expansion into more terrestrial habitats.

Spatial distribution of papionine populations

Broadly, among the papionines, macaques are dispersed across Eurasia, while baboons are principally African in distribution, with the few exceptions in each subgroup noted below. Several other papionine subgroups with more restricted distributions are discussed following an overview of the macaques and baboons (Figure 6.1).

In Asia, macaques are distributed from Afghanistan to as far north as 40 degrees latitude in Japan. To the south they extend from the Indian subcontinent, through Sri Lanka and broadly across southeast Asia, including the Malay Archipelago, Indonesian islands as far east as Timor and Sulawesi, and into the Phillipines. Outside of Asia, macaques are represented in North Africa and Gibraltar by the Barbary 'ape,' really a tailless monkey. These appear to be relict populations from a formerly more continuous distribution extending from parts of Europe and northern Africa through western Asia (Lindburg, 1980).

The distribution of baboon populations is given by Jolly (1993). In relation to macaque populations, baboons occur further south in Africa. At the far western end of Africa's northern savanna belt is a small area occupied by guinea baboons. At the eastern extreme are the hamadryas baboons in the lowlands of Ethiopia and Somalia, and, across the Red Sea, in the highlands of the southwestern part of the Arabian peninsula. A few scattered populations of anubis (olive) baboons are found in the Sahara Desert, with most other anubis populations found in the Subsaharan area and broadly south through the rainforest belt of central Africa, from Sierra Leone in the west to the Sudan and Ethiopia in the east. Further south and west are the yellow baboons, which are distributed in an arc running west and south of the equatorial forest belt to central Angola. The kinda baboons of Angola and western Zambia are distributed largely to the west of typical yellow baboons, with some overlap in parts of Zambia, Zaire (now known as Democratic Republic of Congo) and Tanzania. To the south of the range of yellow and kinda baboons are the chacma baboons, which are subdivided into typical, gray-footed, Transvaal and Kalahari populations.

In addition to macaques and baboons, there are several other related taxa of semi-terrestrial and terrestrial monkeys that are closely related to the populations surveyed above. Geladas are found in central and northern Ethiopia, chiefly in the rocky, mountainous regions around Lake Tana and southwards toward the Ethiopian capital of Addis Ababa (Hill, 1970). The mandrills and drills are a closely related pair of taxa, with drills found in a small area in the vicinity of the border between Cameroon and Nigeria, and on Bioco Island. Mandrills are more widespread, ranging from southern Cameroon to the Zaire River, including parts of Gabon and the Congo (Groves, 1989; Hill, 1970). Mangabeys, unlike the predominantly and terrestrial macaques and baboons, are chiefly animals of the rain forest.

Figure 6.1. Present distribution of papionine primates. In many regions of Africa and Asia the ranges of different taxa overlap, reflecting substantial discontinuities between phenostructure and zygostructure. Some of these discrepancies appear to have persisted for periods as long as several million years. Empirically, morphological difference provides an unreliable guide to genetic continuity or discontinuity. Distribution data from Fooden (1980), Fittinghof & Lindburg (1980), Jolly (1993), and Hoelzer & Melnick (1996).

Populations range over a fairly wide area of Africa from French Guinea, Gabon and Nigeria to western Uganda and Kenya. Some groups are almost exclusively arboreal while others are largely ground-living.

Temporal distribution of papionine primates

As inferred from the fossil evidence (Delson, 1980), within the Old World monkeys, cercopithecines diverged from the leaf-eating colobines about 15 Ma. During the Late Miocene, somewhere between 11 and 5 Ma, dental remains known from Ongoliba, Zaire and Marceau, Algeria could be attributed to macaques (though Delson noted that since among papionines the teeth of macaques are considered conservative or primitive, this allocation remains uncertain). By 6 Ma at Wadi Natrun in northern Egypt, partial jaws with some teeth are known. These were designated as *Macaca libyica*, but are within the size range of *M. sylvanus*, suggesting that this taxon could predate the subdivision of the genus into Mediterranean and Asian lineages. Numerous sites across Europe have yielded macaque teeth of broadly Middle Pleistocene age (from about 1.0 to 0.125 million years ago). The situation is less clear in Asia. The earliest somewhat equivocal specimens are represented by two mandibular fragments from northern India of Late Pliocene age (about 3 Ma). All other Asian fossil macaques are Pleistocene in age and many can be referred to extant taxa.

At the end of the Miocene, tectonic movements caused the Mediterranean Sea to shrink dramatically, to the point of being almost completely dried up. Related to this event was the formation of a semidesert barrier across the Sahara (Delson, 1975, 1980), which might have influenced the subdivision of papionines into three subgroups: gelada baboons in the wet lowlands, papio baboons and mangabeys in more forested regions, and macaques in a variety of northern habitats. Foley (1995) places the peak taxonomic diversity among baboons at about two million years ago, while geladas and other savanna baboons have been phenotypically distinct for a minimum of four million years.

Phenotypic features of the papionines

The basic descriptions provided here are based on Hill (1970, 1974), supplemented with material provided by Napier & Napier (1967). Jolly (1993) provides much more detailed descriptive information on the phenotypic features of baboons, including material that is highly useful in understanding the interactions of these terrestrial monkey populations with each other and with the various ecological zones and geographic regions that they inhabit.

Macaques are large, stockily-built monkeys with robust fore and hind limbs of roughly equal length. Tails vary greatly in length from one taxon to another, from absent in Barbary macaques to about the equal of body length in *M. sinica*. There is marked sexual dimorphism in body size, with males commonly half again as heavy as females. Coat colors are various shades of brown through black. Muzzles are moderately prognathous. Locomotion is quadrupedal, with considerable variation in the amount of time spent in trees.

Baboons are larger on average than macaques, and exhibit even more pronounced sexual dimorphism. In many groups, males are twice as heavy as females. Coats are dense, with considerable regional differences in color, marking patterns, presence or absence of manes, etc. Tails are moderately long and generally tufted at the end. Faces are long with prominent muzzles and jaws; canines are projecting, particularly in young males. Hands, and especially fingers, are rather short. Locomotion is quadrupedal, with digitigrade forelimb stance being typical. Hind limbs are moderately longer than forelimbs, with the distal limb segment (composed of radius and ulna) being longer than the proximal (humeral) segment, resulting in a high brachial index. As noted in detail by Jolly (1993), baboon populations inhabit an exceedingly wide range of vegetational zones, from rain forest through savanna to subdesert.

Like baboons, the drills and mandrills are large animals with strong sexual dimorphism. Both sexes exhibit massive muzzles with prominent swellings on either side of the snout (larger in mandrills than in drills). In mandrills, coats are long and dense, medium gray to deep brown in color, shading to lighter tips. Tails are stumpy. In male mandrills the nose is bright red and paranasal eminences are bright blue, with the same colors marking the genital region as well. In drills the facial mask is intensely black with white cheek tufts and beard; the genital area is even more strikingly colored than that of the mandrill. Stance and gait are similar to those of baboons.

Geladas are massive animals, with pronounced sexual dimorphism in body length and weight, thickness of mane and canine tooth projection. In both sexes muzzles are prominent but rounded in outline, projecting below supraorbital ridges that shadow deep-set eyes. The chest bears a bright reddish-pink patch of skin that is either heart-shaped or divided in two (usually in males); in females, below this patch is a chain of nodules resembling a necklace. The gait is quadrupedal, with nearly all daytime spent on the ground. Principal gelada habitats are grassy slopes at bases of mountains, edges of cliffs, and gorges. Trees are scarce in its ranges, so refuge and sleep occur on small ledges jutting from cliff faces.

Mangabeys are medium-sized monkeys, similar in body dimensions to macaques and somewhat smaller than most baboons. Their limbs and tails are long and slender. Sexual dimorphism is moderate. Background coat colors range from medium browns and grays to black; markings differ widely from one taxon to another, including white cheek tufts and ruffs in some, and vertical pointed crests in others. Muzzles are moderately elongated, about on a par with macaques. The gait is predominantly quadrupedal, suited to locomotion on the ground and in the trees. Some mangabey groups are almost exclusively arboreal while others largely ground-living.

The adaptive capacities of papionine primates

As already noted, papionine primates are widely distributed across Africa and Eurasia, often overlapping extensively with human populations. Consequently, they have been widely observed under field conditions in the wild, in monkey centers that may be either semi-naturalistic or widely different from original locations and habitats (for example, macaques have lived for several decades on Cayo Santiago near Puerto Rico), and in the artificial settings that exist in laboratories. The resultant body of data on papionine primates is formidable. Rhesus macaques alone have been so widely used that until recently in the medical literature they were simply referred to as 'the monkey.' It is possible to draw only selectively on this extensive literature describing adaptive mechanisms influencing numerous biological and behavioral characteristics of papionines.

Short-term acclimations

So many physiological phenomena have been explored in papionine groups that a thorough review is beyond the scope of this chapter. As just one example, in their native habitats in India and surrounding countries, rhesus macaques show a seasonal cycle of reproduction; ovulation takes place in autumn and winter months, with birth occurring in the following spring or summer. However, rhesus females housed indoors can have their initial ovulation in any season (Tanner *et al.*, 1990). Evidently, features as basic as reproductive biology are open to direct influence of environmental stimuli.

Some physiological and behavioral adjustments studied under naturalistic conditions can be highly informative about the capacities of primates to adjust to some of the environmental extremes that in all probability were faced by earlier hominids. Armstrong (1993) described Conrad Brain's studies of chacma baboons living in the Namib desert under conditions of extreme aridity. The troop regularly went without drinking for up to 11 days at a time, and in one case all of these monkeys were continuously without water for 26 days. When drinking water is unavailable, the baboons consume foods that have a high moisture content – *Salvadora persica* (mustard tree) berries, which have about 70 percent water, *Ficus sycamorus* (wild fig) fruits, which have about 80 percent water, and other similarly moist food items. The baboons even have discovered that by stripping off the tough outer bark of *Acacia albida* trees they can gain access to the succulent inner bark, from which they suck liquid and then spit out dry, fibrous wads.

The Namib baboons also cope with their chronic water shortages behaviorally. During extremely hot, dry periods the animals lie on their backs in the shade provided by trees or cliffs, with their limbs extended to expose bodily parts that are more sparsely covered with hair. Some male baboons scoop up and pour cool sand over their chests, a trick that can decrease skin temperature by 5 to 7 °C within minutes. Other aspects of behavior may increase the probability of short-term survival of some individuals at the expense of others; infant mortality in the group is high because some females without infants of their own commonly kidnap and kill offspring belonging to other females. Ultimately such behaviors could, of course, threaten survival of the troop itself; life in a marginal environment forces harsh compromises. In such a setting, the extent of influence exerted by the availability of water was summed up by Brain's comment, 'It was like watching two different troops when they had water and when they didn't.' As an important general inference from this example, it would be difficult to underestimate the significance of facultative behavior patterns in the adaptation and evolution of higher primates.

Developmental plasticity

The flexibility of physical growth patterns among papionines has been widely documented. In one large-scale study Hamada (1994) compared 2886 macaques (*M. fuscata*) living under laboratory and semi-natural conditions in Japanese 'monkey parks.' Investigations of this sort have provided details about age-related changes in body weight and skeletal growth. They also have discovered some differences among populations in patterns of sexual dimorphism in growth velocity and adult size, as well as expected variations occurring under different regimens of population density, food availability, patterns of light and temperature, and other environmental influences.

One interesting example that has emerged from studies of papionine behavior could be interpreted as developmental plasticity, but it also exhibits complex elements that shade into acclimation at one extreme and genetic adaptation at the other. Kummer (1971) carried out a series of experimental studies under field conditions on socialization of female anubis baboons into hamadryas troops and the reverse transfer of hamadryas females into anubis troops. Savannah-dwelling anubis baboons have a multimale troop structure in which males and females form consort pairs for relatively brief periods. In hamadryas groups that live among rocky cliffs, social subunits are formed by a single male and his harem of females. The hamadryas females are maintained in close proximity to the male by his attention and reinforcement; females who stray are pursued and, if necessary, nipped on the neck to reinforce allegiance.

Hamadryas males reared without contact with adult hamadryas models manifest these gender-specific mating-related social behaviors expected for their taxon, suggesting a genetic role in their development. To investigate the genesis of characteristic female behavior patterns, Kummer trapped anubis females and released them into hamadryas troops. Once they were there, males rapidly conditioned them to become 'follower females' in the hamadryas style. In reciprocal experiments, hamadryas females accommodated readily to the less restrictive patterns of male–female interaction. Kummer's inference was that the pattern of behavior in female hamadryas had a higher learned component than in their male counterparts. To the extent that the necessary learning period in both groups of female baboons was brief, the behavioral adjustments could be considered acclimations. However, since the changes could last as long as the females remained in their foster groups, for periods that could be measured in years, the change exhibits the stable features of developmental plasticity hardened into a new mold – with dimensions of the mold being determined by gene-conditioned male behavior patterns.

Genetic adaptations

Papionine primate genetic analysis presents a picture that is relatively simple at the karyotypic level and considerably more complex at the molecular level. A comprehensive chromosomal phylogeny of papionine primates was published by Dutrillaux and colleagues (1982). Long before, Chu & Giles (1957) and Bender & Chu (1963) studied the chromosomes of some macaques and baboons and found a diploid number of 42. However, the decisive early recognition of very broad genetic commonalities among these widely-distributed and morphologically diverse monkeys was made by Brunetto Chiarelli. Beginning in 1958, Chiarelli began an extensive and productive research program that rapidly placed primate karyology on a firm footing, (Chiarelli 1958, 1961a,b,c, 1962a,b,c,d, 1963a,b, 1965, 1966a,b; Chiarelli & Vaccarino, 1964).

Among the many important generalizations arrived at by Chiarelli was that all of the macaques, baboons, geladas, mangabeys, drills, and mandrills share strikingly similar karyotypes, characterized principally by a common diploid chromosome number of 42 and detailed correspondences in banding patterns (visible through staining and microscopy) among about 10 of the individual chromosome pairs of all of these taxa. This pattern was the converse of that seen in guenons (members of the genus *Cercopithecus*), which exhibit great diversity in chromosome numbers (with diploid complements ranging from 48 to 72) and some very similar chromosome banding patterns, but relatively less diversity in body form and morphological features. Externally, guenons exhibit great diversity in coat colors and marking patterns.

Chiarelli drew an important conclusion about the papionines – although animals such as mangabeys and geladas were very diverse in appearance, because of their unusually similar complements of genetic material they should be closely related phylogenetically. He also signaled his grasp of the further implications of this evident closeness of relationship by collecting data on the abundant papionine interspecific and intergeneric hybrids. Subsequent analyses have confirmed and elaborated the details of karyotypic patterning just described. Thus Dutrillaux *et al.* (1982) and Stanyon *et al.* (1988) have argued for an especially close relationship among taxa in *Cercocebus* and *Mandrillus* based on chromosome banding patterns.

Relationships among papionines inferred from karyotypic data have been refined further by molecular studies. In this realm, Morris Goodman's group made substantial contributions (Prychodko *et al.*, 1971; Tashian *et al.*, 1971; Weiss *et al.*, 1971, 1972; Barnabas *et al.*, 1972; Weiss & Goodman, 1972; Moore *et al.*, 1973) even in the early days of electrophoretic studies (Lewontin, 1991). Goodman and his colleagues were not alone in their initial studies, as indicted by contemporaneous publications of others (Ishimoto *et al.*, 1970; Nakajima *et al.*, 1970; Oliver & Kitchen, 1968;

Omoto *et al.*, 1970; Wade *et al.*, 1970). However, the research agenda carried out by Goodman's group was central and integrative, as indicated by numerous cross-group collaborations (e.g., Prychodko *et al.*, 1971; Weiss *et al.*, 1972).

Many of the earlier molecular studies of papionine groups grappled with systematic problems. For example, Weiss *et al.* (1972) noted that there was then no general agreement on the number of species in the genus *Macaca*, estimates varying from a minimum of 11 (Ellerman & Morrison-Scott, 1951) to a maximum of 16 (Kellogg, 1945), with an expanded numerical spread (ranging from 13 to 18) if the celebes monkey populations were subsumed into the genus as well. Fooden (1980), an acknowledged expert on macaque systematics, referred to the 'enigmatic pattern of taxonomic differentiation within each of the major groups of macaques.'

Regardless of the perspective taken, papionine relationships tradition-ally have been seen as unusually complex and controversial, even for a mammalian group as closely scrutinized and debated as the primates. At first the molecular evidence was used to supplement morphological obser-vations such as cranial measurements, tail length, coat coloration, hair length and direction, and so on. More recently, primatologists trying to sort out systematic relationships have given increasing weight to molecular data (e.g., Cronin & Sarich, 1976; Sarich & Cronin, 1976; Cronin & Meikle, 1979). As a result, characteristics that are more complex and environment-ally labile are becoming increasingly the subject of investigations into adaptive mechanisms.

Within the last several years intensive, detailed molecular studies of macaques and baboons have done much to clarify their relationships. A key study was that of Disotell *et al.* (1992), which used sequence data on the cytochrome c oxidase subunit II gene. Their data supported the combina-tion of savannah baboons (*Papio*) and geladas (*Theropithecus*) into one clade, with the drills and mandrills (*Mandrillus*) combined with the manga-beys (*Cercocebus*) into another, and all macaques into a third unit. Of particular note for the study of evolutionary dynamics was the comment by Disotell and his colleagues that it is 'difficult if not impossible to differenti-ate fully the individual lineages from their common background' (Disotell, 1992:10).

The macaques received more detailed study at about the same time by Melnick *et al.* (1993) as well as by Ya-Ping & Li-Ming (1993). In the first of these studies, Melnick and colleagues used restriction-site polymorphisms, and found substantial intraspecific mitochondrial DNA (mtDNA) diver-sity within macaque species. Ya-Ping and Li-Ming also used restriction endonuclease analysis of mitochondrial DNA, and obtained results that were relatively conventional at the first level of analysis, dividing the macaques studied into four groups: (1) *Macaca mulatta, M. fuscata, M. cyclopis* and *M. fascicularis*; (2) *M. arctoides*; (3) *M. nemestrina;* and (4) *M. assamensis* and *M. thibetana*. However, the divergence values among the taxa were not great, with the lowest value (0.024) being lower than some values obtained in comparisons among populations of the same species (0.029 to 0.052). Incorporating evidence from a previous study by Fa (1989), who found there to be a relative absence of important isolating mechanisms in macaques, Ya-Ping and Li-Ming inferred that 'macaques have not yet completed the process of speciation.'

Papionine population dynamics, adaptation, and evolution

As a result of studies carried out over the last several years, a new sense of order is emerging as molecular studies, powerfully detailed in themselves, have been multiplied in value by the broader context provided through long-continued, intensive observations in the field. The combined result is rather like an oil painting by an impressionist master. Up close one cannot help but admire the technical expertise represented by each painstakingly-applied dot of color – but the truly powerful aesthetic experience is created by the pattern in its entirety when seen at some distance. Jolly's (1993) detailed overview is a composition of this sort. He has combined a host of conventional studies into an integrated overview that is striking in its separate inferences and convincing in its total effect.

As a result of Jolly's synthesis, the previously stable picture offered by conventional taxonomy has been effaced. While taxa studied by naturalists, primatologists, and systematists have continued to be defined largely on the grounds of morphology and distribution, the behavioral, ecological, molecular, and other genetic data compel a different pattern entirely. It is not so much that old taxa or groupings of taxa have been replaced by new ones, or that numbers of taxa have been reduced or increased markedly. Rather, to a very considerable extent the hypothetical taxonomic walls believed to separate papionine taxa have been shown, through the new levels of detail emanating from studies of chromosomes, nuclear genes, and mtDNA sequences, to be riddled with holes – channels through which genes flow from population to population. The result of this research is not a reorganization of the relationships among genera and species, but a demonstration that the hierarchical model at the core of Linnaean taxonomy can no longer summarize adequately the increasingly abundant and detailed empirical data coming not only from molecular research but also from field studies of distribution, ecology, and behavior.

Building on the wealth of new data, much of it generated by his own group's research, Jolly's (1993) overview of 'species, subspecies and baboon systematics' contrasted what he termed the *phenostructure* and *zygostructure* of extant populations. The phenostructure comprises the observable characteristics in a given set of animal populations, while the zygostructure describes the results of past and present movements of genes among the same populations. These two concepts are related but distinct. Although the theories of speciation and population genetics predict that in general phenostructure and zygostructure should tend toward concordance, discrepancies are produced by particular instances of selection (which can result in morphological convergence among populations) or gene flow (which can introduce genes from one species into the gene pool of what is perceived at the phenotypic level as another).

At one level, Jolly's (1993) representation of baboons presents a seemingly straightforward picture. There are five principal parapatric 'forms' that are distinguishable on the basis of external characters: guinea, anubis, hamadryas, yellow, and chacma baboons. To these he added the kinda, a smaller version of the yellow baboon named for its type locality in Zaire (now known as Democratic Republic of Congo – DRC); and the gray-footed baboon, which often is lumped with the chacma. But with the exception of the Arabian and Saharan isolates, all of the baboon populations are linked by gene exchange that has been observed in some places and must be inferred from evident results in numerous others. As a consequence of the potential for gene exchange among formally-recognized species populations, it would theoretically be possible for a gene to be passed from Dakar in Senegal to Dire Dawa in Ethiopia and Cape Town in South Africa (Jolly, 1993:87).

At another level, some baboon populations – those in arid stretches of the Sahara and Arabian deserts – effectively are genetically isolated, although they are categorized as parts, respectively, of the anubis and hamadryas 'species.' The idea of species as entities united by gene flow clearly does not work here. Metaphorically, the situation appears rather like the wry characterization of the UK and the US as two countries divided by a common language. Even more thought-provoking is the likelihood that an anubis baboon living in central Ethiopia is more likely to produce an offspring with a gelada than with another anubis living in Ghana or Tibesti, or more certainly than with a Kalahari chacma.

Further complexity is added by certain narrow zones in which populations exhibit unusual phenotypic diversity; Jolly interprets these populations as hybrid swarms resulting from ongoing gene flow. The most thoroughly studied such zone lies between the hamadryas and anubis in Ethiopia (Nagel, 1973; Sugawara, 1979; Phillips-Conroy *et al.*, 1991). Another example that has been studied and mapped is situated between the ibean and anubis baboons in Kenya (Maples & McKern, 1967; Kingdon, 1971; Samuels & Altman, 1986). Among the dozen or so other suspected cases that are less well known, in west Africa the brown-colored eastern guinea populations might represent the introgression of anubis genes producing another guinea–anubis hybrid zone similar to the one in the Awash National Park (Jolly, 1993). All of these particularities attest to marked discordance between baboon phenostructures and zygostructures.

There also is evidence that local adaptations may crosscut conventionally-defined taxonomic units such as the subspecies or other zygostructures. Dunbar (in Jolly, 1993:89) reports evidence that gross body size in baboons at any locality is highly predictable from mean annual rainfall. Similar patterns of clinally-distributed adaptive variation are known in macaques, which exhibit chains of populations variously recognized as subspecies or species by different researchers, though all investigators concur in recognizing that hybridization occurs all along the species borders. Resultant chains of populations exhibit clinal variation along a north–south axis, with size increasing and tail lengths decreasing inversely with mean annual temperature, as predicted by Bergmann's Rule and Allen's Rule, respectively (Groves, 1989:142). Processes of acclimation, development and genetic change are analytically separable, but in natural populations they combine and interact to produce fluid patterns of adaptive response through time.

Hominoid primates

The overview of the papionines showed that in higher primate populations with broad geographic distributions that extend across a range of climatic and habitat zones, phenotypes also display wide variations. Morphologies and behaviors are so divergent that division into multiple taxa seems self-evident, with the result that phylogeny inferred from phenostructure can substantially misrepresent evolutionary phenomena related to zygostructure. Since early hominids evolved over expanses of time and space comparable to the papionines, similar cautions about their phylogeny might be in order, but such an inference would be more secure if based on the additional comparative context provided by study of our nearer hominoid relatives, particularly chimpanzees.

Humans stand in a closer relationship to hominoids than to papionines, so there are different inferences to be made from an overview of surviving populations of the group that includes our own ancestry. For one thing, chimpanzee populations show an array of adaptive mechanisms corresponding closely to those that characterize extant humans. Genetic and developmental changes have long been documented for chimpanzees, and recent research confirms the point that this sister group of all hominids exhibits a range of activities to which the term culture deserves to be applied (McGrew, 1998a, b; Whiten *et al.*, 1999). The second point is that morphological variation in chimpanzees is so well-known that it enables us to test directly certain propositions about phylogenetic differentiation in early hominids.

Hominoid systematics

Traditional approaches to primate taxonomy have subdivided the Superfamily Hominoidea into three Families: Hylobatidae (the lesser apes, including gibbons and siamangs), Pongidae (the great apes, including orangutans, gorillas and chimpanzees) and the Hominidae (humans and their non-pongid predecessors). Allocation of the great apes and humans to separate Families was based on anatomical features (such as a trenchant canine and sectorial promolar complex in the dentition, body, and limb proportions related to posture and locomotion) shared among *Pan*, *Gorilla*, and *Pongo* and contrasting with the orthognathous cranial and orthograde postcranial features of *Homo*. More recently, molecular evidence has led to a substantial realignment among these taxa, with orangutans being considered more distant from a group comprising the African great apes and humans. In recognition of the possibility that chimpanzees are most closely related to humans, *Pan* and *Homo* are now sometimes grouped together in a reconstituted Homininae (Miyamoto *et al.*, 1988; Goodman, 1992).

No single review covers the relationship between phenostructure and zygostructure in any of the great apes in the comprehensive manner provided by Jolly (1993) for the baboons. However, just as it was possible in a preceding section of this chapter to use a number of sources to extend Jolly's approach to the macaques, it is possible to take the same approach here to the population biology of chimpanzees, which are widely believed to be our nearest relatives among the hominoid primates.

Spatial distribution of chimpanzee populations

In the genus *Pan*, four taxa commonly are recognized, although there is some disagreement about their respective ranks. At the far west of Africa, populations conventionally classified as *Pan troglodytes verus* are found in Senegal, Gambia, and Guinea Bisseau through Sierra Leone and Liberia to the Ivory Coast, where their expanse approaches or abuts that of centrally located *P. t. troglodytes*. Populations of *P. t. troglodytes* are found chiefly in eastern Nigeria, as well as in contiguous regions of Cameroon, Gabon, and the Congo, as well as in Rio Muni, where their spatial overlap with the gorilla has been studied. *Pan troglodytes schweinfurthii* groups form an arc from the western Congo, where the subspecies boundary with *P. t. troglodytes* is poorly defined, eastward through northern DRC to portions of Uganda, Ruanda, Urundi, and Tanzania. The pygmy chimpanzee or bonobo, *P. paniscus*, is distributed to the south of the *P. t. troglodytes* and *P. t. schweinfurthii* ranges in the southern part of the great Congo basin. These subspecies or species (depending on the somewhat subjective weighting of diagnostic criteria used) are distributed over parts of equatorial Africa in a pattern consistent with the inference that existing populations are relicts of a range that formerly was much more extensive.

Temporal distribution of chimpanzee populations

Chimpanzees have virtually no paleontological record, at least in the sense of fossilized skeletal parts that would be anatomically duplicated in detail by those of extant *Pan* species. In a broader view, however, there are abundant fossil remains of medium to large bodied hominoids preserved in geological deposits of Africa for about 20 million years, with what appear to be moderately later expansions into Europe. Although dozens of binomials have been applied to various specimens, these earlier ape populations often are referred to generically as dryopithecines, after the earliest fossil remains discovered in France that were designated as *Dryopithecus fontani*. Related populations distributed widely over Eurasia and Africa were ancestral to orangutans as well as to gorillas and chimpanzees. Discoveries over the last several decades, including some recent finds in Spain that are described in Chapter 8, make it possible to reconstruct in very great detail significant postcranial as well as cranial morphology of the Eurafrican hominoids that may well have been closely allied to the common ancestors of present chimpanzees and humans.

Phenotypic features of chimpanzees

Chimpanzees are moderately large mammals with long trunks and chests that are deep and broadened laterally compared to quadrupedal primates. Like all extant hominoids, they lack an external tail. Their forelimbs are much longer than their hindlimbs. Chimpanzee feet exhibit great toes that are deeply divided from the others and sufficiently opposable to be used for grasping, in addition to hands that, despite their short thumbs, are suited for manipulation as well as prehension. On the middle digits the skin is thickened in conjunction with knuckle-walking, a common form of locomotion (interspersed with variable amounts of brachiation and facultative bipedalism). On the body, skin is long, sparse and dark, tending toward black; some whitening occurs with age, chiefly on the thighs.

In comparison with extant humans, chimpanzees have more prognathous faces and smaller crania (with endocranial volumes about one-third that of *Homo sapiens*). Sagittal cresting may occur, more commonly in older males. The dentition of *Pan*, like that of *Homo*, includes the same numbers and categories of both deciduous and permanent teeth. Incisors are spatulate, with the central pair usually broader than the latter in both taxa. In contrast with the incisiform canines of living humans, chimpanzees have canines that are conical and project beyond the levels of other teeth in both dental arches, with the maxillary canines of male chimpanzees being notably trenchant.

Particularly when considering phenotypic features, or in cladistic terminology, character states, norms should be considered in the context of abundant variations and polymorphisms at all levels from molecular to morphological (Eckhardt, 1992a; Goodman, 1992; Hasegawa, 1992; Stanyon, 1992). Some chimpanzees, as virtually all humans, have bicuspid lower third premolars, with the lingual cusp tending to be variably smaller; however in most chimpanzees the lingual cusp is either absent or marginally present. Facial coloration is highly variable, ranging from uniformly blackish through light tan with black freckling.

In comparison with *P. troglodytes*, *P. paniscus* exhibits narrower trunk proportions, as well as forelimbs and hindlimbs that are longer and more slender. Among other differences of detail, bonobos have narrower feet with larger great toes, and second and third toes proximally joined. Bonobos tend to be more gracile cranially, with thinner superciliary margins beneath a slightly more bulbous forehead.

Numerous sources provide data on continuous variation in skeletal characters (an integral aspect of phenostructure) and the relationship of morphological variation to problems of species recognition (which is dependent upon inferences about zygostructure). Albrecht & Miller (1993) summarize broad patterns of geographic variation in a variety of primates including the great apes. Shea *et al.* (1993) focus on multivariate cranial variation in chimpanzees. Overall the pattern of variation indicates that discriminant functions based on metric data can separate 100 percent of bonobos from common chimpanzees, against correct categorization of around 75 percent among members of the three chimpanzee taxa commonly ranked as subspecies. Interestingly, there is no clear geographic patterning of metric cranial variation among common chimpanzees. Eastern populations of *P. t. schweinfurthii* are morphometrically more distinct from the more centrally situated *P. t. troglodytes* than from the more distant western groups of *P. t. verus* (Shea *et al.*, 1993).

The adaptive capacities of chimpanzees

Evidence for short-term adaptation among chimpanzees

Among extant humans, enamel hypoplasias record certain life history events of brief duration. Corresponding records of stress have been known to mark the teeth of various nonhuman primates, including chimpanzees, since the observations recorded by Colyer (1936). Limited data on free-ranging chimpanzees also were provided by Jones & Cave (1960), who found transverse enamel hypoplasias in over 46 percent of 13 specimens sampled in Sierra Leone. These observations were extended by Eckhardt (1992b) to a larger sample of free-ranging Liberian chimpanzees that were subject to multiple stresses including heavy predation by humans (with some animals being wounded and healing multiple times before finally being killed). The overall results were similar to those reported by Jones & Cave (1960), with transverse enamel hypoplasias visible on 46.7 percent of maxillary central incisors and 69.7 percent of mandibular canines.

Bourne (1971) noted that intensively studied chimpanzee populations at the Gombe Stream Reserve in Tanzania appear free from malnutrition, but cited indirect evidence from parasite levels that wild chimpanzees might not always consume a diet that is optimum in all respects. Against this background, skeletal evidence of Harris lines and other indicators of short-term stress should be detectable in free-ranging populations of chimpanzees.

Acclimation includes not only physiological but also behavioral responses to environmental conditions. In extant humans perhaps the most distinctive of these short-term adaptive responses is afforded by the behavioral domain that includes activities to which the label culture has been applied. Culture is variously defined (Kroeber & Kluckhohn, 1963). When emphasis is placed on the centrality of language in the transmission of cultural information, then culture becomes a phenomenon unique to humans (Bloch, 1991). However, according to broader definitional criteria used in the biological sciences, cultural behaviors are those that are transmitted repeatedly through social or observational learning until they become attributes of populations (Whiten & Ham, 1992; see also Quiatt & Reynolds, 1993). Behaviors that meet these criteria are known in various species, including some papionine primates (Imanishi, 1957; Huffman, 1996), although each previously documented variation typically occurred in only a single behavior pattern. Now, the review by Whiten *et al.*, (1999) provides extensive evidence for multiple behavioral variants among free-ranging chimpanzee populations in Africa.

Overall, 65 categories of behavior were surveyed in seven chimpanzee groups that had been studied on a long-term basis. The sites that were included in the study ranged from Boussou in Guinea, near the western end of the present distribution of chimpanzees, through the Taï Forest in the Ivory Coast (both groups included in the subspecies *P. t. verus*), through the Kibale Forest and Budongo Forest in Uganda, plus Gombe and Mahale in Tanzania (the Ugandan and Tanzanian groups representing *P. t. schweinfurthii*). The chimpanzee community at each site showed a distinctive pattern characterized by numerous behavioral variants. Repertoires varied as much within the same subspecies (*P. t. verus* at Bossou and Taï, *P. t. schweinfurthii* in Ugandan and Tanzanian sites) as between them. For example, nut-cracking appears as a western cultural variant, but the fact that this behavior occurs over only part of the *verus* range suggests strongly that it is transmitted culturally rather than genetically.

The potential culturally-transmitted behaviors were screened to eliminate activities that either were not habitual in any community (16 traits) or were either customary or habitual at all sites (7 traits). Differences that could be accounted for by ecological factors also were eliminated; there were three such traits. For example, in certain locales chimpanzees will not sleep in ground nests because of predation by lions or leopards, which are absent elsewhere. Ultimately 39 traits remained to document the existence of culturally transmitted behavioral patterns among chimpanzees. As impressive as it is, this tabulation cannot be considered an exhaustive list by any means, since it represents such a small part of the chimpanzee range. The likelihood is that as more chimpanzee groups are studied, additional culturally-transmitted behaviors will be discovered. Even so, given the genetic evidence that points to chimpanzees as our probable sister group, the existence of even a modest shared capacity for culture should raise expectations that similar capacities existed even among the earliest hominid populations whose existence can be documented in the fossil record. Moreover, the fact that such a high proportion of chimpanzee behavior involves material elements holds out the possibility that corresponding physical remains may be recognized also in hominid paleobiological contexts. Even if leaves, twigs, and branches are not preserved, bone fragments that were used as marrow picks, and stones employed as hammers and anvils, should survive as evidence of cultural activities.

Developmental plasticity in chimpanzees

Studies of chimpanzees occur principally in two settings – field and laboratory. Neither situation is optimum for studies of developmental phenomena, which require repeated observations (e.g., of body mass, areas and diameters) under controlled conditions of large numbers of individuals from defined populations. In naturalistic settings, attempts to secure such data would be disruptive to studies of other phenomena. Laboratory colonies allow for more systematic collection of cross-sectional and longitudinal data, but these are on individuals commonly of unknown geographic origin presently living under rather artificial conditions of activity, diet, density, and disease (to name only a few of many important variables). Nonetheless, some useful observations have been recorded. On the whole these studies indicate that chimpanzees exhibit developmental flexibility that is different in some crucial details but comparable to that which has been documented on a much more extensive scale in humans.

As in many other areas of comparative primate biology, Adolph Schultz pioneered in data collection, first compiling information on growth and development of the chimpanzee and then summarizing additional observations on postembryonic age changes (Schultz, 1956a). Overlapping the work of Schultz were studies by Nissen on infant chimpanzees (Nissen, 1942), later these were extended to developmental studies of the deciduous dentition (Nissen & Riesen, 1945), permanent dentition (Nissen & Riesen, 1964), and ossification sequences in the skeleton (Nissen & Riesen, 1949a). Growth changes in the skull, face, jaws, and teeth of chimpanzees were summarized by Krogman (1969).

Gavan (1953) carried out a classic growth study on chimpanzees living in the Yerkes laboratory colony, utilizing longitudinal data that had been collected since 1939 (first at Orange Park, Florida and subsequently in the colony's new location in Atlanta, Georgia, USA). From the limited data set then available he concluded that his sample gave evidence of a human-like spurt in linear growth at the age of puberty. Later reanalysis by the original author (Gavan, 1971) led to the revised conclusion that a smoothly decelerating curve with a very small residual variance gave the best fit to the original data. This inference was reaffirmed subsequently (Watts & Gavan, 1982), although with the suggestion that chimpanzees (as well as rhesus monkeys) show very slight positive deviations in weight and skeletal growth from an exponential regression in early infancy and just following puberty. It is possible that heritable variations in small-scale deviations of this sort were amplified in the evolution of hominids.

An early but particularly valuable study of factors that can influence variation in developmental trajectories was provided by Nissen & Riesen (1949b). Chimpanzees in the Yerkes colony that had been reared under unusual conditions or had been subjected to various experimental procedures were compared with controls. With the single exception of two animals that had undergone brain surgery yet showed no negative effects, all of the other chimpanzees (including those that had been castrated, deprived of light, restricted in their tactile experiences, or reared in human homes) exhibited slower development, as indicated by retardation in the appearance of skeletal ossification centers. Although the causes of developmental perturbations surveyed by Nissen & Riesen (1949b) seem extreme, as already noted, comparable stresses are experienced in natural populations of chimpanzees that are subject to predation (Eckhardt 1992b).

Watts (1986) has stressed that there still is much to be learned about the development of the skeleton in nonhuman primates. Although further studies of developmental plasticity under conditions more comparable to those commonly encountered by humans (including variations in diet, climate, and exposure to infectious disease) would be informative, studies so far suggest that chimpanzee developmental response resemble those of humans in many general respects if not all particular details.

Genetic adaptations

Important information bearing on the zygostructure of chimpanzee populations has been provided by Morin *et al.* (1994) based on studies of eight hypervariable nuclear simple sequence repeat (SSR) loci and two mitochondrial (mtDNA) sequences (a 178 base pair segment of the cytochrome b region and a 345 base pair segment of the control region). The genetic material used in the study was extracted from hairs collected from chimpanzee nests and amplified by polymerase chain reaction (PCR). In all, 67 individuals were sampled from 20 sites representing the eastern, western, and central regions presently inhabited by chimpanzees.

The results of this molecular genetic analysis are broadly consistent with inferences drawn from multivariate craniometric studies (Albrecht & Miller, 1993; Shea *et al.*, 1993), though there are some important points of difference. A phylogenetic tree based on weighted genetic distances corrected for intraspecific polymorphism at the mtDNA control region locus placed *P. t. schweinfurthii* furthest from *H. sapiens*. There was only modest separation of *P. t. troglodytes* from *schweinfurthii*, with *P. paniscus* roughly equidistant between this pair of chimpanzee taxa and the extant human sequence. The *P. t. verus* sample fell roughly midway between other common chimpanzees and bonobos. The relatively close degree of sequence overlap between *troglodytes* and *schweinfurthii* populations is consistent with their close spatial proximity and the absence of a sharp subspecies boundary to their respective ranges. Similarly, the greater genetic distance of *P. t. verus* from other common chimpanzees can be accounted for by the greater geographic separation. These differences were sufficiently great that Morin *et al.* (1994) raised the possibility that *P. t. verus* might warrant a species, rather than subspecies, level of separation from other common chimpanzees. As already observed, however, these inclinations toward recognition of a new chimpanzee species are not supported by analyses of either cultural or craniometric data.

Several observations suggest that factors other than spatial relationships contribute to chimpanzee evolutionary patterning. For one thing, bonobo populations live in closer spatial proximity to both central African taxa of common chimpanzees but are genetically and morphologically more distinct from them than are western populations of *P. t. verus*. It is probable that a major factor contributing to this greater distinctiveness of the bonobo is the ecogeographic barrier to individual dispersal and gene flow posed by the Congo river. The extent of genetic differences between *P. t. verus* and other common chimpanzees are consistent with the greater geographic distance between the western and central African chimpanzee groups. However, the fact that among common chimpanzees the detectable distinctions at the molecular level are not matched at the morphological level reaffirms the observations by King & Wilson (1975) regarding the substantial decoupling of evolutionary phenomena at these two levels.

The implications of primate patterns of adaptation

Two opposing stereotypes about the adaptive capabilities of primates remain widely held but uncritically. On the one hand, present human populations often are believed to cope with the challenges of environmental change through behavioral mechanisms, with heavy reliance on complex material culture to ameliorate environmental challenges; and genetic adaptations are considered to be virtually absent or unimportant. On the other hand, animal populations, including those of nonhuman primates, are conceived as being adapted to particular ecological settings principally by gene-based mechanisms that permit less flexibility in confronting varied habitats or long-term secular changes in the physical and biotic environments. Contrasts of this sort misrepresent reality on both sides.

As seen in the preceding chapter, human populations also display some adaptations based substantially on genetic inheritance, as well as capacities for developmental plasticity and acclimation. The last decade has seen advances in nonhuman primate studies that are working to dispel the opposite misconception. In the context of the comparative frameworks provided by Foley (1987), particularly that of complex pattern recognition and analysis, these abundant new data are likely also to serve better in reconstruction of hominid paleobiology.

7 Hominid phylogeny: morphological and molecular measures of diversity

Introduction

The power of the adaptability approach for ordering data into frameworks for interpreting patterns of variation in living human populations was established in Chapter 5. As a consequence of its value in framing and testing hypotheses about population norms and variations, this research strategy generally has come to be accepted and used productively among human biologists who carry out investigations on the widely distributed populations of our species, particularly those living in extreme environments such as arctic, desert, and high altitude zones.

As shown in Chapter 6, the adaptability framework also can be extended from its original domain to that of living nonhuman primates. Aside from the behavioral realm, where language and elaborate technological mechanisms distinguish extant humans from other species, the modes by which populations adapt to their environments are shared broadly among mammals. Behavioral, physiological, and developmental, as well as genetic, factors come into play as extant primates, nonhuman and human, meet the challenges posed by the settings into which they have spread. An abundance of research, much of which is summarized by Foley (1987, 1995), clearly supports the inference that the same adaptive spectrum was available in various degrees to hominid populations of the past.

This chapter explores the patterns of phylogenetic relationships hypothesized for the hominids who lived and died over the last five or so million years. Studies of the morphological characters preserved in these fossil remains have led some paleoanthropologists to suggest greater species diversity than is supported by comparative molecular data derived from other groups of extant large mammals such as the bears, cats, and dogs. From the theoretical perspective of adaptability studies, the widely accepted proposition that a large number of previous hominid taxa arose by speciation and disappeared by extinction is not an impossibility, but it is a puzzle of sorts. In adaptive terms, evolutionary change results when the limits of intragenerational buffering mechanisms are exceeded and allelic frequencies are altered via differential fertility or mortality among the members of a population, or in a lineage of successive populations. Extinction is even more extreme, resulting when the limits of even intergenerational reorganizations of gene pools are exceeded. Yet nascent hominid populations probably possessed adaptive capacities comparable to those of current chimpanzees, and through time gave rise to successors with greater behavioral flexibility and cultural capacity. The paradox of evidently great phylogenetic diversity in a group characterized by initially large and subsequently increasing adaptive capacities can be resolved, at least in part, by integrating the perspective offered by analysis of patterns of variation at the molecular level.

How many hominid taxa existed?

During the century following the publication of Darwin's *Origin of Species*, 10 or more taxa of fossil hominids were commonly recognized, with the numbers of genera and species ranging from as low as three to as high as about 15. Somewhat surprisingly, given the huge advances that have been made in the body of fossil evidence, the exponential increase in comparative data on extant nonhuman primates, and great strides made in genetic analysis, the present situation remains rather similar. As often is characteristic in studies of human evolution, there is no general consensus. However, perhaps a start toward one can be made by examining several of the more commonly cited phylogenies of fossil hominids. Following that overview it is possible to approach the question of whether there might be some means other than comparing character states among specimens for establishing numbers of taxa and assessing relationships among fossil hominid populations.

   Recent publications in paleoanthropology (e.g., Johanson & Edgar, 1996) seem to build on a cladogram taken from Tattersall (1995) and a phylogenetic tree from Wood (1994). Wood's phylogeny appeared in a *Nature* 'News and Views' commentary on the occasion of the report by White *et al.* (1994) describing the then newly-discovered fossil hominid material from Aramis, Ethiopia. These schemes are similar to those of other papers (e.g., Wood & Chamberlain, 1986; Wood, 1992).

   Wood (1994) listed 13 named hominid taxa (Table 7.1). Johanson & Edgar (1996) recognized 14 hominid species, incorporating all of the same taxa as Wood, as well as adding the subsequently designated taxon *Australopithecus anamensis* (Leakey *et al.*, 1995) and renaming *Australopithecus ramidus* as *Ardipithecus ramidus* following the published revision of White and colleagues (Day, 1995), plus an additional node labeled only *Homo* sp.

Table 7.1. *Hominid taxa recognized from fossil evidence (Wood, 1994)*

Australopithecus	*Paranthropus*	*Homo*
A. ramidus	P. aethopicus	H. rudolfensis
A. afarensis	P. robustus	H. habilis
A. africanus	P. boisei	H. habilis
		H. ergaster
		H. heidelbergensis
		H. neanderthalensis
		H. sapiens

The shift in genus name from *Australopithecus* to *Ardipithecus* already has fulfilled part of the prediction by *Nature*'s Henry Gee (1995), that by the year 2000, *Australopithecus ramidus* would be removed to a new genus and *A. afarensis* will have dissolved into two or three different species.

Wood (1994), Tattersall (1995) and Johanson & Edgar (1996) share the assumption that all of the hypothetical hominid taxa that they recognize evolved after the last common ancestor of extant humans and chimpanzees. The total number of species-level fossil hominid taxa (excluding *Homo sapiens*) is 12 for Wood, 11 for Tattersall, and 14 for Johanson and Edgar. If the australopithecine taxa indicated by these investigators as occupying side branches are eliminated from the totals, then the minimum number of fossil hominid taxa, represented as being on the direct line of evolution connecting the last common ancestor of extant chimpanzees and humans, is five for Wood, five for Tattersall, and seven for Johanson and Edgar (who incorporate the more recently discovered material referred to as *Australopithecus anamensis*). These estimates of numbers of hominid taxa are empirically based, since they appear to derive largely from the perception of morphological differences that are believed to warrant recognition of genetic differentiation at the species level or above. However, there are other approaches to estimation of levels of hominid diversity.

As one approach, it is possible to estimate hypothetical numbers of hominid taxa from broader comparative and theoretical perspectives. For example, a widely cited generalization is that it takes about a million years for the evolution of a new mammalian species (Mayr, 1965). This induction can be combined with another commonly repeated figure, a date about five to six million years ago for the origin of hominids by a speciation event that split the first members of our lineage from a chimpanzee-like ancestral population. If the origin of hominids took place five million years ago and descendant populations bifurcated again every million years, with all of the daughter species surviving (perhaps at least long enough to leave a few of their remains in the fossil record), the resultant number of hominid taxa would be 2^4 or 16. This estimate appears remarkably close to several of the current phylogenies based on morphological criteria.

However, it should be borne in mind that this number is largely the product of several assumptions. If we had chosen a date for hominid origins of 6 Ma instead of 5 Ma, all other things being equal, the hypothetical number of hominid populations would have been 32 (i.e. 2^5) rather than 16, assuming that all of them survived. Moreover, there is no requirement in nature that requires species to bifurcate rather than to trifurcate, or to follow any other mathematically regular pattern (Hoelzer & Melnick, 1994); these numerical values are employed just to explore some possibilities. In that context, if three-way splitting had been the norm, then given an origin via a splitting event five million years ago, the potential number of hominid species would be 81 (i.e. 3^4), and shifting the origin back to six million years would raise the number to 243! This is a very large number, but not an utterly inconceivable one, since under unusual circumstances extraordinarily large numbers of differentiated vertebrate populations can come into existence over what appear to be rather short time spans. Perhaps the best known example of such a case concerns the cichlid fish of Lake Victoria in Africa, where over 200 populations are believed to have evolved from a single ancestor over about 200 000 years (Stiassny & Meyer, 1999). However, fish are not mammals, and an extensive array of evidence indicates that for reasons related to body size, food requirements, and generation times, large mammals speciate at relatively lower rates than smaller animals.

The last point suggests that ecological considerations are pertinent to questions about hominid speciation. In fact, an ecological approach toward estimating the numbers of hominid taxa was taken by Foley (1991). His results were in accord with an estimate of about 13 species, lending independent support to some of the recent morphologically-based diagnoses of hominid species. Foley was appropriately cautious in arriving at his figure, commenting that 'the precise number will never be known, and anyway the species concept is almost certain to break down when temporal variation is taken into account. On the one hand, we can argue that the fossil record is incomplete, and therefore there are still more species out there to be discovered. On the other hand, it might be argued that the anatomical minutiae have been overinterpreted, resulting in too many spurious distinctions, and that the number is more likely to be toward the lower figure of eight' (Foley 1995:93).

Overall, current estimates based on morphology and ecology yield numbers of hominid species on the order of Foley's lower estimate of about eight, plus or minus about five, and these are not contradicted by more abstract quantities derived from general inferences about the speciation process. Nor, for that matter, are any of these numbers very different from the estimates made around the turn of the twentieth century, when more explicitly typological considerations were the norm. Present and previous estimates could roughly coincide for a variety of reasons. To begin with, the classifications could be convergent because they represent reality, regardless of the process used to derive the categories. After all, field naturalists have discovered that some folk taxonomies yield results that are amazingly close to their own (Mayr, 1997:131). Independent achievement of the same categorical partitioning is not a surprising finding, given the probability that classifying or categorizing of some sort must have been a mental activity of humans since distant times in prehistory. It is also possible, of course, that the estimates of fossil hominid species diversity have converged on a number in the range of about eight or ten or a dozen by convention, based partly on accurate perception of real morphological distinctions, and partly by subjectively settling on a manageable and familiar number of categories into which the morphs can be sorted.

Against this background, and the striking discrepancy between phenostructure and zygostructure pointed out by Jolly (1993) in some primates, it is worth pursuing the alternative avenue of analysis that is provided by analyses of the molecular loci, which are only very loosely associated with morphological characters.

Genetic similarity of humans and chimpanzees

Over two decades of studies in molecular genetics have shown that *Homo* and *Pan* share about 99 percent of their genetic material. It would be reasonable to expect that the degree of genetic similarity among all hominids, living and fossil, logically must be even greater. Less evident alternatives could be suggested (for example, it could be hypothesized that some process operated to heighten genetic diversity among fossil hominids without having any detectable effect on the genetic distances observed among surviving hominoid primates). However, arguments of this sort would seem strained. Assumptions about the generality of evolutionary processes (which are not at all the same as faith in such particulars as molecular clocks that keep perfect time) are important in this case, because of the desirability of using common standards to assess past and present diversity.

Genetic distance measures among extant populations comprise important components of these reference standards. Research in this area is very active, with the result that there is an expanding set of comparative data. However, because the figure of 'less than one percent difference between humans and chimpanzees' is a data point that has become nearly apocryphal, it is worth reviewing how this striking genetic similarity first was established.

In 1975, Mary-Claire King and Allan Wilson wrote a classic paper titled 'Evolution at two levels in humans and chimpanzees.' Their central thesis was that evolutionary changes in form and function may be based more often on loci controlling the expressions of genes than on sequence changes in proteins. In particular, King and Wilson suggested that regulatory gene mutations could account for the major biological differences between humans and chimpanzees.

Much of the empirical research summarized by King & Wilson (1975) provided a basis for the induction that the average human protein is more than 99 percent identical in amino acid sequence to its chimpanzee homologue. Three areas of evidence were adduced in support of this inference. First, King and Wilson compared a set of proteins (technically, partial sequences from polypeptides such as myoglobin, the hemoglobin alpha, beta, gamma and delta chains, as well as cytochrome c, lysozyme, and so on). Of the 2633 total amino acids surveyed in this portion of the work, only 19 differed between humans and chimps. Dividing the difference by the total yielded an adjusted rate of 7.2 differences per 1000 amino acids, which is the usual way that molecular geneticists express an evolutionary divergence of 0.72 percent.

The sequencing results were reinforced by data on amino acid differences between the two hominoid taxa, in this case the substitution of one amino acid by another being detectable by protein electrophoresis. This laboratory technique is based on the fact that intact proteins have positive or negative electrical charges due to chemical differences in their particular amino acid sequences. Of the commonly-occurring amino acids, three (arginine, histidine, and lysine) have positively-charged side chains, while two others (aspartic acid and glutamic acid) have negatively-charged side chains. Electrophoresis can detect only amino acid substitutions that change the net charge of the protein studied, so a correction was made for the subset of substitutions that should be detectable electrophoretically, as well as for the average size of the polypeptide subjected to electrophoresis. The adjusted estimate of the differences detectable via electrophoretic analysis was 2.41 amino acids. Converting this figure again to a rate per 1000 amino acids resulted in an estimate of 8.2 substitutions per site (taking the standard error into account, the estimated range was 7.5 to 9.1 amino acids per 1000).

The two numbers, 7.2/1000 from sequencing and 8.2/1000 from electrophoresis, comprise the empirical results underlying the common phrase 'chimps and humans differ by less than one percent of their genetic material.' The resultant impression of genetic similarity was reinforced by findings from immunology and nucleic acid hybridization. These collateral lines of evidence were expressed in terms of an overall measure of genetic distance, called D (Nei & Roychoudhury, 1974). This value obtained, $D = 0.62$, was less than the average distances between congeneric species, and roughly in the middle of the range for sibling species (taxa that are genetically isolated but phenotypically indistinguishable).

King and Wilson stressed that the molecular similarity between chimpanzees and humans is extraordinary because these two taxa differ far more than the usual sibling species in their anatomy and way of life. This viewpoint was reinforced by a subsequent paper (Cherry *et al.*, 1978) that used data on other vertebrates to document just how much human morphology had changed from that of chimpanzees relative to far more modest underlying molecular divergences. Clear structural differences between humans and chimpanzees can be found in the brain, jaws, and limbs. These physical contrasts are matched and, though difficult to quantify precisely, even exceeded by contrasts in modes of locomotion, subsistence, and communication.

The estimate of less than one percent difference between chimpanzees and humans probably remains the most widely cited point of the paper by King and Wilson. But this finding really was their basis for making a point that, arguably, was even more important because of its wider implications for the interpretation of evolution among hominoid primates – that rates of molecular and morphological evolution were decoupled. Decoupling implies a relatively high degree of independence among various genetically-based developmental systems; a decade and a half later, this remains an area of research that is still relatively unexplored.

The emphasis on decoupling among several developmental levels also has helped to direct attention to the more objective standard provided by molecular data, as opposed to other lines of evidence, such as comparative anatomy, that have been used to estimate degrees of relationship. This new molecular standard was accepted by some traditional paleontologists. For example, Gould (1985) commented 'I do not fully understand why we are not proclaiming the message from the housetops. We finally have a method that can sort homology from analogy.' Studies of anatomical and morphological characters remain important, but it is increasingly being recognized that their value is greater in studies of adaptation than affiliation.

It is probable that acceptance of the conclusions by King & Wilson (1975) was facilitated by an earlier but equally attention-getting publication by Sarich & Wilson (1967), which eventually forced general acceptance of a pongid–hominid split only half as old as that which had been accepted by many paleoanthropologists. Wilson's group always had a knack for choosing a problem of wide interest that could be attacked with some of the most advanced molecular methods of the day (Wilson *et al.*, 1974; Maxson *et al.*, 1975; Cherry *et al.*, 1978; Stewart *et al.*, 1987). Although they didn't invariably get it right – the 'mitochondrial Eve' episode, as documented by Ayala and his colleagues (1994) and Templeton (1993), was a bridge too far – Wilson's group often broke new ground and always made the science sound exciting.

In fairness to other investigators, though, it should be noted that recognition by human biologists of the value of molecular evidence did not begin with the work in Wilson's laboratory. Since just after the turn of the twentieth century, serological studies had indicated a great similarity between humans and the African apes (Nuttall, 1904), and over the decades other investigators pursued similar studies in various groups of vertebrates. In particular, since the early 1960s, Morris Goodman and his colleagues at Wayne State University in Detroit, Michigan, USA, had been carrying out a solid program of research on the molecular evidence for primate relationships. Goodman was among the first investigators to stress firmly and consistently the likelihood of temporal closeness for the speciation events that led to the lineages now recognized as human, chimpanzee and gorilla. He also noted that relationships within the trichotomy would be difficult to resolve. Three decades and many technical advances later, some uncertainty remains, although at this time there is a broad consensus that humans and chimpanzees are the nearest neighbors among the hominoids. One group of researchers even has taken the step of announcing their resolution of the African hominoid trichotomy in favor of a chimp–human clade (Ruvulo *et al.*, 1991); however, a subsequent publication by one scientist in the same group (Ruvulo, 1997) urging consensus on this 'resolution' leaves the impression of lingering doubt rather than undoubted confirmation.

Are molecules and morphologies in conflict?

Consensus on points of major scientific importance – such as resolution of the evolutionary relationships within the extant hominoid primates, or the numbers of hominid taxa that ever existed – is likely to be reached only if there are common standards regarding what constitutes persuasive evidence. Such standards do not always exist, particularly across the boundaries of different disciplines (in this case, molecular biology and paleoanthropology) even if their members are working on what appears to be a common problem. Difficulties in coming to terms with unfamiliar evidence and reasoning may help to explain why some paleoanthropologists who were strong exponents of a pongid–hominid split at about 14 to 15 million years ago accepted the re-calibration of this event to about six to eight million years ago only after a delay of a decade and a half (e.g. Pilbeam, 1982). The same reluctance also may explain why some anthropologists (such as Schwartz, 1984) continue to insist that, among hominoids, orangutans are the nearest neighbors of humans despite overwhelming evidence to the contrary (Janczewski *et al.*, 1990).

In certain cases, strong commitment to a particular conclusion (such as the idea that hominids originated far from African hominoids in time and space, which is a necessary consequence of postulating an orangutan ancestry for humans) may be reinforced by a more general reluctance to concede that one area of research in anatomy – elucidation of phylogeny – now is being refined by molecular biology. A more positive view of the prospects for anatomical or morphological study is that, freed from its role as a principal anchor for phylogenetic inference, this line of research can concentrate on that to which it may be better suited by far – the investigation of relationships between form and function. Suggestions of this sort are resisted by some anatomists and paleoanthropologists. A clear example is provided by Schwartz (1988: 83):

'While it is becoming popular to ask how morphology might be interpreted given a particular biomolecularly based phylogenetic arrangement of taxa, it would seem to be equally viable to ask the question the other way round. If the chimpanzee is closely related to the gorilla, and if the orang-utan is closely related to humans, what are the possible consequences?'

An appropriate scientific response to this question is that the two propositions are not 'equally viable.' If the second alternative, which is preferred by Schwartz, did turn out to be the case (though it is difficult to imagine how), then an entire body of well-developed theory in molecular genetics, and an extremely large and rapidly growing body of highly consistent research results, would have to be discarded. Abandonment of the well-established discipline of molecular evolutionary genetics is unlikely. It is more probable that molecular data will be used for certain rate calibrations, leaving researchers interested in functional morphology increasingly free to pursue investigations into the adaptive implications of different structural variations.

In times past, studies of comparative anatomy or morphology may have been hindered by the assumption that similarity of form indicated closeness of phylogenetic relationship, since this position implied the further assumption (counter-intuitive but little questioned nonetheless) that differences in form were neutral or negative indicators of relatedness. As noted in Chapter 4, there was not much awareness of the potential for adaptive processes to influence morphological characters via developmental plasticity or natural selection. That this situation still persists in some quarters is documented by recently published reports (Holliday, 1997) as well as some earlier papers (Trinkaus, 1981).

The same tacit assumption, that similarity of structure indicates relationship rather than also reflecting function, also still is ubiquitous in molecular biology, where it is accepted that molecular changes are nearly always neutral. It must be realized, however, that neutrality is not so much a fixed belief as a convenient fiction. Technically, neutrality is a working hypothesis, and it has been an extremely productive one. Particular exceptions to it are being found, however, as explicit and objective tests of function are being elaborated (Gillespie, 1991). The alteration of this working hypothesis of neutrality to encompass examples of function has followed a course that is reasonably typical in science. When the concept of molecular neutrality was first proposed (King & Jukes, 1969; Kimura, 1983) it met with stiff opposition, because to many biologists it was counter-intuitive. Then followed a period during which the theory was elaborated and, even more important, the power of the operating assumption was demonstrated. The 1967 paper by Sarich & Wilson was a prime example of this sort. Initial success was followed by wider reliance on this working hypothesis, during the course of which procedures were standardized sufficiently that it seemed possible to carry out investigations in a relatively cookbook manner, with predictable results such as the 'mitochondrial Eve' calculations in which wrong computer algorithms were used, error terms ignored or underestimated, etc. Molecular evolutionary genetics is now entering a more introspective phase, during which new sets of theories are being developed to explain why molecular traits are not *always* neutral. However, the assumption that *most* molecular variants are nearly neutral *much* of the time works often enough that it can be relied on across broad timespans.

Some molecular perspectives on hominid diversity

The discipline of molecular genetics has provided objective reasons for some realignment in our views of relationships among the hominoids. Can this domain of research also help us to gain a better understanding of periods in hominid evolution known directly only from the fossil record? An affirmative answer to this question would be given by many investigators. However, most of them would be endorsing the possibility that sequence data – using nucleic acids extracted and amplified from fossil material, then aligned to detect sequence overlaps or discrepancies – will resolve long-standing questions. It would be incautious to bet against such expectations, if only because technological advances along such lines already are impressive and further innovations appear likely (Janczewski *et al.*, 1992). Some sequence data derived from hominid fossil remains already have been published, though the results are controversial. However, one alternative strategy already exists by which already available molecular data on extant taxa can be used to obtain some relatively objective measures of the hypothetical diversity among named hominid taxa as diagnosed from fossil material. This approach, as explained below, is a byproduct of large scale molecular genetic studies of mammalian genomes.

After molecular investigations of hominoid phylogeny in the 1960s and early 1970s produced results that were (by turns) unanticipated, sporadically opposed, and then broadly accepted, molecular techniques were applied to an increasingly broad array of long-standing questions, many of which proved to have exciting answers. Bruce & Ayala (1978, 1979) calculated genetic distances between common and pygmy chimpanzees, establishing that the sample of their isozyme loci studied showed them to be less distant from each other ($D = 0.103$) than the pairwise distance between either two species of gibbons ($D = 0.130$) or between Bornean and Sumatran orangutans ($D = 0.130$). O'Brien *et al.* (1983, 1987a) documented that the levels of genetic variation among cheetahs were so astonishingly low that allografts (transfers of skin from one animal to another) were tolerated, indicating that donor and recipient were very similar genetically. One of their explanations for this similarity was that severe population bottlenecks had occurred in the recent past.

In another set of studies on felid genetics, O'Brien *et al.* (1987b,c) employed one-dimensional gel electrophoresis to establish the very slight genetic distance ($D = 0.010$) between African and Asiatic lions. O'Brien and colleagues (1985) also resolved the relationship between the lesser panda and the giant panda, showing the former to be more closely related to racoons, the latter to bears. Within the primates, using gel electrophoresis to analyze 47 allozyme loci, Forman *et al.* (1986) found that genetic distances among three subspecies of lion tamarins were quite modest ($D = 0.007, 0.010$ and 0.030, roughly a fourfold spread from least to greatest divergence, but all relatively low). Janczewski *et al.* (1990), utilizing both isozyme and two-dimensional gel electrophoresis, reaffirmed the moderate genetic distances between Bornean and Sumatran orangutans (for which distance measures ranged from $D = 0.010$ to 0.025, depending on technique). These results are consistent with the previous discovery of a subspecies specific pericentric chromosomal inversion that makes it possible to distinguish between Bornean and Sumatran orangutans (Turleau *et al.*, 1975).

In addition to the insights into particular evolutionary questions represented by such studies, results such as these are helping to produce an increasingly valuable overall comparative perspective. Furthermore, as one technological breakthrough has followed another, the level of resolution has improved steadily, and increasingly fine degrees of differentiation continue to be detected. Consequently, we now have multiple estimates of genetic distance within species and between species (Table 7.2). These measures are particularly useful because they have been obtained in a single laboratory, often using common protocols (Wayne *et al.*, 1991). Although the data were collected for other reasons, we can now use them to test hypotheses about the numbers of hominid taxa that have existed over the past several million years.

A baseline is established by the genetic distance between humans and chimpanzees. There are two estimates here, for the comparison between humans and common chimpanzees ($D = 0.244$) and that between humans and pygmy chimps ($D = 0.197$). Many investigators feel that, as these figures indicate, humans are more closely related to the latter population. However, the original comparison drawn by King and Wilson used common chimpanzees, which will be relied upon here as a working standard. This approach is more conservative in any case, as it maximizes the contrast between the two hominoid taxa and hence estimates of the molecular distance between them.

If the distance figure of 0.244 is divided by 14, the highest number of hominid taxa postulated (by Johanson & Edgar, 1996) to have existed since a hominid lineage diverged from a chimpanzee-like ancestor, the average estimated genetic distance among the hominid groups would be 0.244/14, or 0.0174. This is less than one-fourth the genetic distance between the common and pygmy chimpanzees ($D = 0.075$), and is even one-third smaller than the difference between Bornean and Sumatran orangutans ($D = 0.025$), which interbreed freely when placed together. This estimate of the average genetic distance among fossil hominids also falls between the difference of 0.010 estimated between one pair of lion tamarin subspecies (*Leontopithecus rosalia rosalia* and *L. r. chrysomelas*) and that for another pair (*L. r. rosalia* and *L. r. chrysopygus*).

Table 7.2. *Genetic distances among closely-related mammalian taxa*

Comparisons among taxa	Genetic distance estimates (D)	
	Isozymes	2-Dimensional electrophoresis
Intergeneric		
Human and common chimpanzee[a]		
(*Homo sapiens* and *Pan troglodytes*)	0.244	0.100
Human and pygmy chimpanzee[a]		
(*Homo sapiens* and *Pan paniscus*)	0.197	0.100
African lion and Bengal tiger[b]		
(*Panthera leo leo* and *P. tigris tigris*)	0.121	
Interspecific		
Common and pygmy chimpanzee[a]		
(*Pan troglodytes* and *P. paniscus*)	0.075	0.020
Wolf and domestic dog[b]		
(*Canis lupus* and *C. familiaris*)	0.042	
Brown bear and polar bear[a]		
(*Ursus arctos* and *U. maritimus*)		0.028
Brown bear and black bear[c]		
(*Ursus arctos* and *U. americanus*)		0.046
Intraspecific		
Bornean and Sumatran orangutan[a]		
(*Pongo pygmaeus pygmaeus* and *P. p. abelii*)	0.025	0.017
Lion tamarins[d]		
(*Leontipithecus rosalia rosalia* and *L. r. chrysomelas*)	0.010	
(*L. r. rosallia* and *L. r. chrysopygus*)	0.030	
(*L. r. chrysomelas* and *L. r. chrysopygus*)	0.007	
Bengal and Siberian tiger[e]		
(*Panthera tigris tigris* and *P. t. altaica*)	0.007	
Bengal and Sumatran tiger[e]		
(*Panthera t. t.* and *P. t. sumatre*)	0.010	
Sumatran and Siberian tiger[e]		
(*Panthera t. sumatre* and *P. t. altaica*)	0.003	
Asiatic and African lion[f]		
(*Panthera leo persica* and *P. l. leo*)	0.009	
South and East African cheetah[g]		
(*Acinonyx jubatus jubatus* and *A. j. raineyi*)	0.004	

[a] Janczewski *et al.*, 1990; [b] Wayne *et al.*, 1991; [c] Goldman *et al.*, 1989; [d] Forman *et al.*, 1986; [e] O'Brien *et al.*, 1987b; [f] O'Brien *et al.*, 1987c; [g] O'Brien *et al.*, 1987a.

Even if the common chimpanzee–human genetic difference of $D = 0.244$ is subdivided among only five taxa – the minimum number of hominid genera and species postulated to be on a direct line from the common ancestor of hominids and chimpanzees to extant humans (Wood, 1994; Tattersall, 1995) – the average estimated genetic distance among the fossil hominid taxa would be 0.244/5, or 0.0488. This rough approximation to a genetic distance figure between fossil hominids differs only at the third decimal place from the genetic distance between domestic dogs and wolves ($D = 0.042$), which mate on contact and produce viable, fertile offspring despite differing substantially in phenotypic appearance. Similarly, the hominid figure is less than half the genetic distance between lions and tigers, which also are interfertile. Living lions and tigers are disjunct phenotypically, recognizably different at a glance on the basis of coat color; however, characters of the skull that differ between lions and tigers are not absolute (Kitchener, 1999). Many systematists hold the view that instances of hybridization between taxa in zoos, or in other situations where natural circumstances seem disturbed, have little bearing on questions of species recognition. However, if the focus of attention is not taxonomy *per se*, but instead the degree of genomic overlap and associated reproductive implications, then the patterns recognized by O'Brien and other molecular geneticists do have considerable relevance to interpreting hominid phylogeny.

Additional reference points for assessing numbers of hypothetical hominid taxa are provided by studies among the Ursidae. As in the lion–tiger comparison, the quantity estimated for distances among hominid taxa is less than half the distance between American black bears and brown bears, which interbreed in captivity. Of even greater interest is the fact that the hominid figure is less than half the distance between brown bears and grizzly bears. Although these ursid lineages are estimated to have diverged during the middle Pleistocene (Kurtén, 1964), they still are interfertile on contact (see references in Thenius, 1953). Yet brown bears and grizzly bears exhibit multiple character states that allow them to be distinguished by systematists. Kurtén describes numerous features of size, proportions and morphology – in the limb bones, skull and dentition – that are used in recognizing various ursid taxa.

Contrasts between molecular and morphological divergences among related taxa within numerous mammalian groups provide a context for reconsidering the large numbers of hypothetical fossil hominid genera and species now being included in many phylogenies. If other mammals provide a valid general standard, then the hypothetical hominid taxa cannot have differed from each other very much in genetic terms.

To this point, all of the comparisons here have been made in terms of genetic distance because of the large set of directly comparable figures built up by O'Brien and his colleagues. Similar comparisons can be conceived in terms of percentage differences in genetic material. However, these would have been more difficult to make, for a variety of reasons. For example, taxa differ in overall genome size as well as other characters, so comparisons in percentage might be misleading across taxa that are widely separated. However, chimpanzees and humans are close enough to allow a meaningful comparison to be drawn. King & Wilson (1975) noted that the difference between these two taxa was less than one percent. As we saw earlier in this chapter, the average of their two measures of 7.2 and 8.2 substitutions per 1000 nucleotides is 7.7, or a difference of about 0.77 percent. Dividing this by one of the lowest conventional estimates of hypothetical fossil hominid taxa gives us 0.77 percent/5 or 0.154 percent (that is, fifteen- or sixteen-hundredths of one percent). Dividing the largest number of hypothetical hominid taxa (14) would have all of them differing on average by 0.77 percent/14, or 0.055 percent (between five- and six-hundredths of one percent) of the genome. These are minute differences.

When judging the implications of all these figures, paleoanthropologists should recall the original points that were made by King & Wilson (1975) and Cherry *et al.* (1978) that morphological features commonly *overestimate* the genetic differentiation among hominoid primates. Real and visible as the morphological features of many fossil hominids are, such character states could constitute rather unreliable guides to species diversity (Figure 7.1).

Against the background posed by this dilemma, it may be useful to distinguish among several issues that seem to be aspects of a single problem, but which really are separable for analytical purposes. The first question is whether two given fossil hominid specimens are morphologically distinguishable on the basis of one or more character state differences. The second question is whether these specimens were sampled from separate groups that themselves can be reliably distinguished by the same criteria. A third question is whether the groups represented separate populations, as opposed to subgroups of a single population (another way of phrasing this question is whether the populations represented would have been genetically distinguishable if we were able to sample and analyze their genetic material, as we can with extant taxa). A fourth question concerns whether the populations were sufficiently differentiated genetically that, if they came into contact, they would be unable to exchange genes, and whether any gene exchange, if it occurred, would result in offspring that were viable and fertile. A fifth question concerns the

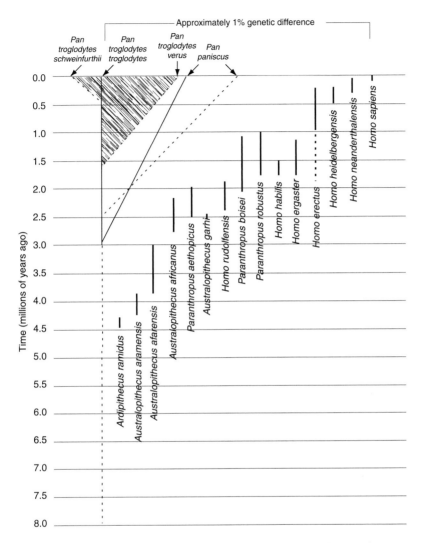

Figure 7.1. Relative genetic differences among actual present and proposed past hominoid taxa. The dotted lines (bounding *Pan troglodytes schweinfurthii*, *P. t. troglodytes*, and *P. t. verus*, all of which are interfertile as indicated by continuous shading) and extending to *P. paniscus*, represent genetic differentiation assessed by Morin *et al.* (1994) using mitochondrial loci. On the graph, physical distances between *P. troglodytes* and *P. paniscus* (solid lines), as well as between *P. troglodytes* and *Homo sapiens*, are proportionate to genetic distances obtained by Janczewski *et al.* (1990) from electrophoretic data (see Table 7.2). The approximately one percent genetic difference between *P. troglodytes* and *H. sapiens* is divided proportionally among 14 other proposed hominid taxa represented only by fossil remains. Depending on the measure used, the genetic distances between several pairs of *Pan* taxa would encompass four or more hypothetical hominid taxa. Hominid taxa based primarily on Wood (1994) supplemented by data from Wood & Collard (1999) and Asfaw *et al.* (1999).

appropriate nomenclature for the two populations. Each of these questions will be considered in greater detail.

Distinguishing between two specimens is a matter of observation. Experience and training are important in the task, of course, since fossils commonly are incomplete, distorted, broken, weathered, and obscured by adherent matrix. The preparation of the specimen and the level of anatomical knowledge of the observer are important factors that will condition the outcome of study at this level.

Judgments about the assignment of specimens to groups is only partially a matter of observation, and more substantially a matter of experience with the group of organisms and the extent and patterning of variation within it. As for the morphological aspect of the question, two specimens could differ from each other because of developmental influences that might be conditioned by age or sex. Moreover, when making such determinations we should beware of simple, single-cause explanations. Age, sex, and other factors influence development in various ways, but their effects necessarily will be expressed jointly in the characters of any given individual. Still further, patterns of sexual dimorphism themselves can differ within a single species and even from one portion of the skeleton to another. Sampling from different spatial localities and temporal horizons can add further complexity.

Concerning the question of whether the groups are themselves differentiable, somewhat different criteria apply at morphological and molecular levels. Groves (1989:7) discusses the traditional 75 percent rule for subspecies – 75 percent of the individuals classified in one subspecies are distinguishable from 100 percent of the individuals belonging to the other subspecies. He notes elsewhere (1989:13) that 'there is no qualitative difference between species and subspecies. The sorts of differences one finds between species are the same as those between subspecies, or indeed between morphs; indeed, the very same characters may be involved . . .' For the molecular level, Groves cited Ayala's (1975) study of *Drosophila willistoni* groups. Using Nei's concept of I (genetic identity), Ayala found that morphologically distinguishable species averaged values for I of 0.352.

On the potential for gene exchange between members of different populations, morphological and molecular criteria again send a mixed message. The existence of any reliable morphological standard is debatable due to the existence of several widely-occurring phenomena, such as sibling species and polytypic species. Sibling species, as noted earlier, are natural populations that are morphologically indistinguishable even though reproductively isolated. Polytypic species include a number of populations that are phenotypically recognizable. Subunits of polytypic species may be in contact and able to freely interbreed and exchange genes, or may be geographically isolated and exhibit greater morphological divergence. Molecular measures can gauge the underlying genetic differentiation among subunits in some cases. Ayala's (1975) work yielded values of 0.563 for comparisons between sibling species, 0.748 for semispecies, and 0.970 for local populations. However, the ranges of genetic identity overlapped extensively among categories.

What about the matter of appropriate nomenclature for distinguishable samples? On the one hand, there is a strong belief on the part of some paleoanthropologists that we are in the midst of a systematic revolution that will provide an objective basis for species recognition. According to Kimbel & Martin (1993:540):

'it would be difficult to overestimate the impact of Hennig's (1966) *Phylogenetic Systematics* and Eldredge and Gould's (1972) "Punctuated Equilibria: An Alternative to Phyletic Gradualism," contributions that emphasized new "ways of seeing" evolution for paleontologists and neontologists alike. Hennig's cladistic approach to phylogenic reconstruction logically entailed an isomorphic relationship between the relative temporal ordering of speciation events and the hierarchical structure of the Linnaean system.'

The situation is seen in a different light by one of the most experienced systematists of the twentieth century, Ernst Mayr (1997: 132, 133):

'According to the phylogenetic species concept, adopted by many cladists . . ., a new species originates when a new "apomorphy" originates in any population. This apomorphy may be as small as a single gene mutation. Rosen, finding that the species of fishes in almost any tributary of the Central American rivers had locally endemic genes, proposed that all of these populations be raised to species rank. One of his critics rightly remarked that with the high frequency of neutral gene mutations, every individual is apt to differ from its parents by at least one gene. How would one then decide when a population was different enough to be considered a separate species? This observation clearly showed the absurdity of trying to apply the cladistic concepts of microtaxonomy to the species problem . . .'

Mayr is more accepting of punctuated equilibrium, perhaps because it overlaps with his own belief in the importance of peripherally isolated founder populations as ideal starting points for new phylogenetic lineages. However, critical assessments of value of punctuationism in particular and expressions of doubt about the decoupling of macroevolution from micro-evolution are offered by Dennett (1995) and particularly Dawkins (1986, 1996), who has accurately characterized punctuationism as 'rapid gradualism,' and as such a phenomenon that is firmly within the neo-Darwinian synthesis.

These theoretical considerations shape the context for the interpretation of the data on which reconstructions of hominid phylogeny are based. The morphological features of the fossils represent one set of data, and these data are believed to support the existence of several related phylogenies that incorporate diverse arrays of 5 to 14 hominid taxa. In contrast, estimates of the total genetic diversity available to be partitioned among all of these formally recognized hominid taxa are objectively rather low (about one percent in total) in comparison with the levels of genetic differentiation among a wide variety of other groups of extant mammals.

Given these contrasts, several responses are possible. The overall contradictions outlined here can be ignored. As a second alternative, these contradictions can serve as the focus of a prolonged debate, with specialists trained in different disciplines occupying entrenched positions. There is yet another possibility, which can lead to new ways of thinking about hominid paleobiology and evolution.

At the terminological level, accommodation may require nothing more radical than a reduction in rank of some currently recognized species to subspecies, and an acceptance of the possibility that other putative taxa may be temporal or spatial subdivisions of clinally continuous lineages. A review by Kitchener (1999) presents an impressive case of this sort for tigers, which diverged from the other large cats about two million years ago. Tigers have an extensive geographic range and occupy habitats ranging from tropical jungles to Siberian steppes, with extensive variation in marking patterns, body size, and cranial characters. Yet the pattern of phenotypic variation among living tigers is most efficiently described in terms of clines rather than discrete subspecies, and the only tiger species other than extant *Panthera tigris* are fossil specimens not yet subjected to genetic analysis.

Conceptually, a shift away from formal taxonomy would coincide with the broad realization that several important attributes of species (morphological distinctiveness, genetic isolation, and so on) very commonly do not coincide. As noted by Mayr (1963: 580), 'Morphological differentiation, leading to the recognition of subspecies, is not a halfway point toward the acquisition of isolating mechanisms. Even in a species where it takes only 10,000 years to develop a well-defined island subspecies, it might well take 100,000 or perhaps 1,000,000 years for the completion of the speciation process. Our ignorance is nearly complete.' The realization that the critical attributes of species are acquired on timescales that can differ by one or two orders of magnitude is not a denial of the reality or utility of the species category, but rather a recognition of the complexity inherent in a natural world that has evolved prodigious diversity over time and space.

From the standpoint of understanding human paleobiology in particular – the modes of adaptation that shaped the fit between earlier hominid populations and their environments – the formal taxonomic names that are given to fossil hominids are less important than understanding whatever genetic relations may have existed among the actual populations that lived in the past. If the average differences among currently recognized hominid taxa were at about the same level as between dogs and wolves, or between Bornean and Sumatran orangutans, then gene exchange should have been generally possible among whichever of the hominid groups were synchronic (living at the same time) and sympatric (overlapping in their distributions). If that were the case, then from the standpoint of clear communication of meaning, it would seem desirable to use formal generic and specific designations with caution, since these names imply (to many biologists) genetic isolation, a proposition that is at best uncertain. From a practical standpoint, even if formal Linnaean binomials are used sparingly, it remains possible to refer unambiguously to fossil hominids by use of specimen numbers (AL 288–1) or site names (Hadar hominids). It is reasonable to believe that eventually some more elegant system will be designed.

These suggestions should not be construed as an attempt to disparage the current taxonomic conventions used in paleoanthropology. Rather, they reflect concern that such practices may be developing as a highly formalized area of scientific endeavor, pursued without full regard for the implications that systematic study has for more dynamic questions about the ecology and evolution of our ancestors. Adaptation, character state change, polymorphism, the evolution of coadapted genomes, and mate recognition systems are all populational phenomena. For these reasons, it is critically important that we make correct diagnoses of the levels at which populations were differentiated. If two groups of contemporaneous hominids are diagnosed as different species, then similar increases in brain size in both would be interpreted in terms of parallelism or convergence. Yet the alternative diagnosis of the same groups as geographically proximate subpopulations of one species could be accounted for in terms of shared gene systems responding to common environmental challenges.

Among the possible objections that might be raised to the suggestion made here, that low levels of genetic differentiation imply modest phylogenetic complexity among previous hominid populations, is that the resultant situation might mark a return '. . . to the days when it was widely believed that human evolution was unilineal. . .' (Groves, 1989:191). That is not implied at all. The days of a 'ladder of life' are long past, and the hominid fossil record clearly reflects the operation of complex evolutionary processes over long reaches of time and space. The challenge before us is to find appropriate models for this complexity, not to deny its existence. Some extant nonhuman primates provide some help here, though it must be realized that no particular surviving group resembles our early direct ancestors in all respects.

A papionine perspective on hominid paleobiology

The populations of terrestrial and semi-terrestrial monkeys that were surveyed in Chapter 6 are amenable to study along the lines discussed by Foley (1987, 1995) and outlined earlier in this chapter. As a group, the macaques, baboons, and their other near relatives constitute a natural experiment, allowing for an interplay of observation and hypothesis testing. Among the papionines, phenostructure and zygostructure do not coincide, with the result that phylogenetic inferences based on morphological data commonly misrepresent patterns of evolutionary relationships. On the one hand, gene flow among formally recognized taxa is fluid, while on the other, the fit between gene pool and environment is enhanced by various non-genetic adaptive processes, including developmental plasticity and behavioral flexibility. Rapidly expanding knowledge about papionine evolutionary biology may have broader implications.

Papionine populations are of particular value for comparative purposes, not only because they evolved and dispersed over much of Africa and Eurasia at about the same time as did hominids, but because they continue to occupy many portions of that broad range. One contrast, however, is just as important as all of the commonalities. Unlike extant humans, but like earlier hominids, the surviving macaques and baboons plus their close relatives exhibit considerable morphological diversity in body size, craniofacial dimensions and dental details. Since present humans exist only as a single surviving species, these terrestrial and semi-terrestrial monkeys provide an opportunity to measure directly the degrees of genetic differentiation (at the chromosomal, protein, and DNA sequence levels) that accompany morphological differentiation in higher primate populations that range from geographically dispersed to contiguous and even overlapping. All of these features combine to make macaques, baboons, and their close relatives valuable in providing a context for resolving some of the existing problems in hominid paleobiology.

As mentioned, the papionines are descendants of Old World monkey populations that adapted to life on the ground at about the same time (within the last 10 million years) that our ape ancestors were doing the same thing, and for much the same reason. They were responding to a common ecological imperative, a massive reduction in the extent of tropical forests and woodlands due to increasing aridity over much of Eurasia and Africa.

But the outcome of these adaptive responses to the common set of ecological opportunities and challenges was radically different. As noted by Foley (1995:117), papionine populations are descended from monkeys that had tree-living ancestors which may have resembled the surviving guenons, members of the genus *Cercopithecus*. Hominids descended from apes that probably were similar to those surviving in Africa today. As both the monkey and ape lineages became increasingly terrestrial, they did so from different arboreal heritages. The monkeys ancestral to papionines were arboreal quadrupeds that had moved through the trees by keeping all four limbs on the upper surfaces of branches as they ran, and jumping from one horizontal surface to another. Our hominoid ancestors also usually used all four limbs, but to support themselves vertically as they progressed by holding simultaneously to multiple branches above and below; this reliable multipoint support sometimes alternated with brachiation, in which their bodies were suspended by the arms beneath branches. These different starting points led to radically divergent evolutionary outcomes.

On the ground, the former arboreal quadrupeds basically exchanged one substrate for another, evolving into the terrestrially quadrupedal papionines. But the arboreal apes brought to the ground bodies with compact trunks supported at the front by rather long arms and at the back by relatively shorter legs. Quadrupedalism was structurally more awkward and energetically less efficient. Bipedalism offered a workable short-run resolution of the problem (though over the longer term, probably spanning many generations, there was a cost to be paid in terms of selection).

Between the papionines and the hominids there was another longer term, larger scale difference in outcome. In terms of conventional paleoanthropological standards, for the first several million years of hominid evolution there was a diversity of morphotypes that commonly are referred to as species. Sometime before the present, these numbers converged on the one hominid taxon that we know to exist through direct observation – our own.

For reasons that we do not yet understand, papionine primates instead have persisted as dozens of recognizable subgroups, with their constituent populations designated in formal taxonomic terms variously as separate subspecies, species, and even genera. Yet the chromosomal and molecular studies summarized above, reinforced by Jolly's (1993) detailed documentation of hybridization and other types of reproductive continuity across the 'boundaries' of many phenotypically distinguishable papionine populations, document how unreliable morphology is as a guide to gene flow. These substantial discrepancies between phenostructure and zygostructure are pervasive and enduring. Geladas and savanna baboons readily exchange genes in the wild, producing viable, fertile offspring as a result – although populations with their phenotypic attributes have persisted for several million years. No pairs of postulated hominid taxa are likely to have existed in parallel for a duration anywhere near as long.

Given these considerations, perhaps it is time to reconsider some of the uses that we are making of paleobiological data. Instead of asking how many taxa existed – or whether the appropriate level of taxon recognition in the fossil record is at the species level, above it, or below it – we should ask whether some of the many hypothesized examples of parallel evolution might be explained instead in terms of genetic contacts among hominid populations, however those populations are defined, and, in particular, however distinguishable some specimens are morphologically.

There is one last point to bear in mind about the evolutionary pattern represented by the papionine primates. As our knowledge of the genetic and reproductive biology of this group has improved, its formal taxonomy has become – in the opinion of some primate taxonomists – more problematical. As one example, we have the comment on *Macaca* that, 'The most detailed consideration . . . has failed to uncover a single derived feature that is shared by all species of the genus' (Groves 1989:140). As in the situation with fossil hominids, it appears that some of the recurrent problems arise from attempting to summarize dynamic aspects of population relationships within the confines of a system that is inherently dichotomizing. The larger lesson of the papionine case study is that if we desire to achieve taxonomic precision, detailed knowledge can bring confusion. If, however, we aspire to comprehend evolutionary dynamics, each additional detail carries us to a fuller understanding of our intricate evolutionary past.

By convention, human phylogeny is represented as a 'tree of life' or even more commonly as a bush with a great mass of intertwined stems. Familiarity with the image should not keep us from realizing that the bush is not itself reality but a metaphor – and, as observed by Paul Valéry (1895), Leonardo da Vinci's commentator, we should be aware of '. . . the folly of mistaking a paradox for a discovery, a metaphor for a truth . . .'

Although there are risks to departing from convention, another metaphor might be offered to help reshape thought about some phases of hominid evolution. In place of the conventional bush, consider the alternative image of a capillary bed. These complex anatomical structures usually have a unitary source in an artery, which then subdivides into a vast array of tiny channels, down to the level of the capillaries themselves. These capillaries anastomose, uniting to form a complex web of alternative pathways for the flow of blood, with the mass of interconnected tributaries eventually coalescing again into a vein. The advantage of this metaphor is that it creates a mental image incorporating a single origin (as from a chimpanzee-like ancestor), followed by branching into multiple pathways that are largely independent but have some interconnections (as may have been the case for phyletic lineages of polytypic early hominid taxa), and later continuing as a channel of much greater diameter (abundant humanity in the historical present). Furthermore, as with the passage of genes among hominid populations through time, flow through the metaphorical capillary system is unidirectional. The chief limitation of this image is that it implies that, as virtually all of the capillary passages feed through to the venous drainage, the majority of early hominid lineages contributed to present populations; in reality some must have become extinct. After all, metaphors (including this one) are only symbolic representations of reality, and as such cannot represent the natural world in a completely accurate fashion.

8 Plio-Pleistocene hominids: the paleobiology of fragmented populations

Introduction

Plio-Pleistocene hominid populations occupied a narrow genetic zone bounded by the genomes of extant chimpanzees and humans (but only approximately, because no living populations can be expected to have gene pools that have remained unchanged over millions of years). Judged from our present vantage, the outcome of hominid evolution represents a great anatomical step across this narrow genetic transition zone. The one percent DNA sequence difference between humans and chimpanzees, objectively small even now, must have been virtually indiscernible when the earliest hominid populations diverged onto their independent evolutionary pathway six to eight million years ago. At the phenotypic level, however, the evolution of hominids from ancestral apes was swift and pronounced, resulting in lasting morphological remodeling of the postcranial skeleton for upright posture and bipedal locomotion, along with other changes in cranial and dental characters.

Evolutionarily, these morphological changes establish that the adaptive capacities of early hominid populations were challenged and their gene pools restructured. Given the known extent of decoupling between molecular and morphological levels, it is probable that the first several million years of hominid evolution were characterized by discrepancies between phenostructure and zygostructure similar to those shown by the papionine populations spread across similar terrestrial ecosystems today. From the standpoint of adaptability, there is every reason to believe that in meeting these challenges, early hominids utilized capacities for flexible responses at several levels (behavioral, physiological, developmental, genetic) that we know are relied upon not only by humans, but also by papionines and to an even greater extent by chimpanzees, whose cultural capacities are increasingly well documented.

Our knowledge of the populations that existed on both edges of the transition zone – the last apes and the first hominids in our lineage – is increasing almost yearly with new discoveries of important fossil material. The nature and extent of those accumulating finds are summarized here, first from the still sparse ape side and then from the increasingly rich hominid side. Although a few key fossils are described in detail, the primary focus is not on phenotypes of individuals or the diagnoses of taxa. The fossil material is used instead to construct a framework that supports broader inferences about phenostructure, the patterns of distribution of the attributes of hominid populations over space and through time.

Hominid antecedents: the Eurafrican hominoid fossil record

The accumulating molecular evidence establishes Africa as the central focus for intensive scrutiny of fossil material around the time of transition. Recent developments in paleogeographic studies widen this spatial horizon somewhat, since for significant parts of the later Tertiary period, Africa and Europe were united in a single province which was separated from much of Asia by the climatic shift that dried up the Mediterranean Sea.

The fossil record for hominoid evolution in the Eurafrican faunal province is extensive (Gregory, 1922; LeGros Clark & Leakey, 1951; Napier & Davis, 1959; Pilbeam, 1969; Eckhardt, 1975). Until recently, however, this record has consisted chiefly of jaws and teeth from sites that were concentrated toward the earlier phases of the Miocene hominoid evolutionary expansion. As a result we have known more about where and when our direct hominoid ancestors lived than what they looked like, especially in the postcranial region. One of the few exceptions was provided by the partial juvenile skeleton of *Dryopithecus* (*Proconsul*) described first by Napier & Davis (1959) and elaborated on three decades later by Ruff *et al.* (1989).

Proconsul exhibited a horizontally-oriented spinal column that was long and flexible. Its axial skeleton supported a rib cage that was deep along the anterior–posterior axis but narrow from side to side. Forelimbs were attached to the thorax through scapulae that had elongated vertebral margins and were laterally directed, consistent with a locomotor complex characterized by an intermembral index that was relatively high (Ward *et al.*, 1993; Rose, 1994). The overall pattern exhibited by *Proconsul* is that of a lightly-built, quadrupedal primate with considerable trunk flexibility. Members of such early ape populations were capable of a variety of climbing and suspensory movements not too different from those of extant arboreal monkeys (Moyà-Solà & Köhler, 1996).

Until very recently, between this juvenile proconsul at about 18 Ma and AL288–1 at 3.1 Ma there was a gap of about 15 million years. The principal postcranial material known during this gap was from *Oreopithecus* (Hürzeler, 1954; Harrison, 1986; Jungers, 1987). The relationship of *Oreopithecus*, either to other hominoids or to other groups of higher primates, has long been disputed. Because of this anomaly arising from the patchiness of the fossil record, one review (Rose, 1994) of the postcranial anatomy of Miocene hominoids concluded that aside from *Oreopithecus*, there was effectively no fossil evidence for hominoid skeletal anatomy and locomotor characteristics. As a result, inferences about the adaptive changes that can be seen in early hominids, such as AL 288–1 and its immediate relatives, were at best indirect.

That gap in the fossil record now has been filled. As a result of paleontological fieldwork carried out from 1992 through 1994 by Moyà-Solà & his colleagues (Moyà-Solà & Köhler, 1993, 1995, 1996) there now exist numerous postcranial elements of a large hominoid primate, specimen number CLl-18000 (classified as *Dryopithecus laeitanus*). The fossil material all comes from a Late Miocene site at Can Llobateres, near Sabadell, Spain. During the Miocene this region was part of a large Eurafrican faunal region. The site has been dated to approximately 9.5 Ma, and the relatively few associated faunal remains (of turtle and rhino) are consistent with a gallery forest setting along a watercourse. The skeletal elements were found over an area of about 900 m^2, and the taphonomic evidence indicates that all of the bones belonged to a single adult male.

The CLl-18000 skeleton has a number of features that point toward the orthograde posture associated with extant pongids. The lumbar vertebrae are relatively short (Ward *et al.*, 1993; Sanders & Bodenbender, 1994), and both transverse and spinous processes of the vertebrae indicate a reduced mobility of the lumbar region. Articular details of the thoracic vertebrae are consistent with a laterally-broadened thorax. The clavicle is relatively long, as in hominoids that exhibit suspensory postures. Forelimbs also are relatively long and powerful, terminating in a large hand interpreted as being adapted for powerful grasping. Characteristics of the hind limb suggest a great extent of hip mobility, including abduction (Ward *et al.*, 1993). The limb dimensions, converted to relative measures such as the intermembral index, humero/femoral index and brachial index, all are far more similar to those of higher primates that exhibit suspensory rather than pronograde postures (such as baboons). The total morphological pattern seen in CLl-18000 clearly stands in contrast to the pattern described for earlier Miocene hominoids such as *Proconsul*, which still retained postcranial patterns more suited to pronograde posture.

The discovery of CLl-18000 makes an important contribution to our view of what the more immediate antecedents of hominids might have looked like. It is therefore perplexing that its discoverers have made some formalized interpretations within a cladistic framework that removes the population represented by CLl-18000 from direct ancestry to extant African apes and humans (Moyà-Solà & Köhler, 1993). This outcome assigned *Dryopithecus* to a Eurasian clade identified as the Ponginae, which also included the fossil taxa *Graecopithecus* as well as *Lufengpithecus* and *Sivapithecus* but only *Pongo* among extant hominoids. This arrangement would leave humans with no nearer known fossil antecedent than *Proconsul*.

Relegation of the taxon represented by CLl-18000 to a largely Asian clade rests on some highly particularized inferences from a very limited anatomical region. Two subsets of morphological features were used by Moyà-Solà and Köhler to argue for membership of the CLl-18000 dryopithecine material in a *Pongo* clade: the first comprised limb dimensions and proportions; while the second included a suite of craniofacial characters. This is a case in which a shift in focus from arbitrary cladistic analysis of character states to an understanding of the underlying biology of the characteristics can help to resolve a specific problem in paleobiology with important implications.

The limb dimensions and proportions used by Moyà-Solà and Köhler to argue for membership of the CLl-18000 dryopithecine material in a *Pongo* clade are features that have been characterized by Pilbeam and colleagues (1990) as adaptively labile. In this context, the level at which lability occurs is principally genetic – limb lengths can respond rapidly to selection for modes of locomotion suited to more terrestrial or to more arboreal substrates. A parallel instance is found among members of the genus *Cercopithecus*.

On the basis of chromosomal and other evidence, Eckhardt (1979) noted that the talapoin and patas monkeys were very closely related despite presenting striking contrasts in body size, form, and limb proportions. Patas monkeys have up to 10 times the body mass of talapoins, and extremely elongated limbs used in rapid cursory locomotion. Talapoins, in contrast, are small animals with a ratio of limb length to body length more similar to other *Cercopithecus* monkeys. It has been suggested that these differences evolved in fewer than a million years, and quite possibly substantially less time (Leakey, 1988), yet the taxa are sufficiently different that these monkeys commonly are placed in separate genera, or more recently as subgenera of the genus *Cercopithecus*, respectively as *C.* (*Miopithecus*) *talapoin* and *C.* (*Erythrocebus*) *patas*. More recently a close relationship between the talapoin and patas has been supported by molecular evidence (Ruvulo, 1988) as well as a methodologically painstaking quantitative study of craniodental characters (Martin & MacLarnon, 1988). Body and limb sizes and proportions appear to be aspects of functional morphology that are highly responsive to genetic selection. By the same reasoning, the postcranial morphology of CLl-18000 is far more informative about the adaptive strategy of an ape living in a forest ecosystem than about its phylogenetic relationships inferred from cladistic analysis of a few relatively modifiable characters.

With regard to the craniofacial features of CLl-18000, Moyà-Solà & Köhler (1993) argued that the zygomatic process preserves a suite of derived characters that show the *Dryopithecus* population from which it was sampled to be related to the Ponginae, as defined above, and not to the African ape/human clade. Yet these phenotypic features, like those of the postcranial skeleton, also are part of character complexes that serve particular biological functions, and vary in patterns that reflect genetic variation and developmental plasticity. Two of the characters, the robusticity of the zygomatic bone and the high placement on it of the zygomaxillary facial foramina, are matters of relative proportion that were not quantified in CLl-18000. As a result, these characters cannot be tested explicitly against comparative data, although it is known in general that craniofacial features, including bone robusticity as well as discrete or discontinuous features such as patterns of sutures and foramina, vary substantially from individual to individual in extant hominoid populations (Eckhardt, 1987; Hauser & DeStefano, 1989).

The awareness of the extent of skeletal variation in assessment of the phylogenetic significance of these features is as important as knowledge of their functional morphology. Zygomaxillary facial foramina have a definite function, serving as orifices for the zygomatico-facial nerve and blood vessels that develop relatively early in embryonic life (Lang, 1985). Postnatally, zygomaxillary facial foramina are highly variable, with observed numbers from zero to eight in hominoids. Although the modal number in chimpanzees is two, individuals with three foramina (the character state in CLl-18000) occur in 10 percent of a large sample of Liberian chimpanzees. In fact, zygomaxillary facial foramina constitute a classic structural polymorphism, with numbers varying widely in all hominoid taxa for which data are available. For example, although in *Pongo pygmaeus* the mode is three, the range is from one to eight, and if the specimens with one and two foramina are taken together, these outnumber the specimens with three. In *Symphalangus syndactylus* the mode (2) and range (1 to 5) are the same as in *Pan troglodytes*. In the gibbon taxon

Hylobates lar carpenteri the mode is three, as in *Pongo*. But in *Hylobates lar entelloides* the mode is two, while in *Hylobates muelleri funereus*, even though the range among a small sample of 19 animals extends to four foramina, the mode is one (Eckhardt, 1995).

These data resolve, in a manner that would be unexpected by many investigators who rely on cladistic analysis of morphological features, the apparent contradiction about the phyletic position of *Dryopithecus laietanus* as inferred from CLl-18000. The Can Llobateres specimen exhibits certain anatomical features (such as three zygomaxillary facial foramina) that are encountered more commonly in *Pongo* than in *Pan* (or in *Gorilla*, for that matter). But correspondence in such variable details of functional anatomy provides no support for removing *Dryopithecus* from a position ancestral to the extant African hominoids and humans. This is because, in formal terms, neither two nor three (nor any other single number of) zygomaxillary facial foramina can be accepted either as the plesiomorphic (primitive) or the apomorphic (derived) character state. Instead, the primitive condition that was present in ancestral hominoids almost certainly was the same as is encountered today in the taxa that are descended from them. This ancestral condition is a polymorphism of considerable phenotypic and ontogenetic complexity. Like skeletal metric variation (Eckhardt, 1987; Eckhardt & Protsch von Zieten, 1988), meristic and other discrete polymorphisms are pervasive in hominoid taxa (as in other mammals).

Attention to such polymorphisms is critical to understanding the phylogenetic relationships among hominoid taxa (including the more restricted group of hominids). The pioneering cladistic investigations (Hennig, 1966) had recognized character state polymorphisms that later tended to be overlooked. Within the 1990s, however, the complex dimension of anatomical reality represented by structural polymorphism is again attracting renewed attention (Kennedy, 1991; Hauser, 1992; Lipscomb, 1992; Barriel & Tassy, 1993; Hoelzer & Melnick, 1994). In studies of phylogeny, fossils should be seen not as artifacts displaying taxonomic 'markers,' but as portions of once-living individuals sampled from populations as variable as those now living. Fossil remains should be understood as preserving traces of ontogenetic development that differed from individual to individual. The high levels of variation reinforce the importance of basing phylogenetic inferences on the phenostructures of populations rather than the phenotypes of individuals. Single specimens or very small samples cannot accurately represent polymorphic character states, and inferences from them should be appropriately limited.

Ancient trans-species polymorphisms comprise one category of vari-

ation that should be expected in fossil samples. Trans-species polymorphisms represent morphological variants that are sufficiently stable that
their sets of multiple underlying alleles are maintained through the splitting of populations. The existence of such character states already is
accepted in molecular studies (Figueroa & Klein, 1988; Howard, 1988;
Hughes & Nei, 1988; McConnell *et al.*, 1988; Takahata *et al.*, 1988;
Takahata, 1990; Hughes, 1993) and karyotypic analyses (Stanyon *et al.*,
1988). Many of the conflicts that persist in studies of primate and human
phylogeny would be resolved if levels of detail in different analyses were
taken into account. It is misleading to compare cladistic analyses of nuc-
leotide-by-nucleotide gene sequences with cladistic studies based on com-
pilations of morphological character states that ignore intrapopulation
data on structural variations and polymorphisms, or that erroneously treat
complex multifactorial traits as unit characters.

Plio-Pleistocene hominids

Systematics

Several contrasting views on the numbers and relationships among hominid populations were discussed extensively in the preceding chapter and
need not be repeated. Rather than descriptions of taxa, the perspective
employed here will emphasize the temporal and spatial distribution of
functional complexes useful in understanding the biology of past hominid
populations.

Distribution in time and space

There is a substantial body of evidence that forms a secure base for
describing the earliest hominids – the nature of their physical remains, when
and where their populations lived, and the ecological settings over which
they roamed and within which they died. Some of these data are provided
by the hominid fossils themselves. Other categories are inferred from the
associated remains of other animals and plants, as well as related geological
indicators of climatic conditions. The recent authoritative summary of this
information provided by Conroy (1997) is drawn on here. The discussion
that follows is organized by site, emphasizing the primary observations
about the times and places where hominid populations lived, rather than
inferences that have been made about their taxonomic relationships.

Lothagam and Tabarin, Kenya (≥ 5.0 to 4.0 Ma)
The documented hominid fossil record in East Africa goes back beyond five million years if one includes such long-known but equivocal remains as the partial mandible from Lothagam, Kenya (Patterson *et al.*, 1970; Behrensmeyer, 1976; Corrucini & McHenry, 1980; Brown *et al.*, 1985b; Kramer, 1986; White, 1986; Hill *et al.*, 1992). Broken at both ends of the mandibular body and containing a single tooth that probably is a first lower molar, this fossil's dimensions place it solidly within the range of present chimps and gorillas, making it conceivable that it might even represent a late dryopithecine population (Eckhardt, 1977), although some later studies (e.g. Kramer, 1986) have stressed its similarities to early australopithecine remains. The equivocal nature of this specimen documents nicely the extent of overlap in many anatomical regions between the earliest hominids and their hominoid ancestors.

More recently, the Tabarin site in the Chemeron Formation near Lake Baringo, Kenya, has yielded a mandible and a humeral fragment estimated to date from about 5 Ma (Pickford *et al.*, 1983; Ward & Hill, 1987; Hill & Ward, 1988). Once again, these fossils inform us more of spatial and temporal continuity than of distinguishing anatomical features or key adaptive characteristics.

Kanapoi, Kenya (4.2 to 3.9 Ma)
An isolated humeral fragment was discovered in the early 1960s at the Kanapoi site (Patterson & Howells, 1967; Leakey *et al.*, 1995). Although an entire humerus would by its length and proportions tell us something about the relationships and much about the way of life of its possessor (as in the case of CLl-18 000), a distal humeral fragment by itself is not very diagnostic. While a complete humerus of a present human is readily distinguishable from that of a chimpanzee because of the differences in length and proportions, the distal joint surfaces alone are pervasively similar. Later, this first postcranial find was supplemented by a fragment of fibia, plus limited dental remains (Leakey *et al.*, 1995). Characteristics of the tibia have been interpreted as indicative of complete bipedal locomotion.

Middle Awash, Ethiopia (4.5 to 2.5 Ma)
The Aramis locale appears to date to approximately 4.4 Ma (Woldegabriel *et al.*, 1994). The remains initially discovered were of the sort characteristic of most early sites, comprising the partial bases of two crania, the mandible of a child, most of a set of teeth from one individual and scattered teeth from one or more others, and a few bones from the postcranial skeleton (White *et al.*, 1994, 1995). Later finds (Asfaw *et al.*, 1995) added numerous

cranial and postcranial specimens, including the partial skeleton of an adult, represented by portions of the upper and lower limbs, as well as cranial and mandibular fragments.

A few teeth dating to approximately 4 Ma have been recovered from the locality of Fejej in the southern part of Ethiopia (Fleagle *et al.*, 1991; Kappelman *et al.*, 1996). So far, these additional remains serve mainly to extend the known range of early hominids in the Ethiopian region.

More recently still from the Middle Awash region is the discovery of cranial and dental remains of a specimen designated BOU-VP-12/30. The material emanates from the Hata Member of the Bouri Formation (Asfaw *et al.*, 1999), dated through biochronological and argon/argon (Ar/Ar) methods to about 2.5 Ma. Additional finds (principally BOU-VP-11/1 and BOU-VP-12/1A-G) of cranial and postcranial fragments from nearby sites in the same time horizon indicate the presence of early hominids that combined an ape-like upper arm to lower arm ratio with a humeral: femoral ratio more like that of later humans. Associated material included abundant catfish remains and fossils of medium-sized bovids, some of which bore cut marks (de Heinzelin *et al.*, 1999). The combined evidence suggests that behavioral changes indicated by lithic technology and carnivory may have provided a basis for the evolution of more advanced hominids.

Koobi Fora and Nachukui Formations, Kenya (≥4.0 to 1.4 Ma)
Koobi Fora and Nachukui are situated around the northeastern and western shores, respectively, of Lake Turkana. Explorations of these areas have continued from 1967 through the present time, and have yielded many important fossil finds, beginning with KNM-ER 406, the robust skull of an old adult. Although a few specimens come from deposits exceeding four million years in age, the bulk of the finds date to less than 2 Ma. As might be expected for a large range spanning several million years (Brown & Feibel, 1986, 1988; Feibel *et al.*, 1989; Brown, 1994), characteristics of the finds, taken together, are quite varied in degree of completeness (from small fragments to the substantially complete skeleton of an adolescent male, KNM-WT 15000); in morphology (from gracile to the robust 'Black Skull' KNM-WT 17000); and in ecological setting (Williamson, 1985).

Laetoli, Tanzania (3.7 to 3.2 Ma)
A comprehensive overview of this site, including its age and paleoecology, has been provided by Leakey & Harris (1991). Hominid remains have been known from the area since Louis Leakey found an isolated lower left canine of uncertain affinity in 1935 (White, 1981). A subsequent survey

carried out over half a century ago by Kohl-Larsen's German research group from 1933 through 1939 (Kohl-Larsen, 1940) recovered an occipital fragment and a partial maxilla containing the third and fourth upper premolars from a young hominid, as well as an isolated upper third molar from an older individual. These materials were later restudied in detail (Protsch, 1981 a,b; Puech *et al.*, 1986).

Expeditions carried out during the 1970s recovered more abundant and complete remains. These were attributed preliminarily (Johanson & Coppens, 1976) to several early hominid taxa, an interpretation that was later revised (Johanson *et al.*, 1978, 1982; Johanson & White, 1979) to a single upright, bipedal australopithecine species, a view that nevertheless remains vigorously disputed in some quarters (e.g. Senut & Tardieu, 1985).

Striking confirmation of the bipedal nature of the very early hominids at Laetoli came from the discovery of footprints in 1978 (Leakey & Hay, 1979). These impressions were preserved in a fresh fall of light volcanic ash, wet by rainfall to make a light paste that was first walked in and then later dried and hardened by sunlight. As might be expected, this collateral line of evidence about hominid locomotor characteristics has garnered considerable attention and generated diverse interpretations (Day, 1985; Tuttle, 1985, 1987; White & Suwa, 1987; Tuttle *et al.*, 1991).

Hadar, Ethiopia (3.6 to 3.2 Ma)
The dating of the Hadar site as well as nearby areas along the Middle Awash River of Ethiopia has been covered in a number of sources (Aronson & Taieb, 1981; Walter & Aronson, 1993; Walter, 1994). Explorations began in 1972 and the earliest report was published several years later (Johanson & Coppens, 1976). The first fossil remains recovered there were postcranial, including proximal portions of right and left femurs as well as a distal femoral end with an associated proximal tibia. Within the decade the sample had been expanded to about three dozen separate individuals represented by between 200 and 300 fossil fragments, including at least 13 individuals from a single site (AL 333) plus the 40 percent complete skeleton of Lucy (AL 288–1), all dated to 3.2 Ma (Johanson *et al.*, 1982; Johanson & White, 1979; Radosevich *et al.*, 1992). Taken together, these remains have done much to shape present views of early hominid structure and function, as well as intrapopulation variation.

Shungura and Usno Formations, Omo Group, Ethiopia
(3.3 to 1.4 Ma)
The earliest fossils from this region were discovered at the beginning of the twentieth century. By 1933 the French paleontologist Camille Arambourg

had carried out a geological and paleontological reconnaissance that established a basis for all later work in the area. In 1966 the American paleoanthropologist F. Clark Howell, along with Yves Coppens of France and Richard Leakey of Kenya, constituted the International Omo Research Expedition. The American and French investigators found abundant hominid remains at nearly a hundred scattered localities (Howell & Coppens, 1976; Howell *et al.*, 1987; Feibel *et al.*, 1989). Over the years assignments of specimens to particular hominid taxa have been relatively diverse and fluid (Hunt & Vitzthum, 1986; Suwa, 1988; White, 1988; Grine, 1993; Wood *et al.*, 1994).

Olduvai Gorge, Tanzania (1.9 to <1.0 Ma)
Although numerous stone tools and scattered fossils had been known for decades, the first relatively complete hominid skull was not unearthed at Olduvai until 1959. Discovered by Mary and published on by Louis (Leakey, 1959), it was a cranial specimen notable for its robusticity and unexpectedly early date (revisited in Drake & Curtis, 1991). Its original taxonomic status was challenged almost immediately (Robinson, 1960) and forthwith defended (Leakey, 1960). More complete studies have provided extremely detailed contextual (Leakey, 1967) and comparative (Tobias, 1967) perspectives. Soon afterward, more gracile hominid remains also were discovered (Leakey *et al.*, 1964). As with the robust skull, their taxonomic status has been a continuing source of disagreement.

Following these influential early finds and the interest that they generated, Olduvai Gorge has received continuing study, which has been consistently rewarded by a steady stream of hominid fossil material, including more recently the fragmentary and controversial remains of OH 62 (Johanson *et al.*, 1987), the interpretation of which is examined in Chapter 9.

Transvaal sites, South Africa (3.0 to 1.0 Ma)
Makapansgat (3.0 to 2.4 Ma) Makapansgat is a cavern containing limestone of high purity that was quarried starting in 1925. However, organized paleontological research was not carried out at this site until after the conclusion of World War II. The first fossil, an occipital fragment, was discovered on a dump outside the cave in 1947 and described in Dart's characteristically swift style the following year (Dart, 1948a). Within the same year infant cranial fragments and an adolescent mandible were added to the sample. Even more important, the adolescent remains included pelvic fragments which provided the first independent direct postcranial confirmation of the upright posture that had been hypothesized by Dart on the basis of the Taung skull alone. The age range represented at the site is

relatively narrow (White *et al.*, 1981; Delson, 1984; Partridge, 1986) and has been supported by faunal correlations with East African sites (Vrba, 1985).

Taung (2.5 to 2.0 Ma) As noted in Chapter 3, the South African site Taung yielded the first fossil identified as an australopithecine. Despite deter-mined professional opposition to its hominid status in particular and to his research in general, for three decades Raymond Dart and his associates continued to find an ever-expanding array of related fossil material in the Transvaal region. It would be a further three decades before the sequence of East African finds, which began with the Leakeys' discoveries at Ol-duvai. Eventually the East African finds came to surpass those from South Africa in abundance and antiquity, but the early finds from the Transvaal sites and their interpretations did much to shape subsequent views about the pattern of early hominid evolution.

Sterkfontein (2.5 to 1.7 Ma) Dart's preparation and description of the Taung child was followed in 1936 by Robert Broom's recovery at Sterkfon-tein of the first fossil described as an adult australopithecine (Broom, 1936, 1937, 1938). Despite delays occasioned by World War II, further fossils were soon added (Broom & Robinson, 1947). Overviews of the full range of finds made to date have been provided (Kuman, 1994a,b; Tobias & Baker, 1994). Stratigraphic units at this site have been divided into members numbered from 1, the oldest, through 6, the youngest; so far hominid fossils have been discovered only in members 2, 4 and 5 (Partridge, 1978). Hom-inid finds include foot bones recently recovered from member 2 (Clarke & Tobias, 1995) as well as a wide range of cranial and postcranial remains that have accumulated over the previous decades. It is notable that in morphological and metric attributes of the dentition, specimens found in Sterkfontein Member 4 alone exceed the range encountered in specimens attributed from 'hyper-robust' to gracile advanced hominids in East Africa (see Clarke, 1988, 1994; and particularly Conroy & Vannier, 1991).

Kromdraai (2.0 to 1.0 Ma) This site, which samples the time range from approximately 2 to 1 Ma, so far has yielded dental, cranial and postcranial remains only of relatively robust australopithecines over an extensive period of study (Broom, 1950; Dart & Craig, 1959; Berger *et al.*, 1994).

Swartkrans (1.8 to 1.0 Ma) Excavation commenced at this site in 1948 by the somewhat unconventional means of blasting with dynamite to fracture the consolidated brecchia deposits. Results were successful, however, with dental and mandibular remains being found at once and described in a publication the following year (Broom, 1949). Since then a total of over 130 fossils have been recovered. These include mandibles (Grine & Daegling, 1993), craniodental remains (Grine, 1989, 1993; Grine *et al.*, 1993), bones of the foot (Susman & Brain, 1988) and hand (Susman, 1988), and a radius (Grine & Susman, 1991), among other postcranial remains (Susman, 1989, 1993; Grine & Strait, 1994). Roughly 40 percent of the hominid remains are pre-adult, and since many of these have been recovered since the 1980s, Mann's (1975) classic paleodemographic analysis established a basis for their study. Overviews have been provided by Brain & Watson (1992) and Brain (1993, 1994).

Phenotypic features of Plio-Pleistocene hominids

Limitations of the evidence

The sites summarized above are distributed geographically in Africa along an axis that extends from Ethiopia, through the Great Rift Valley of East Africa, down nearly to the southern tip of the continent. Temporally the strata from which the hominid remains have been recovered range from more than five million years ago to about a million years before the present, for a total timespan of about four million years. It is difficult to give the exact number of individual hominids known from this expanse of time and space, for a number of reasons. Remains are fragmentary, so it is not always clear whether several fossils represent multiple hominids, or only one.

Sometimes specimens catalogued separately are found to be parts of a single individual, thereby reducing the known number of early hominids. For example, Ron Clarke of the University of the Witwatersrand, South Africa, realized that the facial portion of a skull from Swartkrans, SK 847 (which originally had been classified as member of the genus *Paranthropus*), fitted perfectly with SK 80, a maxillary fragment originally designated as *Telanthropus capensis* (Clarke *et al.*, 1970). The composite specimen now is assigned to the genus *Homo* by some workers (e.g., Clarke & Howell, 1972; Wood, 1993). In the other direction, the new discoveries being made virtually every year (such as BOU-VP-12/30, discovered in 1996 and described in 1999, Asfaw *et al.*), steadily augment the totals. At this point an estimate of about 1500 hominid specimens from Africa in the time period from about 5 to 1 Ma would be the right order of magnitude (Locke, 1999). It should be expected that this large hominid sample from Pliocene and Pleistocene deposits would display appreciable diversity. The challenge is to put the observable differences into some context that helps us to make sense of the extent and causes of the observed variation.

To begin with, all humans from the Pliocene through the present are unique. This ultimate in individuality is assured in an abundant species with a large genome possessing numerous loci, many of which are occupied by alternative alleles that are reshuffled anew each generation by sexual reproduction (Eckhardt, 1979). Added to virtually infinite genetic diversity is developmental flexibility which is so great that even identical twins exhibit some phenotypic differences. Enhancing this base of intrinsically high variation are the dual multipliers of ecological diversity and temporal duration. The spatial range occupied by Plio-Pleistocene populations was substantial, and included environments as varied as savannas, grasslands, and woodlands. The range in time, approximately four million years, encompassed significant evolutionary changes, such as structural remodeling of the postcranial skeleton for upright posture and bipedal locomotion. Over the same period, endocranial volume more than doubled. In addition to these major anatomical changes, there is such abundant craniodental variation among specimens that no two individuals are alike. All of the changes just summarized are matters of observational reality, regardless of how they are interpreted phylogenetically. Their magnitude is unaffected however the variation was generated – by cladogenesis producing numerous species, by anagenic change within a single lineage, or by far more complex and fluid interrelationships among hominid semispecies, subspecies or local populations at shifting levels of genetic differentiation.

In addition to variation within populations due to age, sex, and the other factors that differentiate individuals, plus contrasts between populations attributable to local adaptation and evolutionary change through time, accidents of sampling have played a role that is important to recognize, however difficult it is to quantify. A large part of the problem is comprehending the nature and extent of the underlying distribution being sampled. A common metaphor warns about losing sight of the forest by concentrating on the trees. For the Plio-Pleistocene, whole trees (skeletons) are so rare that there is a fascination even with partial trunks and fragments of branches (individual bones and teeth). And since the forest itself disappeared millions of years ago and no longer can be seen, there is a tendency to underestimate how vast it might have been. Under the circumstances, even a very rough approximation can provide useful perspective.

African Plio-Pleistocene sites are arrayed for 3000 miles from Ethiopia to South Africa. The extent of their distribution to either side of this line is as yet unknown, but if a strip 500 miles (*c.* 805 km) wide is hypothesized, the resultant total area would approach 1.5 million square miles (*c.* 3.9 million km^2). Population density also is unknown, but aborigines living in desert-like areas of southern Australia, where rainfall is less than 25.4 cm per year, have densities just over one person per 100 square miles (*c.* 260 km²). If Plio-Pleistocene hominids had comparable densities on average, then over the entire area some 15 000 hominids might have lived in each generation. If an early hominid generation interval were 20 years (which probably is a slightly conservative overestimate), then four million years there would have encompassed approximately 200 000 generations. The product of these two estimates (15 000 hominids per generation and 200 000 generations) yields a total sample on the order of three billion hominids who might have lived and died between five million and one million years ago.

This is admittedly an extremely rough figure, and might be scaled down in various ways. For example, assume that only ten percent of the 1.5 million square miles (*c.* 3.9 million km²) were habitable by early hominids. Furthermore, allow that the density of occupation was only one individual per 1000 square miles (*c.* 2600 km²) rather than one per 100 square miles (*c.* 260 km²). Taken together, these two adjustments would reduce the hypothetical total of early hominids who lived over the four million years in East and South Africa by two orders of magnitude to a figure on the order of thirty million (which probably is too low). But even at that much reduced figure, the set of about 1500 known Plio-Pleistocene hominid specimens represents sampling of only one individual out of every 20 000 that lived during the entire timespan. That's on about the same scale as representing a motion picture with a few still photos, from which one has to guess both the players and the nature of the plot that structured their relationships; it is inevitable that a lot must be missed.

Although entire populations are represented by only a few specimens, and many generations not yet sampled at all, it is reasonable to expect that the overall situation will improve, perhaps markedly. Even if relatively few earlier hominids have survived as fossils, the total number that might yet be found could be large. The basis for this guarded optimism is statistical. Although the number of hominids alive in any given geographic area may have been small, the numbers of generations that existed over time were large, so the product must have been substantial as well. Nevertheless, until the known sample of Plio-Pleistocene hominids increases substantially, accidents of death, preservation and discovery will exert major influences. Which factors will have exerted the greatest influence on what has come down to us as 'data' in any given instance will depend, in good part, on these accidents of sampling, as well as on the patterns of adaptation that were themselves undergoing evolutionary change. This point was first made in Chapter 3, and is reemphasized by the force of greater detail here.

The environmental settings that hominid populations had to deal with probably were as diverse as those known to shape the varied adaptive characteristics of extant papionines. Because of the discrepancy between phenostructure and zygostructure in papionines (Jolly, 1993) and to some extent in chimpanzees (Morin *et al.*, 1994), as well as the persistent disagreements about taxonomic relationships among Plio-Pleistocene hominids, it might be good to begin by surveying what is a very basic biological characteristic – size. Although conceptually simpler than craniofacial features, body mass and stature have major ecological implications. What were the central tendencies and variations in these characteristics among Plio-Pleistocene hominids?

Body size

An animal's body size is determined by past evolutionary influences and present circumstances. In turn, size exerts a major influence on locomotion, risks from predation, interactions with conspecifics, food sources and feeding behaviors, thermoregulation, and so on. As a result, body size or mass is adjustable within and between generations.

The discussion here begins with information assembled systematically by McHenry over a number of years and summarized by him in 1992 (Table 8.1). The data were presented as the male and female means for each taxon. Thus the body weights of male and female *Australopithecus afarensis* are given as 45 kg and 27 kg, respectively. The corresponding statures given for these taxa are 151 cm and 105 cm. The Plio-Pleistocene fossil hominids generally recognized by paleoanthropologists for the timespan between five and one million years include (in addition to the early taxa *Ardipithecus ramidus* and *Australopithecus anamensis*, not treated by McHenry) *A. afarensis, A. africanus, A. robustus, A. boisei,* and *Homo habilis. Homo erectus* is generally accepted as having arisen at the end of the timespan considered here. Excluding *H. erectus* and *H. sapiens,* the range in body weight is from 27 kg for the female in the taxon of smallest average size (*A. afarensis*) to 52 kg for the male in the taxon with the greatest average size (*H. habilis*), who thus was 93 percent heavier, or more technically had a body mass 1.93 times greater. For stature, the low and high averages were 105 cm and 157 cm, respectively, setting a total span of 50 percent (the tallest being 1.50 times the stature of the shortest).

For context, McHenry listed corresponding values for *Homo sapiens,* in which the male average was given as 65 kg as against 54 kg for females (establishing a ratio of 1.2:1 for the weight averages), with the correspond-

Table 8.1. *Body sizes of some past and present hominids*

Taxon	Body mass (kg)		Stature (cm)	
	male	female	male	female
Australopithecus afarensis	45	27	151	105
A. africanus	41	30	138	115
A. robustus	40	32	132	110
A. boisei	49	34	137	124
Homo habilis	52	32	157	125
H. sapiens	65	54	175	161
H. sapiens (US military data)				
sample size	1774	2208	1774	2208
mean	78.49	62.01	175.58	162.94
standard deviation	±11.10	±8.35	±6.68	±6.36
range	47.6–127.8	41.3–96.7	149.7–204.2	142.8–187.0

Sources: Hominid data in upper half of table based on McHenry (1992) and Conroy (1997). Data on living humans (i.e. US military data) based on Gordon *et al.* (1989).

ing statures being 175 cm and 161 cm (yielding a ratio of 1.09:1 for the stature averages).

It is informative to extend McHenry's comparisons more widely, from means to measures of intraspecific variation. Many reference sources are available for such an exercise. The principal one used here is the *1988 Anthropometric Survey of US Army Personnel* (Gordon *et al.*, 1988). For 1774 male subjects included in the sample, the mean body weight was 78.49 kg (range 47.60 to 127.80; standard deviation 11.1). The corresponding figure for females, based on a sample of 2208, was 62.01 kg (range 41.30 to 96.70; standard deviation 8.35). Respective male and female statures were 175.58 cm (range 149.7 to 204.2; standard deviation 6.68) and 162.94 cm (range 142.8 to 187; standard deviation 6.36). It should be borne in mind that the US Army study sample was by its nature one in which variation would be *reduced* by various factors, including age, health status, certain restrictive physical standards (such as minimum statures required and maximum body weights permitted). In addition, despite the diversity of the US population from which these military personnel are sampled, many of the world's human groups are represented minimally or not at all.

Even within those constraints, the variation represented in this sample, which includes both sexes but a relatively restricted span of age, is noteworthy. The total number in the combined male and female sample was 3982 individuals. The heaviest male weighs 2.7 times as much as the lightest, and more than 1.6 times the mean. The heaviest female weighed twice as much as the lightest male, over 1.2 times the male average, and, in terms of frequency, she weighed more than 94 percent of all the males in the sample. More strikingly, at 127.8 kg, the heaviest male weighed over three times as much (3.09 times, to be precise) as the lightest female, whose weight was 41.30 kg. This range among a sample of living humans is substantially greater than the estimated range for the entire hominid sample studied by McHenry excluding extant humans.

Although the stature ratios are less dramatic, they exhibit a similar pattern. The tallest female is 1.3 times the stature of the shortest female, 1.25 times the stature of the shortest male, and over 1.06 times the male average. The tallest male had a stature of 204.2 cm, while the shortest female had a stature of 142.8 cm; thus the tallest male was 1.43 times taller than the shortest female. The very large but age-restricted military sample represents at most one or two generations of both sexes, but the range of stature exceeds by about nine percentage points the range for the entire Plio-Pleistocene hominid sample that spanned about four million years.

These comparisons are cited not for their own intrinsic interest, but for the perspective that they provide for topics of interest in the paleobiology and evolution of past hominid populations. It is not difficult to imagine how limited, and possibly misleading, an impression might be formed if the US generations from which these nearly 4000 humans were sampled happened to be represented by a restricted number – say two – even if that pair happened by luck to be one male and one female. Still greater complications arise when the samples are not only small but are of uncertain date – as many fossils are. If two specimens are far apart in time, then evolutionary changes in their body proportions could be considerable, even if they are sampled from the same lineage. But even if two finds are close in time, then differences due to evolutionary change could be swamped by, say, sexual dimorphism. If we have only one specimen from each site or locality, then the assumption that each is typical of its population may be made (though more varied and interesting alternative assumptions are explored in Chapter 9). For such cases a whimsical caution has been voiced by Locke (1999), 'If a future paleontologist found the bones of a professional basketball player, twentieth-century humans might seem a species of giants. If the skeleton were that of a jockey, we would appear to be small, battered bipeds.'

The military data should not be construed as indicating that modern humans are more variable than were morphologically defined taxa of their Plio-Pleistocene hominid predecessors. Instead, it is overwhelmingly likely that effects of highly differential sample sizes dominate the comparisons of body size variations within and between past and present hominid populations. Modern humans are more numerous, but it remains to be explained why for a sample of any given size they would be substantially more variable than Plio-Pleistocene fossil hominid remains collected over a comparable geographic range and time horizon. On the contrary, since Plio-Pleistocene samples are drawn from vastly greater expanses of time, any directional evolutionary change – regardless of whether it were gradual or punctuational – should act to increase the observed variation.

The case for pursuing the implications of hominid body size in a context free of taxonomic considerations gains additional support from the empirical research of Henneberg and his colleagues (Henneberg, 1990, 1992; Mathers & Henneberg, 1995). They set out to answer three questions: (1) Was there an overall increase in body size (weight and height) during hominid evolution? (2) Was the change gradual, or was it punctuated at the times of emergence for various hominid taxa? (3) Has hominid evolution taken place within a single lineage, or is it necessary to hypothesize that some branching has occurred? In attempting to answer such questions these investigators surveyed the scientific literature for all available reconstructed body weights and statures of hominids.

The total sample employed in their investigation included 638 weight and 153 height determinations for earlier hominids. These estimates had been derived by numerous investigators using a variety of statistical techniques (reduced major axis or least square regressions, calculation of the ratio of bone to body size, reconstruction of the skeleton), but steps were taken to reduce the effects of methodological variation. Wherever possible, the taxonomic assessments used were those of the authors who carried out the original body size reconstructions; where these were lacking, the taxonomic diagnoses used were those of Oakley & Campbell (1977) or Clarke (personal communication to Mathers & Henneberg, 1992).

Results showed that hominid weights and statures increased steadily over time until about 32 000 years ago, from which point until the present there has been a gradual decrease in body size (Figure 8.1). There was a significant positive relationship between body size and time, establishing that on average specimens with earlier dates were smaller than those with more recent dates. This evident increase in body size over time was detectable regardless of whether the two genera *Australopithecus* and *Homo* were treated separately or treated as part of a single lineage. When the sample was further subdivided into species, no clear relationship could be perceived; no significant difference in stature or weight was observed between any coeval species. In particular, comparisons of regression lines for two alternative hypotheses (single lineage versus multiple lineage) showed no

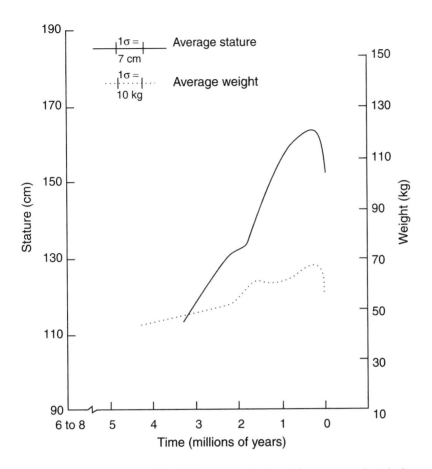

Figure 8.1. Trends in hominid stature and body weight over approximately three to four million years. Both measures appear to have increased until about 32 000 years ago. During the period encompassing the positive trend lines, stature gained 1 to 2 cm and body weight approximately 1 kg every 100 000 years. Redrawn from data in Mathers & Henneberg (1995), following their convention using scales for height and weight based on equality of standard deviations.

difference in the relationship between size and date regardless of whether robust australopithecines (and in later time periods, Neanderthals) were included in the hominid lineage or not; neither robust australopithecines nor Neanderthals appeared to differ significantly in body size from other contemporaneous hominids. Overall, tests for linearity of regression indicated that neither the trend in height nor the trend in weight deviates from the pattern that would be predicted if only gradual change had taken place within a lineage. Mathers & Henneberg (1995) concluded that they could not reject the null hypothesis that all coeval hominids belonged to a single species, and suggested that patterns of change in hominid body size could be explained in terms of gradual microevolutionary change that had acted cumulatively over time.

Studies of past and present hominid populations can be brought into common perspective in part by changing the scope of inference from fossil hominid samples. It is preferable to ask 'How tall was the individual represented by the AL 288–1 remains?' rather than 'How tall were *Australopithecus afarensis* females?' or 'How tall was *A. afarensis*?' or 'What was the difference in stature between males of *A. afarensis* and *A. africanus*?' This shift in focus is critical conceptually because the existence of AL 288–1 and of *Australopithecus afarensis* are not known in the same way. The first question deals fairly directly with an aspect of tangible reality – though even there, statures reconstructed from incomplete bones combine observation with estimation, and estimates based on incomplete specimens can be substantial. But the last three questions compound observation and estimation with less direct – and far less secure – inferences about the relationships between specimens and populations, between populations at different sites (such as Laetoli and Hadar, or Laetoli and Sterkfontein) and all of the factors that could contribute to the variation among the hominids that lived at such sites. Problems of this sort have been recognized by some paleoanthropologists, as indicated by Conroy's (1992) comment, 'One reason evolutionary scenarios are so contentious is that paleoanthropologists name fossil species and then create scenarios on the artificial constructs they have just created.'

Thanks to the work of McHenry and Henneberg, among others, in answer to the question 'How large were Plio-Pleistocene hominids?' there are now two different types of answer. McHenry's is taxon-specific. As one example, it indicates that males of the 'gracile' australopithecines classified as *Australopithecus africanus* averaged 1 kg (2.5 percent) heavier and 6 cm (4.6 percent) taller than males of *A. robustus*, while females of the 'robust' taxon averaged about 2 kg (6.7 percent) heavier but 5 cm (4.3 percent) shorter than 'gracile' females. Henneberg's inferences can be read from Figure 8.1. Between about 4 Ma and 1 Ma, hominids gained, very approximately, 40 cm in stature; and from just under 3 Ma to 1 Ma, the same hominids added roughly 20 kg in body mass. These overall gains would translate to between 1 and 2 cm in stature, and 1 kg in body mass, every 100 000 years (Figure 8.1).

Whichever approach one prefers, it should be understood that the actual hominid populations alive then, however delimited, would have exhibited variation on the same scale as that found within extant humans and other hominoids, far more than usually is allowed for in descriptions and comparisons of paleospecies. Our Plio-Pleistocene ancestors differed from population to population and from generation to generation – but had we been there, in all probability we would have been more readily aware of individual differences than contrasts among regional groups or temporal cohorts.

Consideration of the existing data on hominid body size – past *and* present – within a human adaptability framework shows how the limited data from the fossil record may have far greater value from a paleobiological perspective than from a taxonomic one. For example, if the remains attributed to the gracile and robust australopithecine groups constitute valid samples (or if other samples are constituted by site or region rather than morphological criteria), the ecological implications of their body size differences can be analyzed within the sort of framework utilized productively by Foley (1984). That is, body mass and stature may not provide particularly useful information concerning assignment to species taxa, but still be useful in understanding the relationships among body form, energetic expenditure and ecological opportunities and constraints. Such an analysis would follow the same lines of inquiry, for example, as comparing the energetic requirements of African Pygmy and Bantu populations living contiguously.

Posture and locomotion

Stature is a topic of central interest in human biology, and can be treated from a common standpoint over millions of years, as in the preceding section. This broad perspective is based on recognition that the adaptive patterns of all hominids have much in common while differing from those of even closely related hominoids such as chimpanzees. As a matter of common practice, primatologists do not report statures of chimpanzees. Like other mammalogists, they record measurements of total head and body length (Napier & Napier, 1967). This is because although chimpanzees stand up under certain circumstances, such behaviors are facultative. But in all hominids known so far, upright posture is a shared, defining characteristic. That is not to say that the functional morphology associated with bipedal locomotion is the same in all hominids; as we will see in Chapter 10, important changes have continued to evolve in members of the genus *Homo* even within the last million years. However, upright posture and bipedal locomotion had profound implications for hominid biology even in the earliest structural phases that can be identified so far.

The Can Llobateres hominoid CLl-18000 helps to establish a structural baseline for comparison of locomotor characteristics that can be reconstructed for Plio-Pleistocene hominids. As noted, Can Llobateres bears strong resemblances to extant chimpanzees in its body and limb proportions. These morphological factors, along with the paleoecological data, suggest that the population from which it was sampled were forest-dwelling apes similar to extant chimpanzees.

In contrast, as early as the range of 3.7 to 3.2 Ma hominids such as AL 288–1 from Hadar exhibited structural adaptations for upright posture and bipedal locomotion, including structural modification of the pelvis and hind limb. The related anatomical changes legitimately could be considered the largest scale reorganization of a morphological complex in all of hominid evolution. The fossil footprints preserved in hardened volcanic ash at Laetoli (dated in the range of 3.2 to 3.6 Ma) cement this relationship, so to speak, between a functionally hominid pelvic morphology and the impressions of plantigrade feet.

There has been disagreement about the details of gait patterns that might have been possible (Jungers, 1982; Wolpoff, 1983). However, it is now generally accepted that although hominids such as Lucy may have had a broader locomotor repertoire than present humans, including retention of the capacity for movement in trees (Tuttle, 1981; Stern & Sussman, 1983; Susman *et al.*, 1994), the range of locomotor behaviors included bipedal striding.

In the interpretation of evidence for upright posture and bipedal locomotion in early hominids, structural differences of modest scale among various specimens from one site sometimes are used to postulate taxonomic heterogeneity at the species level or above (Senut & Tardieu, 1985). As we already have seen in the data on body mass and stature in extant humans, within-species variation is very high. Above and beyond these levels encountered in populations during relatively static phases of a lineage, research in developmental and evolutionary genetics indicates that there are grounds for expecting greater levels of morphological variation during the early stages of transformation in a character complex (Heads, 1985; Panganiban, 1997). This theoretical consideration may help in deciding the significance of a hominid tibial fragment with some chimpanzee-like features in the Member 4 deposits (dated in the range of 2.6 to 2.8 Ma) at Sterkfontein (Berger & Tobias, 1995). Puzzling in terms of standard phylogenetic interpretations (White *et al.*, 1981), this specimen may document either the retention of high levels of variation from earlier adaptive levels or complex responses of a population's coadapted genomic complement to modification of a level deep enough to approach its *Baup-*

lan. It is even conceivable that changes in the location of some structural loci within the genome could have been associated with the early stages of hominid bipedalism. In any case, no geologically instantaneous transformation to an entire coadapted gene complex was required in the evolution of the hominid locomotor complex. Incremental changes in characters needed only to improve adaptation, not make it perfect. Improvements can accrue later, in minor ways as well as major, and often at rather uneven rates.

Limb proportions

Discussions of limb proportions in Plio-Pleistocene hominids are complicated not only by the relative rarity of relatively complete skeletons, but also by the patterns of variation in body size discussed previously. For example, the femur of AL 288–1 is absolutely very short (as is the femur of STS 14 from South African deposits roughly a million years later in time). But were Lucy's arms long relative to her legs, or were her legs short relative to her arms? Comparisons with extant humans (Wolpoff, 1983) establish that the reconstructed trunk and humeral lengths of AL 288–1 can be closely matched in modern pygmies, while the length of her femur (280 mm) was well below the minimum (326 mm) in a sample of 81 pygmy females. Lucy was very small overall, but by modern standards her legs were short even relative to the rest of her body.

Just as Plio-Pleistocene hominids increased in size through time, limb proportions changed as well. By about 2.5 Ma, BOU-VP-12/130 from the Hata beds of Ethiopia's Middle Awash possessed a humerus very similar to that of AL 288–1, but in combination with a longer femur. As a result the Hata hominid shows an overall humeral/femoral ratio that is more like that of later humans. However, its antebrachium (lower arm) was absolutely longer than that of AL 288–1, and apparently relatively longer as well, indicating that fully modern limb proportions had not yet been attained.

Although postcranial characters sometimes are used as indicators of taxonomic status (Wood, 1993), among hominid fossils some of their functionally more important attributes appear to change through time irregularly along a morphocline from more chimpanzee-like to more modern human-like. Limited materials preclude any detailed analysis of direct environmental effects in Plio-Pleistocene hominid fossils, though the potential for these influences should be borne in mind. Both trends in limb proportions and developmental influences are examined in greater detail in Chapter 9.

Craniofacial features

Cranial and dental features of Plio-Pleistocene hominids have been studied extensively and intensively for decades. Both general patterns and exceedingly fine details have been the subject of so many works that only a few can be cited among the numerous excellent monographs (Tobias, 1967; Mann, 1975), books (Le Gros Clark, 1967; Rak, 1983), and edited volumes (Jolly, 1978; Grine, 1988), so treatment here will be brief. In addition to abundant presentation elsewhere, however, there is another reason for moderate coverage in this context. To a considerable extent, descriptions and analyses of the discernible phenotypic features of the skull have confounded discussions of adaptive processes with issues of taxonomy and phylogeny. For example, in his 'dietary hypothesis' Robinson (1954, 1956, 1963) related early hominid craniodental morphology to aspects of behavior and ecology. However, in this work he made very sharp distinctions between the total morphological patterns of gracile and robust australopithecines that have not been borne out by the much more abundant finds made subsequently. More recently, there have been attempts to relate patterns of cranial vascular sinuses that drain blood from the brain to locomotion and thermoregulation (e.g., Falk, 1986). Much of this research also has been used to reinforce conventional distinctions such as those between gracile and robust early hominids, despite the observation that some gracile and some robust early hominids exhibit both types of vascular patterns (Tobias & Falk, 1988; Brown et al., 1993). Against this background, the material provided below is intended only to review a few phenotypic features that have broad implications for understanding the paleobiology of Plio-Pleistocene hominids.

Among the more striking features of the skull in our Plio-Pleistocene antecedents is the combination, unexpected in hominids prior to Dart's discovery discussed in Chapter 3, of a small braincase and large jaws. Both of these features are consistent with an ancestor similar to the adaptive level represented by hominoids such as CLl-18000. Hominid endocranial volumes initially overlapped those of chimpanzees but expanded with time, a point that is taken up in greater detail in Chapter 9. However, among the Plio-Pleistocene hominids more of the vault is visible above the level of the supraorbital region, proportionate to the amount of braincase expansion. Bones of the cranial vault were relatively thin; even in skulls characterized as robust, the enlarged portions of bones tended to be heavily pneumatized and thus reduced in weight.

Attached to the cranial walls are several muscles. At the rear of the skull is the nuchal crest, a shelf of bone highly variable in the extent of its development that provides additional area for attachment of the neck muscles that help to maintain skull balance. Along the sides of the cranial vault is an extensive area for attachment of the temporalis muscle. This is so large in some early hominid skulls that its area of attachment is elevated superiorally by development of a sagittal crest. Postorbitally, constriction of the braincase contributes to the large temporal fossa through which this muscle passes to its area of insertion on the mandible.

Although individual specimens vary in numerous details, the faces of early hominids are less prognathous than those of apes because the mandible is aligned more directly under the anterior portion of the braincase and midfacial region. This functional arrangement allows production of greater bite force through the dental arcade, particularly for the cheek teeth situated along the sides of the jaw.

The dentitions of early hominids exhibit morphological trends through time – though again, these usually are presented in terms of differences among taxa. The fossil remains from Aramis, Ethiopia, dated to about 4.4 Ma and classified as *Ardipithecus ramidus* show thin dental enamel and canine teeth that are larger than later hominids. The canine and third lower premolars together form a functional complex that differs from the same teeth in later hominids in a direction that resembles the condition in extant chimpanzees and antecedent dryopithecines. In accord with these features, the cheek teeth remained relatively small.

Material from Kanapoi and Allia Bay, dated to between 4.2 and 3.9 Ma and classified as *Australopithecus anamensis* retains large-rooted canines, but in combination with thicker dental enamel and buccolingually expanded molars that suggest the beginning of trends carried through subsequent hominids (Leakey *et al.*, 1995).

Extensive fossil remains from Laetoli in Tanzania and Hadar in Ethiopia, classified as *A. afarensis*, fall still later in time, between 4 and 3 Ma. Hominids from these sites show larger upper central than lateral incisors, which are in turn separated by a slight gap or diastema from the canines. Although variable in size, these fall in the range bounded by those found in the preceding two samples and later hominids. Specimens from these two sites are sufficiently abundant to show that third lower premolars are polymorphic for cusp number and size, as is the case in extant chimpanzees. Cheek teeth are large.

The newly described hominid from Garhi, designated by White and colleagues as *A. garhi*, is dated to about 2.5 Ma. It has thicker dental enamel than the hominids from the earlier sites described above. Its cheek teeth are massive; the anterior dentition also is large, with breadths of central incisors and canines equivalent to or exceeding the largest known early hominids classified as *Australopithecus* or *Homo* (Asfaw *et al.*, 1999).

East African finds known before the discovery of *A. garhi* had been assigned to a variety of early hominid taxa including *A. aethopicus*, *A. boisei*, *Homo habilis*, *H. rudolfensis* and *H. ergaster*. Specimens assigned to this large number of taxa show dental variations that can be differentiated in some details, but overlap or extend many of the patterns that had been observed in the classic South African sites that are distributed over about the same range of dates, from about 2.5 or 3.0 to 1.0 Ma. Hominid fossils from Taung, Sterkfontein (Members 2 and 4), and Makapansgat (Members 3 and 4) usually are classified as *Australopithecus africanus* while those from Kromdraai and Swartkrans are assigned by many workers to *A. robustus*.

The cranial and dental differences between gracile and robust australopithecines were the stimulus for Robinson's dietary hypothesis, as noted previously. The central idea was that gracile and robust australopithecines presented sharp contrasts in their total morphological patterns. Gracile australopithecines were characterized as having cranial vaults that were relatively narrow, elevated more above the supraorbital margins, and rarely showed traces of sagittal cresting. The lower face was more prognathous, and the jaws held anterior teeth that were large relative to the cheek teeth. The combination was thought to imply a diet that was omnivorous, including some meat eating, and an evolutionary trajectory that led to the evolution of the genus *Homo*.

Robust australopithecines, in contrast, were said to have had broader cranial vaults that extended less above the upper facial region, and commonly were surmounted by sagittal crests that increased the area available for attachment of the temporal muscle. Resultant great masticatory stresses were transmitted through well-developed supraorbital tori and a heavy midfacial region including anterior pillars of bone that extended inferiorly from the midorbital region through the lateral margins of the piriform aperture to the alveolar margins just above the canine teeth. Lateral to the anterior pillars were robust roots for the zygomatic processes, and behind the canine and incisor teeth was an anteriorly thickened palate. All of these features were seen as adaptations to consumption of a coarse vegetarian diet comprising such items as roots and tubers. This regimen was seen as adaptively so constrained as to result in extinction of the robust lineage.

Among the dental features mentioned as distinctions between gracile and robust australopithecines are the sizes of anterior and posterior teeth (Robinson, 1954). However, even when the samples of Plio-Pleistocene hominid teeth were not as extensive as they are today, it could be seen that the metric differences were not extreme. Eckhardt (1979:474, based on data in Wolpoff, 1971) noted that specimens categorized as robust australopithecines have lower canines that are smaller, and upper fourth premolars that are larger, than those described as gracile australopithecines. For other teeth, the differences between the two groups of early hominids were less than those which are known to exist within living human populations. When the total crown areas (length × breadth) of all three anterior teeth (central incisors, lateral incisors, and canines) were divided by the corresponding areas of all posterior teeth (third premolars through third molars), robust australopithecines do have relatively smaller anterior teeth. However, this is chiefly because the posterior teeth are absolutely larger, while the anterior teeth are very similar in size in both groups.

Increasingly large samples of Plio-Pleistocene hominid material from East and South Africa have extended ranges of dental variation for individual teeth, and also have generated patterns of dental dimensions (as well as other craniofacial characteristics) not previously seen in earlier, more limited samples. The Garhi remains from Ethiopia already have been mentioned in this regard (Asfaw *et al.*, 1999). As another example, the STW 252 fragmentary cranium from Sterkfontein (Clarke, 1988) combines very large posterior teeth with large anterior teeth, particularly a pointed maxillary canine that projects beyond the levels of the adjacent teeth. Among the proposals to accommodate each of these specimens that presents a new morphological pattern is the recognition of new species. However, resolutions of this sort only intensify the paradox raised by the molecular data reviewed in Chapter 7.

Just as there are questions about the morphological basis of the early distinctions drawn between australopithecine taxa, later studies also have cast doubt on narrow conceptions about the food resources exploited by higher primates. Field studies have shown that chimpanzees are omnivorous, with diets including not only a wide variety of seasonally and regionally varying plant materials but also insects, as well as meat obtained through hunting (Teleki, 1973). Similarly, papionine food regimens include a great variety of vegetable materials such as fruits, seeds, roots, and tubers. In addition, baboons also consume insects (Dunbar, 1976, 1977), and exhibit carnivorous behaviors in relatively arid habitats (Altmann & Altmann, 1970). It is difficult to conceive a theoretical basis for the position that early hominids would have been less flexible in satisfying their nutritional needs than chimpanzees or papionines.

Evidence from another, more technical, area of analysis lends support to the belief that the diets of Plio-Pleistocene hominids were less narrowly taxon-specific than had been hypothesized decades ago (Conroy, 1997). It is now possible to measure the strontium/calcium (Sr/Ca) ratios in fossil teeth as a basis for indirectly assessing dietary components. The underpinning for these studies is the finding that vertebrate digestive systems favor absorption of calcium over strontium, with the result that Sr/Ca ratios decline from lower to higher levels in the food chain. Herbivores consequently have lower Sr/Ca ratios than the plants that they ingest, and carnivores have still lower ratios than those found in the tissues of the herbivores that they, in turn, consume. By extension, Sr/Ca ratios in omnivores should be inversely proportional to the amount of meat in their diets.

At Swartkrans, hominid fossil remains assigned to *A. robustus* yielded Sr/Ca ratios indicative of an omnivorous diet including some meat rather than one that had been restricted to plant materials. Similarly, Swartkrans fossils attributed to early *Homo* gave ratios indicating that their diets included significant amounts of plant foods, particularly the roots, tubers, and other underground energy storage units that Robinson had seen as the mainstay of robust australopithecines (Sillen, 1992; Lee-Thorp & van der Merwe, 1993; Lee-Thorp *et al.*, 1994; Burton & Wright, 1995). Additional complexities in the interpretation of these results are introduced by other physiological influences, such as sex differences in Sr/Ca metabolism, with females usually having higher Sr/Ca ratios than males due to calcium reductions in bones and teeth because of the demands of pregnancy and lactation. With such factors in mind, Thackeray (1995) has suggested that SK 847, originally assigned to *Paranthropus* (now *A. robustus*) and then reassigned to *Homo*, as noted previously, could in fact be a female of *A. robustus*.

In assessing the meaning of these isotopic studies and the possibilities that they raise, it is worth noting that although the SK 847 specimen attributed to early *Homo* was determined to have a moderately higher Sr/Ca ratio than the SK 27 specimen and others assigned to *A. robustus*, values for all of these early hominids, whatever their taxonomic status, fell within the expected range (mean $\pm$ one standard deviation) for the fossil baboon taxon represented at the same site, *Papio robinsoni* (Sillen *et al.*, 1995). This may be another instance in which multiple taxonomic categories established decades ago can be maintained in the light of new paleobiological data – but only by the elaboration of numerous subsidiary hypotheses that are at variance with interpretive frameworks based on extant human and nonhuman primate populations.

Given the increasing number of early hominid cranial and postcranial remains that have been recovered since the 1970s, wider anatomical comparisons have become possible. One very preliminary indication of the scope for such investigations was explored in a paper by Mitlo (1986), who compared the morphometric variation in 10 papionine taxa (*Macaca irus, M. mulatta, M. nemestrina, M. nigra, Papio anubis, P. cynocephalus, P. hamadryas, P. papio, P. ursinus,* and *Theropithecus gelada*) with that in 12 fossil specimens (MLD37/38, SK48, STS5, OH5, OH24, KNM-ER 406, KNM-ER 407, KNM-ER 732, KNM-ER 3732, KNM-ER 1805, KNM-ER 1813, and KNM-ER 1470) that have been assigned to a variety of early hominid taxa. The seven measurements included were selected to match those commonly provided in published descriptions of the hominid fossils. These included maximal cranial length, minimum frontal breadth, bimastoid breadth, breadth at postorbital constriction, superior facial breadth, inner orbital breadth, and palatal length. Comparable measurements were taken by the investigator on museum specimens of the extant papionine taxa. For all of the dimensions, the absolute ranges of the composite sample of interfertile papionine taxa exceeded that among the hominid taxa, often by a very wide margin.

Numerous criticisms could be leveled at Mitlo's study. The papionine sample sizes ranged widely, from as low as 6 to as high as 85. As a statistic, the range is influenced heavily by sample size. Some taxa were represented by males alone, and only univariate comparisons were made. These are substantive problems, but rather than dismissing the findings, a more appropriate response would be to carry out a similar study according to more rigorous methodological standards of the sort illustrated by the work of Albrecht & Miller (1993). Independent observations lend support to this recommendation.

In discussing analogies and interpretation in paleoanthropology, Wolpoff (1978:481) stressed that 'baboons are consistently more variable than any partitioning of the early hominid sample (including the sample of all Plio-Pleistocene hominids) for every tooth.' Since the year in which that statement was made, many more early hominid specimens have been recovered, suggesting that the underlying analysis should be repeated for the expanded database. But regardless of details of any renewed comparison, the fact remains that papionine primates constitute an appropriate and highly variable standard of reference.

To this point, most of the cranial and dental features discussed have been explicitly or implicitly metric. As already observed at the beginning of this chapter with reference to assessment of the phyletic position of CLl-18000, it is also the case that the extent of nonmetric trait variations and polymorphisms within hominoid species is underestimated, with consequent distortions of perceived phylogenetic patterns.

In a series of papers, Olson (1978, 1985a,b) argued that several highly distinctive patterns in the shapes of nasal bones and their articulations with the maxillary and frontal bones were diagnostic of specific extant hominoid and fossil hominid taxa. Building on this assumption, Olson allocated the immature Plio-Pleistocene hominid AL 333–105 to a *Paranthropus* lineage and the Taung child to a *Homo* lineage. However, Eckhardt (1987) demonstrated high degrees of polymorphism for these character states in all extant pongid taxa. In particular, the upwardly divergent or 'keystone-shaped' nasal bone configuration supposedly diagnostic of *Paranthropus* occurred at a frequency of about 10 percent in a combined sample of orangutans, gorillas, and chimpanzees. A later study (Eckhardt & Protsch von Zieten, 1988) showed that the *Paranthropus* pattern was represented in 25 percent of a large sample of Liberian *Pan troglodytes*.

Eckhardt & Protsch von Zieten (1992) used the same chimpanzee population sample to test another hypothesis advanced by Olson (1978), that the anterior nasal spine is an apomorphic feature diagnostic of the genus *Homo*. Once again, it was possible to demonstrate that of 263 chimpanzee specimens, 10.7 percent exhibited bilateral anterior nasal spines. Thus designating the absence of an anterior nasal spine in some hominid specimens from a single site as plesiomorphic, and the presence of this feature in another specimen (SK 847) as apomorphic, runs the risk of dividing single populations or lineages into multiple taxa, some of which may never have existed as other than typological constructs.

Studies of the incisive foramen produced a similar outcome. Schwartz (1983, 1984a,b, 1988) held that the presence of a single incisive foramen near the anterior margin of the palate is a character state shared by extant humans and orangutans but not gorillas and chimpanzees, which exhibit two separate canals separated by a bony septum. In studies of 514 hominoid skulls, Eckhardt & Protsch von Zieten (1995) and Kiessling & Eckhardt (1990) demonstrated the presence of the supposed *Homo* character state in *Pan*, and the African ape character state in extant humans. Overall, it was possible to show that in large samples of hominoid crania, specimens intergrade continuously from one idealized character state to another. The morphology of the incisive foramen varies in many ways, aside from the question of whether there is one channel or two passing from the palate to the nasal cavity. The foramen may be wider or narrower, longer or shorter, subdivided internally or externally, accompanied by multiple accessory foramina or none, and so on.

The common inference from these several studies of discontinuous characters is that hominoid taxa share much underlying diversity in the genetic material that controls the development and expression of morphological characteristics. Moreover, the gene complexes that contribute to the character states observable in numerous morphological features are modified by environmental influences during development. For all of these reasons, it is expected that Plio-Pleistocene hominids, like extant hominoids, should exhibit substantial variation within each taxon. For these theoretical reasons, as well as the preceding examples that are consistent with them, paleobiologists should be inherently suspicious of cladistic analyses that incorporate untested assumptions about monomorphic character states.

The adaptive capacities of Plio-Pleistocene hominids

From the standpoint of human adaptability theory, the acceptance of large numbers of hominid taxa requires not only high rates of species origin, but also high levels of extinction. This fate, in turn, implies the termination of a population and its unique store of genes plus environmentally appropriate behaviors – the developmental outcomes that result from the interactions among these two information sources are critical to evolutionary continuity.

Many discussions of Plio-Pleistocene hominid taxa focus on their sets of defining character states, and embody explicit statements or implicit assumptions that these features are relatively uniform and highly heritable. In this sense, if adaptation were occurring, then its primary mode among Plio-Pleistocene hominids must have been genetic. And there are also other models used in discussions of hominid phylogeny, in which species are not modified by genetic selection at all, but replaced by other species; this is the idea of species selection or clade selection (Eldredge & Gould, 1972).

Against this background, a few examples must serve to establish the point that not only genetic change, but also a variety of adaptive levels were utilized by Plio-Pleistocene hominids.

Short-term adaptations

Increasing acceptance of the cultural capacities of Plio-Pleistocene hominids already has been discussed. This conceptual shift is being aided by studies of cultural behaviors in chimpanzees such as those documented in Chapter 6, as well as discoveries of stone tools and modified bones in direct or indirect association with hominid fossil remains.

Less dramatic than the expanding capacity for culture in Plio-Pleistocene hominids is one observation that gives an intriguing insight into the behavioral activities of one individual hominid, L.894–1 from Member G of the Shungura Formation at Omo in Ethiopia, dated to about 1.8 Ma. This specimen is very incomplete, comprising cranial fragments and teeth. But particularly interesting from the standpoint of behavioral adaptation is the mention in the description of the specimen (Boaz & Howell, 1977) of approximal or interproximal grooving on both the left and right upper third premolars. Microscopically, these grooves are lined with fine, parallel scratches.

Grooves of this sort are found sporadically through the hominid fossil record, marking molars attributed to *Homo erectus* at Choukoutien, China (Weidenreich, 1937), various cheek teeth from numerous Neanderthal sites (Martin, 1923; Frayer & Russell, 1987), and extant human populations as widely separated as Australia and South America (Eckhardt & Piermarini, 1988, 1987). Various explanations have been offered for these dental modifications, with the consensus favoring repetitive use of a probe or sinew, functionally similar to a toothpick or dental floss. The behavioral activities that produced the grooves seem too simple to require a hypothesis of cultural transmission. More probably they imply a sporadic behavior activity repeatedly discovered by hominid populations over the course of nearly two million years. But even the repeated rediscovery of how simple materials can be used for basic maintenance activities can help to illustrate some of the mental attributes shared by hominids over long spans of time.

Developmental plasticity

Defects of the dentition, such as transverse enamel hypoplasias, were introduced as examples of developmental plasticity in discussions of adaptive responses in extant humans (Chapter 5) and chimpanzees (Chapter 6). Enamel hypoplasias also have been observed in samples of teeth from Plio-Pleistocene hominids. For example, Bombin (1990) found a frequency of 91.2 percent for enamel hypoplasias in a sample of 31 specimens attributed to *Australopithecus africanus*, in comparison to a frequency of 80.0 percent in 5 specimens identified as *Homo habilis*. This discrepancy of 11.2 percent was used as a basis for implying a level of adaptive superiority for the latter taxon. Interpretations of this sort stand in contrast to those drawn from comparable samples of extant humans. It is doubtful that a human biologist studying two samples of children differing in enamel hypoplasia frequencies by 10 percent to 15 percent would discuss the problem in the context of probabilities of survival of the two groups rather than in terms of socioeconomic status in general, or adequacy of diet and maternal care in particular.

Attention should be paid to appropriate levels of inference from data sets that reflect comparable phenomena in physiologically similar organisms separated chiefly by great expanses of time. The alternative is to believe that our more limited knowledge of past hominid populations can support broader conclusions than the more abundant, detailed, and verifiable knowledge of extant human and nonhuman primate populations.

Genetic adaptations

As has been noted previously, not all adaptations can be character-ized operationally as entirely developmental or entirely genetic. The documented occurrences of enamel hypoplasia are as certain to have resulted from environmental stresses acting on genetically-programmed developmental systems in Plio-Pleistocene hominids, as they do in extant chimpanzees and humans. Other features, such as the karyotypic com-plement, are far more effectively insulated from direct environmental influences.

External body covering: skin and hair

Extant apes have heavy coats of hair, as is consistent with their activity patterns. Chimpanzees spend part of the day moving about on the ground and part clambering about in trees, but usually not at high enough levels of activity, or rapid enough rates of energy expenditure, to generate great stress on the thermoregulatory system.

In contrast, early hominids, abroad during the day to seek food and water and carry out other activities in savannah settings, would have been exposed to the full force of tropical sunlight. If their behavioral repertoires required rapid movements from place to place, the heat load would have been considerable. Among potential causes for this heat load, hunting comes immediately to mind, particularly given recent discoveries of hom-inid remains associated with stone tools and bones bearing cut marks in deposits dated to about 2.5 Ma (de Heinzelin *et al.*, 1999) and the evidence for hunting in chimpanzees (Teleki, 1973). Representing the opposing view, more than a few authorities have argued against hominids having been hunters during the early phases of our evolution. Regardless of how this question is resolved, however, even if the earliest hominids obtained meat only by scavenging, they at least needed to be able to flee quickly to avoid being eaten themselves. Escape from predators was an essential part of early hominid activity patterns, and one in which they were not always successful, as indicated by Brain's graphic description of an australopithecine skull from Swartkrans bearing two puncture marks with the exact spacing of leopard upper canine teeth.

Some physiological models have placed the evolution of a reduced hair covering and related sweating mechanisms with the evolution of modern limb proportions and striding bipedalism (Chaplin *et al.*, 1994). However, it is reasonable to see the changes in limb proportions as morphological responses to antecedent behavioral changes that pushed the previous locomotor system near to its limits, thereby generating selection pressures that would have led to fitness differentials and genetic repatterning for functional improvements. Wolpoff (1983) has argued that the legs of AL 288–1 already would have permitted an effective stride, but the research of Jungers (1982) can be interpreted as indicating the potential for further biomechanical efficiencies.

For a variety of reasons, then, early hominids would have had to move swiftly, placing a considerable load on their cooling systems. Whenever this pattern of behavior became predominant, it would have led to selection for hair loss, exposing relatively naked skin which itself yields a thermoregulatory advantage by reducing the need for evaporative dissipation (Wheeler, 1996). Hair reduction was accompanied by the evolution of an increased number of sweat glands, especially on the face (Cabanac & Caputa, 1979; Falk, 1990) that could raise the maximum level of evaporative cooling. Fluid produced by eccrine sweat glands could evaporate freely from exposed skin, with the evaporative heat loss helping to maintain body temperature homeostatically.

The interaction among factors such as body size, bipedality, and thermoregulation is intricate (Ruff, 1991; Quieroz, 1996; Wheeler, 1996) and has implications for energetics (Hammond & Diamond, 1997) and other ecological factors (Purvis & Harvey, 1997). In this case of hominid adaptive responses to environmental challenges, as in many others, it is good to be wary of single-cause explanations. Selection must have acted in many ways on populations of hominids, who always have led complex lives.

Jablonski & Chaplin (2000) theorize that the integument of the earliest hominids resembled that of chimpanzees that have a covering of dark hair over the skin on the body which is lightly pigmented due to a dearth of active melanocytes. Chimpanzee facial pigmentation is polytypic and polymorphic. *Pan paniscus* has a black face, while that of *P. troglodytes verus* bears a butterfly-shaped mask, *P. t. troglodytes* is mottled and *P. t. schweinfurthii* is more uniformly light. In all of the chimpanzee groups with relatively light pigmentation, facial skin coloration darkens with age and exposure to ultraviolet (UV) radiation (Napier & Napier, 1967; Post *et al.*, 1975) indicating that the potential for induction of melanogenesis in exposed skin is the primitive condition in primates (Erikson & Montagna, 1975). The complex genetic basis of skin color is known (Byard, 1981), as is the existence of a substantial norm of reaction. Tanning occurs relatively rapidly and to varying degrees in different populations. As norms of reaction in skin color have been documented in chimpanzees as well as in extant humans, it is parsimonious to accept their existence in Plio-Pleistocene hominids as well.

When hominids lost their coat of body hair, in theory as part of adaptive processes that improved thermoregulation, the underlying integument would have been more exposed to strong UV radiation. The resultant selective pressures would virtually certainly have favored dark skin color due to its heavier concentrations of melanin pigment. Although it has long been believed that increased melanin pigmentation in tropical regions is protective against elevated exposure to UV radiation, it has been difficult to provide conclusive evidence for a selective mechanism. The effects of skin exposure to UV in present human populations include sunburn and blistering in the short run, and heightened risk of skin cancer in the long run (Fitzpatrick, 1965), as well as nutrient photolysis (Branda & Eaton, 1978), with the greatest damage occurring in more lightly pigmented individuals. However, because these effects appear to have minimal influence on reproductive success, it has been argued that differences in levels of melanin pigmentation are only slightly adaptive or nonadaptive (Blum, 1961). For example, the effects of squamous and basal cell carcinomas accrue only after reproductive age (Blum, 1961; Roberts, 1977; Robins, 1991), and even malignant melanomas have an age of onset beyond the age of first reproduction (Johnson *et al.*, 1998).

Without denying the possibility of some modest selective effects attributable to sunburn and skin cancers, recently it has been suggested that a more powerfully selective agent for increased skin pigmentation has been the impact of UV radiation on folate levels (Jablonski & Chaplin, 2000). Folic acid levels can influence both differential fertility and differential mortality. With regard to fertility, chemically induced folate deficiency has been shown to produce spermatogenic arrest in rodents (Mathur *et al.*, 1977; Cosentino *et al.*, 1990), and blockers of folate metabolism have been considered as male contraceptives in humans. Concerning mortality, there is a connection between defective folate metabolism and neural tube defects.

Neural tube defects comprise a family of congenital abnormalities ranging in severity from spina bifida occulta, in which a single neural arch fails to fuse but is unaccompanied by herniation of enclosed neural tissue and may remain undetected throughout the course of a normal life, to anecephaly or failure of the entire neural tube to close, leaving exposed a dorsal mass of undifferentiated brain tissue and invariably resulting in death. Anecephaly and the more severe forms of spina bifida are common in lightly pigmented populations, and accounted for 15 percent of all perinatal mortality and 10 percent of all postperinatal mortality in certain populations prior to the introduction of nutritional supplementation (Elwood & Elwood, 1980).

Adequate levels of folate prevent 70 percent of neural tube defects in humans, by regulating pyrimidine biosynthesis needed for DNA production (Minns, 1996; Fleming & Copp, 1998). Levels of this metabolite in the body represent a balance between dietary intake and destruction by UV light, particularly UVB. Evolutionarily, populations living in areas characterized by high levels of UV radiation gained protection against UV photolysis through increases in the melanin concentration in the skin. This process could have operated extremely rapidly, at least on the scale of geological time, a point that is taken up in Chapter 10.

Chromosomes

Chromosomes supply useful information in studies of adaptation and evolution due to their position intermediate between genotype and phenotype. These structures are transmitted across generational boundaries. They tend to be conserved within species, and since chromosomal reorganizations are rare relative to changes at the nucleotide level, those that do become fixed generally allow discrimination between primitive and derived conditions (Stanyon & Chiarelli, 1991). Thus although chromosomes do not fossilize, they nevertheless are useful in reconstructing some features of hominid paleobiology independent of hard tissue remains, and give some indirect information bearing on the evolution of the present human species.

One fundamental genetic discontinuity between humans and chimpanzees is the diploid chromosome number – humans have 46, while the great apes have 48; although chimpanzees, gorillas, and orangutans share a common diploid number, their karyotypes differ in many structural details. The evolution of a 46 chromosome diploid number could, in theory, have occurred at any time after the divergence of hominids from African (then Eurafrican) apes about six to eight million years ago.

The timing of the reduction in human diploid chromosome number has implications for later events in hominid evolution. For example, if hominids dispersed from a local African population into Eurasia several times, with each subsequent wave completely replacing its predecessors, then it is conceivable that a diploid chromosome number of 46 could have evolved just before the most recent radiation that is hypothesized to have occurred between 100 000 and 200 000 years ago. Alternatively, if there had been one primary expansion from Africa into other parts of the world sometime between one and two million years ago, followed by continuous gene flow among regions, then the existence of the shared human karyotype makes it more likely that evolution of the modern human diploid chromosome number of 46 occurred substantially earlier.

Supporting the idea that the diploid number was reduced from 48 to 46 early in hominid evolution is the suggestion that fixation of a chromosomal novelty would have been easier in a small population (Hamerton & Klinger, 1963). This argument reinforces the likelihood that numerical reduction occurred soon after the divergence of hominids rather than much later, when populations would have expanded numerically as well as geographically. On balance it seems more likely than not that the reduced human diploid chromosome number arose early in hominid evolution.

While the timing of hominid karyotype evolution may be uncertain, the changes involved are not. The large metacentric human chromosome pair number 2 arose via a telomere-to-telomere fusion of two shorter, submetacentric chromosomes similar to those found in chimpanzees. If the numbering system used for chimpanzee chromosomes is followed, the centromere of present human chromosome 2 was derived from the region on a chromosome corresponding to pair 12 in chimpanzees, while the centromere homologous to that of chimpanzee chromosome pair 13 was lost or inactivated. Still further, detailed studies of banding patterns indicate that proximal to the region identified as 2q21 in the human genome, there are inverted arrays of the vertebrate telomeric repeat in a head-to-head arrangement. These juxtaposed telomeric sequences should mark the point where the telomeres of the two ancestral chromosomes fused.

As with timing, the dynamics of earlier hominid chromosome evolution are less certain than the mechanics, but intriguing to consider nonetheless. It is difficult to know, for instance, how long early hominid populations might have remained polymorphic, with some individuals retaining the ancestral unfused submetacentric chromosomes corresponding to chimpanzee pairs 12 and 13, others possessing a pair of the new metacentrics corresponding to human 2, and yet others having one metacentric and one each of submetacentric 12 and 13. Among hominoid primates, some chromosomal polymorphisms have been maintained in multiple phylogenetic lineages, suggesting that they have survived speciation events. This has led some researchers (such as Stanyon, 1992) to conclude that numbers in most speciating populations of the large-bodied hominoids were never extremely low. There is no formulaic basis for resolving this point, because for each species the karyotype itself appears to be part of the multi-level adaptive system that extends from genotype to phenotype, and genomes of other primate lineages have not remained static since the divergence of lineages leading to our own.

While it is unlikely that patterns of karyotypic evolution in early hominids can ever be reconstructed with assurance, comparative studies of nonhuman primates provide some useful perspectives. Gibbons show the results of a very high rate of chromosome evolution that has produced species differing in diploid chromosome numbers ($N = 38, 44, 50$ and 52) reflecting numerous translocations that have contributed to massive karyotypic reorganization. Jauch *et al.* (1992) suggest that rapid fixation of translocations may have been facilitated by gibbon ecology and social structure, which is characterized by arboreality, monogamous matings, and nuclear family units.

In marked contrast to gibbons, papionine primate karyotypes are pervasively similar across taxa, and Jauch *et al.* (1992) have related their karyotypic commonality to features of ecology and social structure, including terrestriality and life in large groups with multiple male and multiple female matings. Against this background, the finding that rates of evolution at the nucleotide and chromosomal levels have slowed down in the human line in comparison to the African great apes has important implications. Extant human karyotypes show relatively high levels of uniformity (though there are some widely-distributed polymorphisms at levels of a few percent). Karyotypes of papionines are far more uniform than those of gibbons, despite the vastly greater geographic range and ecological diversity encountered by papionines than by gibbons. The levels of karyotypic diversity in extant papionine populations might comprise a potentially useful model system for making it possible to gain some understanding of the zygostructure of Plio-Pleistocene hominids.

Blood group polymorphisms

Paleobiological inferences can be made about other characters that existed in our early hominid ancestors despite the absence of any fossil evidence *per se*. Just as with chromosomes, antigens located on the outer surfaces of red blood cells leave no trace that can be detected in skeletal material with certainty beyond a few thousand years ago, or perhaps a few tens of thousands of years ago. Experimental evidence remains equivocal on this point. Yet it is possible to state with certainty that these antigens were expressed in our Plio-Pleistocene hominid ancestors.

The key to our ability to make such an inference is the uniformitarian perspective that is one of the foundations of paleobiological reasoning. Comparative studies (e.g., Wiener & Moor-Jankowski, 1971) have established that blood group antigens homologous to those in present humans occur in all of the living hominoid primates as well. As long ago as 1925, Landsteiner and Miller demonstrated that chimpanzee blood gives isoagglutination reactions that are indistinguishable from those of human blood. More extensive tests have demonstrated that in the ABO blood group system, chimpanzees exhibit the presence of only two blood groups, O and A. We do not, however, know whether Plio-Pleistocene hominids were similarly restricted in their ABO blood group phenotypes. Yet to be resolved are interesting complexities arising from the observation that gorilla red blood cells exhibit no agglutination reactions, although the presence of the antigenic substance for type B (and its precursor) is demonstrable in gorilla saliva. Adding to the puzzle is the observation that orangutans, by molecular criteria more distantly related to humans than are the African apes, exhibit the red cell antigenic phenotypes A, B and AB. At this point it is all but certain that our Plio-Pleistocene ancestors had the genes to produce ABO blood group antigens, and in all likelihood their populations were polymorphic for several, though perhaps not all, of these.

Research into the role of adaptation at the molecular level suggests how such polymorphisms may be maintained. In a recent large scale search for genes on which positive selection may operate in various species, Endo *et al.* (1996) screened 3595 groups of homologous sequences. Overall, only about 17, or one half of one percent (0.5 percent), of the sequences showed evidence of positive selection. Yet 9 of the 17 gene groups were surface antigens of parasites or viruses, presumably to foil the immune systems of their hosts. Such findings dovetail nicely with the earlier studies of Hughes & Nei (1988, 1989) demonstrating the operation of natural selection in the maintenance of trans-species polymorphisms at the MHC locus. Trans-species and intraspecific polymorphisms in discontinuous traits, as well as polytypic and clinal variation in continuous characters preserved in fossil skeletal remains, are part of the data for understanding the nature and dimensions of population–environment interactions. Detailed analyses of such data will affirm the dynamic aspect of human paleobiology, and help to place it squarely within the realm of modern population biology.

Evolutionary patterns and adaptive capacities of Plio-Pleistocene hominids

It is generally agreed that Plio-Pleistocene hominids were highly diverse. The extent, patterning, and causes of this diversity remain highly debated.

As discussed in Chapter 7, some paleoanthropologists hypothesize that approximately 10 or more genera and species of fossil hominids lived between about five and one million years ago, and suggest that this may be an underestimate, since taxa as yet unknown remain to be discovered or recognized. One important example of these many new discoveries is BOU-VP-12/130, which was uncovered in 1996 and diagnosed in 1999 as another new taxon, *Australopithecus garhi*.

Representative of another phenomenon, making new taxonomic assignments of remains previously known, is a composite specimen assembled from fragments discovered in the 1950s that originally were assigned to *Parathropus robustus* (SK 847) and *Telanthropus capensis* (SK 80), and now combined and reallocated to *Homo ergaster*. Pushing interpretation toward the opposite pole are studies of the sort carried out by Henneberg and his colleagues (e.g., Henneberg & Thackeray, 1995) on hominid body size, indicating that a single lineage model fits the existing data.

Other perspectives converge on an intermediate view of Plio-Pleistocene hominid diversity. White *et al.* (1995: 20) stated their belief that the early phases of human evolution 'can be accommodated in the time-successive, ancestral-descendant series of *A. ramidus* – *A. anamensis* – *A. afarensis*' and argued against either a single species hypothesis or cladistic approaches that generate a picture of a heavily branched phylogenetic tree for early hominids. In their informal language, 'even bushes have trunks.' The genetic data reviewed in Chapter 6 accord with this more moderate view of diversity, but cannot by themselves entirely resolve the situation. Rather, they indicate that partitioning the genetic distance between human and chimpanzee genomes among a large number of taxa would create hypothetical units that differed very little genomically, however diverse they appeared on the basis of detailed analyses of craniofacial morphology.

It is against this unresolved background of conflicting evidence and theory that the Plio-Pleistocene hominid remains might usefully be conceived as representing fragmented populations. Some of the fragmentation, or in this sense separation, perhaps about half, is temporal in nature, representing allochronic populations separated beyond possibility of direct contact and gene exchange. The remaining half of the diversity perceived by many paleoanthropologists corresponds to measurable morphological and morphometric diversity that cannot all be allochronic. Nor can it simply be ignored. But what is its paleobiological significance?

The papionine model might provide an important component of the answer to this question. Their populations exhibit variable but generally high levels of sexual dimorphism. Synchronic papionine populations are spatially dispersed and morphologically diverse, yet involved in the exchange of mates with adjacent groups, and through contact at multiple nodes in the web of populations across broad expanses of Africa and Eurasia. The same sort of discordance between phenostructure and zygostructure could have existed for much of the phase of early hominid evolution reviewed here. However serviceable the analogy, though, Plio-Pleistocene hominids were not baboons. Their descendants transcended the early phase of their evolution with greater cultural capabilities and lower levels of morphological diversity. The next chapter explores these emergent patterns.

9 *Character state velocity in the emergence of more advanced hominids*

Introduction

During the Miocene, our ancestors had been part of an enormous network of hominoid populations distributed widely across tropical forests and more open woodlands that covered much of the Eurasian and African continents. Possibly as early as ten million years ago, but in any case by six to eight million years ago, climates changed and forests across those regions contracted. Somewhere in Africa clusters of ape populations crossed a transitional adaptive zone, becoming distinguished at first by ecology and behavior, and only later by genes and morphology. Their evolution followed a mosaic pattern, with one of the earliest recognizable components of hominid status being the functional complex including upright posture and bipedal locomotion, followed by craniodental changes and brain expansion. As we saw in Chapter 8, hominids evolved for four or five million years, producing morphologically diverse and adaptively successful populations that spread over East and South Africa. From among those groups, about which much is known but more is uncertain, biologically and behaviorally advanced hominids later arose.

Foley (1995) refers to the populations resulting from the first transition to upright posture as hominids, and reserves the term human only for the much later populations (circa 100 000 to 150 000 years ago) characterized by distinctive patterns of anatomical structure and behavior. Between the diverse and fragmented populations of earlier hominids and later populations that are recognizably human lies another zone of transition occupied by what many paleoanthropologists believe are members of the genus *Homo* who have not yet achieved fully human status. The formal taxonomic designation that traditionally has been applied to these transitional hominids is *Homo habilis*, though as noted below, this taxon is subdivided by some investigators. Important common features include upright posture and bipedal locomotion, in combination with endocranial volumes averaging half again as large as those encountered in earlier

Plio-Pleistocene hominids. Diverse interpretations of these postcranial and cranial character complexes raise questions about evolutionary tempos and modes that are explored in this chapter.

Distribution in time and space

Fossil remains attributed to *Homo habilis* span the period from about two million years ago to one and a half million years ago. The inclusion, or exclusion, however, of particular specimens introduces further temporal uncertainty on the order of several hundred thousand years.

The first fossil remains attributed to *Homo habilis* were recovered from the FLKNN site at Olduvai Gorge in 1960. These included portions of the cranial vault, partial mandible, and hand bones of a juvenile hominid. Subsequently other specimens from Olduvai Bed I and the lower parts of Bed II also were referred to this taxon (including OH 4, 6, 8, 13–16, 24, 37, 39, 62). Finds at sites elsewhere in East Africa (among others, L. 894–1 at Omo, and KNM-ER 992 and 1813 at Koobi Fora) and South Africa (Swartkrans, Sterkfontein) have swelled the sample (Wood, 1987). As is the case with the time range, discussions of morphological and adaptive characteristics are complicated by the belief that *H. habilis* may represent more than one taxon (for this reason, some points discussed here will overlap with issues considered in Chapters 8 and 10).

From time to time there are suggestions, based on morphological attributes or chronological position (or both) that certain Asian hominids may be attributable to *Homo habilis*. Tobias & von Koenigswald (1964) drew attention to the similarities between the '*Meganthropus*' mandibular fragments and the *Homo habilis* type mandible from Olduvai Gorge Bed I, and suggested that these fossils may represent the same grade of hominid evolution. Other examples are the 'Modjokerto child' (Perning 1), first described by von Koenigswald in 1936, that has been dated to approximately 1.8 Ma (Swisher *et al.*, 1994), and, more recently, a mandibular fragment and teeth associated with a stone flake and battered cobble from Longgupo Cave in China (Wanpo *et al.*, 1995). These finds suggest the beginning of a wider dispersal of hominids that will be discussed in Chapter 10.

Systematics

Authorities who believe that taxonomic diversity exists within *H. habilis* are further divided on the point of whether some of the specimens represent gracile australopithecines or more advanced hominids (variously referred to as *H. ergaster* and *H. rudolfensis*). One of the most prolific writers on this taxon is Bernard Wood, who has provided various overviews (e.g., Wood, 1993; Wood & Collard, 1999). In addition, Conroy (1997) has presented a valuable comparison of the divergences in material allocated to this taxon by various workers. Most of these discussions focus on details of craniofacial anatomy. In contrast, the primary emphasis here will be on functional aspects that relate postcranial structure to function, and on endocranial volumes that undergird behavioral and cultural capacities.

Phenotypic features

Following Stringer (1986), Klein (1989) notes that *Homo habilis* is difficult to characterize because specialists disagree on what specific fossils it includes. However, there seems to be somewhat more agreement on the morphology of these transitional populations taken together than in the taxonomic assignments of the individual specimens. They generally are held to present a combination of features found in gracile australopithecines and later *Homo*.

Crania are more lightly built and cheek teeth are longer and narrower than those of the larger australopithecines. The initial delineation of the taxon (Leakey *et al.*, 1964) emphasized the combination of hands suited for manipulative ability and a brain that was moderately enlarged; bipedal locomotion was accepted as a given. However, some recent finds have raised interesting questions about adaptive patterns in this taxon, and how perceptions of them are intertwined with problems of preservation and dating, as well as knowledge of the factors that influence variation in extant human populations.

Adaptive levels in relation to evolutionary interpretations

Developmental perspectives on postcranial evolution

Contrasting views on the tempo and mode of evolution among early hominids were brought into sharp focus by the discovery and interpretation of OH 62 from lower Bed I at Olduvai Gorge, dated indirectly to about 1.8 Ma (Johanson *et al.*, 1987). The OH 62 skeletal material came from a scrappy surface find that comprised a total of nearly 18 000 separate fragments of bones and teeth from a variety of different animals ranging from fish through giraffes. The numerous hominid elements were distinguishable in part by differential coloration.

The find included small cranial vault fragments, parts of a maxilla that could be fitted together, isolated teeth, portions of the right humerus, ulna and radius, and part of a left femur including the femoral neck and part of the shaft. Formally the material was referred by its finders to the taxon *Homo habilis* and colloquially is referred to by them and others as 'Lucy's daughter.' The informal nomen refers to the fact that OH 62 lived and died later than a previous discovery by Johanson and his colleagues, AL 288–1 ('Lucy') at Hadar in Ethiopia (Johanson *et al.*, 1982).

From the fact that the third molar had erupted, and from the heavily worn occlusal surfaces of its teeth it was argued that OH 62 was a relatively old adult. From the diminutive size of the limb bones, particularly the femur, which is even smaller than that of AL 288–1, it was postulated that OH 62 was a female, with stature estimated to be about 1 m. Some data and extrapolations are given in Table 9.1 for comparison and context.

Despite the damaged and incomplete nature of the find, Johanson and his colleagues proposed that analysis of OH 62 supported several important conclusions. First, they felt that the body size indicated that this individual was as small as, or smaller than, any other known fossil hominid. Second, as noted previously, they saw important anatomical and proportional similarities between the skeletons of OH 62 and AL 288–1. Third, if OH 62 is a representative of *Homo habilis*, as they believed, then this specimen would represent the first instance in which limb elements could be assigned securely to that taxon. Building further on that taxonomic inference, they drew attention to the contrast between the 'postcranially primitive *Homo habilis*' at about 1.8 Ma and a 'relatively derived *H. erectus* postcranium' at about 1.8 Ma (KNM-WT 15000), which they felt might 'imply an abrupt transition between these taxa in eastern Africa (Johanson *et al.*, 1982).'

The key dimensions on which these inferences were arrived at are as follows. The OH62 humerus length was given as 264 mm, which is 27 mm longer than the corresponding arm bone of AL 288–1. Further, if 'the length of the OH 62 femur was no greater than that of AL 288–1 (280 mm), the Olduvai individual would have a humerofemoral index of close to 95 percent.' That ratio would imply that the bone of the upper arm was nearly as long as the bone in the upper leg.

The contrast between the very fragmentary nature of the remains and the strong inference that this evidence supports the hypothesis of a rapid evolutionary transition was a matter for concern. Among human biologists working with extant populations, in general the more indefinite the evidence, the more tentative should be the inferences derived from it.

Table 9.1. *Comparison of postcranial features of three fossil hominids*

	AL 288–1	OH 62	KNM-WT 15000
humerus	237 mm	264 mm	319 mm (actual)
femur	280 mm	280 mm	432 mm (actual)
		(if same as AL 288–1)	
humerofemoral index	0.8464	0.9429	0.7384

It was in this spirit of caution that one of the more thoughtful reconsiderations of the OH 62 problem was offered by Korey (1990). While noting that the humerus and femur of OH 62 are badly damaged and that consequently their lengths are not directly measurable, Korey realized that it was possible to use relatively intact reference materials from a representative sample of extant humans to derive the error term that would be associated with the reconstruction of femoral length. Using the approximate variance of the ratio mean (Kish, 1965), Korey was able to show that the error term associated with the humerofemoral index is so substantial that it is only possible to situate the index somewhere between the distributions for extant *Homo* and *Gorilla*, and quite possibly not above the index for AL 288–1 itself. This analysis illustrates, once again, the value of efforts to place fossil finds into the broader inferential perspectives made possible by much larger samples representing better-known populations of living primates, human and nonhuman.

It is possible to build upon Korey's comparative perspective by utilizing the heuristically robust human adaptability framework. As mentioned, the OH 62 specimen was introduced to the world as 'Lucy's daughter' because of the discoverers' belief that this skeleton, found at Olduvai Gorge in Tanzania, represented a female who lived later in time than the well-known specimen from Hadar in Ethiopia. Apparently OH 62 had longer arms in relation to legs than did AL 288–1, at least as inferred from the relative lengths of humerus and femur in the respective fossils. The significance of this comparison stands out against the background provided by extant apes and humans, as already indicated above.

For example, it has been noted by Leakey & Lewin (1992) that chimpanzees have a humerofemoral index of 100; that is, the respective bones of their upper arms and upper legs are of equal length. In contrast, modern humans are said to have a humerofemoral index of 70 – the humerus is only 70 percent as long as the femur. Against these background data stand the observations that the humerofemoral index of AL 288–1 was 85, evidently midway between chimps and modern humans, while that of OH 62 was 95 – ostensibly more apelike, thus posing a problem in reconstructing relationships. But does it? Is a difference of 10 index points in a measure of limb proportions too great to be encompassed within a single species such as *Homo habilis*? More broadly, if these specimens are considered as time-successive members of a single lineage, would the respective limb proportions of OH 62 and AL 288–1 really require an evolutionary reversal so great as to be impossible, or at least unlikely, in a lineage connecting Plio-Pleistocene hominids with those of the middle Pleistocene?

In answering questions such as these, it is crucial to realize that the evidence commonly provided by the fossil record comprises the remains of individuals, but the inferences made are – ostensibly at least – about relationships among the populations from which the individual specimens have been sampled. Consequently, the appropriate reference standard for evaluating individual observations from the fossil record must be data from extant *populations*.

Observations on populations of living humans provide a broader context for a variety of related questions. How much variation is there within populations for proportions such as the humerofemoral index? Does that variation differ in its distribution among demographic categories, such as age and sex? Is it influenced by environmental factors, such as nutrition, disease, and temperature that could differ between generations, and even, over time, shape secular trends of longer duration? If there are trends, do they seem to be unidirectional, or are they reversible? Are there significant differences between populations living in different geographic areas, and if so, to what extent might these differences be partitioned among proximate environmental and genetic influences?

Shortly after the turn of the twentieth century, as discussed in Chapter 5, Franz Boas (1912) realized that concerns of citizens living in the United States about large-scale immigration could be turned to some advantage in funding scientific research into some fundamental questions about the factors that might influence human growth and development. Fortunately, because of the questions raised, the work of Boas was followed by a number of further investigations characterized by increasing precision and controls. One particularly well-executed example of these subsequent studies, published by Shapiro in 1939, compared Japanese offspring born in Hawaii to their own migrant parents and to relatives of their parents who remained in Japan.

The data collected by Shapiro and his associates in Hawaii and Japan comprised anthropometric measurements on living subjects, so they are not directly comparable to dimensions of fossil bones. However, some measurements on past and present human populations are closely comparable, particularly for most estimates of limb size and proportions. The upper arm length in a living subject reflects closely the length of the humerus as an isolated skeletal part, and the upper leg length represents mainly the length of the femur. In both instances the presence of soft tissue will slightly increase the dimension in a living subject over that of a separate bone, but these differences largely cancel out in the calculation of a composite measure such as the humerofemoral index.

For analytical purposes, proximal limb segment indices can be calculated from the summary statistics provided by Shapiro (1939). Data for females are used here, reflecting published inferences that AL 288–1 and OH 62 both were females. For Japanese females who remained in Japan, the index is 82.3; in migrants to Hawaii, the index is a very similar 82.5; and in the Hawaiian-born daughters of the immigrants, the index drops to 80.9, largely because upper leg length increased by about 2 cm in length while upper arm length increased by only about 1 cm. The corresponding figures for males are quite similar: for non-migrants, 82.2; for migrants to Hawaii, 78.3; and for Hawaiian-born males, 80.9. All of these samples from populations of Japanese ancestry – females and males, non-migrants, migrants, and offspring of migrants – cluster around a proximal limb segment index of about 80. This aggregate value is 10 points higher than that of the unspecified modern human sample cited by Leakey and Lewin, and only five points lower than that of AL 288–1. More striking yet is the observation that the difference of ten points between the unspecified modern human sample used by Leakey and Lewin and Shapiro's Japanese sample, is no greater than the difference between AL 288–1 and OH 62. That is, in the case of the fossils we might be dealing with a difference that does not have to be attributed at all to evolutionary change, but merely to sampling from a different population of the same species.

Limb proportions also vary substantially even within subpopulations. Unfortunately, although Shapiro computed 21 different indices from his data, the humerofemoral index was not among them. However, his summary tables do include ranges for both components of the index (see Table 9.2).

For example, in Hawaiian-born Japanese females (Table 9.2) upper arm length varies between 24 and 32 cm; that is, the maximum value is almost exactly one-third greater than the minimum, with the average (28.01 cm) nearly precisely at the midpoint. Upper leg length has an even wider absolute range, from 25 to 42 cm, with the maximum value exceeding the minimum value by some 68 percent. It is all but certain, therefore, that the range for the humerofemoral index *within* the Japanese samples would approach or even exceed the difference *between* AL 288–1 and OH 62,

Table 9.2. *Proximal limb segment (PLS) index – Japanese females*

Trait	Non-immigrants		Immigrants		Hawaiian-born	
	X + s.d.	range	X + s.d.	range	X + s.d.	range
Upper arm length	26.88 +1.55	23–30	27.82 +1.78	24–32	28.01 +1.68	24–32
Upper leg length	32.68 +3.30	25–40	33.72 +4.08	23–44	34.76 +3.36	25–42
PLS index	82.3		82.5		80.6	

Source: Shapiro (1939).

which may have been separated by 10 000 generations of 20 years each.

This inference is supported rather effectively by Shapiro's closely related data on the intermembral index (Table 9.3), which is the total length of the upper limb divided by the total length of the lower limb. Indeed, it is probable that paleoanthropologists would have preferred to use a measure approximating the intermembral index if sufficiently complete skeletal remains for AL 288–1 and OH 62 had been available for analysis.

Even from these limited data it is easy to see that the intermembral index, which closely parallels the humerofemoral index values, shows a range of over 20 to 30 points in every subsample, and a combined range over the six closely related subsamples of nearly 40 points. These ranges within an extant human population parallel the differences observed between AL 288–1 and OH 62, while their magnitude dwarfs the differences between the fossils.

As the last part of this exercise in judging the significance of the difference in limb proportions between AL 288–1 and OH 62, notice should be taken of the changes that can accrue even over a time period as brief as that encountered in comparing two subsequent generations. In Shapiro's study, there was a mean change in the proximal limb segment index (anatomically comparable to the humerofemoral index in the fossils) from 82.5 to 80.6, for a reduction of 2.3 percent in a single generation, probably from environmental influences and behavioral choices (possibly affecting the composition of the samples of who chose to migrate and who did not).

What lesson might be drawn from all of these numbers? Quite simply, that adaptation and evolution are complex phenomena, so that any given observation may have more than one explanation. Interpretations should be made within as comprehensive, and comparative, a biological context as possible. It is conceivable that one Olduvai hominid differs from a given Hadar hominid because both of the two individuals accurately reflect comparable differences between their respective populations. But it also is

Table 9.3. *Intermembral index in the Japanese migrant study*

	N	Mean ± s.d. (cm)	Range
Japanese non-migrants			
males	171	94.98 ± 4.94	78–109 = 31
females	91	95.54 ± 4.64	84–107 = 23
both sexes combined	262	NA	
Japanese migrants			
males	178	94.98 ± 4.94	84–117 = 33
females	91	94.46 ± 5.64	80–113 = 33
both sexes combined	269	NA	
Hawaiian-born Japanese			
males	186	93.90 ± 4.10	82–107 = 25
females	91	92.44 ± 4.58	82–103 = 21
both sexes combined	277	NA	
Total range over all subsamples			
combining sex and location	808		78–117 = 39

Intermembral index: total length of upper limb divided by the total length of the lower limb.
Source: Shapiro (1939).

possible that their individual differences represent only the particular events of development, death, deposition, destruction, and discovery. In this case, it is possible that limb proportions in the underlying populations may have been distributed quite similarly, or even have diverged in the opposite direction. Ages at death of the individuals could have influenced the observations. It is even conceivable that the apparent stratigraphy and dating is sufficiently in error as to reverse the sequence of the populations.

Scientists interested in the comparative aspects of human biology – whether their materials are drawn from the present or the past – should use population-based models that accept the existence of substantial amounts of intraspecific variation. They also should consider the dynamic processes of adaptation, to see the full range of implications for the fossils we now have. The recognition that each fossil specimen represents an individual who lived life as part of a population of young and old, male and female, shorter and taller individuals means that variability and its adaptive correlates must be key constituents of the modern evolutionary framework in paleobiology. In response to this suggestion, a paleoanthropologist might propose an alternative antidote for problems of this sort: find more fossils! Fortuitously, with reference to the OH 62 example just discussed, appropriate fossils were found several years after Korey's paper was published, also following the preceding calculations made from Shapiro's work. Commenting on the new fossil material, White *et al.* (1999) observed that 'The new Bouri VP-12/1 specimen is only the third Plio-Pleistocene hominid to provide reasonably accurate limb length proportions. The Olduvai Hominid 62 specimen of *Homo habilis* has been erroneously argued to show humerus-to-femur proportions more primitive than those of 'Lucy'. . . but its femur length cannot be accurately estimated.' Present and past perspectives coincide here to cast doubt on this suggested instance of postcranial punctuation.

Brain expansion: compounding the hominid heritage

The million year timespan often assumed for the emergence of *Homo habilis* from smaller-brained hominids seems brief, when considered in the abstract. But even seemingly short spans of time allow for the compounding of gains, even if each increment is so slight as to be scarcely noticeable in itself. What Einstein, like Darwin, saw in compounding – the physicist, because of his mathematical mind, explicitly, the naturalist perhaps intuitively – was the vast power of cumulative growth. A financial analogy is useful here. Given a starting sum of 10 dollars and an objective of turning that small amount of capital into a million dollars, most people would believe that their only possibility would be to take their chances on a potentially 'punctuational' event, with a lottery. If they followed this impulse, the odds are that nearly all of the players would lose and be entirely wiped out. But suppose that every person who so desired could get a rate of return that was certain, such as the coupon on a government guaranteed bond. Further, let's assume that the interest rate on the bond is three percent (which while not very exciting is utterly reasonable, given that British gilts and US long-term treasury securities that are indexed for inflation have a current yield of about 3.5 percent).

At a rate of three percent, compounded annually, 10 dollars will grow to just over a million dollars in 390 years. That calculation will leave most people unimpressed since they realize that they will have cashed out mortally long before they could have done so financially, when the magic number of a million dollars was reached. Presumably this is the sort of situation that Lord Keynes (1936) had in mind when he remarked in the context of finance that 'In the long run we are all dead.' But consider this. If the investment perspective is not that of an individual, for whom death is a certainty, but that of a lineage, which has a finite probability of continuing to exist for a very long period of time (millions or tens of millions of years), the outcome changes dramatically.

For any entity that is long-lived or potentially even immortal (a corporation, college, or lineage), rates of compounding that are infinitesimally low are not at all uninteresting. If the population stays in the game, the gain is close to a sure thing. The evolutionary implications of this point are profound. Suppose here for a first approximation that we are not dealing with a mammal (*Homo sapiens*) having a lifespan measured in decades and who is hoping for an unrealistically high payoff in terms of return on capital within that period (for many individual members of our species, such hope is one aspect of the human condition). Imagine instead that the compounding period is not a year but a generation, and the outcome is not having 10 currency units grow into a million of the same counters, but having body size or the dimensions of some structure increase at the same rate – by 100000 times in under 400 generations (analogous to $10 growing to $1 000 000 in 390 rounds of compounding). Even with a generation time on the human scale of about 20 years this transformation could be accomplished in fewer than 8000 years, or less than the span of recorded history. Put in those terms, the outcome of compounding at three percent is not so slow as to be boring; it is so astonishingly swift as to strain credulity.

A caution is appropriate here. When comparing the real world of nature with the rather more abstract realms of mathematics or finance (which really is an area of applied mathematics), it is important to realize that different constraints apply. When desiring to limit expectations to some reasonable level, investment managers will sometimes remark 'Trees don't grow to the sky,' meaning that one cannot extrapolate current returns endlessly into the future. In the biological world that same statement is literally true. Trees don't grow to the sky because they can't; there are physical limits to the growth of living organisms. One of them is set by simple geometry. For any increase in linear dimensions, cross-sectional area increases roughly as a square of the linear dimension and volume as a cube – so after some point, a tree of ever-increasing size would break and fall of its own weight. All other real organisms are constrained by similar physical limitations, as recognized in the splendid title and contents of Pennycuick's (1995) book *Newton Rules Biology*.

In the context of human paleobiology, Ruff (1991) has shown convincingly how corresponding physical limitations, interacting with climatic variables, have directly influenced the evolution of human body shape, and indirectly through it such behaviorally significant features as the birth process and secondary altriciality. In the domain of human evolutionary biology, therefore, size is significant for proportions, and shifts in proportions can lead to the emergence of novel developmental and behavioral properties. Matters of scale are critical here. Even a tenfold increase in the size of some body part would be enormous, and experience leads us to expect that millions of years, or even far more, would be required for such an increase, or even one of more modest degree, to be accomplished (if it were possible at all, which it might not be due to physical constraints). For example, as we saw in Chapter 8, for reasons that are not agreed upon, body masses and statures of Plio-Pleistocene hominids, particularly those that lived at about the same time, fall in a range so narrow as to be puzzling.

With these cautions in mind, we can return to the different conceptual problems concerning rates of compounding. For example, in financial terms, a three percent rate of change seems unsatisfying – yet its results seem dizzyingly swift in terms of the evolutionary record. How might we arrive at a biologically more plausible compounding function? One approach might be to just play around with the numbers. In physics, heavily influenced by German culture and also being accustomed to hypotheses on a grand scale but limited opportunities for experiment, these disciplined speculations are referred to as *Gedanken Versuche*, 'thought experiments.' Such conceptions take the form of 'what if?' For example, if three percent compounded produces results that seem excessive in terms of the magnitude of change after some period of time, the rate might arbitrarily be scaled down by a factor of 100. If so, what would be implied?

With such a reduction, the rate of change per generation would not be three percent, but instead three one-hundredths of one percent (0.03 percent or 0.0003) for each compounding period. In that case the original objective of a 100 000 fold gain (ten dollars to a million) would be realized only after 38 383 generations. Next, let not only the compounding rate, but also the objective be scaled back to a 'mere' tenfold change, comparable to growing our original 10 dollar stake to 100 dollars. The result is that the number of compounding periods would be fewer than 8000 (7677 to be precise). If the compounding periods represented generations, at 20 years per generation the time elapsed would be 153 540 years.

The timespans just calculated for abstract amounts of change might seem more or less 'reasonable' to many paleontologists or paleoanthropologists, in the sense that they correspond to intervals of time that actually are encountered in the fossil record. But note that, to arrive at them it has been necessary to scale down both compounding rates and outcomes drastically, with the result that the hypothetical changes per generation are so tiny that they almost certainly could not be measurable in real samples of fossil material. That is, if we were looking at a characteristic in two successive generations that differed by 0.0003 (i.e. three-hundredths of one percent) it would be virtually impossible for conventional measuring instruments employed in the study of skeletal remains to detect the differences. Even if a change were there to be found, the increment would be dwarfed by mere errors in measurement.

Exercises of this sort underscore the value of the *Gedanken* experiment approach, which makes it possible to visualize phenomena in the mind that the eyes really cannot see in the physical world. There is no evidence indicating that Darwin made calculations of this sort explicitly, and in fact it is rather likely that he did not. However, it is known that he was a successful private investor, and quite possibly had an intuitive grasp of long-term returns on invested capital. Like Einstein in a later scientific era, Darwin must have realized the power of compounding over long intervals of time.

Compounding functions in hominid evolution

Calculations of the sort just discussed actually can have some direct applications to problems in human evolution. One phenotypic characteristic that lends itself particularly well to such approaches also is unmistakably prominent in the evolution of the lineage that leads to present humans – brain size. In the fossil record the usual proxy for brain size is endocranial volume. There is not a one-to-one relationship between the two measures, but they are very closely correlated.

Before looking at particular questions and fossils, it is a good idea to establish the outer boundaries of the area of inquiry. Extant humans, obviously, are near the upper end of the range (although some Neanderthals actually attained moderately higher averages about 100000 years ago). Modern chimpanzee populations offer a reasonable beginning point, not because we are descended directly from them (they are our contemporaries, not our ancestors) but because adaptively they appear to be close to the populations that actually did give rise to Plio-Pleistocene hominids.

In the case of the endocranial volume estimates, the errors arise from incompleteness of some specimens, and a need to estimate internal volumes from external dimensions in cases where endocranial cavities are filled with mineralized matrix, and so on. For estimates of geological age, error terms arise from intrinsic methods of calculation and, less predictably, from problems in judging the association between datable material and the fossils themselves. It is important not to ignore or discount these error terms, since in scientific inquiry they are as real as the central values calculated. At the same time, it should be realized that methodological advances over the last several decades have vastly improved our knowledge of the intervals of time separating various population samples in the hominid fossil record.

One rather important instance in which understanding rates of change can help to gain a useful perspective on a problem in human evolution concerns the evolutionary significance of KNM-ER 1470, found at East Rudolf, Kenya in 1972. The first report of this discovery was made by Richard Leakey (1973). Because of its high endocranial volume (given initially as over 800 cm^3, later adjusted to about 750 cm^3) and early date (initially stated to be probably 2.9 Ma), this find immediately attracted wide attention, both popular and professional. In his preliminary description and diagnosis in *Nature*, Leakey attributed this individual to an undetermined species of the genus *Homo* (more recently it has been reclassified as *Homo rudolfensis* by Alexeev, 1986). In support of the original assignment, Leakey noted that 'to include the 1470 cranium from East Rudolf within the genus *Australopithecus* would require an extraordinary range of variation of endocranial volume for this genus. This seems unacceptable and also other morphological considerations argue strongly against such an attribution' (Leakey, 1973).

The other morphological features included relatively weak supraorbital tori, absence of a continuous supraorbital sulcus, and forward placement of both the glenoid fossae and external auditory meati. Other descriptive features are given by Groves (1989) as well as Alexeev (1986). However, the aspect of KNM-ER 1470 that has attracted and held the attention of those writing about it from the time of its first discovery (see, as examples, Jerison, 1973:421; and Tattersall, 1995:133) is the high endocranial volume, particularly when that feature is combined with its early chronometric date.

The caveat that has been articulated by some neuroscientists is that brain size is not significant in itself; it is the organization of the brain that is important. The position of Jerison (1991:36) seems preferable, that both brain size and organization are important. This viewpoint seems close, as well, to that articulated by Holloway (1983). In fact, it is not possible to find many cases in which material size changes are not accompanied by shape or structural reorganizations. Furthermore, it is difficult to imagine why the substantial size changes seen in the evolution of the human brain would have occurred unless they *were* important. That is what human biologists believe adaptation is all about, although there are alternative perspectives. Groves (1989:320), who acknowledges the influence of Blumenberg (1983), views brain size as an exaptation in the sense of Gould & Vrba (1982). Finally, size is particularly critical for understanding the evolution of mind as well as behavior, both of which appear to be central adaptive features for human evolution. With these points made, it is possible to go back from general considerations to the particular example of KNM-ER 1470.

The reference sample that Richard Leakey chose for comparison with KNM-ER 1470 comprised six small Plio-Pleistocene hominids (Taung, MLD 37/38, STS 5, STS 19/58, STS 60, STS 71) whose crania had been studied by Ralph Holloway (1970). These specimens were stated (Leakey, 1973) to have a mean volume 422 cm³ (erroneously, since Holloway's published average actually was 442 cm³). Around the same time, Phillip Tobias (1973) made a comparable study of the same specimens, for which he estimated a mean endocranial volume of 441.2 cm³. Tobias (1973) suggested that around 3 Ma, or perhaps earlier, a branch of *Australopithecus africanus* underwent strong selection for cerebral enlargement out of proportion to body size, giving rise to the *Homo* lineage. Like Leakey, Tobias then believed KNM-ER 1470 to be the earliest member of the genus *Homo*.

On the basis of these data and related assumptions it is possible to calculate the implied rate of expansion in endocranial volume. To build on Einstein's insight, and because the logic and mathematics are easier to follow than for many alternatives, a compounding approach is used here. The exercise can be made to look neat and formal by introducing a tailor-made formula. The one used below really is just the standard compound interest formula, re-labeled to fit the nature of the input data used in the example:

$$V_f = V_i(1 + r)^n$$

where V_i is the mean volume in the population represented by the earlier sample, V_f is the mean volume in the population represented by the later sample, n is the time, expressed in generations, and r is the rate of compounding.

Here, the final volume is 750 cm³, the measured endocranial volume of KNM-ER 1470, assuming that the specimen was drawn from the mean of its population. Groves (1989:264) gives the volume as 770 cm³, but this difference would not affect the calculations very much. To determine how much change would be required if KNM-ER 1470 were to be considered a lineal descendant of a population represented by this particular known sample of Plio-Pleistocene hominids, it is possible to use Holloway's determination of 442 cm³ as the initial size, as others have (the data of Tobias give virtually the same results). Another assumption, in the direction of conservatism, is to set generation time in Plio-Pleistocene hominids at 20 years, the figure conventionally used for extant humans. In all probability the figure for earlier populations was lower, closer to 15 or even

10 years, which would allow for more generations between the two samples, regardless of the absolute time interval.

What was the timespan? For a first approximation, provisionally accept the same 2.9 Ma for KNM-ER 1470 that Leakey did, and use the 3.0 Ma of Tobias for the preceding Plio-Pleistocene sample. This nominal 100 000 year interval is empirically intriguing. All radiometric dates have an intrinsic error term; in this case the original publication (Fitch & Miller, 1970) gave the date as 2.61 ± 0.26 Ma. If the error term is taken at face value, the spread around the potassium/argon age determination could easily be half a million years (0.26 Myr either way), substantially more than the hypothetical 0.1 Myr interval allowed. Divided by 20 years per generation, the 0.1 Myr interval would be but a small fraction of the spread possible between the two hominid samples given the magnitude of errors inherent in the dating methods. Yet this 'geological instant' still would allow for 5000 generations separating the two populations represented by the samples of six australopithecine crania and KNM-ER 1470, respectively.

Taking into account all of these assumptions and substituting the resultant numbers into the general formula given above, the actual expression would appear as

$$750 \text{ cm}^3 = 442 \text{ cm}^3 (1 + r)^{5000}$$

Solving for r this would give a value of 0.000106; that is, a change in the mean of a little over one one-hundredth (106 ten-thousandths to be precise) of a percent per generation.

What are we to make of a number of this magnitude? Clearly, it is very small; in fact, it is so minute that it is difficult to contemplate in the abstract. To put it into some perspective, return to the situation of someone comparing a lottery's risk with the surer return via compounding. With a rate of return set at 0.000106, ten dollars would increase to a million dollars eventually, of course, but only after over 100 000 compounding periods (108 618 to be precise again). If each of these compounding periods were a year, the wait would seem very long, indeed; the payoff would not come for over 1000 centuries. Seen from one end of a timeline, looking toward the future, in this example a human would wait a long time for 10 dollars to compound to a million. If the perspective were reversed and payoff were to come during the lifetime of someone now living, at a rate of return of 0.0106 percent, the 'investment' of 10 dollars would have had to have been made sometime well back into the Middle Paleolithic.

There is another comparison that can be made, this time from the standpoint of functional biology. The modern human brain has approximately 10 billion neurons in its average volume of 1345 cm³. If there were a roughly proportionate relationship between endocranial volume and numbers of neurons, then brains in the same Plio-Pleistocene hominid sample used above would have about 442/1345, or about 33 percent as many neurons as modern humans (a rough estimate indeed). For perspective another caveat should be added here. The relationships among endocranial volume, brain size, and numbers of neurons are not simple (Tobias, 1971). For example, there are developmental influences; in present humans, at birth over 94 percent of cranial capacity is represented by actual volume of the brain, while at age 20 brain volume is only 80 percent of cranial capacity. In comparisons among species, neuron density is on the order of 100 000 neurons per cubic millimeter of motor neocortex in the mouse, while in humans it is an order of magnitude lower at about 10 000 per cubic millimeter (Jerison, 1991:34). Even more to the point, knowledge of internal reorganization in the brain during hominid evolution still is soberingly inadequate.

With these cautions in mind, a tentative direct extrapolation from present to past hominid brain sizes suggests that members of the small Plio-Pleistocene hominid sample might have had somewhere on the order of 3.3 billion neurons. If the compounding rate were only 0.000106 as calculated, this would mean that the next generation would have an additional 349 800 neurons, and the generation following the first would have that initial increment plus an additional 349 837 more than the preceding increase (note the additional nominal 37 neurons attributable to just one round of compounding), and so on. Against baseline numbers in the billions these gains might not seem to be very large increments, but collectively they are equivalent to adding the entire brain of a mouse every 100 generations for the first few iterations, with the absolute values of additions increasing even more thereafter. The possibilities can get even more interesting, as will be seen from some further examples.

The preceding case incorporated a working hypothesis that the brain of KNM-ER 1470 was representative of the average in the population from which it was sampled. This is the usual assumption that is made, of course, for isolated specimens, and it is justified on the grounds of probability. However, it is also known that there exists considerable variation in endocranial volume in hominid populations. For example, in the sample published by Holloway (1970), the range from smallest (428 cm^3) to the largest individual (530 cm^3) specimen is 102 cm^3, with the spread representing 23 percent of the sample mean. The two largest specimens, with endocranial volumes of 530 cm^3, are 4.1 standard deviations above the sample mean. Suppose that KNM-ER 1470 also might have represented an unusually large-brained individual, but not one so extreme as to be more than four standard deviations above the mean of its population. Consider, instead, the relatively more conservative possibility that KNM-ER 1470 were only two standard deviations above its respective population mean.

By the very nature of size distributions in natural populations, outliers should be discovered now and then in the fossil record. Given properties of the normal distribution, brain sizes of two or more standard deviations above the mean represent a bit over two percent of populations (and because brain size distributions are positively skewed, perhaps even a little more than that), so perhaps about one specimen in 50 would be unusually large but not impossibly rare. To see what effect this assumption about the position of KNM-ER 1470 in its population would have on rate calculations, some estimate is needed for the value of a standard deviation in a hominoid population, the mean endocranial volume of which is unknown (since this specimen was an isolated find). Such an estimate could be derived in various ways. One source might be Holloway's (1970) sample, in which one standard deviation was 21.59 cm^3. Another approach that would make it possible to avoid statistical extrapolation from the earlier Plio-Pleistocene sample itself (which, with only six specimens included, is very small) would be to assume that variation in endocranial volume among these early hominids was roughly comparable to that found in a large sample of living chimpanzees. This latter approach is likely to furnish quite a conservative estimate, both because chimpanzees are among the least variable in cranial capacity of the larger living hominoid primates, and because their mean endocranial volumes are lower than those known for fossil hominids.

According to Tobias (1971), in a composite sample of 363 male and female chimpanzees with a mean endocranial volume of 383.4 cm^3, one standard deviation is 37.14 cm^3. Therefore, two standard deviations on either side of the mean would total 74.28 cm^3. Subtracting this amount from the 750 cm^3 estimated for the endocranial volume of KNM-ER 1470 would yield a hypothetical population mean of 675.72 cm^3. Leaving all other assumptions as before, the compounding equation would be:

$$675.72 \text{ cm}^3 = 442 \text{ cm}^3 \, (1 + r)^{5000}$$

Solving this expression for r would produce a notional compounding factor of 0.0000849, or about 85 ten-thousandths of one percent. Note how merely changing the assumption about where in a population's continuum an individual might be situated changes what seems to be asked of character state velocity in evolution. This last rate is only 80 percent that of the first calculation, based as that was on KNM-ER 1470 being just at the mean of its population during life. If it is assumed that much of observed increase in brain size was due to natural selection, then in the second case, the intensity of this force of evolution could be measurably lower, while the outcome remained unchanged. Or, alternatively, if the rate had stayed the same, at 0.000106, from the same starting point of small-brained hominids averaging endocranial volumes of 442 cm^3, the metric gap could be closed in far less time – 4000 generations of 20 years instead of 5000. The resultant temporal reduction of about 20 000 years might seem to be slight on a geological timescale, but it can be biologically meaningful. In evolutionary terms, 20 000 is roughly twice as long as selection has taken to transform a wolf-like ancestor into all of the domestic dog breeds – from St. Bernards to chihauhas. It is about half the time that separates extant humans from the latest Neanderthals.

In combination with the rate calculated previously, this number (about 85 ten-thousandths of one percent) – tiny though it is – gives some insight into the effects that assumptions have on interpretations of the past. It is possible to entertain the idea that, during life, KNM-ER 1470 might have been an unusually large-brained individual – perhaps comparable, among humans in the historical present, to Daniel Webster and Ivan Turgenev (who had brain sizes of about 1900 cm^3), but perhaps not as extreme as either Lord Byron or Oliver Cromwell with brain sizes of about 2200 cm^3. Examples of this sort give the force of detail to general statements that variation is the raw material on which selection can act, and that most character state changes do not require much in the way of selective differentials among genotypes. Before this exercise in exploring the internal dynamics of evolutionary change is closed, another example is in order, one that factors in a changed assumption of another sort.

Well over a decade after the announcement of the discovery of KNM-ER 1470 and the pronouncement that this specimen 'fit no previous model of human beginnings,' repeated paleontological and geological studies forced a re-assessment of the age of the deposits that had yielded this attention-getting find. Among other papers, two by Frank Brown and his colleagues (Brown & Feibel, 1986; Feibel *et al.*, 1989) were centrally important in shifting the date accepted for the lifetime of KNM-ER 1470. The bed from which this specimen was recovered is identified as Area 131 in Member UBU of Level KBS-36m. It now has been given a date of approximately 1.9 Ma, a shift that brings it one million years nearer to the present, and hence that much more distant from the Plio-Pleistocene hominid sample with which it has been compared here and by its discoverer. This massive alteration in reported date allows roughly 55 000 twenty-year generations between the initial sample of Plio-Pleistocene hominids if the sample studied by Holloway and Tobias remains dated at 3.0 Ma. This far longer interval exceeds by more than an order of magnitude the 5000 generations that were allowed in the two previous examples.

The quantitative consequences of this shift follow from the relationship below:

$$750 \text{ cm}^3 = 442 \text{ cm}^3 (1 + r)^{55000}$$

Now, $r = 0.00000963$, which is (not surprisingly) also more than a whole order of magnitude lower than the very first case considered, when the number of generations was believed to be only 5000. Building on a base of 442 cm³, the hypothetical first generation increment would be a minuscule 0.0043 cm³, or just 29 853 neurons added to the initial 3 100 000 000. Reducing the timespan between the two hominid samples by one million years, or about a third of the original estimate, changes the rate of compounding by a factor of 10. This alteration makes a profound reduction in what is asked of evolutionary change. Puzzlingly, however, some paleoanthropologists still refer to KNM-ER 1470 as 'exceptional' (e.g., Tattersall, 1995:138). Such a position can be held only if one considers the specimen outside of any temporal context. It is possible to ignore time, of course; in fact, the thesis that comparisons among samples representing taxa can be made independently of the times when their members lived and died is an operating assumption implicit in much cladistic work. However, the idea that time is irrelevant in assessing the likelihood of various ancestor–descendant relationships is not part of evolutionary biology in any of that discipline's conventional or traditional senses.

To return to one of Darwin's central operating principles, a large overall gain, here in brain size, need not imply a rapid *rate* of gain, as long as the elapsed geological time is sufficiently great. Small-brained hominids can be lineally ancestral to much larger brained hominids *even if* the amount of evolutionary change is small in an entire series of successive generations. A Darwinian perspective on long-term evolution makes sense on a geological timescale.

The explicit calculations made above underscore the point that the several million years that constitute the hominid fossil record are sufficient for substantial metric and morphological transformations, again even if rates of change in each successive generation are incredibly small. The actual compound interest calculations make it possible to get a feel for quantitative differences between populations, and how our perspectives on these are – or at least should be – affected once the times separating populations are taken into account.

Rates of change: an alternative approach

At the beginning of this exercise in exploring some quantitative aspects of hominid evolution, using endocranial volume as an example, differences between populations were expressed in absolute terms. Then calculations were added that made possible comparisons in terms of estimated rates of change. These seem small, but it would be good to have some more objective yardstick for making judgments about the numerical results. At what point do hypothetical rates of change become too large to be plausible?

Fortunately, there are objective ways of tackling these problems of evolutionary tempo and character state velocity. As a matter of fact, so many methods have been developed for measuring rates of change in evolution that not all of them can be considered here. Fortunately, many of them can be ignored, such as the numerous approaches that are geared to tracking rates of increase or decrease in numbers of taxonomic units over time, since such operations take us far from the paleobiological characters themselves. As Dawkins (1996) noted, in order to understand what happened as populations were pursuing adaptive peaks through time, it is necessary to know their basic features of size and shape. Then it is necessary to know by how much these features of hominids have changed as the result of organism–environment interactions through time.

Because morphologies can vary widely among invertebrates and vertebrates, a uniform metric is needed to make wide comparisons possible. Realizing this situation nearly half a century ago, J.B.S. Haldane (1949) offered a general solution. His approach was in keeping with his general belief that scientific knowledge is not particularly useful until it has been quantified. Haldane began by defining a standard unit of evolutionary change that he called the darwin. A darwin (abbreviated d) is defined to be the change by a factor e per million years, where e is the commonly used symbol for natural logarithms. Because Haldane's approach has become widely used, there are abundant comparative data to which it has been applied. A large number of these findings about evolutionary changes and the rates at which they occurred were summarized in a very useful paper by Gingerich (1983).

Gingerich summarized 521 cases in which rates of morphological evolution, measured over intervals of time from 1.5 years to 350 million years, were calibrated in darwins. He found that the rates fell into four major categories:

I. very high rates, averaging 60 000 d, determined in laboratory selection experiments;

II. high rates, averaging about 400 d, associated with colonization events, when populations expand into areas previously unoccupied by them;
III. moderate rates of about 4 d, associated with faunal changes following Pleistocene glaciation;
IV. low rates of about 0.1 d, common to changes recorded on longer timescales in the fossil record.

In his paper, Gingerich made an elegant argument for the necessity of carefully calibrating temporal scales and making due allowances where this cannot be managed. For example, the low rates commonly estimated over longer time periods in the fossil record span such long intervals that differences in morphologies or character states probably are swamped by interval length. This apparent interaction of absolute time and relative rate probably exists because the longer the time interval that is sampled in the fossil record, the more that periods of stasis and even reversals in the direction of change are likely to be averaged into the observed outcome. These cautions, like the overall mathematical strategy itself, apply with equal force to the compound interest approach used previously.

Quantitative methods used to calculate evolutionary rates share certain basic assumptions, advantages, and limitations, therefore it is possible to translate the previous calculation based on a compound interest approach to one given in terms of darwins, as follows:

$$\frac{\ln\ (750\ cm^3) - \ln\ (422\ cm^3)}{1.1\ my} = 5.75\ d$$

This rate is only moderately above the geometric mean for Gingerich's rate category III, post-Pleistocene mammals. Using either method, it appears that for the conditions specified, there is no problem in linking KNM-ER 1470 lineally to earlier, smaller brained Plio-Pleistocene hominids by rates of evolution that are as moderate in comparative terms as they had appeared from our first overview using a compound interest approach.

Regardless of how any rate of evolutionary change in character state is calculated, some basic points that bear on the reconstruction of hominid evolution must be made explicit. For one thing, there is still little consensus on the dating of the South African hominid sites, and some that have yielded small-brained hominids (such as Taung) have been dated to as recently as about 2.2 Ma. After following the several examples that have been worked through to this point, a reader preferring any alternative chronology or sampling assumptions should be able to set up the appropriate equation and solve for the corresponding rate; all that is needed is a calculator with a y^x function key (for the compound interest approach) or a natural log key (for Haldane's approach).

The various calculations performed here yield evolutionary rates that are constant over the respective time periods for each example. Some paleoanthropologists may raise the objection that we do not know that rates of change through time are constant, or even that we know that rates are *not* constant. This caveat is entirely proper, scientifically. As already noted, it is all but certain that over most intervals of time in the geological record, rates of change must be variable. Rate constancy is not an empirical observation, it is an assumption often used in the absence of more detailed information. But by now it should be clear that constancy is not a necessary assumption. It is possible to work up schedules of rates that fluctuated in magnitude and even in sign, negative as well a positive. But as long as the beginning and end points of the character state differences, as well as the time intervals separating the populations that manifest them, remain the same, so will the average rates of change that the calculations yield (Figure 9.1). The operating assumption of constant average rate constitutes no more than a practical working arrangement that must serve until better data on actual rate irregularities (which surely existed) become available through further research that subdivides the geological timescale into finer subdivisions with better chronological markers. Note that from the standpoint of explicit quantitative models, more and better data are expected to improve reconstructions of human evolution, not make them more intractable.

Those who might object to constant rates of change in morphological or metric traits of organisms should realize that they accept, knowingly or unknowingly, exactly comparable assumptions in other areas of work on which most researchers rely for the basic temporal framework of fossil finds. For instance, determinations of chronometric dates for geological deposits and the fossils contained in them are also based on assumptions of regularity in various physical and geological processes. As a very general case, radiometric dates are based on assumptions about constancy in rates of conversion of one isotope to another. The same generalization applies to stratigraphic scaling in geology. Thus the important paper on the Omo group deposits (in Turkana, Kenya, and Ethiopia) by Feibel *et al.* (1989:601) notes at one point: 'If one assumes that the rate of accumulation of sediments (including diastems) in a particular area is constant, then estimates of the age of undated strata can be made by linear interpolation between levels at which the age has been measured isotopically or otherwise. . .' Subsequently they noted 'Using reasonable estimates of the sediment accumulation rate it is found that the time between initial deposition and redeposition is on the order of 0.03 my' (Feibel *et al.*, 1989:602).

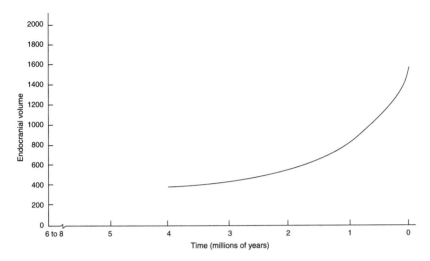

Figure 9.1. Trends in hominid endocranial volume over approximately four million years. The double exponential curve was fit to data of K. L. Beals by Henneberg (1988). Time range extended here in accordance with a hypothesis of hominid divergence from non-hominid primates about six to eight million years ago. The timespan from hominid origins to about four million years ago may represent a period of approximate stasis, since endocranial volume in a large sample of extant chimpanzees (Tobias, 1971) had an average of 383.4 cm³.

These assumptions of constancy, arbitrary as they may seem, are just as necessary in studies of human evolution as is a positive audience response in *Peter Pan*. In that famous children's play of the book, after Tinker Bell has drunk poison and is dying, Wendy comes to the front of the stage and implores the audience to 'Clap if you believe in fairies.' If they clap, Tinker Bell will revive and action in the play will proceed. While it is doubtful that most audience members really believe in fairies, they do want the show to go on, and nowhere in the history of the play's presentation is it recorded that an audience has failed to applaud as required. Conventions, like assumptions and the scientific models that incorporate them, are not necessarily true, but they are truly necessary.

Uneasiness surfaces in science whenever assumptions are made. Accepting conventions that we know are fundamentally untrue, or at least are oversimplified, may seem to entail unwelcome risks. The resultant feeling of unease certainly is justified, and some may feel that proceeding on such a basis is as unsatisfactory as building on sand. The core of the problem is that there are genuine difficulties in interpreting the hominid fossil record, and even close reliance on what appear to be established empirical facts can lead to substantial errors, as we already have seen in the chronometric age estimates of KNM-ER 1470.

Brains and behavior: acclimative potentials enhanced by evolution

What were early hominids doing with relatively large brains that increase volumetrically so markedly from the past to the present? Just as we used modern chimpanzees to establish a rough baseline for endocranial volumes that might be expected in early Plio-Pleistocene hominids, we can do the same thing for data on behavioral capabilities. Hominid ancestors from the base of our lineage had brains that already were larger than chimps, so there is no reason to hypothesize that their behaviors must have been any the less rich or flexible (also see Jerison, 1991:81).

The last several decades have seen detailed documentation of behavioral complexity among chimpanzees that would scarcely have been credited as recently as the 1950s. These African hominoids are capable of infanticide, grieve for their dead, hunt and kill other animals for food, and share some of the resultant meat with supplicants as well as collaborators. They also use natural objects to serve as tools, either unmodified as in the case of leaves used to staunch blood flow from wounds, or with trimming and shaping as in the case of sticks used to harvest termites. Documented cases of stones used to crack nuts are of particular interest in attempts by paleoanthropologists to interpret the archeological record, since the stones employed by chimps as hammers show no marks afterward that would distinguish them as tools. The failure of use to leave a definitive mark should be a caution against considering absence of evidence as evidence of absence. The archeological record has yielded tools from several areas known to have been inhabited by Plio-Pleistocene hominids, but direct associations between stone tools that must have been made by hominids and hominids that probably used tools are tenuous. At this point, with a fossil record for hominids approaching five million years and a record of stone tools only about half as long, one of the few safe bets is that documented instances of tools made by hominids will trend to earlier dates.

The capacity of chimpanzees to learn and transmit language is a topic of enormous complexity and controversy. One sceptic of chimpanzee linguistic capabilities (Jerison, 1991) stresses that in extant humans, language is controlled by an enormous neocortical system. This in turn implies that the human linguistic system is a perceptual–cognitive adaptation. The situation might have been different during the early stages of the pre-hominid–hominid transition, with this complex of perceptual and cognitive abilities arising first to meet one whole set of complex challenges, then – with the brain that had been modified by selection to meet early challenges – being used later for others such as language. Early communication systems might have provided a functional basis for human language as we know it.

Jerison envisioned early hominids shifting from forest to savanna for ecological imperatives, into the niche of a carnivorous predator. Of course, hunting and eating meat does not guarantee that large prey will be taken at all, nor does it preclude inclusion in the diet of other food sources. Wolves get a lot of calories by hunting mice, bears eat berries, and reindeer have been observed grazing on lemmings during the population peaks that result in the migrations of these small rodents. But there are special demands of a savanna hunting niche, including navigation of a large range by a socially integrated group. In wolves a typical territory is on the order of several hundred square kilometers, in contrast to a typical daily range of only a few hundred square meters (Pickford, 1988). To be successful a predator must have a good cognitive map of its area over time as well as space. To accomplish this, wolves have an elaborate scent-marking system and corresponding anatomical equipment (including olfactory bulbs fifty times as large as those of humans). The map of the real world is constructed by wolves from olfactory data processed by hippocampal, paleocortical, and neocortical structures.

Given the limited olfactory equipment of all higher primates, the paleobiological problem for a protohominid population adapting to the niche of a social predator could well also have used the hippocampus as a neural central processing unit for cognitive adaptation. This structure is polysensory, accessed not only by olfaction but also by other types of input. Jerison's theory is that the transition to a hominid grade was related to the evolution of the auditory–vocal channel that already is highly developed in primates. His picture is of an ancestor moving about its territory for purposes of marking, not by urinating and sniffing, but by vocalizing in various locations and sensing the sounds, talking in primitive tongues. Vervets are known to have a vocabulary comprising three 'words' respectively for eagles, leopards and snakes (Struhsaker, 1967; for a review see Quiatt & Reynolds, 1993). The hominid vocabulary could have been enlarged to encode more abundant environmental features, which also would have presented more combinatorial possibilities such as trees with and without fruit, and so on.

An interesting feature of Jerison's speculation is that human language could have begun as a cognitive rather than as a system of command-like signals and responses. Once there had evolved a cognitive system for knowing an extended range and naming its components, that knowledge could be communicated to other members of the population – along with other kinds of knowledge. Whatever one individual knew would become part of what another individual could know by merely listening to the vocalizations. This is the case, in fact, with echo-locating bats, which can interpret the calls and echoes of conspecifics. In the case of humans, linguistic communication produces a sharing not only of external reality but also of consciousness. In a rudimentary form, this sort of awareness might have catalyzed the shift that first separated us from the forest-based niche more common for apes. It also could have set the stage for the brain expansion already evident more than three million years ago, and elaboration of the complex behavior that has become a hallmark of human adaptation to environmental challenges.

10 *The paleobiology of widely dispersed hominids*

Introduction

Prior to the profound environmental changes that led to the evolution of semi-terrestrial and terrestrial papionines and hominids, vast tropical forests and woodlands in Eurasia and Africa had been occupied by ancestral monkey and ape populations (Andrews, 1992). Many of these disappeared with the increased aridity that caused the near-obliteration of the Mediterranean Sea. Thus when later hominids expanded numerically and geographically, they reoccupied a Eurasian territory that had become radically different – i.e. one that was more arid over broad areas and ecologically much patchier.

The evidence indicates that evolving hominids met these new challenges by adaptive strategies in which material culture and more flexible behavior patterns played relatively greater roles than had ever been the case among primates, including ancestral hominoids and the earlier African hominids descended from them. These new patterns exceeded those of papionines that, using their own complex of adaptive strategies, also had expanded across much the same area of Eurasia and Africa over a broadly comparable time period. It has been suggested that the advent of greater use of material culture in more advanced hominids may be attributed to the capacity for observational learning made possible by enhanced cognitive abilities (Beck, 1974).

Until hominids accomplished their major range expansion beyond Africa, much variation would have reflected evolutionarily-accrued adaptations to the variety of habitats available on that continent – e.g., desert, open savanna, woodland savanna, tropical forest – superimposed, of course, on characters of heritage. These characters of heritage sometimes are described as biological levels that have been added to successively in the past in much the same way as the build up of strata on the ocean floor, or the layers of an onion. The adaptations of organisms, however, accrue more like the structural elements in a habitation of venerable age. An analogy would be the lasting physical framework of a house that supports a roof now made of shingles instead of thatch; the heating system could include old fireplaces supplemented with gas heaters, as well as an air conditioner to deal with summer heat; and a garage that has been converted to a family room. In such a complex the latest bits stand out, but it is not always evident that some of the elements that seem new have been made over from older components.

In much the same way, the hominids who expanded from Africa retained, for example, grasping hands with flexibly manipulable fingers. These are features shared with all of the anthropoid primates for at least 35 million years. Onto this base was added differentiated power and precision grips. The nomen *Homo habilis,* literally 'handy man,' had been coined to reflect the belief that the hominids discussed in the previous chapter had these enhanced manipulative abilities. The new hominids also had evolved (through adaptations favored during previous major adaptive shifts) moderately large body size, a shortened lumbar region, a laterally-broadened trunk that facilitated thermoregulation (Ruff, 1991), and limb proportions that already reflected several million years of genetically-based biomechanical adjustments in proportions to meet the needs of walking, running, and striding, along with brain sizes that were at least double those encountered in ape and earlier hominid populations. All together, these features provided the adaptive basis for a significant range expansion by the middle Pleistocene hominid populations that commonly are referred to, though not universally, as *Homo erectus.* That geographic extension was accompanied by further expansion of brain size that brought members of these Old World populations into overlap with the lower end of modern values. This chapter explores the nature of that territorial expansion and its paleobiological consequences.

Systematics

The scientific literature on the systematics of archaic hominids is extensive and cannot be reviewed fully here. More detail can be found in the volume devoted to *Homo erectus* by Rightmire (1990) and a subsequent overview (Rightmire, 1998).

In discussions concerning the relative diversity or cohesiveness of hominids dispersed throughout Africa and Eurasia, over the course of about a century the broad range of opinion has swung, pendulum-like, from elaborated to minimalist, and back again. As noted in Chapter 3, the earliest discoveries from Java in the 1890s were classified as *Pithecanthropus erectus.* Similar (with endocranial volumes overlapping the lower end of the modern range, and on average only moderately larger than the Javan specimens), but not morphologically identical, fossils found several decades later in China were designated as *Sinanthropus pekinensis*. Repeated reconsiderations, during the 1950s and 1960s, tended toward a common assignment of these and other materials from Eurasia and Africa that were broadly similar in age, appearance, and associated artifacts to *H. erectus*.

In the 1980s, several researchers pointed out a number of cranial features (vault thickening, frontal keeling, an angular parietal torus, etc.) present in Far Eastern specimens but not in those from Africa. From a strict cladistic standpoint the features seen in the Asian skulls were considered by some investigators to be uniquely derived (autapomorphic) variants that marked the Asian clade as a side branch of human evolution. African populations were held to represent the phylogenetic mainstream. With the nomen *H. erectus* restricted to the Asian populations, African materials were designated variously as *H. ergaster* (Wood, 1994) and *H. leakeyi* (Clarke, 1990, 1994a,b).

Other workers in this area (Rightmire, 1986, 1990; Kennedy, 1991; Bräuer & Mbua, 1992; Harrison, 1993; Kramer, 1993; Bräuer, 1994) have maintained the position that the specimens from Africa as well as Asia belong to *H. erectus*. Judgments vary not only on the definition of this taxon but also on the specimens allocated to it. For Asia, Rightmire (1998) includes Trinil, Sangiran 17 and Ngandong in Java as well as Zhoukoudian Locality 1; in Africa his sample takes in Olduvai Hominid 9, KNM-ER 730, KNM-ER 3733, KNM-ER 3883, and KNM-WT 15000. Depending on where temporal and morphological limits are established, a number of European specimens, discussed below, also are considered to pertain to this taxon.

As a further complication, there is substantial phenotypic overlap between the hominid taxa *Homo habilis* and *H. erectus*, with the result that certain critically important specimens such as SK 847 from South Africa and KNM-ER 3733 and KNM-WT 15000 from East Africa are allocated to one or the other (or to *H. ergaster*, *H. rudolfensis*, or *H. leakeyi*) by various authorities.

Temporal and spatial distribution

The period of about one and a half million years beginning about 1.8 Ma and extending to approximately 0.25 Ma encompassed evolutionary advances within Africa, territorial extensions over much of Eurasia, and attendant increases in the total numbers of hominids living across the Old World.

On the basis of age and morphology, Africa has the earliest and most continuous record of advanced hominid populations. As noted above, regardless of their precise taxonomic assignment, specimens such as KNM-WT 15000, KNM-ER 3733 and KNM-ER 3883, as well as KNM-ER 1808, establish the presence of larger-brained hominids in East Africa as early as 1.6 to 1.8 Ma. The line is extended by L.996–17 at Omo, between 1.3 and 1.4 Ma, and Olduvai Hominid 9 at about 1.2 Ma. Specimens from Ternifine, Algeria, bring some of the African populations closer geographically to Eurasia, and also nearer in time, to about 0.5 Ma.

Many of the morphologically comparable hominid populations from Asia have been considered to have lived in the more recent past, with the long known Javan material from Djetis and Trinil horizons dated between 0.8 and 0.3 Ma, the classic Zhoukoudian Locality 1 specimens between 0.5 and 0.25 Ma, and more recently discovered Chinese hominids from Gongwangling, Jianshi, Yuanmou, Chenjiawo and Hexian may be distributed across the same half million year span between 0.75 and 0.25 Ma (Klein, 1989). However, according to some workers, Gongwangling in China may date from about 700 000 years ago (Woo, 1964, 1966), while dental remains from Yuanmou have a controversial date of as much as 1.7 Ma (Woo, 1966; Howells, 1980), consistent with the age of 1.6 to 1.7 Ma given for a fragmentary mandible from Longgupo Cave in Sichuan Province (Wanpo *et al.*, 1995).

In favor of the younger range of dates is the evidence that most or all of the first known hominid fossils in Asia – i.e., those from Java – are younger than a million years in age (Pope, 1983, 1988; Pope & Cronin, 1984). This view was conditioned by the belief that Javan faunas were dominated by endemic groups having few species in common with mainland Asia (de Vos, 1985). This was quite possibly due to the operation of a selective filter of some sort that restricted the movement of large mammals such as equids and hominids alike. One likely possibility for such a filter would be stretches of water, and it was reasoned that humans and other large mammals could have reached Java only during phases of low sea level that episodically exposed the Sunda shelf, roughly 3, 1.25, 0.9, and 0.45 to 0.65 million years ago (Pope & Cronin, 1984; Pope, 1988; Pope & Keates, 1994). During those periods, Java was connected to Borneo, Sumatra, Malaysia and thence to what now is continental Asia.

As mentioned in Chapter 9, the recent redating of several Javan specimens to much greater antiquity would make the Asian temporal distribution coeval with that in Africa. Swisher *et al.* (1994) report that potassium/argon analyses of geological samples associated with the skull of a hominid child from the Modjokerto site suggested an age of about 1.8 Ma, while other mineral samples associated with Sangiran sites may be from about 1.8 Ma. Nevertheless, there are questions about the reliability of the association between the hominid remains and the geological samples (Lewin, 1994).

The situation is similar for the European portion of the range. The Mauer (Germany) mandible as well as crania from sites such as Petralona (Greece) overlap morphologically in certain features (a robust mandible with receding chin for Mauer; a low, thick-walled cranial vault for Petralona) with some of the earlier African and Asian specimens. However, because some other features appear more advanced (Mauer has molars within the size range of extant humans, and at 1200 cm^3 the cranial capacity of Petralona is also in the modern range), these and other European specimens such as those from Arago, France, commonly have been referred to as 'archaic sapiens' populations. Uncertainties in dating of these specimens have fostered the idea that no European hominid fossils could be dated with certainty to before about 0.5 Ma.

The last several years have recorded a number of new finds, some of which appear to reinforce traditional chronologies. One is 'Boxgrove man,' known from a tibia found in Boxgrove in Sussex, England. Although this find was originally estimated to be about half a million years old, more recent revisions have indicated an age closer to 0.36 to 0.42 Ma (Bowen & Sykes, 1994; Roberts, 1994; Roberts *et al.*, 1994) . Yet other hominid fossils and associated tools appear to be older, with the site of Gran Dolina in the vicinity of Atapuerca, Spain, yielding age estimates in the vicinity of 0.8 Ma (Carbonell *et al.*, 1995; Pares & Perez-Gonzalez, 1995). Suggestions that hominids may have reached the western end of Eurasia sooner than previously accepted (Morrell, 1994; Roebroeks, 1994) have received further tentative support from finds at Dmanisi in the Caucasus region of East Georgia, where a hominid mandible associated with Oldowan tools is said to be associated with a Villafranchian fauna dated to about 1.8 Ma (Gabunia & Vekua, 1995).

Based on either *a priori* theoretical considerations or the fossil evidence – or both – the Eurasian hominids could have occupied these wider regions at any time from the emergence of advanced hominids in Africa to as much as half a million to three-quarters of a million years later. Discriminating between these two alternatives (or any variety of temporal possibilities in between) is a matter for future research. Although some of the newer finds nearly double the antiquity of hominid expansion out of Africa and into Eurasia and therefore might modify views about the tempo of evolution in the more recently occupied areas of the Old World, they pose no unusual problems for understanding the biology of earlier human populations. For now it is enough to know that approximately a million or so years ago the hominid range did expand dramatically.

Whenever this expansion occurred, the adaptive implications are the same, and of considerable interest.

Out of Africa: a population expansion

Regardless of just when it occurred, it is crucial to comprehend accurately the nature of hominid dispersal beyond the African continent. Despite increasing theoretical sophistication on the part of many biological anthropologists and other evolutionary biologists, the term 'migration' still is commonly applied to this movement or spread of hominids over a million years ago (e.g. Vigilant *et al.*, 1991). Such terminology is a curious, logically uncritical holdover from nineteenth century anthropology. In the early days, many of the scholars had received fine classical educations that gave them a great knowledge of history, including awareness of the vast population movements that had swept over parts of Eurasia from around the second century BCE – Angles, Burgundians, Franks, Huns, Jutes, Lombards, Ostrogoths, Saxons, Suevians, Visigoths, and the like. Many of these movements were genuine migrations, and the groups that were shifting or expanding their ranges were not deterred by the human populations that already occupied each region from earlier times. In some cases resident populations were displaced, in others they suffered great numerical reductions, and in yet other instances they were absorbed. In all the regions entered by new migrants, population structures were affected, as the incoming migrants churned up gene pools and left their marks on cultural and historical records. As we saw in Chapter 2, however, around the time that scholars first were writing about events in human prehistory, the geological timescale was very imperfectly known. In particular, the human evolutionary past was believed to have had a very much shorter duration than the weight of later evidence has established. Yet the scientific literature still contains accounts and maps that uncritically illustrate the 'migrations' of early hominids and even of their nonhuman primate predecessors (Nei, 1993). In some quarters it still is thought that, as a matter of course, that was how humans and animals got from one region to another – they migrated.

As a matter of fact as well as logic, large-scale human movements are overwhelmingly unlikely to succeed – or even begin – unless groups have two critical elements in their material culture. The first is some efficient means of transportation, and the second is a supply of food that can nourish the migrants on their journey. The means of transportation could be sleds or wagons, the last depending on the invention of the wheel.

Domesticated animals could be ridden (horses) or used for draft (oxen, sled dogs). Without these elements, however, movement of a mass of people – the troops of hundreds to thousands involved in the historical migrations – are all but impossible. For example, infants and very young children could hardly be included without risk of loss from exhaustion in a group covering long distances without transport. Exclusion of young offspring also would preclude many women in their fertile years; most of them already would have one or more children that simply could not be abandoned. Depending on the route to be traveled, an alternative to draft animals would be watercraft of some size and sophistication, implying the invention of steering mechanisms, oars or sails, and so on.

With regard to food supply, a large migrant population moving through unfamiliar territory could not be certain of obtaining sufficient food by hunting or collecting. We all have heard of armies on the move 'living off the land,' but the phrase is a euphemism. Armies without their own supplies did not live off the land, literally. They lived off the productive labors of its existing inhabitants, confiscating the livestock, crops, and stored foodstuffs of the populations unfortunate enough to live in the area traversed.

Only the earliest human range expansions, those that the fossil record suggests took place from Africa into Eurasia between one and two million years ago, could have moved people into unoccupied territories. Those hominids were members of bands of hunters and gatherers. For their small groups, areas previously untapped by intelligent, behaviorally flexible culture-bearing large mammals initially would have been so rich in resources that they would have supported rapid demographic expansions of populations, which rapidly would approach carrying capacities at levels sustainable by Paleolithic technologies. At a first level of approximation, if every pair of parents produced only four surviving offspring, populations could double every generation. More sophisticated demographic analyses would modify this estimate without altering very much its force. Successive generations of progeny would form a wavefront, expanding wherever not checked by physical barriers such as lakes and oceans or unsuitable ecological zones such as deserts (Bartholomew & Birdsell, 1953). Paleoindians expanding through the Americas provide one reasonably well-documented example of this phenomenon in a context free of taxonomic complexity.

The joint requirements for transport and food make it improbable in the extreme that mass migrations occurred much before the Neolithic period (when tools of ground or polished stone replaced Paleolithic or Mesolithic chipped stone tools), about 8000 to 10000 years ago. The same cultural conditions that engendered the domestication of plants and animals also led to the invention of writing, initially for temple record keeping, a few millennia later. As the outcome of these interconnected developments, the last few thousand years – the period of recorded history – have included precisely the time in which migrations were the most likely to have occurred.

Paleolithic populations did not migrate – they expanded their numbers and territories. These range expansions were done without very much movement of people at all, merely small bands of foragers budding off and relocating just a few kilometers further in search of food each generation. As a natural consequence of such slight ripples outward, new areas would become populated, and these newly-populated regions in turn would constitute the edges of the base populations from which the next generation would move out. The inevitable consequence of this expansion pattern is that all areas along the way became occupied by hominids, to whatever local carrying capacity was permitted by ecological factors.

This detailed treatment of the pattern by which Pleistocene hominids spread is provided as the basis for a corollary. That is, as populations expanded and territories became occupied, the result would not have been a few scattered, separate human groups isolated from each other by large distances, but, rather, broad networks of populations in which the more distant groups maintained genetic contact through numerous intermediates. Under such circumstances, gene exchanges among these groups would be the norm. Furthermore, the adaptive genetic and phenotypic changes that accrued then continue to exist now. These have been documented in detail by human biologists who have studied adaptations of extant humans to heat, cold, and other specific environmental challenges. Human biological diversity is maintained despite the expected homogenizing tendencies of gene flow. This persistence is an implicit argument for the action of evolutionary forces (probably a combination of selection and genetic drift) that produce and maintain some degree of regional differentiation among human populations, without the need for speciation.

Regional differentiation in the face of gene flow is an uncomfortable concept to many anthropologists, since it is widely believed that any appreciable degrees of genetic and morphological differentiation require isolation, lest the alleles underlying the traits be swamped. Yet as we saw in Chapter 6, there are data that contradict the idea that gene flow necessarily swamps genetic differentiation. To return to a point made there, Jolly (1993:85) has noted that hamadryas baboons evidently evolved derived characters, both physical and behavioral, presumably through adaptation to desert habitats. However, 'this evolutionary change in the population's phenostructure demonstrably did *not* [Jolly's emphasis] entail the appearance of genetic isolation.' In Jolly's terms, hamadryas baboons did not have to become a fully differentiated species to be genetically, morphologically, and behaviorally distinguishable – or to remain biologically adapted to the environments in which they live. He notes, however, that the question of just how hamadryas became specialized without speciating is an issue of some interest; important work remains to be done in this area.

Whatever zygostructures might have characterized middle Pleistocene hominids are unknown. However, archeological evidence suggests that prior to the Neolithic period most humans lived in small bands that inhabited relatively stable territories. Most gene flow presumably would have occurred through matings between members of immediately adjacent populations. For example, human hunter–gatherer groups that survive today have systematic (and often highly complicated) arrangements for mate exchange among adjacent bands, either to make up for a shortage of mates of appropriate demographic characteristics or to ensure amicable relationships, or for other reasons.

Based on what we know from studies of other large mammals species, the most suitable model for understanding the initial human spread out of Africa is one of gradual or episodic numerical expansion over increasingly vast territories by networks of populations that continued to exchange mates. This is not to say that no area ever became secondarily depopulated. There must have been some areas once occupied that later became uninhabited. These gaps have come about as the result of special, changed circumstances (that is, some areas became uninhabited because they became uninhabitable), or else expansion through the area would not have taken place to begin with.

The argument that Eurasia was populated by population expansion, rather than direct migration, still rests on logic rather than physical evidence, except of the negative sort. The archeological record from about a million or so years ago is devoid of evidence for means of transport other than bipedal locomotion. Therefore, when hominids first went from anywhere in Africa to the areas of Eurasia occupied within the last two or so million years, the method must be: they walked. That the journey was spread across generations of hominid populations whose collective lives spanned multiple millennia is not an observed fact but seems more plausible than any of the other possibilities.

Lewin (1994) estimated that the Middle Pleistocene hominids, even at a modest rate of territorial expansion of 10 km per generation, could have covered the distance from East Africa to Java in about 25 000 years. The same distance conceivably could have been covered by a few particular hominids, walking at a rate of about 10 km a day, in under a decade. Despite the striking contrast between 250 centuries and a tenth of one century, though, the quantitative difference between these two hypothetical modes of expansion is so small that it would be dwarfed by the error term in any radiometric determination for the age of datable materials.

Phenotypic patterns

The expansion beyond Africa and into Eurasia took place after hominids had undergone considerable amounts of morphological change from the levels reached by various Plio-Pleistocene hominid populations. Endocranial volume increases were accompanied by expansion in the postorbital region of the skull, various dental reductions, and moderate changes in trunk and limb proportions.

Once human populations began to spread across the wider areas of Eurasia as well as Africa, the potential existed for further morphological and genetic differentiation. It might be expected, *a priori*, that these changes would have taken place on an expanded scale. As we will see later, there does seem to have been biological adaptation to a variety of climatic zones along the lines expected (e.g. Roberts, 1978). But while the patterns followed predictable lines, the extent of variation is less than was the case for earlier hominids restricted to Africa alone. Although hominids expanding from Africa into Eurasia roughly doubled the area inhabited, and entered a greater range of ecological zones, the resultant populations are less diverse biologically than the Plio/Pleistocene hominids taken all together, at least as far as we are able to infer from known remains (Rightmire, 1990).

This reduced diversity is at least in part a consequence of temporal scaling. The known African hominid fossil record exceeds four million years in duration, and the differentiation of a lineage that gave rise to hominids probably began as far back as six or eight million years ago. In contrast, after hominids expanded into Eurasia as well as Africa, the subsequent fossil record extends over perhaps half that span, or less, with most estimates clustering in the range of one to two million years.

If evolutionary differentiation were proportionate to time alone, the expected diversity in middle Pleistocene hominids would be about half that in the previous African record. Putting the increased geographic range and the decreased time together, at the roughest first approximation we might expect the two factors to approximately cancel out. However, the actual extent of variation seems to be even less than expected, although any treatment of this subject raises a question of how the diversity should be measured – in taxonomic, morphological, molecular, or other terms. This point will be revisited later, but a relatively lower level of morphological and metric variation is broadly accepted.

Discussions of the reasons have persisted for decades. Weidenreich (1947) supported the existence of just one hominid species from the Middle Pleistocene until the present, a viewpoint that has been reiterated by Wolpoff and colleagues (1994), among others. In contrast, Tattersall (1995, 1998) has argued that the dozen or more hominid species recognized by Wood (1987, 1992, 1993, 1994) and others (Wood & Chamberlain, 1986; Wood & Collard, 1999) on morphological grounds actually underestimate the number of separate taxa that existed, since not all variation is expressed in skeletal traits. He is correct in his perception of the existence of diverse morphotypes, but as we have seen in previous chapters, morphological diversity and species definition are different phenomena.

The lesser amount of hominid biological diversity since the Middle Pleistocene suggests the operation of some other factor. Cultural influences represent a category worth considering in discussions of hominid adaptation and evolution from at least the Middle Pleistocene. Archeological evidence increasingly is building toward documentation that material culture appeared earlier in the evolutionary record than formerly thought, with Oldowan assemblages now reliably dated to as far back as 2.5 million years ago (Semaw *et al.*, 1997). This picture is complicated by the appearance of what has been termed 'technological stasis' in the Oldowan complex for over a million years. Whether the inference of a long period without cultural change is accurate, or whether that impression is erroneously conditioned by the fact that the record is limited to lithic remains for the most part, is uncertain.

Some authorities have combined aspects of several of the preceding points – the existence of multiple hominid species in relatively narrow time zones with little variation within each species – to the point of theorizing that the taxon *H. erectus* was characterized by biological stasis (Howells, 1980; Delson, 1981; Rightmire, 1981; Stanley, 1981; Kennedy, 1983; Day, 1982). This position was examined in detail by Wolpoff (1984), who used up to 13 different craniodental measurements on 92 individual *H. erectus* fossils subdivided into three broad groups that he characterized as low resolution temporal samples. The variables included cranial capacity plus eight linear measurements on the cranium and three on the mandible, as well as breadth of the first lower molar. The fragmentary nature of the fossils ensured that not all measurements could be taken on every specimen.

Wolpoff's results showed that, with few exceptions, the differences between earlier and later *H. erectus* samples were marked and significant. Taking into account estimates of the time separating the samples, he was able to calculate evolutionary rates in darwins (one of the approaches used in Chapter 9 for cranial capacity). Rates varied from −0.16 for breadth of the mandibular corpus at the level of the first lower molar to 0.27 for cranial capacity (which was reduced to 0.09 through dividing the reported rate by three to make the volumetric rate more comparable to a linear rate). In eight out of the 13 traits, the rates exceeded the geometric mean of rates observed by Gingerich (1983) for fossil vertebrates, and the average for all 13 traits was 0.10 darwins. Overall, the pattern was one that combined an expanding vault with reductions in the masticatory structures, thus casting doubt on any hypothesis that the changes in vault dimensions could be accounted for by a hypothetical overall increase in body size. Wolpoff concluded that the hypothesis of stasis in *H. erectus* can be rejected, and noted further that since this taxon has repeatedly been cited as one of the best examples of stasis in the fossil record, then stasis may be less common overall than generally is thought.

Adaptive capacities of Middle Pleistocene hominids

In the paleontological record, detection of evidence for various adaptive mechanisms is constrained by the nature of the available data, as has been seen already in Chapters 8 and 9. Fortunately, as the populations studied approach our own more closely in time, the amount of evidence increases and some of the adaptive strategies and mechanisms seem more familiar.

Short-term behavioral and cultural acclimations

Relatively simple stone tools of the long-continued Oldowan tradition were found with the remains of hominids discussed previously in Chapters 8 and 9. It appears that in some parts of the world, the period of relative constancy in the cultural record was broken by the appearance of the Acheulean complex at about 1.6 to 1.5 million years ago (Isaac & Curtis, 1974; Asfaw *et al.*, 1992; Dominguez-Rodrigo, 1996). This event falls in the time range of the initial hominid expansion beyond Africa, which generally has been placed in the vicinity of a million years ago, but as noted above, may have taken place up to nearly two million years ago (Swisher *et al.*, 1994).

A useful overview of the material culture of broadly Middle Pleistocene hominids is given by Klein (1989). As already noted, across Africa and Eurasia stone artifacts are associated with their skeletal remains. Views dating to the work of Movius (1944, 1948, 1949, 1955) have held that during this phase of human evolution there were two different cultural traditions, the Acheulean area extending from Europe and Africa eastward to India, characterized by the production of hand axes; and another area extending eastward and southeastward into the remainder of Asia, characterized by the manufacture of choppers and chopping tools. More recent finds have tended to blur this sharp distinction. Western sites such as Vertesszöllös in Hungary, Clacton in England, and Bilzingsleben in Germany lack hand axes. In the other direction, hand axes have been recovered at some eastern Asian early Paleolithic sites such as Lantian in China and Chon-Gok-Ni in South Korea. Among other suggestions is the possibility that the absence of hand axes at many sites may be due to the lack of stone with the necessary qualities for their production.

Where Acheulean technologies could be used, they produced sharper-edged tools, at the same time making more efficient use of raw materials. Butzer (1971) has shown that Acheulean artisans were able to turn about 0.5 kg of stone into 20 cm of cutting edge, about four times as much as that produced by the earlier Oldowan toolmakers. This was managed by prior preparation of a stone block in such a manner that each flake required little or no further retouching. The gains seem to have resulted both from more careful selection of raw materials and improved manual dexterity.

It sometimes is remarked that Middle Pleistocene hominids made re-markably little use of bone and that there were no animal bones that had been deliberately fashioned into standardized tools (Klein, 1989:217). However, as documented by the extensive work of Mary Leakey (1971), at least 105 animal bones from Bed II at Olduvai Gorge show modifications reflecting human use. These include parts of long bones, some of the longer ones having been split lengthwise and flaked or otherwise worn on the broken ends. There also are shoulder blades with chipped and battered edges. Massive knee caps and foot bones from elephants and other large mammals show pitting and battering that suggests that they were used as anvils. There also is at least one bovid tibia flaked to a point, and a bifacially flaked hippopotamus tibia. Although these bone artifacts are more modest quantitatively and qualitatively in comparison to patterns exhibited culturally by later humans, like the lithic evidence, they suggest continuity rather than discontinuity of cultural traditions.

Certain other categories of implements known from later periods, such as recently discovered wooden spears dated to approximately 400000 years ago (Dennell, 1997; Thieme, 1997), would not have survived in deposits five to ten times older, as would have been necessary for them to have formed part of the Oldowan record.

There is one fascinating minor behavioral similarity to that exhibited by a previous hominid found at Omo, mentioned in Chapter 9. This is the occurrence at Konso-Gardula in East Africa of a mandible attributed to *H. erectus* that shows interproximal grooving that suggests the use of either sinews or probes made of bone or wood inserted between the teeth. Similar grooving appears on the teeth of Neanderthals and later humans at many sites over the world.

Developmental plasticity

Environmental influences on bone remodeling

The femur that was discovered at Trinil in Java as the result of paleontological research carried out by Eugene Dubois in his 1891–92 field season was significant primarily because it helped to establish the existence of early humans in Java in ancient times, as discussed in Chapter 3. This same fossil also provided some scope for application of the Dutch scientist's medical training.

The Trinil femur's feature of primary phylogenetic significance was a long straight shaft entirely consistent with upright posture. Although a commonplace observation now, this point was highly controversial when the same behavioral correlate was disputed even for Neanderthals (e.g. by Boule, 1913). In addition, though, the Trinil femur exhibits an extensive bony growth near the upper end of its shaft. This feature long has been considered abnormal by anatomists and anthropologists, but the nature of the pathology was disputed. Rudolf Virchow, the nineteenth-century German anatomist and pathologist, diagnosed the growth's cause as syphilis. Others have suggested that the projecting mass represented the overgrowth of bone following a badly healed fracture.

Much later, Soriano (1970) suggested an alternative cause for the Trinil femur pathology – fluoride poisoning. Soriano, working at the University of Barcelona, Spain, discovered a strikingly similar pathology on the femur of a man undergoing autopsy following his death from cirrhosis of the liver after long-continued alcoholism. Further inquiries identified additional cases in the area, all of them among habitual drinkers of a local table wine to which the manufacturer had illegally added sodium fluoride (which is colorless and tasteless) to control fermentation. Analysis of the patients' bones documented a concentration of 8 ppm of sodium fluoride, twice the level diagnostic of bone fluorosis.

In the case of the Trinil hominid population, there was a different potential source of fluorine contamination – one that was entirely natural. The Javan hominid remains were associated with thick beds of ash from volcanic eruptions; in fact, these beds have been used to date the fossils. Soriano's search of the literature uncovered cases in which sheep grazing in a volcanic region of Iceland had developed bone fluorosis following eruptions that left fluoride-containing residues on grasses and plant leaves. Soriano's suggestion was that the fruits and vegetables consumed by some members of early Javan populations may have been contaminated by an ancient form of air pollution.

Alternative explanations also have been proposed. Conroy (1997) notes that lesions similar to those on the Trinil femur can be produced by myositis ossificans, an inflammatory disease of voluntary muscle characterized by the deposition of bone. Similar symptoms are shared with diaphyseal aclasia, a disease of autosomal dominant inheritance. Littleton (1999) discusses criteria for differential diagnosis between skeletal fluorosis and other disorders producing similar symptoms.

As an added controversial note, questions have been raised about the association of the Trinil femur with the skullcap, and suggestions have been made that the evidently more modern morphology of the long bone may indicate that it represents a more advanced hominid rather than another example of mosaic evolution (Day & Molleson, 1973; Day, 1984). Whichever of these several explanations for the characteristics of the Trinil femur survives reanalysis, other examples establish that injuries and pathologies were not uncommon among earlier hominid populations.

Another example illustrating the richness of our knowledge about later phases of the hominid fossil record focuses on a specimen from the Upper Member of the Koobi Fora Formation near East Lake Turkana in Kenya. Beginning in 1973, B. K. Kimeu made the first in what has become a continuing series of finds that, together, have yielded much of the skeleton of an adult female individual designated as KNM-ER 1808 (Walker *et al.*, 1982). Her remains comprise one of the most complete specimens attributed by paleoanthropologists to *H. erectus* prior to the discovery of KNM-WT 15000.

The geological age of KNM-ER 1808 was given as about 1.6 ± 0.1 Ma. The specimen's sex was diagnosed as female by comparison of the innominate parts with corresponding skeletal elements of KNM-Er 3228 (Leakey, 1976) and Olduvai Hominid 5 (Day, 1971), which are considered to be male and female specimens, respectively.

Appendicular regions of the KNM-ER 1808 skeleton exhibit pervasive pathological lesions. These comprise subperiosteal diaphyseal deposits of bone with a coarsely woven texture, up to 7 mm thick in places, with thinning toward the metaphyses. Pathology is confined to the outermost cortex, where the coarse new bone includes enlarged, randomly placed lacunae that are sharply demarcated. In contrast, there is no remodeling of the underlying bone. These manifestations all are consistent with a diagnosis of chronic hypervitaminosis A (Walker *et al.*, 1982).

Cases of this disorder are exceedingly rare in modern times and apparently limited to highly unusual circumstances. The few suggested occurrences have been among polar explorers, who reported acute toxic effects after the consumption of livers from polar bears, seals, or husky sled dogs (Gerber *et al.*, 1954; Shearman, 1978). Rodahl & Moore (1943) identified the toxic ingredient of seal and polar bear liver as vitamin A. The symptoms of acute hypervitaminosis A include vomiting, diarrhoea, headache, convulsions, and peeling of the skin. The condition can be fatal. The chronic form of the disorder, which is uncommon and more difficult to diagnose, has been recognized only more recently (e.g., Pease, 1962).

The suggestion initially advanced to account for evidence of hypervitaminosis A in KNM-ER 1808 was related to a dietary shift among hominids. The first recorded association in the Koobi Fora succession of stone artifacts with animal bones occurred roughly 200000 years before the KNM-ER 1808 specimen lived and died. Following the onset of meat consumption, it was theorized that hominids might have taken some time to learn which parts of particular animal carcasses might be toxic. With 'learning' spread over 10000 generations, some selection for behavioral elements might have taken place (many modern children dislike the taste of liver). In any case, carnivore livers contain much higher concentrations of vitamin A than do comparable organs from herbivores. While hominid diets may have involved the consumption of some carnivores early in the history of meat eating, evidently such practices decreased later. Under this interpretation, KNM-ER 1808 represents an instance in which the physiological consequences of experiments in cultural evolution remain evident.

While accepting the diagnosis of vitamin A intoxication made by Walker and colleagues, Skinner (1991) has proposed an alternative source for the ingested toxic material – consumption of broods in the nests of the East African bee *Apis mellifera*. Under this interpretation, the search for bee brood and other immature insects could have been a component in foraging behavior, within a generalized subsistence strategy of the sort evident in chimpanzees (Wrangham, 1975; Goodall, 1986).

Further work might establish whether vitamin A hypervitaminosis in KNM-ER 1808 was the result of dietary continuity with nonhuman primate predecessors (as suggested by Skinner), or a shift to new behavioral modalities (as hypothesized by Walker and his colleagues). The principle remains, however, that the fossil record can and does record cases where pathologies can not only be detected, but linked to rather specific instances of earlier humans behaving recognizably as living individuals.

Adolescent growth spurt

In chimpanzees the evidence for an adolescent growth spurt is at best equivocal, as noted in Chapter 6, and there is little, if any, evidence bearing on this point for Plio-Pleistocene hominids. But the Nariokotome skeleton, KNM-WT 15000, is complete enough to allow this point to be addressed for a specimen attributed to *H. erectus* or a closely allied taxon.

Smith (1993) used three developmental indicators (stature, epiphyseal closure, and dental maturity) to estimate the physiological age of the Nariokotome hominid, and concluded that the estimated dental age of 11 years was at variance with the estimated skeletal age of 13 to 13.5 years. Against a mean stature of 152 cm reached in many populations in the age range of 12 to 15 years, the Nariokotome youth's stature was estimated at 160 cm (Ruff & Walker, 1993). Smith therefore inferred that he showed stature consistent with a chronological age of about 15 years. Proceeding from the assumption that all maturity indicators are in agreement in modern adolescents in their respective growth spurts, Smith further concluded that *H. erectus* had not yet evolved the extant human developmental pattern that includes a clear cut adolescent growth spurt.

Using a collection of eighteenth- and nineteenth-century British skeletons from the Spitalfields collection as a reference sample that included 10 juveniles of known ages (between 5.4 and 18.5 years), Clegg & Aiello (1999) showed that in all but one specimen, estimated dental maturity underestimates age, by amounts ranging from ten months in the youngest to five years in older individuals. As in an earlier study by Lampl & Johnston (1996) they affirmed the difficulty of estimating age from maturity indicators. Although the Nariokotome youth's age for stature was greater than that predicted from his skeletal maturity, Clegg & Aiello concluded that their study lends no support to the hypothesis that *H. erectus* lacked a modern human growth spurt. Before this matter can be considered resolved, however, there is a great need for larger samples, including skeletons of known age, for a diversity of populations other than those of European ancestry.

Genetic adaptations

Climate and body form

The far wider geographic distribution of populations at this level than had been the case for earlier hominids makes it possible to test more fully the applicability of general ecogeographic rules such as those formulated by Bergman (1847) and Allen (1906), discussed in detail in Chapter 5. Christopher Ruff (1991) has carried out a major investigation of this sort that examined the relationship between climate and body shape in human evolution.

As has been pointed out by Roberts (1953, 1978) and others, the ecogeographic rules relate body morphology to climate, being special cases of the more general theoretical relationship among body mass, surface area, and ambient temperature. If predictions are followed, the ratio of surface area to body mass should increase in warmer regions and decrease in colder ones. In general, these predictions are met for humans as for other animals.

Ruff used a cylinder as the simplest regular geometric model that reasonably approximates the shape of the human body. An interesting property of this model is that in order to maintain a constant ratio of surface area to mass with changes in stature, breadth (i.e. the diameter of the cylinder) must remain constant. From this he made two predictions: first, that within similar temperature zones, variations in height should be accompanied by little or no variation in body breadth; and second, that between different temperature zones, absolute breadth should vary by increasing in colder climates and decreasing in warmer climates. In applying this model to living and fossil hominids, Ruff used bi-iliac breadth as his proxy for body breadth. This variable is commonly measured in anthropometric studies of living populations, and can be reconstructed for some fossils. It has further advantages of being based on identifiable bony landmarks and being affected relatively little by sexual dimorphism.

The data from extant human populations accorded well with expectations. Within similar temperature zones, populations differing in average stature varied little in average bi-iliac breadth, thus becoming more linear as they increase in stature. Furthermore, populations living in different temperature zones manifested large systematic contrasts in bi-iliac breadth, with those in colder climates having wider bodies.

Three fossil hominid skeletons were sufficiently complete that bi-iliac breadths and statures could be estimated with reasonable accuracy: the A.L. 288–1 and STS 14 australopithecines, the KNM-WT 15000 *H. erectus*, and the Kebara 2 Neanderthal. Results showed that the pelves of the two australopithecines were wide relative to their overall body sizes, while the Nariokotome specimen had a much narrower pelvis relative to stature, though just below the range of sample means in living human populations (Figure 10.1). The Kebara specimen was wider than that of any of the African hominids, and above sample means for extant European and northern Asian population samples – as would be expected for the temperate zone that it inhabited.

In a thoughtful discussion, Ruff noted doubts in some quarters that the associations between body form and climate observable in populations represented by fossils should still be found in living groups. For example, it has been suggested that buffering via technological innovations such as clothing, shelter, and fire is so successful that genetically-based morphological adjustments represented by ecogeographic rules should not be necessary (e.g., Scholander, 1955, 1956). Similarly, it has been argued that physiological acclimatization is more important than inherited differences in body form (Strydom & Wyndham, 1963). In response, Ruff stressed that all adaptive modes should be additive rather than necessarily offsetting each other, and that a small physiological advantage that might be useful only rarely could be selected for in the long run. Additionally, not all climatic stresses are avoidable; working out of doors in the heat or cold is widespread still in many human populations. Last, even given the possibility that cultural buffering against environmental stress has increased from the past to the present, it is reasonable to assume that unless the genetically-based morphological adaptations were selected against or at least selectively neutral, they should be retained, as appears to be the case.

One role that Ruff did see for technology is a possible reduction in the need for physical adaptations to become so different among human populations that they would have contributed to speciation. Instead, like Mayr (1956), he saw the likelihood that gene flow would contribute to the establishment of clines, particularly after human culture made it possible for our ancestors to expand into regions of the world that previously had been uninhabitable.

Skin color

Unlike body proportions, soft tissue variations usually cannot be documented directly from the remains of fossil hominids. However, as we saw in Chapter 8, much the same kind of inferences about the geographic distribution of skin colors follow from an understanding of environmental factors and the nature of their influences on human phenotypes. In Chapter

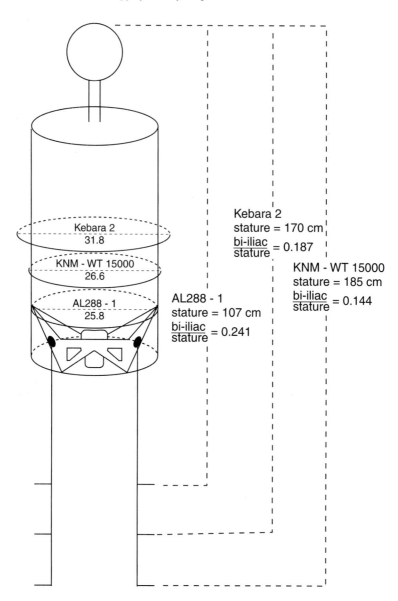

Kebara 2
stature = 170 cm
$\dfrac{\text{bi-iliac}}{\text{stature}} = 0.187$

KNM - WT 15000
stature = 185 cm
$\dfrac{\text{bi-iliac}}{\text{stature}} = 0.144$

AL288 - 1
stature = 107 cm
$\dfrac{\text{bi-iliac}}{\text{stature}} = 0.241$

$\dfrac{\text{Kebara 2}}{31.8}$

$\dfrac{\text{KNM - WT 15000}}{26.6}$

$\dfrac{\text{AL288 - 1}}{25.8}$

Figure 10.1. Pelvic bi-iliac diameters and statures for three fossil hominids. Small
australopithecines (e.g., AL 288-1) as well as very tall later hominids (e.g.,
KNM-WT 15000) have absolute body breadths within the modern human
subtropical–tropical range, while hominids from cold temperate climates (e.g.,
Kebara 2) have absolutely wide body breadths combined with relatively shorter
statures. Similarly, among extant modern humans, variation in stature greatly
exceeds variation in body breadth with the resultant shape patterns chiefly
reflecting thermoregulatory considerations. Based on data and inferences in Ruff
(1991).

8 it was hypothesized that following a shift to living in open areas and the evolution of morphological adaptations to bipedal locomotion, very early hominids lost the covering of hair that had been the primitive condition in their chimpanzee-like ancestors. This sequence was followed by the evolution of higher levels of melanin production in the integument.

Following their expansion from Africa to Eurasia, the later hominids discussed in this chapter would have become the first populations of our ancestors to exhibit a range of skin colors approaching the diversity seen today. According to the arguments developed by Jablonski & Chaplin (2000), dark pigmentation would have been retained in tropical regions to protect against UV-induced photolyis of folate, a metabolite essential for normal embryonic neural tube development and for spermatogenesis. Outside the tropics, the prior evolution of deeply pigmented skin would have been reversed, in order to permit the synthesis of previtamin D_3 in the skin. This compound is subsequently converted to vitamin D_3, a compound that is essential for calcium absorption and normal development of the skeleton.

Deficiency of this vitamin can cause death, impairment of movement, and also pelvic deformities that can interfere with normal childbirth (Neer, 1975). High levels of melanin in the skin increases the length of time needed for exposure to UV light needed to induce synthesis of previtamin D_3. Where the duration of UV exposure is suboptimum for appropriate vitamin synthesis, the risk of rickets is heightened, an occurrence documented in recent migrants from the Indian subcontinent to the UK, in whom hypovitaminosis D and rickets show a marked north–south gradient that is inversely proportionate to UV dosage (Henderson *et al.*, 1987).

Geographic zones representing different potentials for UV-induced vitamin D_3 synthesis have been defined. Zone 1 is the area in which the average UV medically equivalent dose (UVMED) was sufficient to catalyze previtamin D_3 throughout the year. This zone comprises the area from five degrees north of the Tropic of Cancer to five degrees south of the Tropic of Capricorn. Zone 2 is the area in which the UVMED was not sufficient for previtamin D_3 synthesis during at least one month of the year. This zone covers large areas of human occupation in the northern hemisphere. Zone 3 comprises the area over which the daily UVMED dose, averaged over the entire year, was not sufficient to catalyze synthesis of previtamin D_3. This zone includes northern Eurasia and northern North America where skins are lighter (Jablonski & Chaplin, 2000).

Populations that are believed to have inhabited their current locations for the last 10000 to 20000 years conform closely to predicted values for skin reflectance. These findings for the distributions of populations with various skin colors conform extremely well to the predictions made by Livingstone (1969). The model that he hypothesized assumed polygenic inheritance with four unlinked loci. Assuming no dominance at these loci, just a six percent difference between the genotype with optimum fitness, and that most strongly selected against, could produce the entire known range of human skin color phenotypes within 800 generations. With dominance the rate of evolution would be slower, taking about 1500 generations to produce the same outcome. Given a human generation length of 20 years, these models predict that human skin colors could be transformed from dark to light, or the reverse, in 16000 to 30000 years. Such changes would appear instantaneous in the human fossil record.

Prospects for further paleobiological study

The inferences drawn in the preceding section represent only a sample of the types of questions that can be explored within a paleobiological framework for populations of dispersed hominids. Ideally, all of these questions would be framed in the form of testable hypotheses, in the manner that corresponding research topics are treated in the study of living human populations. Much of the research summarized in this chapter suggests that considerable progress is being made toward the unification of human biological studies in past and present populations.

11 *Paleobiological perspectives on modern human origins*

Introduction

Following their spread from Africa to Eurasia a million or more years ago, hominids entered a prolonged phase of contact across these areas that allowed for the multidirectional transfer of two kinds of information – cultural and genetic. The cultural contact is documented, straightforwardly, by the association of human remains across the entire inhabited area with one or another manifestation of the Developed Oldowan/Acheulean tool complex. Tools of these related traditions are found at sites that arc from Kabwe in South Africa through Bodo in East Africa, westward through Europe at sites such as Arago in France and Steinheim in Germany, and eastward from Zuttiyeh in Israel through Narmada in India to numerous localities in China, including Dali and Maba. These continuities of material culture in themselves imply human contact and hence gene flow. This implication is supported further by the numerous broad phenotypic similarities among the human fossil remains discussed in greater detail below.

At the same time, other patterns delineate *in situ* adaptation to local and regional environments. There are contrasts in tool complexes between sites in the eastern and western ends of the Eurasian geographic continuum, of which just one major example is the lack of an Asian Acheulean (Pope & Keates, 1994; Schick, 1994). It is known that identifiable Levallois flakes and hand axes do occur at some Chinese sites, although infrequently (Pope, 1997). As a partial explanation of cultural differences in ecological terms, Pope (1983) has argued that early Asian (i.e. Oriental) populations adjusted to the scarcity of stone by using other suitable materials for toolmaking in areas that were densely vegetated or characterized by extensive karst limestone deposits by, for example, substituting bamboo as a raw material. Similar patterns are duplicated in Europe. In France, for example, Tayacian lithic assemblages that are contemporaneous with Acheulean sites elsewhere lack bifaces but have high concentrations of sidescrapers and other flake-based tools that prefigure the Mousterian (Klein, 1989). Again, as in Asia, explanations include differences in the local availability of raw materials or site-specific activity patterns (Pope, 1983).

The African record presents a coherent continental mosaic made up of component local variants over time and territory that has continued without any break until the present period, suggesting half a million years of interrelated biocultural evolution extending to the present. It should be noted that this continuity does not equate to simplicity, since there is abundant and compelling evidence (summarized in Lahr, 1996:281) for multiple cultural contacts, human dispersals, and cultural distinctions within Africa. As just one example, Masao (1992) has made a case for environmental specializations represented by two temporally overlapping traditions represented in the middle Pleistocene of Tanzania. There, the more archaic appearing Stillbay appears in open sites, while the Sangoan and Charaman assemblages are associated with riverbeds and more heavily forested coastal settings. In the case of Africa, these differences in cultural traditions are not used to support hypotheses about biological differentiations among human populations.

There is less agreement on the degree and duration of continuity outside of Africa, with the cultural and biological records being read differently. Klein (1989:251) has noted that 'from a strictly archeological perspective, there is little to distinguish early *H. sapiens* from *H. erectus.*' Some investigators see the same continuity in hominid fossil remains, while others argue for complete replacement of previous Eurasian hominids by a relatively recent wave of anatomically more modern humans emanating from Africa between 100000 and 200000 years ago. In the context of understanding modern human origins, it is all but impossible to ignore the debates over continuity versus replacement, because these commonly juxtaposed alternatives pervade nearly every question in human paleobiology over the last quarter of a million years. Although the questions raised about modern human origins are widely ranging (literally, they cover much of the Old World), they come into their sharpest focus in considerations about the fate of one regional group of populations, the Neanderthals of Europe and the Near East. In these debates, names sometimes have taken on great symbolic significance, so that designation of this group as a subspecies of anatomically modern humans, *H. s. neanderthalensis*, implies a rather different evolutionary fate than the species-level designation, *H. neanderthalensis.* Yet at another level, the problem of modern human origins is considerably more complex than can be encompassed within the limits of an inherently dichotomizing taxonomic system, as was discussed in Chapter 2. The closer we come in time to the present, the more obtrusive this historically-determined interpretive framework becomes. Part of the reason for dissatisfaction with it is that nearer in time, the paleontological record itself becomes more continuous

– with more abundant fossils, many character state distinctions become less sharp. Another part of the reason is that taxonomic dichotomization, however it can be made to fit the morphological data, fails at the molecular level in populations as closely related as the ones in this time frame. Finally, in the behavioral and cultural phases extending from the Middle and Upper Paleolithic to the present, we are grappling with neither just biological issues of character state change nor only ecological matters of territorial expansion and contraction, but at a higher level, with what, in Foley's terms, it means to become human (Foley, 1995).

Systematics

In traditional taxonomic terms, the human populations discussed in this chapter begin with *H. erectus* and end with *H. sapiens*. Framed in nomenclature that simple, the central paleobiological problem would seem to constitute an exercise in explaining the pattern of species succession – how did one widely-distributed hominid species give rise to another that has become even more widely distributed? In fact the problem was conceived in terms this simple, or simplistic, just several decades ago (Coon, 1962). The confusion and misunderstandings generated by the answers given in that work have had continuing negative consequences for research in this area.

Coon's interpretation of the hominid fossil record of the last million years held that the *H. erectus–H. sapiens* threshold was crossed independently several times in the Old World. The conceptual contradictions inherent in such a view helped to polarize later workers (although the roots of the divergent views had been present much earlier). At one end of the interpretive continuum, Wolpoff *et al.* (1994) have argued that the taxon *H. erectus* should be sunk, and all of the material attributed to it and later populations included in a single lineage leading to extant humans. At the other extreme, Tattersall (1986) has advocated designating multiple distinctive hominid morphs as species, with the consequence of recognizing several taxa, including *H. sapiens*, *H. neanderthalensis*, and *H. heidelbergensis* as recent descendants of *H. erectus* (or *H. ergaster*).

Taxonomic disagreements of this sort can influence interpretations of the biology of present populations as well as those of the past. Regarding past populations, Brace (1997) has noted that a common solution that recognizes the morphological differences between Neanderthals and their successors is to designate the former as *H. s. neanderthalensis* and the latter as *H. s. sapiens*. Marks (1997) examines the implications of such an approach for discussions about relationships among extant human groups. If Neanderthals are classified as a subspecies, then some anthropologists find it disturbing to have no formal category that reflects the still smaller differences that exist among extant human populations inhabiting major geographic areas of the present day world – traditionally referred to as races. Fortunately, this aspect of the problem has been dealt with definitively by Templeton (1998) and the broad implications of his research will be discussed later in this chapter.

The situation is not improved very much if the nomenclature is made less formal, as long as the conceptual dichotomization remains. Thus designating Neanderthals (or their predecessors) as 'archaic *H. sapiens*' in contrast to 'anatomically modern *H. sapiens*' does not solve the problem. As noted by Brace (1997) it still is necessary to find some suitable term for populations or specimens commonly accepted as 'anatomically modern *H. sapiens*' (such as those from the Skhul site at Mount Carmel, Israel) but that are phenotypically more archaic than extant human populations.

Regardless of what these earlier populations are called, several large questions remain concerning their fates. As outlined cogently by Foley & Lahr (1992), the way toward their resolution lies in recognizing that the last million years has not encompassed just a single event but in all likelihood several, the joint outcome of which has been the global distribution of modern *H. sapiens*.

Distribution in time and space

Considered in the broadest terms, the archaic *sapiens* group existed in the time range of about 500 000 years to 200 000 years ago, succeeding the populations widely referred to as *H. erectus* in Africa, the Far East, Near East, and Europe.

In Africa, the time frame from about 200 000 to 100 000 years ago encompasses specimens such as Kabwe in South Africa and LH 18 from the Ngaloba Beds at Laetoli, Tanzania. According to Smith (cited in Foley & Lahr, 1992) LH18 may be one of the uncommon African specimens in this group for which the association between the hominid and the dated material is certain rather than only probable. Resembling both Kabwe and Ngaloba are two crania from the Jebel Irhoud cave in Morocco. In many of their dimensions, the North African specimens overlap the range of variation in European Neanderthals.

In the same time period, the Asian fossil record is quite abundant and, also, morphologically complex. Important specimens derive from

Chaoxian, Changyang, Dali, Dingcun, Jinniu Shan, Maba, and Xujiayao (Conroy, 1997). Similar to the situation in Africa, some of these specimens bear resemblances to those seen in Neanderthals. For example, the Dali cranium bears pronounced supraorbital tori, and Maba combines this feature with rounded orbital outlines similar to those seen in La Chapelle and other 'classic' Neanderthal specimens.

Within Europe, the older archaic *sapiens* group (including Arago, Bilzingsleben, Mauer, Petralona, and Saccopastore, among others dating back several hundred thousand years) preceded and showed gradual evolutionary trends leading through two time-successive groups with increasingly marked shifts toward what later coalesce into the Neanderthal pattern. The first of these groups comprised Atapuerca, Biache, Swanscombe, and Steinheim; the second, Ehringsdorf, Krapina, and Saccopastore.

Based on the samples noted briefly here, some authorities believe that the transition from archaic *sapiens* to anatomically modern populations to have taken place along a temporal gradient that commenced earlier in Africa and variably later in Eurasia. However, matters of preservation, as in the case of the Klasies River Mouth material, and associations between datable materials and hominid specimens, as with Border Cave (Wolpoff & Caspari, 1997) exert considerable influence on all of the interrelated interpretations.

Phenotypic features

Abstractly considered, treatment of the origin of modern humans from their predecessors should be an easier task in paleobiological analysis than the comparable exercises undertaken in previous chapters. There are serious conceptual difficulties involved in reconstructing aspects of the paleobiology of Plio-Pleistocene hominids, which stood and walked erect much as we do, but had to cope with life's challenges using brains at the outset no larger than those of chimpanzees, augmented by marginal levels of material culture. Neither this niche nor its occupants exist any longer. In contrast, hominids of the later Pleistocene had skulls that, despite their visible morphometric differences, enclosed endocranial volumes that matched and exceeded those of extant humans (Henneberg, 1988). These early humans employed their mental abilities in the production of material cultures, including the Mousterian, that in some ways were functionally equivalent to those of the Upper Paleolithic (Movius in Brace, 1997). The extent and intensity of disagreement on the issue of modern human origins attests, nonetheless, to the problems of paleobiological reconstruction that remain large even as the temporal distance from our predecessors becomes small.

In a comprehensive approach to this problem, Lahr (1996) gives an insightful suggestion for the persistence of these problems in the interpretation of the recent human paleobiological record. In her view, the evolution of modern populations combines two issues: the origin of modern humans from an archaic ancestor and the origins of the differences among living populations. These are separable in theory, but they commonly are treated together.

Against the background of an intensive decade in research on modern human origins (Smith & Spencer, 1984; Mellars & Stringer, 1989; Trinkaus, 1989; Bräuer & Smith, 1992; Hublin & Tillier, 1992; Nitecki & Nitecki, 1994), Lahr's publication, *The Evolution of Modern Human Diversity* (Lahr, 1996), provides one of the most comprehensive and widely ranging overall treatments of the subject. The core of the work provides a refreshingly modern treatment of craniological data. One of the volume's methodological distinctions is an extensive appendix that provides descriptions and photographs of the grades used in scoring the morphological regional continuity traits. Anyone who has done this sort of work can readily appreciate the painstakingly detailed effort that has gone into it. Everyone who has tried to interpret other treatments in which morphological traits are discussed in more general terms will grasp its value in advancing discussions of future research in this area, even if they do not concur with all of the investigator's conclusions.

Although the origin of modern humans is a worldwide matter (Foley & Lahr, 1992), there are multiple reasons why a disproportionate amount of attention has focused on Europe. First, as discussed in Chapter 3, hominid fossil material was recognized there first, and the original Neanderthal find was among the earliest. Second, the European Neanderthal specimens comprise one of the largest fossil hominid populations, sampling over 60 sites with more than 10 relatively complete specimens: Spy 1 and Spy 2 from Belgium; La Quina, Le Moustier, La Ferrassie, La Chapelle-aux-Saints, and St. Césaire from France; Monte Circeo from Italy; Forbes Quarry from Gibraltar; and the Neander Valley from Germany.

In the cranial skeleton, Neanderthals had braincases that were long and wide but lower than those of present humans. At the rear they had an occipital bone commonly with a bulging occipital bun and suprailiac fossa. Anteriorially, above a brow ridge that was continuous or arched strongly above each eye socket, the forehead rose moderately. Below the brows the midfacial region projected prominently and the malar bones sloped backward. The chin was absent or only weakly developed, and at the posterior end of the dental arch on each side was a retromolar gap. The incisors and canines were large, and the molars commonly were taurodont, enclosing large pulp cavities.

Postcranially, Neanderthal skeletons had a more massive overall appearance than those of present humans. Many specific anatomical details are related to this pervasive feature. Thus the vertebral column is heavy, the scapula is broad and exhibits a dorsal sulcus on the axillary border, uncommon in subsequent populations (it does occur at levels of several percent in human population samples in which other skeletal features exhibit independent correlates of high levels of physical activity). The humerus is strongly developed, and the radius tends to be laterally bowed. In the lower limb the femur has a cylindrical shaft with a stout cortex. The tibia is short and relatively massive, and the kneecaps are relatively thick. Not all features reflect robusticity alone, however; for example, in addition to having ilia that are rotated dorsally, there are thin and elongated pubic rami.

There is always the risk that a summary description of this sort will emphasize differences at the expense of commonalities (in cladistic terms, Neanderthals are said to be characterized by numerous autapomorphic traits) and form without reference to function. It should be noted, therefore, that some aspects of Neanderthal morphology overlapped features of anatomically modern humans. The simplest example of such an overlap concerns endocranial volume. Although sample sizes are small, so that the observed range appears to be lower than in living human populations, the average exceeded that in extant humans (Henneberg, 1988).

Not all of the morphological features that are thought to distinguish Neanderthals from anatomically modern humans stand up to close scrutiny. One example of a hypothetical distinction was offered in a recent restudy of the long-known temporal bone from Arcy-sur-Cure. Various human fossils have been recovered from the site since 1859, which is reported to be one of the latest known occurrences of the Chatelperronian industry, and a particularly valuable one since it includes a rich bone and ivory industry and ornaments such as pierced and grooved animal teeth and ivory rings. At Arcy-sur-Cure the Chatelperronian has been dated to 33 000 years ago (Leroyer & Leroi-Gourhan, 1983; Leroyer, 1987). Among Upper Paleolithic industries, the Chatelperronian of northern Spain and central through southwestern France is considered by some to be critically important for understanding the Middle to Upper Paleolithic transition in western Europe. This is because the Chatelperronian seems to have developed from certain Mousterian industries, and combines Middle Paleolithic elements with Upper Paleolithic blade and bone technologies.

Hublin *et al.* (1995) proposed several possibilities to explain the Chatelperronian genesis. One of their alternatives saw Chatelperronian and Aurignacian traditions emerging at several different locations as parallel technological inventions by modern humans, perhaps with Neanderthals making some genetic contribution. A second alternative saw modern human invaders introducing the Aurignacian, with the Chatelperronian arising through acculturation of the latest western Neanderthals during a period of contact with modern humans.

The biological affinity of the Chatelperronian toolmakers was held to be critical in differentiating between these two alternatives, but the available skeletal material has been considered ambiguous. Although the remains from layer Xb at the Arcy site included a temporal bone preserving the petrous, mastoid and tympanic regions, the estimated age at death of the individual (about one year) had made difficult identification of its population affinity by traditional morphological criteria.

Noting that the bony labyrinth within the temporal bone attains its adult morphology before birth, Hublin *et al.* (1995) were able to make use of computerized tomography to measure its dimensions. They compared these with known Neanderthal and Upper Paleolithic populations as well as extant humans. Their reported conclusions were that the Arcy-sur-Cure juvenile temporal bone was closer to the mean of Neanderthals in three dimensions (semicircular canal radii) and one index that reflected the relationship of the posterior canal to the horizontal plane formed by the lateral canal. Going beyond that point, however, Hublin and his colleagues (Hublin *et al.*, 1995) also maintained that in the Neanderthal labyrinth 'apparent lack of continuity with modern human morphology could be seen as an argument in support of distinguishing between neanderthals and modern humans at the species level.'

In fact, the semicircular canal radii of Neanderthals are not discontinuous with those of later humans (Figure 11.1a–d). They overlap extensively (approximately 50 percent, depending on the dimension) among Neanderthal, Upper Paleolithic and extant anatomically modern humans (Eckhardt *et al.*, 1997). Moreover, data on mammalian hybrids show that there is no reliable relationship between labyrinthine dimensions and probability of exchanging genes between pairs of taxa. As just one example, *Macaca niigra* and *Papio cynocephalus* are part of the broadly interfertile papionine group, but have canals with percentage differences about three times greater than those between Neanderthals and anatomically modern humans.

This current example illustrates well the extent to which questions about the relative roles of behavior, physiology, development, and genetics can become confounded. It appears that Hublin and his colleagues are inferring reasonably that the Arcy-sur-Cure juvenile was a member of a Neanderthal lineage, and lived in a context that suggests that other group members employed an advanced technology. But nothing about the data or analysis supports any sharply-drawn discontinuity between Neanderthals and their anatomically distinguishable successors. Indeed, the anatomical features studied support continuity. Since that is the case, it is simpler to infer that anatomical and cultural continuity were part of a process of transformation rather than replacement. A similar argument can be made for the case of St. Césaire as well (Mercier *et al.*, 1991).

From the first Neanderthal discovery in Germany through finds that are continuing in a rather steady stream still (e.g., Rak *et al.*, 1994; Akazawa *et al.*, 1995), however, it is clear that members of these populations that preceded anatomically modern humans did have some distinctive characteristics. Yet from that point until now the more important questions have concerned the biological significance of these characters. Often they have been used as symbols of taxonomic status and phylogenetic relationship, sometimes with implications that they are non-adaptive markers of ancestry rather than parts of a functioning organism. As noted previously in several places (Chapters 9 and 10), however, morphological or morphometric distinctions do not constitute automatic bars to ancestor–descendant relationships between populations. Methods exist for dealing with such differences in continuous phyletic lineages..

Discontinuous traits often are proposed as apomorphies, unique character states believed to be restricted to a given taxon and hence diagnostic of it; yet new (and larger, or differently constituted) reference samples often illustrate occurrences in other populations. In this regard, Frayer (1992) demonstrated that several traits suggested as Neanderthal apomorphies, such as the horizontal-oval form of the mandibular foramen, do occur in appreciable frequencies in anatomically modern humans from European subfossil samples.

Differences in continuous morphometric traits also are used to argue against certain ancestor–descendant relationships. Frayer (1997) has taken up this question as well, comparing a large array of craniofacial and dental dimensions among several samples – early Neanderthals, late Neanderthals, Upper Paleolithic, Mesolithic, and Neolithic. Time estimates were used to convert average metric differences among samples into rates of change measured in darwins.

For anterior tooth lengths and breadths, rates of change between the Neanderthal and Upper Paleolithic samples do not represent the highest evolutionary rates in the study. The most rapid rates of change in these

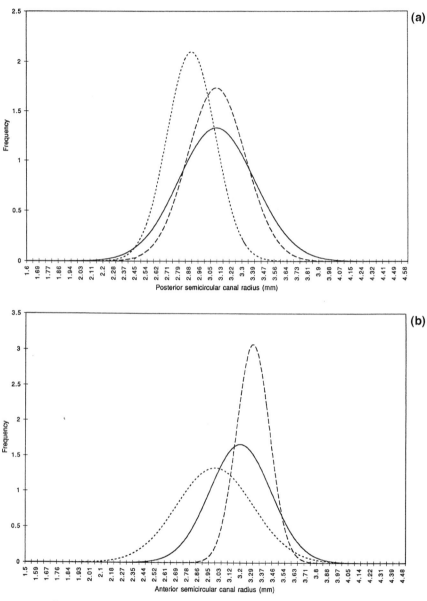

Figure 11.1. Normal distributions of human semicircular canal radii. Curves are
bounded by solid lines (extant modern humans, M), long dashes (Upper
Paleolithic humans, UP), and short dashes (Neanderthals, N). For the posterior
semicircular canal (a), total overlap among all three curves is 58.12 percent, with
overlap between EM and UP samples (87.52%) exceeding N with UP (62.74%)
or N with EM (63.89%). For the anterior semicircular canal (b), total overlap
among all three curves is 41.51 percent, with greater continuity between N and
EM samples (69.94%) than between UP and EM. For the lateral canal (c),

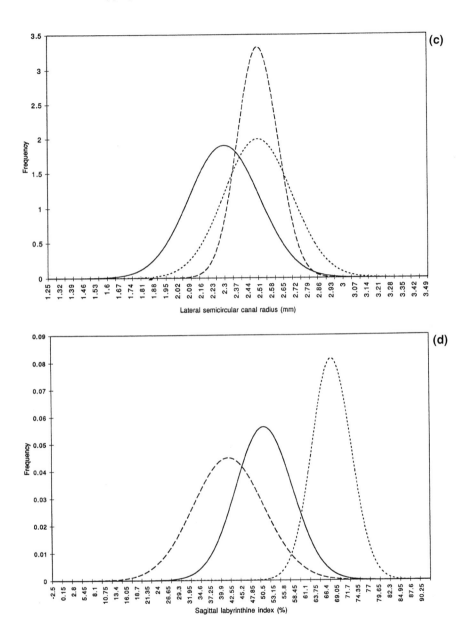

overlap among all three curves is 50.14 percent with both the N and UP (75.80%) as well as N and EM samples (62.52%) overlapping more than do UP and EM (50.59%). The sagittal labyrinthine index $[(i/(s + i)) \times 100]$, (d), shows greatest overlap between UP and EM (56.63%), less between N and EM (15.32%), and modest continuity between N and UP (5.66%). Note that the index appears to understate dimensional overlap among human populations in semicircular canal measurements. Data from Spoor *et al.* (1995).

dental dimensions were observed between the Mesolithic and Neolithic samples, which were approximately 20 times the rates of change observed between Neanderthals and their successors in Europe. None of the evolutionary rates in the study was particularly high; all actually fell within the lowest of the four rate categories delimited by Gingerich (1983). Rates of change between both the early and the late Neanderthal samples and the early Upper Paleolithic sample were within the magnitude of change for the same traits found among later groups of recent *H. sapiens*. Frayer concluded that, contrary to the commonly stated argument that not enough time exists for European Neanderthals to be ancestral to subsequent Europeans, no acceleration in evolutionary rate is required for acceptance of an ancestral–descendant relationship.

Adaptive capacities

Acclimation

Mousterian tool assemblages, which include various sizes of flaked stone points, both short and elongated, side scrapers, plus Levallois flakes and points, often are compared unfavorably with the Upper Paleolithic toolkits that succeeded them. These earlier perspectives, however, are changing. By now it is known that at least some of these 'rudimentary' Mousterian-era stone tools were hafted using a sort of bituminous glue (Boeda *et al.*, 1996). Wooden spears also were fabricated and used to great effect, as witnessed by the tip of one lodged some 120 000 years ago in the rib cage of an elephant at Lehringen, Germany. Other implements and ornaments made from bone, antler, and ivory also are now known (Mercier *et al.*, 1991).

Before their skeletal remains were identified as representing populations of humans earlier than our own, Neanderthals were known from remains of their material culture, the Mousterian. After associations were found, the relationship was so recurrent that it gave rise to the assumption that if Mousterian tools existed at a site, they must have been made by Neanderthals; and when Neanderthal skeletal remains were discovered, they must have represented hominids who had produced Mousterian tools. This biocultural equation, long accepted, was brought into question by the discovery of the St. Césaire specimen in association with an Upper Paleolithic Chatelperronian assemblage; coupled with Bordes' view that the Chatelperronian is an outgrowth of the local Mousterian, this find is compatible with suggestions of biological continuity. As with the Arcy-sur-Cure temporal fragment, as noted earlier in this chapter, it is difficult to separate behavioral and cultural evidence. Both are immediately pertinent to understanding acclimations and their direct effects, and to distinguishing these influences from others that are more likely to arise from developmental or genetic factors.

Among the more readily distinguishable short-term environmental effects visible in Neanderthal skeletons are high levels of trauma, as noted by Trinkaus (1989). When these studies were updated (Berger & Trinkaus, 1995) it was established that virtually every complete Neanderthal skeleton above the ages of 25 to 30 years at the time of death displayed some type of injury. More detailed analysis disclosed that nearly one-third of the specimens studied exhibited head and neck trauma. Parallels were drawn with similar patterns seen in rodeo cowboys, with the inference that Neanderthals, too, may have had frequent close contact with medium to large-sized ungulates. Hunting activities, in particular using thrusting spears, could be one explanation.

Jelinek (1994) has built up a more general picture of western European Neanderthals as a human population living near its adaptive limits – exposed over much of its range to a cold climate, from which it was sheltered by modest levels of technology. In this view, each healthy individual would have had to spend prolonged intervals engaged in vigorous physical activities to obtain sufficient calories to maintain the core temperature necessary for survival. While cultural mechanisms could have palliated stresses of this sort, over numerous generations there could have been feedback effects visible at other adaptive levels. In addition to injuries, Neanderthal skeletal remains are marked by developmental features that are diagnostic of extreme levels of muscular exertion. Over even longer periods, selection could operate to produce the body proportions observed by Ruff (1991) in the postcranial skeleton of the Kebara 2 Neanderthal.

If there were a cultural shift to modern toolkits and related technologies, there is the possibility that a combination of immediate developmental changes (which even could occur between two successive generations), supplemented by relaxed selection operating over longer periods, could have produced some significant morphological changes. In this regard, Brace (1964:12) has emphasized that logically 'the selective forces responsible for these changes [producing skeletal gracilization] had to have taken place in the Mousterian for the key morphological responses to have become apparent in the guise of the 'modern' form that generally coincides with the Upper Paleolithic.'

Developmental

As implied above, short-term acclimations in the cultural realm are likely to have shaped patterns of development through the lifespan. Adjustments made possible by plasticity, in turn, could have helped to buffer Middle Paleolithic populations during periods in which selection could have modified frequencies of genes underlying various morphological complexes to produce results of the sort estimated by Frayer (1997). This sort of pattern resembles what has been described in Chapter 5 as the Baldwin effect.

As in the case of morphology, developmental phenomena sometimes are invoked to accentuate differences between Neanderthals and their successors. For example, in a short publication that is chiefly about the use of computer-based technologies to aid in reconstruction of skulls, Zollikofer *et al.* (1995) commented that 'marked quantitative differences in skull morphology can be demonstrated between modern humans and Neanderthals at an age of only 3–4 years. The existence of these clear quantitative differences at such an early age considerably strengthens the interpretation that Neanderthals and modern humans are separate species.' Such reasoning, while common, does not find much reliable support. Bacteria causing such diseases as tuberculosis can be endemic in populations, present at birth, and cause modifications of the skeleton; the same observation holds for many nutritionally-based disorders such as rickets. Conversely, many conditions known to have a clear genetic basis and skeletal manifestations show late ages of onset, a subject on which there is extensive data (Eckhardt, 1984, 1989).

In addition to the patent injuries discussed in the preceding section, skeletons of Neanderthals from the Shanidar site in Iraq exhibit high levels of osteoarthritis and related joint pathologies (Trinkaus, 1983). These indicators of stress are consistent with a general pattern (including general skeletal robusticity, rugosity of attachment areas, and cortical bone thickness) suggesting extremely high levels of energy expenditure in the course of heavy physical activity. Placing these figures in perspective are observations on athletes who carry out repetitive activities. Jones *et al.* (1977) demonstrated that male tennis players exhibit playing arms in which the distal humeri show 35 percent thicker cortical bone than on the contralateral side; the comparable figure for female tennis players is a 29 percent gain.

There is a burgeoning scientific literature in which developmental observations on populations of living primates, nonhuman and human, are being systematized and applied to the study of past populations. Although much of their work has focused on developmental patterns in earlier Plio-

Pleistocene hominids, Mann and his colleagues (Mann *et al.*, 1990) provide insights that are pertinent to problems of modern human origins. Wood (1996) also has recognized the value of such studies, tracing them back to the pioneering research of Adolf Schultz in 1924 (discussed in Chapter 6), and exploring their specific applications to hominid paleobiology. As an example of one specific finding applicable to the study of modern human origins, Tompkins (1996) has shown that although patterns of dental development have continued to evolve from the Upper Pleistocene to the present, Neanderthal and early modern samples shared similar features. While this expansion of interest in ontogenetic development in Neanderthals and other archaic populations is encouraging, much remains to be done before results can be characterized as other than consistent with some degree of continuity between earlier and later populations.

The role of genetic adaptations in modern human origins

Since the beginning of the 'mitochondrial Eve' controversy (Cann *et al.*, 1987), when genetic studies are mentioned in the context of modern human origins, it is generally expected that reference is being made to molecular studies, particularly discussions about the timing of the hypothetical replacement of antecedent Eurasian populations by a postulated secondary wave of migration out of Africa (Stringer & Andrews, 1988). But there has long existed the potential for studies of genetic adaptation to contribute to an understanding of the multiple, overlapping problems in this realm of research – not only through molecular genetics but also from the areas of population genetics and developmental genetics.

Against this hopeful prospect, it should be realized that attempts to provide genetic perspectives on the evolution of modern populations, and their relationships to more archaic antecedents, have produced rather mixed conclusions. The examples provided here do not constitute an exhaustive review, but rather a sampling of some of the work that has been carried out since the 1950s.

Genetic drift

One of the earliest attempts to explore the potential for concepts from population genetics to understanding Neanderthal paleobiology, including evidence from ecology, anatomy and material culture, was that of Howell (1952). This paper still is cited as a landmark study (e.g., Jelinek,

1994). Howell's thesis was that many of what have been characterized as extreme features of Western European Neanderthals may have resulted from a period approaching genetic isolation (increasing the possibility for genetic drift) of a small population of hominids who were subjected to heavy stress (from natural selection) in a periglacial environment that accompanied the early phases of the last glacial advance. In the theoretical state of paleoanthropology at the time Howell's paper was written, it provided a creative turn from descriptive morphology.

From a later vantage point, some reconsideration might be in order. One component in the argument that the classic Neanderthals represented a substantially isolated hominid group is the belief that Western Europe was, in fact, cut off by glaciers during the Würm. In a population already of limited size, extreme directional selection could, in theory, have further depleted genetic variation. This possibility contributed to the view that drift and selection were synergistic in their action of molding identifying Neanderthal characteristics such as facial form.

Modern satellite mapping and computer generation of possible ecological zone shifts, however, add new perspectives to the view developed by Howell (CLIMAP Project members, 1976; see also West, 1977 in Lahr, 1996). Even after the ice-covered areas are deducted from the land area that would have been available for hominid populations in Europe, the remaining zone comprises up to half a million square kilometers. Most of this territory would have been covered with savanna and dry grasslands. Densities of hunting and gathering populations in comparable regions in the historical present range from 2–3 to 20–25 inhabitants per square kilometer. From these figures it is possible to estimate, though only to a rather crude first approximation, that the Middle Paleolithic population of Europe could have been on the order of tens of thousands per generation (Eckhardt, 1979:552). These estimates are higher than many hypothesized for this time period (e.g. Schnider, 1990), but are consistent with those recently made by Templeton (1998) of a worldwide human population of up to 500 000 people at about that time.

Population sizes on the order of tens of thousands are not really very small from the standpoint of potential for genetic drift, as long as there was gene exchange among the bands or other subdivisions of the overall population. What we know of the distribution of material cultural remains suggest that social contacts did in fact exist, as would be consistent with the observed behaviors of extant hunting and gathering groups.

An alternative view of European Neanderthal paleobiology during this time period sometimes is suggested, with a less numerous population overall and subpopulations more widely dispersed and less frequently in contact. While this reconstruction cannot be ruled out on the basis of direct evidence, its implications for other statements about Neanderthals should be considered. The potential for genetic drift of course would be higher within each of the small population subdivisions. But to the extent that drift did occur, it should have led to genetic differentiation among the various groups. However, one of the most commonly repeated generalizations about western European Neanderthals during this phase of existence is their high degree of morphological uniformity.

More recent studies summarized by Lahr (1996) do not indicate isolation of the European region occupied by Neanderthals under peak glacial conditions, with the possible exception of the Italian peninsula between about 25000 to 35000 years ago. Reductions in population density are possible, but remain to be quantified. Against this background, the hypothesis that genetic drift played some role in the evolution of European Neanderthals cannot be ruled out. However, given the repeated affirmations that many of their morphological characteristics conveyed biomechanical advantages, a suggestion of uniform drift in directions that would have been favored adaptively in any case does not appear necessary.

Hybridization vs. mutation

One of the most puzzling applications of genetic terminology to the Neanderthal problem was carried out by Thoma (1958), who analyzed characters in near eastern Neanderthals in an attempt to distinguish between hypotheses of 'hybridization' or 'transformation.' He studied 27 complex anatomical features: 19 for the skull; two for the dentition; and six for the postcranial skeleton. Characters of the skull included the angle of inclination of the forehead and occiput, form of the occipital torus, shape and robusticity of the supraorbital torus, size of the mastoid process, form of the temporal bone, size of the sphenoid wing, morphology of the tympanic bone, shape of the malar region, proportions of the orbit, characteristics of the maxilla, sizes of the nasal opening and nasal root, angle of inclination of the upper face, breadth of the palate, mandibular robusticity, development of the chin and size of mandibular ascending rami. Dental features included the degree of premolarization of the incisors and canines (that is, the development of basal tubercles on these teeth) and form of the pulp cavity (presence or absence of taurodontism). Postcranial characters included form of the cervical vertebrae, ribs, bowing of the radius and femur, proportions of the ilia, and stature.

Thoma's sample included 14 specimens from Tabun (I and II), Skhul

(I–X), Galilee and Qafzeh 5. Where possible the character state in each specimen was scored as representing trait expressions that corresponded to a state found in (1) a classic Neanderthal; (2) a 'less typical' Neanderthal, with trait expressions exceeding those of Neanderthal predecessors from the Riss-Würm interglacial; (3) a 'somewhat atypical' category intermediate between Neanderthals and modern humans; or (4) a state characteristic of *H. sapiens.*

Thoma interpreted the results of his analysis as indicating a distribution of character states in the Palestine sample that was highly variable and broadly intermediate between his two most different reference groups, classic Neanderthals and anatomically modern humans. His principal conclusion was that the variability and intermediacy were most readily explained by admixture of Neanderthal and modern populations. Proceeding beyond this point he suggested that modern humans were derived principally from a presapiens group (usually embodying features similar to fossils such as Swanscombe and Fontéchevade), with some elements introduced from Neanderthals.

While Thoma's broad conclusions are not unusual, some of the underlying reasoning that he employed should not be overlooked. In examining, and rejecting, the alternative explanation of evolutionary change within the Palestine sample, he made the working assumption that the morphological variation in each characteristic was due to a single gene mutation. He then used estimates of mutation rates based on pathological conditions such as retinoblastoma and chondrodystrophic dwarfism, with then-standard values of one gene/100000 gametes per generation. Assuming that there would be only about 200 surviving offspring per generation over the entire area represented by the fossil sample, generation length of 20 years, and a time interval of 10000 years or 350 generations, Thoma arrived at cumulative population numbers for the region of 70000. Multiplying this total by the mutation rate, he arrived at a total possible number of one to two mutations per locus over the entire time period. Not surprisingly, this was rejected as too low a rate to account for 'transformation' of the Palestine sample by known mechanisms of evolution and thus, consequently, the distribution of characteristics must be explained by hybridization.

At one level, Thoma's work presents at its base some informed, careful morphological description. The results of the observation then are vitiated by the conversion of observations on continuous variates into discontinuous character states (though they are not referred to as such). Then the results are interpreted within a framework of genetic analysis that is flawed by failure to consider the potential diversity and complexity of evolutionary forces that can act on human populations, present or past. These shortcomings are then so exacerbated by apparent misunderstanding of the forces that are analyzed, that the study approaches being a paleobiological caricature. This is an extreme case, but more than a few of its elements surface as a repeating pattern in the application of genetic data to problems of modern human origins.

Molecular and morphological perspectives on modern human origins

Krings *et al.* (1997) have attempted to forge a direct link between molecular and morphological evidence. In their study, mitochondrial DNA (mtDNA) from the hypervariable control region was extracted from the humerus of the original Neanderthal fossil and amplified by a variant of polymerase chain reaction. The material that was identified as Neanderthal mitochondrial DNA (mtDNA) comprised 379 base pairs out of 16 142 in the entire molecule, representing about 2.3 percent of the whole. Among the identified bases, 27 differed from the modern human reference sequence. From this result it was inferred that 'Neanderthals went extinct without contributing mtDNA to modern humans.'

This is a strong inference from the modest amount of material available for comparison (a sample size of one). To place this matter in context, consider its counterpart in morphological terms. A comparable percentage of a human skeleton would comprise the equivalent of about five bones, but distributed as bone fragments from one portion of the anatomy (perhaps the skull, which might be considered analogically comparable to the control region). Whether it would be possible to distinguish between two species on such a basis would depend in part on how large and diagnostic the fragments were.

As another qualifier governing the interpretation of these findings, remember that although molecular geneticists have now determined the entire mtDNA sequences of all extant hominoid primates, the gorilla/chimpanzee/human trichotomy has not yet been resolved to the general satisfaction of qualified workers in the field. The Neanderthal mtDNA results are compatible with the possibility that this hominid population was replaced in Europe, but do not constitute conclusive proof.

From a paleobiological perspective, other forms of molecular traces preserved from the past can be as informative (or uninformative) as those preserving morphological features. Zischler *et al.* (1995) provided one recently-discovered example of a mtDNA insertion into the nuclear genome. After such an event, the inserted material is believed to behave subsequently in evolution as a more slowly-evolving pseudogene. This type of event, a relatively common occurrence (Zullo *et al.*, 1991), is considered by some to constitute a kind of 'molecular fossil' that can be used as an outgroup for assessing relationships among populations. In this particular case, the insertion was used in attempts to reconstruct a phylogenetic tree with a neighbor-joining algorithm. The result was interpreted as providing increased support for an African root to the mitochondrial phylogenetic tree.

Studies of this sort commonly are taken as additional evidence for replacement models, which they are not. Supporters of a multiregional model have not argued against Africa as the origin of extant human populations, questioning only when such an origin occurred, as well as its nature. Was it once only, with subsequent isolation of human populations as they differentiated? Or, was there one main spread with continuing or frequently intermittent gene flow? Or, were there necessarily several waves with each successive one replacing antecedent populations in the regions over which secondary spreads occurred?

Regardless of particular materials or their limitations, it is axiomatic that genetic analyses of data derived from extant human populations will continue to shape views on modern human origins. In fact, to the extent that issues concerning interactions among past populations also involve questions of variation within and among extant populations, pertinent research spans nearly four decades. Coon (1962) hypothesized the independent evolution of several major geographic racial groups from *H. erectus* ancestors. In doing so, he revived an extreme form of the candelabra model (Figure 11.2) for human evolution (characterized by independent branching from a central trunk at several successive levels, with all but one, usually central, branch terminating before a subsequent branching at a higher level). In the same year, Livingstone (1962) published a widely read paper arguing for the non-existence of human races. Shortly afterward, this position gained additional support from the work of Hiernaux (1964).

The techniques and results of electrophoretic analysis were brought powerfully to bear on the question of how variation is apportioned, particularly by Lewontin (1972). Soon afterward he placed the question into a broader perspective (Lewontin, 1974). The finding of greatest generality was that electrophoresis detected much higher levels of genetic variation than had been anticipated. Of particular importance for the understanding of recent human evolution was the discovery that genetic variation within each major human group was on the same order of magnitude as differences between these groups. As noted in Chapter 4, results of this sort were at

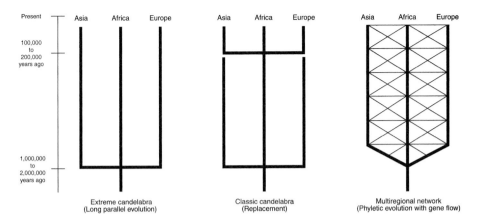

Figure 11.2. Schematic relationships among human populations following
expansion from Africa over a million years ago. The extreme candelabra model,
popularized by Coon (1962), requires extensive parallel evolution among
populations over a long period of hypothetical isolation. The candelabra with
replacement model (long the most widely accepted in paleoanthropology)
requires sequential, parallel evolution of some traits over a relatively short period
of geological time. Various network models that can be traced to the ideas of
Weidenreich (1936, 1937, 1938) on polycentric origins are regaining support (e.g.,
Wolpoff *et al.*, 1994; Templeton, 1998). Network models do not require the
assumption of parallel evolution, instead positing complex interactions among
various evolutionary forces varying over time and space.

variance with classical models of the genome, which had assumed that
levels of within-population variation were small relative to between-popu-
lation differences.

In some regards these papers established a context for the reception of
the mitochondrial haplotype tree published by Cann *et al.* (1987) and
subsequent papers on the subject (Vigilant *et al.*, 1991; Stoneking, 1997).
These publications present the core of recent genetically-based arguments
for revival of a candelabra model for the later phases of human evolution,
also referred to as a replacement model. As observed by Templeton (1998),
Cann and her co-workers make a tripartite argument: (1) that all mtDNA
haplotypes in extant human populations can be traced back to a single
common maternal ancestor (mitochondrial 'Eve'); (2) that the mitochondrial tree is rooted in Africa; and (3) that the tree's branches coalesce to this
African mitochondrial root sometime within the last 200 000 years.

Much of the early support for this model, and criticism of it, lie aside
from its major implications for modern human origins. In terms of support,
the idea that recency of shared ancestry affirms the common humanity of
all extant human populations is unnecessary. The degree of genetic

commonality among living humans is a datum, however it may be explained. Regarding criticism, the initial objection by Hedges *et al.* (1992) and others (that the results were produced by erroneous use of a computer program that led to many more parsimonious trees being ignored) is small in comparison to several objections that are far more weighty. More important, as argued by Templeton (1998), is that the mitochondrial data and analyses published by this group do not discriminate between replacement and what he refers to as a trellis model, which is similar in some ways to those advanced much earlier by Weidenreich (1936, 1938) and to later multiregional theories. Trellis or networks models recognize relationships within regions, but see these as supplemented by continuing interconnections among regional populations through time by gene flow.

Moving beyond criticism of the mitochondrial-based replacement model, Templeton emphasizes several important features of a trellis model. First, it is consistent with an African origin for all modern human populations (as noted in Chapter 10, the fossil evidence is most consistent with Africa having been the locus of hominid evolution until sometime within the last million years or so). A second implication of Templeton's version of the trellis model holds that the taxonomic designations *H. erectus* and *H. sapiens* have only morphological significance, and do not imply reproductive isolation under the biological species concept (Mayr, 1970). As a corollary of this point, anatomically modern traits could evolve anywhere among the populations that are linked by gene flow, including Africa. Thus an African origin for anatomically modern humans is as consistent with a trellis model as it is with a candelabra model. This is another example of a potential decoupling between phenostructure and zygostructure, and one that has broad implications for human paleobiology.

Another major interpretive difference between the two models concerns alternative explanations for interpopulational genetic differences. According to candelabra models (which feature branching topologies), genetic distances reflect the time of divergence from a common ancestral population. According to the trellis model, as long as genetic contact has persisted through prior generations, there has been no divergence; instead, genetic distances between populations reflect levels of genetic interchange. Relationships among extant human populations also are interpreted in divergent manners. The trellis model holds that since there has been no separation of human groups into isolated evolutionary lineages, our species cannot be divided into races, other than by artificial convention (this is a conclusion that had been reached independently by Lahr, 1996).

The clear inferences made by Templeton gain added force from their setting within what is overall a very even-handed perspective. One indication of this balance is the realization that the two models are not irreconcilable. Some human populations, past and present, may be differentiated genetically because they are true historical lineages, while others have diverged quantitatively due to sporadically restricted gene flow. There is no basis in genetic theory for assuming that humans must be either a polytypic species or a single evolutionary lineage; it can be both simultaneously.

The result of the last million or so years of human evolution, in this view, is a human population structure that is characterized by the simultaneous existence of many locally differentiated populations that nevertheless are linked by sufficient genetic contact to form a common evolving lineage.

Implications of molecular evidence for human paleobiology

The findings summarized above are unusually emphatic in their resolution of the relationships among extant humans. Their implications provide a less clear guide to the past. Left untouched, for example, is any detailed understanding of the relationship between genetic distance and measures of morphological resemblance, other than the general suggestion that physical dimensions of the phenotype are less shielded from environmental influences than are nucleic acid sequences.

A prodigious amount of work remains to be done before there will be a clear consensus on the relative roles that have been played by non-genetic aspects of adaptation through time. Perhaps the message for archeologists and paleobiologists is that their future research is needed to produce a sufficiently adequate understanding of human paleobiology at the level of local and regional populations. Only then will the vertical, horizontal, and diagonal lines on the trellis that have been straight since the time of Weidenreich conform to the tangled lines of the paleontological record.

12   *A future for the past*

Limitations of the evidence

The challenge of human paleobiology is to reconstruct the appearances and lifeways of our ancestors over the course of several million years from evidence that is, in the epic epithet most often adopted by critics of the field, 'sparse and fragmentary.' The evidence is limited, and most specimens are far from complete. But this situation poses a challenge that is neither insurmountable nor even especially unique. Parallels are found in many other disciplines. In her history of England's Lollard religious movement, Anne Hudson (1988: 8) acknowledged what others had termed the 'fragility and discontinuity of the existing evidence.' She then went on to state her own philosophical stance, 'evidence does not cease to be evidence because it is not ideal; the rider to this is that the obligation lies upon the researcher to refine or modify his techniques to accommodate the difficulties and obtain results if . . . the picture without new sources is manifestly inadequate. But on the other hand, the problems of the sources must be squarely faced and clearly explained; no useful purpose will be served by offering new evidence which appears to be firm and unambiguous when it is questionable, however much it may complete the perspective.'

It would be presumptuous as well as incorrect to characterize the existing state of human evolutionary studies that has been created by paleoanthropologists as 'manifestly inadequate.' My preference is to borrow a colleague's far more optimistic characterization of the field as 'infinitely perfectible.' In this sense, human paleobiology has come a long way, but it has much further to go. How shall we move forward?

Alternatives to phylogeny

In many recent interpretations of the hominid fossil record, taxonomic and phylogenetic questions have been a primary focus of attention. An alternative perspective is offered here, one which acknowledges the importance of phylogeny, but (along with Rowe, 1991) situates it as part of a broader evolutionary context that places greater emphasis on studies of the velocity of character change and the paleobiological contexts that shaped adaptation and evolution. In the current state of our knowledge, detailed cladograms depicting large numbers of hominid species into which our ancestry has been partitioned probably are less robust – more subject to substantial revisions based on the next discovery – than are estimates of velocities of change in particular characters. The reference to *particular* character velocities is intentional, because of the pronounced mosaic nature of hominid evolution, the patterns of which have been discussed in Chapters 8 through 11. Knowlege of the velocities for state changes in multiple characters, in turn, will make it increasingly possible to reconstruct the phenostructures of hominid populations during various time periods – largely independent of continuing reference to multiple alternative phylogenies.

As stated in the Preface, my own inclination to deal with character state change as much as possible and phylogeny as little as possible arose originally from discussions with a colleague who – although a human biologist of broad experience and scientific distinction – was increasingly daunted by the aura of interpretive complexity that appeared only to grow with each new fossil find. This situation seemed counterintuitive to me, as if some process were obscuring the remarkable gains being made in the abundance and quality of the material evidence being recovered. More fossils are being found every decade. And with rare exceptions, descriptions of the discoveries are being published with far less of a time lag than formerly was the case – athough to be fair, these gains have been on the average rather than at the extremes. To my knowledge, Raymond Dart's elapsed time between receipt and report on the Taung child (Chapter 3) stands as a record in the field. It is an attainment that is unlikely to be exceeded in a scientific climate that has been transformed radically in almost every conceivable way since his time, with attendant losses and gains.

Among the gains influencing our ability to understand the past and, to a limited extent, recreate glimpses into the lives of our ancestors, is the acceptance of interdisciplinarity, the idea that other areas of science hold the potential for multiplying the value of the unique knowledge-base represented by the fossils themselves. For paleobiologists, numerous adjoining fields have generated a prodigious array of techniques that are indispensible for establishing the proveniences of fossils and extracting information from them and their contexts.

Perspectives from molecular genetics

Among the many important collateral sources of evidence that now can be brought to bear on paleobiological problems, molecular genetics has had a major role in shaping the views developed here, in several ways. The most central of these was the exercise, in Chapter 7, of using molecular data to derive an estimate – independent of the fossil evidence – for the number of hominid taxa that have existed since the separation of the lineages leading to extant apes and humans. This approach did not yield an exact solution, but its results should direct the attention of paleoanthropologists toward several alternatives. These possibilities are neither unitary nor mutually exclusive, but any one or combination of them must lead to reassessment of the relationships among hominid populations over the last six or so million years.

Genetic distance data

A large body of evidence is in accord with the working hypothesis that humans and chimpanzees are the two most closely related taxa among the hominoid primates, and are likely to have shared a common ancestor in the range of six to eight million years ago. The proximity of this relationship is expressed in quantitative form by various measures of genetic distance that were summarized in Chapter 7. Based on the work of Janczewski *et al.* (1990), the genetic distance based on isozyme comparisons between extant humans (*Homo sapiens*) and common chimpanzees (*Pan troglodytes*) is 0.244 (the *H. sapiens–P. paniscus* distance is nominally lower, at 0.197, so the higher figure for the *H. sapiens–P. troglodytes* distance is more conservative). If this distance is apportioned *pro rata* among the numbers (approximately 5 to 15) of hominid taxa currently recognized by many paleoanthropologists, the greatest distance is about 0.049 (0.244/5) and the smallest is approximately 0.016 (0.244/15). The larger of these two figures is less than two-thirds the distance between *P. troglodytes* and *P. paniscus* (0.075), while the smaller of the two is less than two thirds the distance (0.025) between Bornean and Sumatran orangutans (respectively, *Pongo pygmaeus pygmaeus* and *P. p. abelii*).

In terms of reproductive behavior and the possibility of gene exchange, *P. troglodytes* and *P. paniscus* are allopatrically distributed in Africa, and there are no reports of hybrids being produced in captivity. The situation is different for orangutans. Until a recent decision to maintain captive animals derived from the two islands as separate stocks, hybrid offspring were common.

Morphologically the picture also is mixed. As discussed in Chapter 6, the multivariate craniometric study carried out by Shea *et al.* (1993) was able to discriminate from 63 percent to 82 percent of *P. paniscus* female crania from those of three *P. troglodytes* subspecies, with the discriminating ability rising to between 62 percent and 96 percent after adjustment for size. After eliminating *P. paniscus* from the sample and carrying out the same size adjustment, the discriminating ability of the technique was moderately lower, correctly discriminating from 41 percent to 82 percent of female crania. In a similar multivariate study on orangutans, Groves *et al.* (1992) found that skulls of *Pongo pygmaeus* from southwestern Borneo were as distinct from skulls derived from the remainder of Borneo as were those from Sumatra.

In relating their results on extant hominoid samples to inferences made about fossil hominid taxa, Shea *et al.* (1993) quoted Tattersall's (1986:186) position that 'it is critical to avoid relegating distinct morphological variants observed in the fossil record to the status of subspecies' and recommending that 'where distinctive morphs can be readily identified it would seem most productive to assume that they represent species.' In response, Shea *et al.* (1993:280) emphasized their finding of distinct morphological variants within *P. troglodytes*, even though these were intraspecific groups rather than species. Among the larger hominoid primates, phenostructure is not a reliable indicator of zygostructure, particularly when estimated genetic distances are low, at or within the boundaries of formal subspecies as estimated here.

Genetic data on papionine populations present a complementary pattern. The work of Scheffrahn *et al.* (1996) provides an important set of benchmark data, derived from studies of genetic relatedness within and between populations of *Macaca fascicularis* on Sumatra and offshore islands in the region. On the mainland of Sumatra, genetic distances presented the classic pattern usually referred to as 'isolation by distance,' which really represents not absolute isolation but rather some quantitative reductions in levels of shared genes proportionate to geographic separation. In the large matrix of genetic distance values that they have calculated for the 14 populations studied, it is possible to screen for values that correspond to the genetic distance values of 0.016 and 0.049 estimated here for average distances among different numbers of hypothetical fossil hominid taxa. None of the genetic distances between *M. fascicularis* populations was as low as 0.016 estimated for hominid taxa; the lowest value was 0.021, for two populations separated by under 5 km. The value of 0.049 could be matched precisely, in this case by two *M. fascicularis* populations separated by approximately 300 km in northwestern Sumatra.

Among the other comparisons made by Scheffrahn *et al.* (1996) there were several made between populations on offshore islands and the Sumatran mainland. Geological sources make it likely that two of the islands have been separated from the mainland for between 100 000 and 1 000 000 years. Genetic distances between these island populations and those on the mainland ranged from a low of 0.061 to 0.247. Macaques on one of these islands, Simeulue, have some differences in coat color that may be interpreted as adaptations to the absence of feline predators, and dominant males there have a specific call that may be used for group spacing. There does not appear, however, to be evidence for strong morphologial differentiation or evidence for speciation. Jolly's (1993) inferences about the disjunction between phenostructure and zygostructure in papionine primates, based in his knowledge of baboons, also apply to the situation in macaques. By papionine standards, even moderately large genetic distances are even less reliable guides to morphological differentiation, and particularly to genetic isolation, than are chimpanzee or other hominoid reference values.

Gene differences

Data are not as abundant for estimation of nucleotide differences among primate taxa as they are for genetic distance measures. However, some approximations are possible. In Chapter 7, the nucleotide difference between chimpanzees and humans was taken as 0.77 percent, based on the values published by King & Wilson (1975). To be on the conservative side again here, this value is rounded up to a one percent difference.

The human genome is estimated to have about 100 000 genes. A one percent difference between chimpanzees and humans would correspond to about 1000 genes. The distribution of these differences by time of origin is unknown, as is their location within the genome. There is no reason for assuming that either the rate of accrual or the genomic distribution has been uniform. Since it is known that at least one major karyotypic rearrangement took place (as discussed in Chapter 8), non-linearity in time and position is more likely than not.

If the time of the pongid–hominid divergence is set at approximately six million years ago and the 1000 gene differences that might have accrued are apportioned among five hypothetical hominid taxa, each taxon would differ at about 200 loci, or a substitution occurring at one locus about every 1500 generations. If all of the underlying assumptions remain the same, except an increase in the number of hominid taxa to 15, the resultant difference among taxa would be about 67 genes, with one locus turning over every 4500 generations. Aside from the one major karyotypic restructuring already noted (Chapter 8), there is as yet no way of knowing whether these genetic changes occurred evenly or very unevenly, whether within lineages or at points of population splitting. But overall, these figures reinforce the pattern established from the genetic distance data, that changes in zygostructure among hominid taxa through time are likely to have been modest.

These comparisons, as already noted, do not yield an exact figure for the numbers of hominid taxa that have existed over the course of our evolutionary history as a clade. But they do suggest that there are some limits on the overall amount and distribution of taxonomic diversity, with these components taken together. One alternative is a very limited number of taxa (very likely fewer than five, perhaps up to two or three) that apportion the modest total genetic distance among them. Because there is no exact correspondence between genetic, morphological, and reproductive discontinuities, some of these taxa might approach the species level in one or more respects. Another possibility is a large number of taxa, up to the 15 recognized by some paleoanthropologists. But if there is a *pro rata* allocation of genetic differences among such units, differences are likely to be very small and to correspond closely to the range of slightly differentiated subspecies or local populations. Of course, any combination among these alternatives also is possible. There might be other possibilities, but it would seem that at least some of these would amount to making a special case of hominids in a direction opposite to that manifested by most groups of large mammals.

Changing definitions of taxonomic categories

A considertion that bears on thoughts about these alternatives was first suggested to me in an informal context. In a discussion of the points above,O'Brien (personal communication, 1999) pointed out that there has been a shift in the meaning of the species category since the nineteenth century. Naturalists of the nineteenth century described the animals that they saw and the specimens that they collected, and as a general rule didn't consider whether the units that they described were or were not differentiated genetically (among other things, as discussed in Chapter 4, the formal concept of a gene was not yet known). That situation changed with the development of a very large body of scientific thought about species definitions and recognition, much of which gives priority to characters related to reproductive incompatibility over those of morphological dis-tinctiveness (Mayr, 1970). As a consequence of this shift, many species categories and concepts may have subtly become 'grandfathered,' having entered the scientific literature according to morphological criteria and having reproductive discontinuity attributed secondarily to them.

Yet another conceptual change has taken place even more recently, with the passage of the US Endangered Species Act (Pennock & Dimmick, 1997). This legislation has shifted the emphasis from genetic differentiation to the necessity for a subspecies also to have historical continuity; that is, to be a distinct evolutionary lineage. This development is favorable from a paleobiological standpoint, since it shifts attention from inferences about reproductive behavior (which cannot be observed in fossil populations in any case) to whatever traits work best in the identification of lineages. Some of the groups in the fossil record that are recognizable as 'morphs' might, if their continuity through time can be established securely, con-tinue to be recognized by formal taxonomic designations, though probably at the level of subspecies. Such outcomes would represent another kind of resolution to the apparent conflict between what appear to be large numb-ers of species but inferred low levels of genetic differentiation.

Species concepts and human paleobiology

By this point, many readers will feel that I have never encountered a species nomen that I didn't dislike. In fact, the reality of species – as phenomena in the external world and as concepts in the internal world of the mind – is beyond reasonable doubt. The problem for me, as a scientist, is that some species concepts require that I accept propositions that appear to be logically unappealing (e.g. that species are individuals, a fashionable idea about which my scepticism is not alone – see Kitcher, 1992; Ruse, 1994). Yet others incorporate elements that are logically compelling (reproduc-tive isolation) but difficult to observe in present populations and all but impossible to demonstrate in those of the past. In fact, among the things that we do know is that some populations (in the sense used in the preceding section) are *not* reproductively isolated but do maintain their distinctiveness (wolves and coyotes, which exchange genes in the wild but have survived as lineages for 0.5 to 2.0 million years).

One recently developed species model that does combine logical and practical appeal is the cohesion species concept (Templeton, 1992). Such species have genetic exchangeability (the ability to exchange genes during sexual reproduction).

A key feature of this concept is its acceptance that the process of adaptation via natural selection can directly alter the traits that influence the extent of demographic exchangeability (which is related to the ecological niche requirements of organisms). One of the most appealing aspects of the cohesion species concept is that it defines speciation as the process by which new genetic systems of cohesion mechanisms evolve within a population. In this sense, a purely environmental alteration in the expression of cohesion can lead to conditions favoring assimilation of the new pattern into the gene pool. The cohesion species concept defines species in terms of the mechanisms that produce cohesion through time, including genetic drift and natural selection as well as gene flow. Under this definition, a species is the most inclusive group of organisms having the potential for genetic and/or demographic exchangeability.

Some of the central ideas in this concept appear to have direct application to resolution of certain long-standing problems in the hominid fossil record. Just one of them might be introduced here. There are many mentions of 'parallelisms' between what commonly are taken as representatives of contemporaneous lineages such as robust and gracile australopithecines or robust australopithecines and 'early *Homo*.' The cohesion species concept readily accommodates the existence of syngaemons, reproductive units above the level of species, several of which are characterized by natural hybridization and gene exchange. Technically, a syngaemon is the most inclusive unit of interbreeding in a hybridizing species group. Units that some paleoanthropologists have long believed, by common convention, to be entirely independent lineages may stand in such a relationship. This idea cannot be rejected simply because the interpretation is unconventional or its underpinning in theoretical population genetics unfamiliar. As noted in Chapter 2, views very similar to these were broached over three decades ago by Philip Tobias, one of paleoanthropology's most productive empiricists – and one of its least dogmatic thinkers.

Lineages and character states

A change in focus, from identification of species on the basis of fossil hominid remains to identification of lineages, is compatible with much of the work included here in Chapters 8 through 11. Unlike hominid species, which often – though, in theory, not necessarily – are identified by shared character states (particularly apomorphies), lineages can be characterized by trends. No particular rates for trends in any characters need be assumed *a priori*. In fact, as shown by the work of Henneberg and his colleagues, the trends need not have uniform rates through time; the more and better the fossil material that is available to work with, the more likely it is that temporal heterogeneities in rates will be detected.

There is an objection that could be raised about the procedure of framing analyses of characters that are important in understanding the paleobiology of past hominid populations in terms of character state velocities rather than phylogenies. The caveat will be made, probably taking the form that it will not be possible to compare hominid samples that have not been assigned to particular taxa. As outlined briefly in Chapter 9, Mathers & Henneberg (1995) have shown the way here. They adopted as a null hypothesis that all coeval hominids belong to a single species, and that this hypothesis must be falsified before a theory of synchronous taxonomic plurality can be accepted. Among their results was the finding that when samples were divided into species, there seemed to be no relationship between date and body size within a single species, and that there was no clear vertical separation in height or weight between any coeval species.

An improved fossil record will help in studies of trait velocities; here, 'better' fossil material has at least two major attributes. The first, of course, is completeness. Most researchers in the field are aware of the enormous influence attributable – with great justification – to just a few specimens. Several of these – CLl-18000, AL 288–1, BOU-VP-12/1, KNM-WT 15000, and to a lesser extent, KNM-ER 1470 – have figured heavily in some of the examples used in this book. We need very many more such specimens. And, given current trends in fieldwork, they will be discovered.

But the time also has come for better use to be made of the many less complete specimens that exist in large numbers. The technology (if not the financial resources) now exists for these to be entered into electronic databases, from which status they could be accessed and used as references to compose samples for testing various hypotheses about size, proportions, and morphometric trends.

It was noted above that in addition to completeness (and accessibility), the other great need for new analyses of fossil material is improved dating methods. Like the new discoveries of fossil remains themselves, gains in this area are occurring relatively rapidly. There also is a need for caution in the use of estimates for the ages of specimens, which usually means the ages of materials that bear some association with the primary fossil material.

The temporal contexts of hominid fossils

There are genuine difficulties in interpreting the hominid fossil record, and even close reliance on what appear to be established empirical facts can lead to substantial errors, as we already have seen in problems arising from the chronometric age estimates of KNM-ER 1470, discussed in Chapter 10.

Anyone wishing to gain some appreciation of the hazards implicit in scientific work need only read the series of papers by Frank Brown and his colleagues dealing with the stratigraphy and dating of the Koobi Fora region of Kenya and adjacent regions (Brown & Feibel, 1986; Feibel *et al.*, 1989). These papers, particularly the first, document in detail how investigators have worked for over two decades in the attempt to provide a reliable chronological setting for important hominid fossils. Behrensmeyer (1970) provided the initial description of sediments in the Koobi Fora region. Vondra *et al.* (1971) supplied a generalized stratigraphic section for the Ileret region. Bowen & Vondra (1973) formalized the stratigraphic nomenclature of the Koobi Fora region and related it to the Ileret and Kubi Algi areas. Findlater (1976, 1978) carried out stratigraphic and paleoenvironmental research based on these correlations.

Along the way, however, diligent work by qualified investigators did not guarantee reliable or consistent results. For example, several different horizons were identified erroneously as a single tuff complex, yet that complex was not even tuffaceous. Strata from different areas were miscorrelated. As one key indication of the scale of problems that proliferated, the type exposures of the Koobi Fora Formation were depicted in one publication as 70 m in depth, while in others the thicknesses of the same interval were given as 130 m, 146 m and 155m. Two related papers published in the same year (Brown & Cerling, 1982; Cerling & Brown, 1982) began documentation of the stratigraphic miscorrelations that had been made. Subsequently, the 1986 and 1989 papers by Brown and his colleagues built on these contributions and have brought us to the current state of affairs, in which over 400 hominid fossils are related in what may now be a more coherent stratigraphic and chronological framework – but only after some important hominid fossils have been shifted in apparent date by a million years or so. In situations of this sort one is tempted to accept the philosophy of the American humorist James Thurber, who commented, 'There is no safety in numbers, or in anything else.'

Scientific inquiry itself is not a linear process, and problems of this sort – and of many other sorts – are virtually inevitable. This is why investigators always should be sceptical of data points that seem to be outliers and claims that are unusually sweeping. Whenever one hears, or is tempted to say, 'We must either discard this specimen or discard all previous theories of human evolution' an internal alarm should go off.

Occurrences of this sort help to underscore the need for a genuine theory-based framework to receive new observations (a theory that has to be revised to accommodate each new discovery is not a theory). It should not be upsetting that errors sometimes are made and revisions of interpretations must occur. The only time that we should really be upset is when the assumptions and (subsequently) errors prove to be directional rather than random. It is in this sense that the initial interpretations of the phylogenetic significance of KNM-ER 1470 leave a feeling of unease.

The most attention-getting feature of this specimen, its cranial capacity, was over-estimated by about 50 cm^3. Cranial capacity in the Plio-Pleistocene hominid sample used for comparison was understated by 20 cm^3 (Leakey, 1973). Estimates of the time that KNM-ER 1470's population had existed were too early by a million years, with the original judgment that the cranium was 'probably 2.9 million years old' (Leakey, 1973) having been reached evidently by taking the potassium/argon dating results (Fitch & Miller, 1970) of 2.61 $\pm$ 0.26 and adding (without also subtracting) the error term, a course of action which happened to give the greatest time depth. Faunal correlations with other areas that suggested more recent dates were discounted by *ad hoc* ecological arguments. Some later investigators even have remarked on what seems to be another oddity: that the fission-track ages published for the KBS Tuff have tended to support the potassium/argon estimate that was current at each respective time, suggesting that, in practice, the two techniques of age estimation may not have been entirely independent (Hurford, 1986; Feibel *et al.*, 1989).

To be fair to the investigators involved in the example cited, over-reliance on the accuracy of scientific data is so commonplace that it should be considered endemic to the scientific enterprise. According to David Lide, head of the National Standard Reference Data System of the US National Bureau of Standards, from 50 percent to over 90 percent of the published raw data believed to provide reliable knowledge of the physical properties of scientific materials cannot be used for that purpose. One illustration of this basic problem was given by W. J. Youden of the National Bureau of Standards, 'Of 15 observations of the mean distance to the sun published from 1895 to 1961, each worker's estimated value is outside the uncertainty limits set by his immediate predecessor' (Macdonald, 1972).

There is a further matter that follows from the discovery, interpretation, and reinterpretation of KNM-ER 1470. The Koobi Fora area was the locus, in the early 1970s, of discoveries that were taken as definitive proof of the contemporaneity of advanced hominids and what many specialists take to be evolutionarily less-advanced robust australopithecines, both at a relatively early date, and continuing on together for perhaps a million years. Now that the geological setting has been interpreted as not only radically different in age from what originally was published, but substantially more tangled (resulting from redeposition of materials and other complexities initially overlooked) it might be time to reconsider alternative interpretations of evolutionary relationships. Adding weight to this suggestion is the publication by Fitch *et al.* (1996), in which it is argued that the appropriate bracketing limits of the deposits from which KNM-ER 1470 was sampled were 'certainly younger than 3.31 Ma, probably younger than 2.5 Ma, but definitely older than 1.9 Ma' (Fitch *et al.*, 1996:277). If substantiated, this age redetermination will, of course, alter all of the compounding rates calculated in Chapter 9. It also appears likely to call into question the temporal relationships among fossil hominids worked out in detail by Feibel *et al.* (1989). Ultimately, such matters will bear on problems of phylogeny, of course, and many of the implications are so great that they must remain to be answered at another time, perhaps along the lines suggested by, for example, Tobias (1967) and Clark (1993).

The principal inference from this example is the desirability of a population-based perspective, which would engender caution in the interpretation of a specimen that appears to be an outlier – particularly a very far outlier.

Paleobiology's 'two cultures' problem

The approach taken in this book represents an exercise in combining what Mayr (1961) has referred to as 'two largely separate fields' in the life sciences: evolutionary biology and functional biology. Evolutionary biology is concerned principally with problems of ultimate causation, while functional biology deals chiefly with matters of proximate causation. To use one of the examples offered by Mayr (1991:53), the proximate cause of sexual dimorphism in bird plumage is a difference in hormone levels; its ultimate cause is sexual selection. Neither mode of explanation is any more fundamental or important than the other.

Another example, in this case from human biology, can be offered from my own experience. Populations native to high altitude in South America combine short statures with massive, barrel-shaped chests that enclose lungs of high respiratory capacity in relation to overall body size. A proximate cause of this allometric relationship is the hypoxic environment that these populations occupy; at 4000 m above sea level, the atmosphere holds only about 70 percent as much oxygen per unit volume as is available at sea level. Larger lungs are needed to extract sufficient oxygen from this hypoxic atmosphere. But the potential for an ultimate causal answer existed as well, to the question of whether these large chests and lungs were developed anew each generation in response to proximate environmental stresses, or whether selection has altered the frequencies of genes underlying the developmental processes that produced absolutely and relatively large thoracic dimensions. As it turned out, the answer was that variations in thoracic dimensions are influenced by both genes and direct environmental conditions (Eckhardt & Melton, 1992).

A further outcome of this research followed from a combination of the archeological evidence documenting that the ancestors of these populations had lived at high altitude for 10000 years, and the physical comparisons that could be made between past and present populations in the highlands and lowlands. This represented a situation in which there were measurably large morphological differences, but no suggestion of taxonomic heterogeneity – yet the rates of evolution exceeded those calculated by Frayer for differences between Neanderthals and anatomically modern populations (summarized in Chapter 11). Functional biology and evolutionary biology, though conceptually separate, can be combined in a productive manner.

Moreover, in living populations, adaptive mechanisms can be seen in their full complexity. In the high altitude Andean setting, cold stress interacts with caloric consumption, contributing to reductions in stature, a situation further exacerbated by a limited nutritional base, and so on. Using studies of present populations as keys to the past rapidly develops a healthy respect for a pluralistic approach to human paleobiology in a limited, empirical context.

Pluralism in the study of human paleobiology is important on a higher and more theoretical level as well. In Chapter 2, after a review of the inherent limitations in the Linnaean taxonomic system, a case was made for a variety of newer approaches to summarizing biological variation. That point is returned to here.

In a discussion of the species question, Kitcher (1992) observed that in the writings of great systematists, there are identifiable passages that recognize the needs of different categories of biologists. 'Typically, these passages precede the moment at which monism takes over and the writer becomes an advocate for a single conception of species which is to answer the interests of everyone.' As an example, Kitcher cites Hennig's classic work on systematics (Hennig, 1966) where he emphasizes the multiplicity of admissible approaches to classification – and then formulates a single general reference system for systematics.

There is no doubt that cladistic approaches – Hennig's conceptual legacy – have made important formal contributions to evolutionary analysis. Now might be the time to recognize the importance of Hennig's other legacy, one of tolerance for approaches that make it possible to look at our hominid ancestors in terms of the successful living beings that they were, rather than evolutionary failures, as they so often have been regarded.

Bibliography

Acheson, R. M. (1959). Effects of starvation, septicaemia and chronic illness on the growth cartilage plate and metaphysis of the immature rat. *Journal of Anatomy*, **93**, 123–30.

Adolph, E. F. (1947). *Physiology of Man in the Desert*. New York: John Wiley and Sons.

Aguirre, E. (1994). *Homo erectus* and *Homo sapiens*: one or more species? *CourierForschungs-Institut Senckenberg*, **171**, 333–9.

Agustí, J. (1996). Can Llobateres: the pattern and timing of the Vallesian hominoid radiation reconsidered. *Journal of Human Evolution*, **31**, 143–55.

Ahern, J. C. M. (1998). Underestimating intraspecific variation: the problem with excluding Sts 19 from *Australopithecus africanus*. *American Journal of Physical Anthropology*, **105**, 461–80.

Aiello, L. (1981). Locomotion in the Miocene Hominoidea. In *Aspects of Human Evolution*, ed. C. B. Stringer, pp. 63–98. London: Taylor and Francis.

Akazawa, T., Muhesen, S., Dodo, Y., Kondo, O. & Mizoguchi, Y. (1995). Neanderthal infant burial. *Nature*, **377**, 586–7.

Albrecht, G. H. (1978). The craniofacial morphology of the Sulawesi macaques: multivariate approaches to biological problems. *Contributions to Primatology*, 13, pp. viii, 151. Basel: Karger.

Albrecht, G. H. & Miller, J. M. A. (1993). Geographic variation in primates. In *Species, Species Concepts, and Primate Evolution*, eds. W. H. Kimbel & L. W. Martin, pp. 123–61. New York: Plenum.

Alexeev, V. P. (1986). *The Origin of the Human Race*. Moscow: Progress Publishers.

Allen, J. A. (1906). The influence of physical conditions on the genesis of species. *Smithsonian Institution Annual Report* (1905), pp. 375–402.

Allen, J. A. (1916). The proper generic name of the macaques. *Bulletin of the American Museum of Natural History*, **35**, 49–52.

Allen, J. A. (1925). Primates collected by the American Museum Congo Expedition. *Bulletin of the American Museum of Natural History*, **47**, 283–499.

Altmann, S. A. & Altmann, J. (1970). *Baboon Ecology*. Chicago: University of Chicago Press.

Amaral, L. Q. (1996). Loss of body hair, bipedality and thermoregulation. Comments on recent papers in human evolution. *Journal of Human Evolution*, **30**, 357–66.

Anderson, J. J. B. (1995). Development and maintenance of bone mass through the cycle. In *Calcium and Phosphorous in Health and Disease*, ed. J. J. B. Anderson & S. C. Garner, pp. 265–88. Boca Raton: CRC Press.

Anderson, J. J. B. & Pollitzer, W. S. (1994). Ethnic and genetic differences in susceptibility to osteoporotic fractures. In *Advances in Nutritional Research*, ed. H. H. Draper, vol. 9, pp. 129–49. New York: Plenum Press.

Anderson, M., Green, W. T. & Messner, M. B. (1963). Growth and predictions of growth in the lower extremities. *Journal of Bone and Joint Surgery*, **45A**, 1–14.

Anderson, S., Bankier, A. T., Barrell, B. G. *et al.* (1981). Sequence and organization of the human mitochondrial genome. *Nature*, **290**, 457–74.

Andrews, P. (1992). Evolution and environment in the Hominoidea. *Nature*, **360**, 641–6.

Anon. (1859). St. Hilaire on the systematic position of man. (Histoire naturelle générale des règnes organiques, tome II, l^e partie, 1856.) *Proceeding of the Royal Society.* (London), **10**, 1–9.

ApSimon, A. M. (1980). The last neanderthal in France? *Nature*, **287**, 271–2.

Armstrong, S. (1993). Real monkeys don't drink water. *New Scientist*, **138**, 34–9.

Arnason, U. & Gullberg, A. (1993). Comparison between the complete mtDNA sequences of the blue and the fin whale, two species that can hybridize in nature. *Journal of Molecular Biology*, **37**, 312–22.

Arnaud, C. D. & Sanchez, S. D. (1990). The role of calcium in osteoporosis. *Annual Review of Nutrition*, **10**, 397–414.

Arnold, M. J. (1997). *Natural Hybridization and Evolution*. Oxford: Oxford University Press.

Aronson, J. & Taieb, M. (1981). Geology and paleogeography of the Hadar hominid site, Ethiopia. In *Hominid Sites: Their Geological Settings*, ed. G. Rapp & C. Vondra, pp. 165–96. Boulder: Westview.

Asfaw, B., Beyene, Y., Suwa, G., Walter, R. C., White, R. D., WoldeGabriel, G. Yemane, T. (1992). The earliest Acheulean from Konso-Gardula. *Nature*, **360**, 732–5.

Asfaw, B., Beyene, Y., Haile-Selassie, Y., Hart, W., Renne, P., Suwa, G., White, T. & WoldeGabriel, G. (1995). *Three Seasons of Hominid Paleontology at Aramis, Ethiopia*. Oakland: Paleontology Society Conference.

Asfaw, B., White, T., Lovejoy, O., Latimer, B., Simpson, S. & Suwa, G. (1999). *Australopithecus garhi*: a new species of early hominid from Ethiopia. *Science*, **284**, 629–35.

Auel, J. *Clan of the Cave Bear* (1980). New York: Crown.

Avise, J. C. (1994). *Molecular Markers, Natural History and Evolution*. London: Chapman and Hall.

Avise, J. C. & Duvall. S. W. (1977). Allelic expression in hybrid macaques. *Journal of Heredity*, **68**, 22–30.

Ayala, F. (1975). Genetic differentiation during the speciation process. In *Evolutionary Biology*, vol. 9, ed. T. Dobzhansky, M. K. Hecht & W. C. Steere, pp. 1–78. New York: Plenum.

Ayala, F., Escalante, J. A., O'Huigin, C. & Klein, J. (1994). Molecular genetics of speciation and human origins. *Proceedings of the National Academy of Sciences, USA*, **91**, 6787–94.

Baker, P. T. (1958). The biological adaptation of man to hot deserts. *American Naturalist*, **92**, 337–57.

Baker, P. T. (1960). Climate, culture, and evolution. *Human Biology*, **32**, 3–16.

Baker, P. T. (1966). Human biological variation as an adaptive response to the environment. *Eugenics Quarterly*, **13**, 81–91.

Baker, P. T. (1969). Human adaptation to high altitude. *Science*, **163**, 1149–56.

Baker, P. T. (1983). Man must adapt, or be damned. *New Scientist*, **4**, 352–5.

Baldwin, J. M. (1898). A new factor in evolution. *American Naturalist*, **30**, 441–51, 536–53.

Bales, C. W. & Anderson, J. J. B. (1995). Influence of nutritional factors on bone health of the elderly. In *Calcium and Phosphorus in Health and Disease*, ed. J. J. B. Anderson & S. C. Garner, pp. 319–37. Boca Raton: CRC Press.

Bar-Yosef, O. (1993). The role of western Asia in modern human origins. In *The Origin of Modern Humans and the Impact of Chronometric Dating*, ed. M. J. Aitken, C. B. Stringer & P. A. Mellars, pp. 132–47. Princeton: Princeton University Press.

Barker, H., Burleigh, R. & Meeks, N. (1969). British Museum National Radiocarbon Measurements VI. *Radiocarbon*, **11**, 289.

Barnabas, J., Goodman, M. & Moore, G. W. (1972). Descent of mammalian alpha globin chain sequences investigated by the maximum parsimony method. *Journal of Molecular Biology*, **69**, 249–78.

Barriel, V. & Tassey, P. (1993). Characters, observations and steps: comment on Lipscomb's 'Parsimony, homology and the analysis of multistate characters'. *Cladistics*, **9**, 223–32.

Bateson, W. (1894). *Materials for the Study of Variation*. New York: Macmillan.

Bateson, W. (1906). A text-book of genetics. *Nature*, **74**, 146–7.

Bartholomew, G. A. & Birdsell, J. B. (1953). Ecology and the protohominids. *American Anthropologist*, **55**, 481–98.

Bather, F. A. (1925). The word *Australopithecus* and others. *Nature*, **115**, 947.

Baxter, J. H. (1875). *Statistics, Medical and Anthropological, of over a Million Recruits*. Washington, DC: US Government Printing Office.

Beck, B. (1974). Baboons, chimpanzees, and tools. *Journal of Human Evolution*, **3**, 509–16.

Behrensmeyer, A. (1970). Preliminary geological interpretation of a new hominid site in the Lake Rudolf basin. *Nature*, **226**, 225–6.

Behrensmeyer, A. (1976). Lothagam Hill, Kanapoi, and Ekora: a general summary of stratigraphy and faunas. In *Earliest Man and Environments in the Lake Rudolf Basin*, ed. Y. Coppens, F. C. Howell, G. Isaac & R. Leakey, pp. 163–70. Chicago: University of Chicago Press.

Bender, M. A. & Chu, E. H. Y. (1963). The chromosomes of primates. In *Evolutionary and Genetic Biology of Primates*, vol. 1., ed. J. Buettner-Janusch, pp. 261–310. New York: Academic Press.

Benveniste, R. E. (1985). The contributions of retroviruses to the study of mammalian evolution. In *Molecular Evolutionary Genetics*, ed. R. I. MacIntyre, pp. 359–417. New York: Plenum.

Berger, L. R., Menter, C. G. & Thackeray, J. F. (1994). The renewal of excavation activities at Kromdraai, South Africa. *South African Journal of Science*, **90**, 209–210.

Berger, L. R. & Tobias, P. V. (1995). A chimpanzee-like tibia from Sterkfontein, South Africa and its implications for the interpretation of bipedalism in *Australopithecus africanus*. *Journal of Human Evolution*, **30**, 343–8.

Berger, T. D. & Trinkaus, E. (1995). Patterns of trauma among the Neanderthals. *Journal of Archaeological Science*, **22**, 841–52.

Bergman, C. (1847). Über die Verhältnisse der Wärmeökonomie der Thiere zu ihrer Grösse. *Göttinger Studien*, **3**, 95–108.

Bernstein, F. (1932). *Die geographische Verteilung der Blutgruppen und ihre anthropologische Bedeutung.* Rome: Instituto Poligraphico della Stato.

Bernstein, I. S. (1966). Naturally occurring primate hybrids. *Science*, **154**, 1559–60.

Bernstein, I. S. (1968). Social status of two hybrids in a wild troop of *Macaca irus*. *Folia primatologia*, **8**, 121–31.

Bernstein, I. S. (1974). Birth of two second generation hybrid macaques. *Journal of Human Evolution*, **3**, 205–6.

Bernstein, R. S., Robbins, J. & Rall, J. E. (1970). Polymorphism of monkey thyroxine-binding prealbumin (TBPA): mode of inheritance and hybridization. *Endocrinology*, **86**, 383–90.

Berry, W. B. N. (1968). *Growth of a Prehistoric Time Scale.* San Francisco: W. H. Freeman and Company.

Black, D. (1927). On a lower molar hominid tooth from Chou-Kou-Tien deposit. *Palaeontologia Sinica*, **7**, 1–28.

Blanco, R. A., Acheson, R. M., Canosa, C. & Salomon, J. B. (1974). Height, weight, and lines of arrested growth in young Guatemalan children. *American Journal of Physical Anthropology*, **40**, 39–48.

Bloch, M. (1991). Language, anthropology and cognitive science. *Man*, **26**, 183–98.

Blum, H. F. (1961). Does the melanin pigment of the human skin have adaptive value? *Quarterly Review of Biology*, **36**, 50–63.

Blumenberg, B. (1983). The evolution of the advanced hominid brain. *Current Anthropology*, **24**, 589–623.

Boas, F. (1910). *Changes in the Bodily Form of the Descendants of Immigrants.* Senate Document 208, 61st Congress, 2nd Session. Washington, DC: US Government Printing Office.

Boas, F. (1912). *Changes in the Bodily Form of the Descendants of Immigrants.* New York: Columbia University Press.

Boaz, N. & Howell, F. C. (1977). A gracile hominid cranium from Upper Member G of the Shungura Formation, Ethiopia. *American Journal of Physical Anthropology*, **46**, 93–108.

Boeda, E., Connan, J., Dessort, D., Muhesen, S., Mercier, N., Valladas, H. & Tisnerat, N. (1996). Bitumen as a hafting material on Middle Paleolithic artifacts. *Nature*, **380**, 336–8.

Bombin, M. (1990). Transverse enamel hypoplasia on teeth of South African Plio-Pleistocene hominids. *Naturwissenschaften*, **77**, 128–9.

Boule, M. (1911). L'homme fossile de La Chapelle-aux-Saints. *Annales de Paléontologie*, **6**, 111–172.

Boule, M. (1912). L'homme fossile de La Chapelle-aux-Saints. *Annales de Paléontologie*, **7**, 21–56, 85–192.

Boule, M. (1913). L'homme fossile de la Chapelle-Aux-Saints. *Annales de Paléontologie*, **8**, 1–70.

Boule, M. & Vallois, H. (1921). *Les hommes fossiles.* Paris: Maisson.

Boule, M. & Vallois, H. (1937, rpt. 1957). *Fossil Men*. New York: Dryden Press.

Bourne, G. (1971). Nutrition and diet of chimpanzees. In *The Chimpanzee*, ed. G. H. Bourne, pp. 373–400. Basel: Karger.

Boveri, T. (1904). *Ergebnisse über die Konstitution der chromatischen Substanz des Zellkerns*. Jena: Gustav Fischer Verlag.

Bowditch, H. P. (1879). *The Growth of Children, a Supplementary Investigation*, pp. 35–62. Boston: State Board of Health of Massachusetts.

Bowen, D. Q. & Sykes, G. A. (1994). How old is 'Boxgrove man'? *Nature*, **371**, 751.

Bowen, F. H. & Vondra, C. F. (1973). Stratigraphical relationships of the Plio-Pleistocene deposits, East Rudolf, Kenya. *Nature*, **242**, 391–393.

Bowler, P. (1997). Paleoanthropology theory. In *History of Physical Anthropology, an Encyclopedia*, ed. F. Spencer, pp. 785–790. New York: Garland.

Boyd, W. C. (1950). *Genetics and the Races of Man*. Boston: Little Brown.

Brace, C. L. (1964). The fate of the 'Classic' Neanderthals. *Current Anthropology*, **5**, 3–19.

Brace, C. L. (1997). Modern human origins: narrow focus or broad spectrum? In *Conceptual Issues in Modern Human Origins Research*, eds. G. A. Clark & C. M. Willermet, pp. 11–27. New York: Aldine de Gruyter.

Brace, C. L., Xiang-qing, S. & Zhen-biao, Z. (1984). Prehistoric and modern tooth size in China. In *The Origins of Modern Humans*, ed. F. H. Smith & F. Spencer, pp. 485–516. New York: Alan R. Liss.

Brain, C. K. (1993). Structure and stratigraphy of the Swartkrans cave in the light of the new excavations. In *Swartkrans: A Cave's Chronicle of Early Man*, ed. C. K. Brain, pp. 23–33. Pretoria: Transvaal Museum.

Brain, C. K. (1994). The Swartkrans palaeontological research project in perspective: results and conclusions. *South African Journal of Science*, **90**, 220–223.

Brain, C. K. & Watson, V. (1992). A guide to the Swartkrans early hominid cave site. *Annals of the Transvaal Museum*, **35**, 343–65.

Branda, R. F. & Eaton, J. W. (1978). Skin color and nutrient photolysis: an evolutionary hypothesis. *Science*, **201**, 625–6.

Bräuer, G. (1984). A craniological approach to the origin of anatomically modern *Homo sapiens* in Africa and implications for the appearance of modern Europeans. In *The Origins of Modern Humans*, ed. F. H. Smith & F. Spencer, pp. 327–410. New York: Alan R. Liss.

Bräuer, G. (1994). How different are Asian and African *Homo erectus*? *Courier Forschungsinstitut Senckenberg*, **171**, 175–84.

Bräuer, G. & Mbua, E. (1992). *Homo erectus* features used in cladistics and their variability in Asian and African hominids. *Journal of Human Evolution*, **22**, 79–108.

Bräuer, G. & Smith, F. H. (eds.) (1992). *Continuity or Replacement? Controversies in* Homo sapiens *Evolution*. Rotterdam: Balkema.

Broberg, G. (1980). *Linnaeus: Progress and Prospects in Linnaen Research*. Stockholm: Almqvist & Wiskell International.

Brooks, A. S. (1993). Behavior and human evolution. In *Contemporary Issues in Human Evolution*, ed. W. E. Meikle, F. C. Howell & N. G. Jablonski, pp. 135–66. Memoir 21. San Francisco: California Academy of Sciences.

Broom, R. (1936). A new fossil anthropoid skull from South Africa. *Nature*, **138**, 486–8.

Broom, R. (1937). Discovery of a lower molar of *Australopithecus*. *Nature*, **140**, 681–2.

Broom, R. (1938). The Pleistocene anthropoid apes of South Africa. *Nature*, **142**, 377–9.

Broom, R. (1949). Another type of fossil ape-man. *Nature*, **163**, 57.

Broom, R. (1950). *Finding the Missing Link*. London: Watts & Co.

Broom, R. & Robinson, J. T. (1947). Further remains of the Sterkfontein ape-man, *Plesianthropus*. *Nature*, **160**, 430–1.

Brown, F. & Cerling, T. E. (1982). Stratigraphical significance of the Tulu Bor Tuff of the Koobi Fora Formation. *Nature*, **299**, 212–15.

Brown, F. (1994). Development of Pliocene and Pleistocene chronology of the Turkana Basin, East Africa and its relation to other sites. In *Integrative Paths to the Past*, ed. E. S. Corrucini & R. L. Ciochon, pp. 285–312. Englewood Cliffs: Prentice-Hall.

Brown, F. & Feibel, C. (1986). Revision of lithostratigraphic nomenclature in the Koobi Fora region, Kenya. *Journal of the Geological Society*, **143**, 297–310.

Brown, F. & Feibel, C. (1988). 'Robust' hominid and Plio-Pleistocene paleogeography of the Turkana Basin, Kenya and Ethiopia. In *Evolutionary History of the 'Robust' Australopithecines*, ed. F. E. Grine, pp. 324–41. New York: Aldine de Gruyter.

Brown, F., Harris, J., Leakey, R. & Walker, A. (1985a). Early *Homo erectus* skeleton from West Lake Turkana, Kenya. *Nature*, **316**, 788–92.

Brown, F., McDougall, I., Davies, T. & Maier, R. (1985b). An integrated Plio-Pleistocene chronology for the Turkana Basin. In *Ancestors: The Hard Evidence*, ed. E. Delson, pp. 82–90. New York: Alan R. Liss.

Brown, B., Walker, A., Ward, C. V. & Leakey, R. E. F. (1993). New *Australopithecus boisei* calvaria from East Lake Turkana, Kenya. *American Journal of Physical Anthropology*, **91**, 137–59.

Brown, P. (1993). Recent human evolution in East Asia and Australia. In *The Origin of Modern Humans and the Impact of Chronometric Dating*, ed. M. J. Aitken, C. B. Stringer & P. A. Mellars, pp. 217–33. Princeton: Princeton University Press.

Bruce, E. J. & Ayala, F. J. (1978). Humans and apes are genetically very similar. *Nature*, **276**, 264–5.

Bruce, E. J. & Ayala, F. J. (1979). Phylogenetic relationships between man and apes: electrophoretic evidence. *Evolution*, **33**, 1040–56.

Buckland, W. (1820). *Vindiciae Geologicae; or the Connexion of Geology with Religion Explained*. Oxford: Oxford University Press.

Buckland, W. (1823–1824). *Reliquiae Diluvianae; or, Observations on the Organic Remains Contained in Caves, Fissures, and Diluvial Gravel, and on other Geological Phenomena Attesting the Action of an Universal Deluge*. London: John Murray.

Buckland, W. (1836, 1837). *Geology and Mineralogy Considered with Reference to Natural Theology (Bridgewater Treatise)*, 2 vols. London: William Pickering.

Buettner-Janusch, J. (1966). A problem in evolutionary systematics: nomenclature and classification of baboons, genus *Papio. Folia Primatologica*, **4**, 288–308.

Buikstra, J. E., Frankenberg, S. R. & Konigsberg, L. W. (1990). Skeletal biological distance studies in American physical anthropology: recent trends. *American Journal of Physical Anthropology*, **82**, 1–7.

Buikstra, J. E. & Ubelaker, D. (eds.) (1994). *Standards for Data Collection from Human Skeletal Remains. Arkansas Archaeological Survey Research Series*, **44**. Arkansas: Arkansas Archaeological Survey.

Burchfield, J. D. (1975). *Lord Kelvin and the Age of the Earth*. New York: Science History Publications.

Burton, J. H. & Wright, L. E. (1995). Nonlinearity in the relationship between bone Sr/Ca and diet: evolutionary implications. *American Journal of Physical Anthropology*, **96**, 273–82.

Busk, G. (1861). On the crania of the most ancient races of man, by Professor D. Schaaffhausen of Bonn. (From Müller's *Archiv.*, 1858, pp. 453.) With remarks, and original figures, taken from a cast of the Neanderthal cranium. *Natural History Review* (April, 1861).

Buskirk, E. R., Anderson, K. L. & Brozek, J. (1956). Unilateral activity and bone and muscle development in the forearms. *Research*, **27**, 127–31.

Butzer, K. (1971). *Environment and Archeology*, 2nd edn. Chicago: Aldine.

Byard, P. J. (1981). Quantitative genetics of human skin color. *Yearbook of Physical Anthropology*, **24**, 123–37.

Cabanc, M. & Caputa, M. (1979). Natural selective cooling of the human brain: evidence of its occurrence and magnitude. *Journal of Physiology*, **286**, 255–64.

Cann, R. L., Stoneking, M. & Wilson, A. C. (1987). Mitochondrial DNA and human evolution. *Nature*, **325**, 31–6.

Carbonell, E., de Castro, J. M. B., Arsuaga, J. L., Diez, J. C., Rosas, A., Cuenca-Bescos, G., Sala, R., Mosquera, M. & Rodriguez, X. P. (1995). Lower Pleistocene hominids and artifacts from Atapuerca-TD 6 (Spain). *Science*, **269**, 826–30.

Castle, W. E. (1911). *Heredity in Relation to Evolution and Animal Breeding*. New York: Appleton.

Castle, W. E. (1916). *Genetics and Eugenics*. Cambridge, MA: Harvard University Press.

Castle, W. E. (1919). Piebald rats and selection, a correction. *American Naturalist*, **53**, 373–6.

Castle, W. E. & Phillips, J. C. (1914). *Piebald Rats and Selection*. Carnegie Institution of Washington Publication no. 195. Washington, DC: Chapman and Hall.

Castle, W. E. & Wright, S. (1916). *Piebald Rats and Selection*. Carnegie Institution of Washington Publication no. 241. Washington, DC: Chapman and Hall.

Cerling, T. E. & Brown, F. H. (1982). Tuffaceous marker horizons in the Koobi Fora region and the Lower Omo Valley. *Nature*, **229**, 216–21.

Chaplin, G., Jablonski, N. G. & Cable, N. T. (1994). Physiology, thermoregulation and bipedalism. *Journal of Human Evolution*, **27**, 497–510.

Charles, R. H. (1893). The influence of function, as exemplified in the lower extremity of the Punjabi. *Journal of Anatomy and Physiology*, **28**, 1–18.

Cherry, L. M., Case, S. M. & Wilson, A. C. (1978). Frog perspective on the morphological divergence between humans and chimpanzees. *Science*, **200**, 209–11.

Chesterton, G. K. (1908). The ethics of Elfland. Reprinted in *Orthodoxy*, ed. P. J. Kavanagh, pp. 254–69. London: The Bodley Head.

Chiarelli, B. (1958). Tavole cromosomiche dei Primati e dell'Umo. *Caryologia*, **11**, 99–104.

Chiarelli, B. (1961a). Chromosomes of the Orang-Utan (*Pongo pygmaeus*). *Nature*, **192**, 285.

Chiarelli, B. (1961b). Ibridologia e sistematica in Primati. I. Raccolta di dati. *Atti Associazione Genetica Italiana, Pavia*, Gen. It. **6**, 213–20.

Chiarelli, B. (1961c). Cariologia e sistematica dei Primati con cenni sulla origine del cariotipo umano. *Comunicazione Societa Italiana Antroplogia ed Ethnologia*, (19 dic. 1961).

Chiarelli, B. (1962a). Karyological evolution in primates and the origin of the human karyotype. *Atti Associazione Genetica Italiana, Pavia*, **7**, 284–5.

Chiarelli, B. (1962b). Some new data on the chromosomes of Catarrhine monkeys. *Experientia*, **18**, 405–07.

Chiarelli, B. (1962c). Comparative morphometric analysis of the Primate chromosomes. I. The chromosomes of the anthropoid apes and of man. *Caryologia*, **15**, 99–121.

Chiarelli, B. (1962d). Comparative morphometric analysis of the Primate chromosomes. II. The chromosomes of the genera *Macaca, Papio, Theropithecus* and *Cercocebus*. *Caryologia*, **15**, 401–20.

Chiarelli, B. (1963a). Comparative morphometric analysis of the Primate chromosomes. III. The chromosomes of the genera *Hylobates, Colobus*, and *Presbytis*. *Caryologia*, **16**, 637–48.

Chiarelli, B. (1963b). Primi risultati di recherche di genetica e cariologia comparata in Primati e loro interesse evolutivo. *Rivista di Antropologia*, **50**, 87–124.

Chiarelli, B. (1965). A marked chromosome in Catarrhine. *Folia Primatalogica*, **4**, 74–80.

Chiarelli, B. (1966a). Caryology and taxonomy of the Catarrhine monkeys. *American Journal of Physical Anthropology*, **24**, 155–70.

Chiarelli, B. (1966b). Chromosome polymorphism in the species of the genus *Cercopithecus Cytologia*, **33**: 1–6.

Chiarelli, B. & Vaccarino, C. (1964). Cariologie ed evoluzione nel genere *Cercopithecus*. *Atti Associazone Genetica Italiana, Pavia*, **9**, 328–39.

Chu, E. H. Y. & Giles, N. H. (1957). A study of primate chromosome complements. *American Naturalist*, **91**, 273–82.

Clark, G. A. (1988). Some thoughts on the black skull: an archeologist's assessment of WT-17000 (*A. boisei*) and systematics in human palaeontology. *American Anthropologist*, **90**, 357–71.

Clark, J. D. (1993). African and Asian perspectives on the origin of modern humans. In *The Origin of Modern Humans and the Impact of Chronometric*

Dating, ed. M. J. Aitken, C. B. Stringer & P. A. Mellars, pp. 148–78. Princeton: Princeton University Press.

Clark, R. W. (1971). *Einstein: The Life and Times*. Cleveland: World Publishing Company.

Clarke, R. J. & Howell, F. C. (1972). Affinities of the Swartkrans 847 hominid cranium. *American Journal of Physical Anthropology*, **37**, 319–36.

Clarke, R. J. (1988). A new *Australopithecus* cranium from Sterkfontein and its bearing on the ancestry of *Paranthropus*. In *Evolutionary History of the 'Robust' Australopithecines*, ed. F. E. Grine, pp. 285–92. New York: Aldine de Gruyter.

Clarke, R. J. (1990). The Ndutu cranium and the origin of *Homo sapiens*. *Journal of Human Evolution*, **19**, 699–736.

Clarke, R. J. (1994a). Advances in understanding the craniofacial anatomy of South African early hominids. In *Integrative Paths to the Past*, ed. R. S. Corrucini & R. L. Ciochon, pp. 205–22. Englewood Cliffs: Prentice-Hall.

Clarke, R. J. (1994b). The significance of the Swartkrans *Homo* to the *Homo erectus* problem. *Courier Forschungsinstitut Senckenberg*, **171**, 185–93.

Clarke, R. J. & Gindhart, P. S. (1981). Commonality in peak age of early childhood morbidity across cultures and over time. *Current Anthropology*, **22**, 574–75.

Clarke, R. J. & Tobias, P. V. (1995). Sterkfontein Member 2 foot bones of the oldest South African hominid. *Science*, **269**, 521–4.

Clarke, R. J., Howell, F. C. & Brain, R. (1970). More evidence of an advanced hominid at Swartkrans. *Nature*, **225**, 1219–22.

Claussen, B. F. (1982). Chronic hypertrophy of the ulna in the professional rodeo cowboy. *Clinical Orthopaedics and Related Research*, **164**, 45–7.

Clegg, M. & Aiello, L. C. (1999). A comprison of the Nariokotome *Homo erectus* with juveniles from a modern human population. *American Journal of Physical Anthropology*, **110**, 81–93.

CLIMAP Project Members (1976). The surface of the ice-age earth. *Science*, **191**, 1131–37.

Collingwood, R. G. (1946). *The Idea of History*. London: Longman.

Colyer, F. (1936). *Variations and Diseases of the Teeth of Animals*. London: John Bale and Sons and Danielsson, Ltd.

Conroy, G. C. (1992). Closing the hominid gap. *Nature*, **360**, 393–4.

Conroy, G. C. (1997). *Reconstructing Human Origins*. New York: Norton.

Conroy, G. C. & Vannier, M. W. (1991). Dental development in South African australopithecines: Part I. problems of pattern and chronology. *American Journal of Physical Anthropology*, **86**, 121–36.

Coon, C. S. (1962). *The Origin of Races*. New York: Alfred A. Knopf.

Corrucini, R. & McHenry, H. (1980). Cladometric analysis of Pliocene hominids. *Journal of Human Evolution*, **9**, 209–21.

Cosentino, M. J., Pakyz, R. E. & Fried, J. (1990). Pyrimethamine: an approach to the development of a male contraceptive. *Proceedings of the National Academy of Sciences, USA*, **87**, 1431–5.

Cronin, J. E. & Meikle, W. E. (1979). The phyletic position of *Theropithecus*: congruence among molecular, morphological and paleontological evidence. *Systematic Zoology*, **28**, 259–69.

Cronin, J. E. & Sarich, V. M. (1976). Molecular evidence for dual origin of mangabeys among Old World monkeys. *Nature*, **260**, 700–2.

Dart, R. (1925). *Australopithecus africanus*: the man-ape of South Africa. *Nature*, **115**, 195–9.

Dart, R. A. (1948a). An adolescent promethean australopithecine mandible from Makapansgat. *South African Journal of Science*, **45**, 73–5.

Dart, R. A. (1948b). The adolescent mandible of *Australopithecus prometheus*. *American Journal of Physical Anthropology*, **6**, 391–412.

Dart, R. A. & Craig, D. (1959). *Adventures with the Missing Link*. New York: Viking.

Darwin, C. (1859). *The Evolution of Species by Means of Natural Selection*. London: Murray.

Darwin, C. (1868). *The Variation of Plants and Animals Under Domestication*, 2 vols. London: Murray.

Darwin, C. (1871). *The Descent of Man, and Selection in Relation to Sex*, 2 vols. London: Murray

Dawkins, R. (1986). *The Blind Watchmaker*. New York: Penguin Books.

Dawkins, R. (1995). *River Out of Eden*. London: Weidenfeld and Nicolson.

Dawkins, R. (1996). *Climbing Mount Improbable*. New York: Norton.

Dawkins, W. B. (1880). *Early Man in Britain*. London: Macmillan.

Dennett, D. (1995). *Darwin's Dangerous Idea*. New York: Simon & Schuster.

Day, M. H. (1971). Postcranial remains of *Homo erectus* from Bed IV, Olduvai Gorge, Tanzania. *Nature*, **232**, 363–87.

Day, M. H. (1982). The *Homo erectus* pelvis: punctuation or gradualism? In L'Homo erectus *et la place de l'homme de Tautavel Parmi les hominides fossiles*, vol. 1, pp. 411–21. Nice: Louis-Jean Scientific and Literary Publications.

Day, M. H. (1985). Hominid locomotion – from Taung to the Laetoli footprints. In *Hominid Evolution: Past, Present and Future*, ed. P. V. Tobias, pp. 115–27. New York: Alan R. Liss.

Day, M. H. (1971). Postcranial remains of *Homo erectus* from Bed IV, Olduvai Gorge, Tanzania. *Nature*, **232**, 363–81.

Day, M. H. (1984). The postcranial remains of *Homo erectus* from Africa, Asia, and possibly Europe. *Courier Forschungsinstitut Senckenberg*, **69**, 113–22.

Day, M. H. (1995). Remarkable delay. *Nature*, **376**, 111.

Day, M. H. & Molleson, T. (1973). The Trinil femur. In *Human Evolution*, ed. M. H. Day, pp. 127–54. London: Taylor and Francis.

de Heinzelin, J., Clark, J. D., White, T., Hart, W., Renne, P., WoldeGabriel, G., Beyene, Y. & Vrba, E. (1999). Environment and behavior of 2.5 million-year-old Bouri hominids. *Science*, **284**, 625–8.

De Quieroz, K. (1988). Systematics and the Darwinian revolution. *Philosophy of Science*, **55**, 238–259.

de Vries, H. (1910). *The Mutation Theory*, 2 vols. (Translated by B. J. Farmer & A. D. Darbishire.) Chicago: Open Court.

de Vos, J. (1985). Faunal stratigraphy and correlation of the Indonesian hominid sites. In *Ancestors: The Hard Evidence*, ed. E. Delson, pp. 215–20. New York: Alan R. Liss.

de Waal, F. M. B. (1998). *Chimpanzee Politics*. Baltimore, MD: Johns Hopkins.

Deacon, H. J. (1993). Southern Africa and modern human origins. In *The Origin of Modern Humans and the Impact of Chronometric Dating*, ed. M. J. Aitken, C. B. Stringer & P. A. Mellars, pp. 104–17. Princeton: Princeton University Press.

Dean, M. C. (1986). *Homo* and *Paranthropus*: similarities in the cranial base and developing dentition. In *Major Topics in Primate and Human Evolution*, ed. B. Woo, L. Martin & P. Andrews, pp. 249–65. Cambridge: Cambridge University Press.

Delson, E. (1975). Evolutionary history of the Cercopithecidae. In *Approaches to Primate Paleobiology*, ed. F. Szalay, pp. 176–217. Basel: Karger.

Delson, E. (1980). Fossil macaques, phyletic relationships and a scenario of deployment. In *The Macaques: Studies in Ecology, Behavior and Evolution*, ed. D. G. Lindberg, pp. 10–30. New York: Van Nostrand Reinhold.

Delson, E. (1981). Paleoanthropology: Pliocene and Pleistocene human evolution. *Paleobiology*, **7**, 298–305.

Delson, E. (1984). Cercopithecoid biochronology of the African Plio-Pleistocene: correlation among eastern and southern hominid-bearing localities. *Courier Forschungsinstitut Senckenberg*, **69**, 199–218.

Dennell, R. (1997). The world's oldest spears. *Nature*, **385**, 767–8.

Dennett, D. (1995). *Darwin's Dangerous Idea*. New York: Simon & Schuster.

Diamond, J. (1991). *The Rise and Fall of the Third Chimpanzee*. London, Radius.

Dierbach, A. (1986). Interspecific variability and sexual dimorphism in the skull of *Pan troglodytes verus*. *Human Evolution*, **1**, 41–50.

Disotell, T. R., Honeycutt, R. L. & Ruvulo, M. (1992). Mitochondrial DNA phylogeny of the Old-World Monkey Tribe Papionini. *Molecular Biology and Evolution*, **9**, 1–13.

Dobzhansky, T. (1955). A review of some fundamental concepts and problems of population genetics. *Cold Spring Harbor Symposia in Quantitative Biology*, **20**, 1–15.

Dobzhansky, T. (1957). *Evolution, Genetics and Man*. New York: John Wiley and Sons.

Dominguez-Rodrigo, M. (1994). *El Origen del Comportamiento Humano*. Madrid: Tipo.

Donoghue, M. J., Doyle, J.A., Gauthier, J., Kluge, A. G. & Rowe, T. (1989). The importance of fossils in phylogeny reconstruction. *Annual Review of Ecology and Systematics*, **20**, 431–60.

Dreizen, S., Currie, C., Gillie, E. J. & Spies, T. D. (1956). Observations on the association between nutritive failure, skeletal maturation rate and radiopaque transverse lines in the distal end of the radius in children. *American Journal of Roentgenology*, **76**, 482–7.

Dreizen, S., Sprirakis, C. N. & Stone, R. E. (1964). The influence of age and nutritional status on 'bone scar' formation in the distal end of the growing radius. *American Journal of Physical Anthropology*, **22**, 295–306.

Dubois, E. (1894). *Pithecanthropus erectus, eine Übergangsform*. Batavia: Landesdruckerei.

Dubois, E. (1896). On *Pithecanthropus* erectus: a transitional form between man and the apes. *Transactions of the Royal Dublin Society*, **2**, 1–18.

Dubois, E. (1899). Remarks upon the brain-cast of *Pithecanthropus erectus*,

(Fourth International Congress of Zoology, Cambridge, 22–27 August 1898, pp. 78–95). *Journal of Anatomy and Physiology*, **33**, 273.

Dubois, E. (1924). On the principal characters of the cranium and the brain, the mandible and the teeth of *Pithecanthropus erectus*. *Proceedings of the Royal Academy of Science, Amsterdam*, **27**, 459–64.

Duckworth, W. L. H. (1925). The fossil anthropoid ape from Taungs. *Nature*, **115**, 236.

Dunbar, R. I. M. (1976). Austalopithecine diet based on a baboon analogy. *Journal of Human Evolution*, **5**, 161–7.

Dunbar, R. I. M. (1977). Feeding ecology of gelada baboons: a preliminary report. In *Primate Ecology*, ed. T. Clutton-Brock, pp. 251–73. New York & London: Academic Press.

Dunbar, R. I. M. & Dunbar, P. (1974). On hybridization between *Theropithecus gelada* and *Papio anubis* in the wild. *Journal of Human Evolution*, **3**, 187–92.

Dutour, O. (1986). Enthesopathies (lesions of muscular insertions) as indicators of the activities of Neolithic Saharan populations. *American Journal of Physical Anthropology*, **71**, 221–4.

Dutrillaux, B., Couturier, J., Muleris, J. M., Lombard, M. & Chauvier, G. (1982). Chromosomal phylogeny of forty-two species or subspecies of Cercopithecoids (Primates, Catarrhini). *Annals of Genetics*, **25**, 96–109.

East, E. M. (1910a). A Mendelian interpretation of variation that is apparently continuous. *American Naturalist*, **44**, 65–82.

East, E. M. (1910b). The role of selection in plant breeding. *Popular Science Monthly*, **77**, 199.

Eckhardt, R. B. (1971, 1975). Hominoid dental variation and hominid origins. Ph.D. dissertation. The University of Michigan, Ann Arbor. Reprinted (1975) in *Occasional Papers in Anthropology*, No. 8, 93–307. University Park: The Pennsylvania State University.

Eckhardt, R. B. (1972). Population genetics and human origins. *Scientific American*, **226**, 94–03.

Eckhardt, R. B. (1977). Hominid origins: the Lothagam mandible. *Current Anthropology*, **18**, 56.

Eckhardt, R. B. (1979). Chromosome evolution in the genus *Cercopithecus*. In *Comparative Karyology of Primates*, ed. B. Chiarelli, A. L. Koen & G. Ardito, pp. 39–46. The Hague: Mouton.

Eckhardt, R. B. (1984). Rapid morphometric change in human skeletal traits: an example from the Andean highlands. In *Hominid Evolution: Past, Present and Future*, ed. P. V. Tobias, pp. 381–6. New York: Alan R. Liss.

Eckhardt, R. B. (1987). Hominoid nasal region polymorphism and its phylogenetic significance. *Nature*, **328**, 333–5.

Eckhardt, R. B. (1989). Evolutionary morphology of human skeletal characteristics. *Anthropologischer Anzeiger*, **47**, 193–228.

Eckhardt, R. B. (1990). Human quantitative genetics: a century of research. In *Human Genetics, New Perspectives*, ed. P. K. Seth & S. Seth, pp. 21–34. New Delhi: Omega Scientific Publishers.

Eckhardt, R. B. (1992a). A comparative overview of some recent research on adaptation and evolution of Andean populations. In *Population Studies on*

Human Adaptation and Evolution in the Peruvian Andes, ed. R. B. Eckhardt & T. W. Melton, pp. 243–6. *Occasional Papers in Anthropology*, No. 14. University Park: Matson Museum of Anthropology.

Eckhardt, R. B. (1992b). Hominid evolution: molecular and morphological perspectives. In *Topics in Primatology*, vol. 1, ed. T. Nishida, W. C. McGrew, P. Marler, M. Pickford & F. B. M. de Waal, pp. 455–69. Tokyo: University of Tokyo Press.

Eckhardt, R. B. (1992c). Tooth crown development: nonhuman primate perspectives on the interpretation of linear enamel hypoplasia frequencies in present and past hominid populations. In *Recent Contributions to the Study of Enamel Developmental Defects*, ed. A. H. Goodman & L. L. Capasso, pp. 293–305. Teramo, Italy: Edigrafital.

Eckhardt, R. B. (1995). Ape family tree. *Nature*, **372**, 326–7.

Eckhardt, R. B., Dean, W. J. & Hildebrand, A. H. (1997). Variants in vestibular form and function document functional responses irrespective of reproductive isolation. *American Journal of Physical Anthropology*, **24** (Supplement), 105–6.

Eckhardt, R. B. & Piermarini, A. L. (1988). Interproximal grooving of teeth: additional evidence and interpretation. *Current Anthropology*, **29**, 668–71.

Eckhardt, R. B. & Melton, T. W. (eds) (1992). *Population Studies on Human Adaptation and Evolution in the Peruvian Andes. Occasional Papers in Anthropology*, No. 14. University Park: Matson Museum of Anthropology.

Eckhardt, R. B. & Protsch von Zieten, R. R. (1988). Nasal region polymorphism frequencies in the Frankfurt *Pan troglodytes verus* collection. *Human Evolution*, **3**, 367–79.

Eckhardt, R. B. & Protsch von Zieten, R. R. (1992). Apes and apomorphies: the anterior nasal spine as a projection of cladistic conceptions. *Zeitschrift für Morphologie und Anthropologie*, **79**, 95–101.

Eckhardt, R. B. & Protsch von Zieten, R. R. (1995). Molecular and morphological congruence in hominoid trans-species polymorphisms. *Human Evolution*, **10**, 185–92.

Ehrich, R. W. & Coon, C. S. (1947). Occipital flattening among the Dinarics. *American Journal of Physical Anthropology*, **6**, 181–6.

Eiseley, L. C. (1954). The reception of the first missing links. *Proceedings of the American Philosophical Society*, **98**, 453–65.

Eldredge, N. (1982). Phenomenological levels and evolutionary rates. *Systematic Zoology*, **31**, 338–47.

Eldredge, N. (1985). *Unfinished Synthesis: Biological Hierarchies and Modern Evolutionary Thought*. New York: Oxford University Press.

Eldredge, N. & Cracraft, J. (1980). *Phylogenetic Patterns and the Evolutionary Process*. New York: Columbia University Press.

Eli, I., Sarnat, H. & Talmi, E. (1989). Effect of the birth process on the neonatal line in primary tooth enamel. *Pediatric Dentistry*, **11**, 220–30.

Ellerman, J. R. & Morrison-Scott, T. C. (1951). *Check-list of Paleoarctic and Indian Mammals 1758–1946*. London: British Museum (Natural History).

Elliot, D. G. (1913). *A Review of the Primates*, 2 vols. American Museum of Natural History, Monograph Series. New York: American Museum of Natural History.

Elwood, J. M. & Elwood, J. H. (1980). *Epidemiology of Anacephalus and Spina Bifida*. Oxford: Oxford University Press.

Endo, T., Ikeo, K. & Gojobori, T. (1996). Large-scale search for genes on which positive selection may operate. *Molecular Biology and Evolution*, **13**, 685–90.

Erikson, K. L. & Montagna, W. (1975). The induction of melanogenesis by ultraviolet light in the pigmentary system of rhesus monkeys. *Journal of Investigative Dermatology*, **65**, 279–84.

Eveleth, P. & Tanner, J. M. (1976). *Worldwide Variation in Human Growth*. Cambridge: Cambridge University Press.

Eveleth, P. B. (1966). The effects of climate on growth. *Annals of the New York Academy of Sciences*, **134**, 750–9.

Fa, J. E. (1989). The genus *Macaca*: a review of taxonomy and evolution. *Mammal Review*, **19**, 45–81.

Fa, J. E. & Lindburg, D. G. (1996). *Evolution and Ecology of Macaque Societies*. Cambridge: Cambridge University Press.

Falk, D. (1986). Evolution of cranial blood drainage in hominids: enlarged occipital/marginal sinuses and emissary foramina. *American Journal of Physical Anthropology*, **70**, 311–24.

Falk, D. (1990). Brain evolution in *Homo*: The 'radiator' theory. *Behavior and Brain Science*, **13**, 333–381.

Falk, D., Gage, T. B., Dudek, B. & Olson, T. R. (1995). Did more than one species of hominid coexist before 3.0 mya?: Evidence from blood and teeth. *Journal of Human Evolution*, **29**, 591–600.

Federation Dentaire International. (1982). An epidemiological index of development defects of dental enamel (DDE Index). *International Dental Journal* **32**, 515–528.

Feibel, C. S., Brown, F. H. & MacDougal, I. (1989). Stratigraphic context of fossil hominids from the Omo group deposits: Northern Turkana Basin, Kenya and Ethiopia. *American Journal of Physical Anthropology*, **78**, 595–622.

Feldesman, M. R. & Lundy, J. K. (1988). Stature estimates for some African Plio-Pleistocene fossil hominids. *Journal of Human Evolution*, **17**, 583–96.

Feldesman, M. R., Kleckner, J. G. & Lundy, J. K. (1990). The femur/stature ratio and estimates of stature in mid- and late-Pleistocene hominids. *American Journal of Physical Anthropology*, **83**, 359–72.

Fennessy, P. (1997). Interspecies hybrids: some thoughts. *Journal of Heredity*, **88**, 353–4.

Ferrozo, G., Morandi, A., Bounaguro, V., Jaafar, J. & Draghi, F. (1990). Significance of Harris lines in fractures of the lower limbs. *Radiologia Medica*, **80**, 638–44.

Festetics, E. (1819). Weitere Erklärung des Herrn Grafen Emerich Festetics über Inzucht. *Oekonomische Neuigkeiten und Verhandlungen* (Prague), **19**, 25–8.

Figueroa, F. & Klein, J. (1988). Origins of H-2 polymorphism. In *H-2 Genes, Products, and Function*, ed. C. S. David, pp. 61–76. New York: Plenum.

Findlater, I. (1976). Tuffs and the recognition of isochronous mapping units in the East Rudolf succession. In *Earliest Man and Environments in the Lake Rudolf Basin*, ed. Y. Coppens, F. C. Howell, G. L. Isaac, & R. E. F. Leakey, pp. 94–104. Chicago: University of Chicago Press.

Findlater, I. (1978). Isochronous surfaces within the Plio-Pleistocene sediments east of Lake Turkana. In *Geological Background to Fossil Man*, ed. W. W. Bishop, pp. 415–420. Edinburgh: Scottish Academic Press.

Fishberg, M. (1905). Materials for the physical anthropology of the American Jew. *Annals of the New York Academy of Sciences*, **16**, 155–297.

Fisher, R. A. (1924) The biometric study of heredity. *Eugenics Review*, **xvi**(3), 189–210.

Fisher, R. A. (1930). *The Genetical Theory of Natural Selection*. Oxford: Clarendon Press.

Fitch, F. J. & Miller, J. G. (1970). Radioisotopic age determinations of Lake Rudolf artefact site. *Nature*, **226**, 226–8.

Fitch, F. J., Miller, J. A. & Mitchell, J. G. (1996). Dating of the KBS tuff and *Homo rudolfensis*. *Journal of Human Evolution*, **30**, 277–86.

Fittinghof, N. A. & Lindburg, D. G. (1980). Riverine refugia in East Bornean *Macaca fscicularis*. In *The Macaques, Studies in Ecology Behavior and Evolution*. ed. D. G. Lindbury, pp. 182–214. New York: Van Nostrand Reinhold.

Fitzpatrick, T. B. (1965). Introductory lecture. In *Recent Progress in Photobiology*, ed. E. J. Bower, pp. 365–373. New York: Academic Press.

Fix, A. G. (1999). *Migration and Colonization in Human Microevolution*. Cambridge: Cambridge University Press.

Fleagle, J. (1988). *Primate Evolution and Adaptation*. New York: Academic Press.

Feagle, J. (1995). Too many species? *Evolutionary Anthropology*, **4**, 37–8.

Fleagle, J., Rasmussen, D., Yirga, S., Bown, T. & Grine, F. (1991). New hominid fossils from Fejej, Southern Ethiopia. *Journal of Human Evolution*, **21**, 145–52.

Fleming, A. & Copp, A. J. (1998). Embryonic folate metabolism and mouse neural tube defects. *Science*, **280**, 2107–9.

Foley, R. (1984). Early man and the Red Queen: tropical African community evolution and hominid adaptation. In *Hominid Evolution and Community Ecology: Prehistoric Human Adaptation in Biological Perspective*, ed. R. A. Foley, pp. 85–110. New York: Academic Press.

Foley, R. (1987). *Another Unique Species*. Essex: Longman.

Foley, R. (1991). How many hominid species should there be? *Journal of Human Evolution*, **20**, 413–27.

Foley, R. (1992). Evolutionary ecology of fossil hominids. In *Evolutionary Ecology and Human Behavior*, ed. E. A. Smith and B. Winterhalder, pp. 131–64. Chicago: Aldine de Gruyter.

Foley, R. (1995). *Humans Before Humanity*. Oxford: Blackwell.

Foley, R. & Lahr, M. M. (1992). Beyond 'Out of Africa': reassessing the origins of *Homo sapiens*. *Journal of Human Evolution*, **22**, 523–9.

Fooden, J. (1964). Rhesus and crab-eating macaques: intergradation in Thailand. *Science*, **143**, 363–5.

Fooden, J. (1969). Taxonomy and evolution of the monkeys of the Celebes. *Bibliotheca primatolgoica*, No. 10, pp. 148.

Fooden, J. (1971). Male external genitalia and systematic relationships of the Japanese macaque (*Macaca fuscata* Blyth, 1875). *Primates*, **12**, 305–11.

Fooden, J. (1975). Taxonomy and evolution of liontail and pigtail macaques (Primates: Cercopithecidae). *Fieldiana: Zoology*, **67**, 1–169.

Fooden, J. (1976). Provisional classification and key to the living species of macaques (Primates: *Macaca*). *Folia primatologia*, **25**, 225–36.

Fooden, J. (1980). Classification and distribution of living macaques (*Macaca* Lacépède, 1799). In *The Macaques: Studies in Ecology, Behavior and Evolution*, ed. D. G. Lindburg, pp. 1–9. New York: Van Nostrand Reinhold.

Forman, L., Kleiman, D. G., Bush, R. M., Dietz, J. M., Ballou, J. D., Phillips, L. G., Coimbra-Filho, A. F. & O'Brien, S. J. (1986). Genetic variation within and among lion tamarins. *American Journal of Physical Anthropology*, **71**, 1–11.

Fraipont, C. (1936). *Les Hommes fossiles d'Engis*. Archives de l'Institut de Paléontologie humaine, Mémoire 16. Paris: Institut de Paléontologie humaine.

Frayer, D. W. (1984). Biological and cultural change in the European Late Pleistocene and Early Holocene. In *The Origins of Modern Humans*, ed. F. H. Smith & F. Spencer, pp. 211–250. New York: Alan R. Liss.

Frayer, D. W. (1992). The persistence of Neanderthal features in post-Neanderthal Europeans. In *Continuity or Replacement? Controversies in* Homo sapiens *Evolution*, ed. G. Bräuer & F. H. Smith. Rotterdam: Balkema.

Frayer, D. W. (1997). Perspectives on Neanderthals as ancestors. In *Conceptual Issues in Modern Human Origins Research*, ed. G. A. Clark & C. M. Willermet, pp. 220–34. New York: Aldine de Gruyter.

Frayer, D. W. & Russell, M. D. (1987). Artificial grooves on the Krapina Neanderthal teeth. *American Journal of Physical Anthropology*, **74**, 393–405.

Frisancho, R. A. & Schechter, D. E. (1997). Adaptation. In *History of Physical Anthropology*, ed. F. Spencer, pp. 6–12. New York: Garland.

Gabunia, L. & Vekua, A. (1995). A Plio-Pleistocene hominid from Dmanisi, East Georgia, Caucasus. *Nature*, **373**, 509–12.

Galton, F. (1889). *Natural Inheritance*. London: Macmillan.

Galton, F. (1897). The average contribution of each several ancestor to the total heritage of the offspring. *Proceedings of the Royal Society*, **61**, 401–13.

Garn, S. M., Rohrmann, C. G., Wagner, B. & Ascoli, W. (1967). Continuing bone growth throughout life: a general phenomenon. *American Journal of Physical Anthropology*, **26**, 313–18.

Garn, S. M. & Schwager, P. M. (1967). Age dynamics of persistent transverse lines in the tibia. *American Journal of Physical Anthropology*, **27**, 375–8.

Garn, S. M., Silverman, F. N., Hertzog, K. P. & Rohmann, V. M. (1968). Lines and bands of increased density: their implication to growth and development. *Medical Radiography and Photography*, **44**, 58–89.

Garrod, A. E. (1902). The incidence of alkaptonuria: a study in chemical individuality. *Lancet* **2**: 1616–20.

Garrod, A. E. (1908). Inborn errors of metabolism. *Lancet*, **2**: 1–7, 73–9, 142–8, 214–20.

Gavan, J. A. (1953). Growth and development of the chimpanzee, a longitudinal and comparative study. *Human Biology*, **25**, 93–143.

Gavan, J. A. (1971). Longitudinal postnatal growth in the chimpanzee. In *The Chimpanzee*, vol. 4, ed. G. Bourne, pp. 46–102. Basel: Karger.

Gee, H. (1995). Uprooting the family tree. *Nature*, **373**, 15.

Geissmann, T. (1986). Estimation of australopithecine stature from long bones: A.L. 288–1 as a test case. *Folia Primatologica*, **47**, 119–27.

Gerber, A., Raab, A. P. & Sobel, A. E. (1954). Vitamin A poisoning in adults. *American Journal of Medicine*, **16**, 729–45.

Gettinby, G. & Glekin, B. M. (1987). The importance of limited exposure to ultraviolet radiation and dietary factors in the aetiology of Asian rickets: a risk factor model. *Quarterly Journal of Medicine*, **63**, 413–25.

Gibbs, H. L. & Grant, P.R. (1987). Oscillating selection on Darwin's finches. *Nature*, **327**, 511–13.

Gillespie, J. H. (1991). *The Causes of Molecular Evolution*. Oxford: Oxford University Press.

Gingerich, P. D. (1979). Paleontology, phylogeny, and classification: an example from the mammalian fossil record. *Systematic Zoology*, **28**, 451–64.

Gingerich, P. D. (1983). Rates of evolution: effects of time and temporal scaling. *Science*, **222**, 159–61.

Gleick, J. (1992). *Genius: The Life and Science of Richard Feynman*. New York: Pantheon Books.

Gloger, C. L. (1833). *Das Abhändern der Vögel durch Einfluss des Klimas*. Breslau: August Schultz.

Golding, W. (1995). *The Inheritors*. London: Faber and Faber.

Goldman, D., Giri, P. R. & O'Brien, S. J. (1989). Molecular genetic-distance estimates among the Ursidae as indicated by one- and two-dimensional electrophersis. *Evolution*, **43**, 282–95.

Goldstein, M. S. (1943). *Demographic and Bodily Changes in Descendants of Mexican Immigrants*. Austin: University of Texas Institute of Latin American Studies.

Goodall, J. (1986). *The Chimpanzees of Gombe: Patterns of Behavior*. Cambridge, MA: Belknap Press.

Goodman, M. (1961). The role of immunochemical differences in the phyletic development of human behavior. *Human Biology*, **33**, 131–162.

Goodman, M. (1962a). Evolution of the immunologic species specificity of human serum proteins. *Human Biology*, **34**, 104–50.

Goodman, M. (1962b). Immunochemistry of the primates and primate evolution. *Annals of the New York Academy of Sciences*, **102**, 219–34.

Goodman, M. (1963a). Man's place in the phylogeny of primates as reflected inserum proteins. In *Classification and Human Evolution*, ed. S. L. Washburn, pp. 204–34. Chicago: Aldine de Gruyter.

Goodman, M. (1963b). Serological analysis of the systematics of recent hominoids. *Human Biology*, **35**, 377–436.

Goodman, M. (1965). The specificity of proteins and the process of primate evolution. In *Protides of the body fluids – 1964*, ed. H. Peters, pp. 70–86. Amsterdam: Elsevier.

Goodman, M. (1967). Deciphering primate phylogeny from macromolecular-specificities. *American Journal of Physical Anthropology*, **26**, 255–75.

Goodman, M. (1992). Hominoid evolution at the DNA level and the position of humans in a phylogenetic classification. In *Topics in Primatology*, vol. 1, ed. T. Nishida, W. C. McGrew, P. Marler, M. Pickford & F. B. M. de Waal, pp. 331–46. Tokyo: University of Tokyo Press.

Goodman, M. & Moore, G. W. (1971). Immunodiffusion systematics of the Primates. I. The Catarrhini. *Systematic Zoology*, **20**, 19–62.

Gordon, C. C., Churchill, T., Clauser, C. E., Bradtmiller, B., McConville, J. T.,Tebbetts, I. & Walker, R. A. (1989). *1988 Anthropometric Survey of US Army Personnel: Methods and Summary Statistics*. Natick: United States Army Natick Research, Development and Engineering Center. (Distributed by National Technical Information Service, Springfield, VA.)

Gossett, W. S. ['Student'] (1933). Evolution by selection. *The Eugenics Review*, **24**, 293–6.

Gould, B. A. (1869). *Investigations in the Military and Anthropological Statistics of American Soldiers. Sanitary Memoirs of the War of the Rebellion*. US Sanitary Commission. New York: Hurd and Houghton.

Gould, S. J. (1980). Is a new and general theory of evolution emerging? *Paleobiology*, **6**, 119–30.

Gould, S. J. (1990). Men of the thirty-third division. *Natural History*, **99**, 12–24.

Gould, S. J. (1985). A clock of evolution. *Natural History*, **94**, 12–25.

Gould, S. J. & Eldredge, N. (1977). Punctuated equilibria: the tempo and mode of evolution revisited. *Paleobiology*, **3**, 115–51.

Gould, S. J. & Vrba, E. S. (1982). Exaptation – a missing term in the science of form. *Paleobiology*, **8**, 4–15.

Gray, A. P. (1972). *Mammalian Hybrids*. Farnham Royal: Commonwealth Agricultural Bureau.

Gregory, W. K. (1922). *The Origin and Evolution of the Human Dentition*. Baltimore: Williams and Wilkins.

Gregory, W. K. (1951). *Evolution Emerging*. New York: Macmillan.

Grine, F. E. (1988). *Evolutionary History of the 'Robust' Australopithecines*. NewYork: Aldine de Gruyter.

Grine, F. E. (1989). New hominid fossils from the Swartkrans Formation (1979–1986 Excavations): craniodental specimens. *American Journal of Physical Anthropology*, **79**, 409–49.

Grine, F. E. (1993). Australopithecine taxonomy and phylogeny: historical background and recent interpretation. In *The Human Evolution Source Book*, ed. R. L. Ciochon & J. G. Fleagle, pp. 198–210. Englewood Cliffs: Prentice-Hall.

Grine, F. E. & Strait, D. S. (1994). New hominid fossils from Member 1 'Hanging Remnant,' Swartkrans Formation, South Africa. *Journal of Human Evolution*, **26**, 57–75.

Grine, F. E. & Susman, R. I. (1991). Radius of *Paranthropus robustus* from Member 1, Swartkrans Formation, South Africa. *American Journal of Physical Anthropology*, **4**, 229–48.

Grine, F. E. (1986). Dental evidence for dietary differences in *Australopithecus* and *Paranthropus*: a quantitative analysis of permanent molar microwear. *Journal of Human Evolution*, **15**, 783–822.

Grine, F. E. & Daegling, D. J. (1993). New mandible of *Paranthropus robustus* from Member 1, Swartkrans Formation, South Africa. *Journal of Human Evolution*, **24**, 319–33.

Grine, F. E., Demes, B., Jungers, W. L. & Cole, T. M. (1993). Description and preliminary analysis of new hominid craniodental fossils from the Swartkrans Formation. In *Swartkrans: A Cave's Chronicle of Early Man.*, ed. C. K. Brain, pp. 75–116. Pretoria: Transvaal Museum.

Groves, C. P. (1989). *A New Theory of Human and Primate Evolution.* Oxford: Clarendon Press.

Groves, C. P. Westwood, C. & Shea, B. T. (1992). Unfinished business: Mahalanobis and a clockwork orang. *Journal of Human Evolution*, **22**, 327–42.

Haeckel, E. (1874). *Anthropogenie; oder, Entwicklungsgeschichte des Menschen.* Leipzig: Englemann.

Hagedoorn, A. C. (1924). *Soortsvorming en Eugeneitca.* Doctoral dissertation. Leiden: Leiden University.

Haldane, J. B. S. (1932). *The Causes of Evolution.* New York: Harper.

Haldane, J. B. S. (1948). The formal genetics of man. *Proceedings of the Royal Society* (London), B, **153**, 147–170.

Haldane, J. B. S. (1949). Suggestions as to quantitative measurement of rates of evolution. *Evolution*, **3**, 51–6.

Haldane, J. B. S. (1951). *Everything Has a History.* London: Allen and Unwin.

Hamada, Y. (1994). Standard growth patterns and variations in growth patterns of Japanese monkeys (*Macaca fuscata*) based on an analysis by the spline function method. *Anthropological Science*, **102** (Supplement), 57–76.

Hamerton, J. L. & Klinger, H. P. (1963). Chromosomes and the origin of man. *New Scientist*, **341**, 483–5.

Hardy, G. H. (1908). Mendelian proportions in a mixed population. *Science*, new series **28**, 49–50.

Harris, H. A. (1931). Lines of arrested growth in the long bones in childhood: the correlation of histological and radiographic appearances in clinical and experimental conditions. *British Journal of Radiology*, **4**, 561–8.

Harrison, G. A. (1966). Human adaptability with reference to the IBP proposals for high altitude research. In *The Biology of Human Adaptability*, ed. P. T. Baker & J. S. Weiner, pp. 509–19. Oxford: Clarendon Press.

Harrison, G. A. et al. (1964). *Human Biology: An Introduction to Human Evolution, Variation, Growth, and Ecology.* London: Oxford University Press.

Harrison, G. A., Weiner, J. S., Tanner, J. M. & Barnicot, N. A. (1977). *Human Biology*, 2nd edn. Oxford: Oxford University Press.

Harrison, T. (1987). A reassessment of the phylogenetic relationships of *Oreopithecus bambolii* Gervais. *Journal of Human Evolution*, **15**, 541–83.

Harrison, T. (1993). Cladistic concepts and the species problem in hominoid evolution. In *Species, Species Concepts, and Primate Evolution*, ed. W. H. Kimbel & L. W. Martin, pp. 345–71. New York: Plenum.

Hartwig, W. C. & Sadler, L. L. (1993). Visualization and physical anthropology. In *Milestones in Human Evolution*, ed. A. J. Ahmquist & A. Manyak, pp. 187–222. Prospect Heights, IL: Waveland.

Hartwig-Scherer, S. & Martin, R. D. (1991). Was 'Lucy' more human than her child? Observations on early hominid postcranial skeletons. *Journal of Human Evolution*, **21**, 439–49.

Hasegawa, M. (1992). Evolution of hominoids as inferred from DNA sequences. In *Topics in Primatology*, vol. 1, ed. T. Nishida, W. C. McGrew, P. Marler, M. Pickford & F. B. M. de Waal, pp. 347–57. Tokyo: University of Tokyo Press.

Hauser, D. L. (1992). Similarity, falsification and character state order – a reply to Wilkinson. *Cladistics*, **8**, 339–44.

Hauser, G. & DeStefano, G. F. (1989). *Epigenetic Variants of the Human Skull*. Stuttgart: E. Schweizerbart.

Hawkey, D. E. & Merbs, C. F. (1995). Activity-induced musculoskeletal stress-markers (MSM) and subsistence strategy changes among ancient Hudson Bay Eskimos. *International Journal of Osteoarchaeology* **5**, 324–38.

Hawkey, D. E. & Street, S. R. (1992). Activity-induced stress markers in prehistoric human remains from the eastern Aleutian Islands. *American Journal of Physical Anthropology*, (Supplement) **14**, 89.

Hayden, B. (1993). The cultural capacities of Neanderthals: a review and re-evaluation. *Journal of Human Evolution*, **24**, 113–46.

Hendersen, J. B., Dunnigan, M. G., McIntosh, W. B., Abdul-Motaal, A. A. & Heads, M. (1985). On the nature of ancestors. *Systematic Zoology*, **34**, 205–15.

Hedges, S. B., Kumar, S., Tamurs, K. & Stoneking, M. (1992). Human origins and the analysis of mitochondrial DNA sequences. *Science*, **255**, 737–9.

Henneberg, M. (1988). Decrease in human skull size in the Holocene. *Human Biology*, **60**, 395–405.

Henneberg, M. (1990). Brain size/body weight variability in *Homo sapiens*: consequences for interpreting hominid evolution. *Homo*, **39**, 121–30.

Henneberg, M. (1992). Continuing human evolution: bodies, brains and the role of variability. *Transactions of the Royal Society of South Africa*, **48**, 159–82.

Henneberg, M. & Thackeray, J. F. (1995). A single-lineage hypothesis of hominid evolution. *Evolutionary Theory*, **11**, 31–8.

Hennig, W. (1950). *Grundzüge einer Theorie der Phylogenetischen Systematik*. Berlin: Deutscher Zentralverlag.

Hennig, W. (1966). *Phylogenetic Systematics*. Urbana: University of Illinois Press.

Heywood, V. H. (1985). The impact of Linnaeus on botanical taxonomy. In *Contemporary Perspectives on Linnaeus*, ed. J. Weinstock, pp. 1–15. Lanham: University Press of America.

Hiernaux, J. (1964). The concept of race and the taxonomy of mankind. In *The Concept of Race*, ed. A. Montagu, pp. 29–45. New York: The Free Press.

Hill, A. & Ward, S. (1988). Origin of the Hominidae: the record of African large hominoid evolution between 14 my and 4 my. *Yearbook of Physical Anthropology*, **31**, 49–83.

Hill, A., Ward, S. & Brown, B. (1992). Anatomy and age of the Lothagam mandible. *Journal of Human Evolution*, **22**, 439–51.

Hill, W. C. O. (1970). *Primates: Comparative Anatomy and Taxonomy, vol. VII: Cynopithecinae (Papio, Mandrillus, Theropithecus)*. Edinburgh: Edinburgh University Press.

Hill, W. C. O. (1974). *Primates: Comparative Anatomy and Taxonomy, vol. VIII: Cynopithecinae (Cercocebus, Macaca, Cynopithecus)*. Edinburgh: Edinburgh University Press.

314   *Bibliography*

Hirschfeld, L. & Hirschfeld, H. (1919). Serological differences between the bloods of different races. *Lancet*, **2**, 675–9.
Hoelzer, G. A. & Melnick, D. J. (1996). Evolutionary relationships of the macaques. In *Evolution and Ecology of Macaque Societies*, ed. J. E. Fa & D. G. Lindburg, pp. 3–19. Cambridge: Cambridge University Press.
Hoelzer, G. A. & Melnick, D. J. (1994). Patterns of speciation and limits to phylogenetic resolution. *Trends in Ecology and Evolution*, **9**, 104–7.
Hogben, L. (1931). *Genetic Principles in Medicine and Social Science*. London: Williams & Norgate.
Holliday, T. W. (1997). Body proportions in Late Pleistocene Europe and modern human origins. *Journal of Human Evolution*, **32**, 423–47.
Holloway, R. L. (1970). Australopithecine endocast (Taung specimen, 1924): a new volume determination. *Science*, **168**, 966–8.
Holloway, R. L. (1983). Human brain evolution: a search for units, models and synthesis. *Canadian Journal of Anthropology*, **3**, 215–30.
Hooton, E. A. (1946). *Up From the Ape*. New York: Macmillan.
Höpfel, F. Platzer, W. & Spindler, K. (Eds.) (1998). *The Man in the Ice*, vol. 5. Vienna: Springer Verlag.
Hopwood, A. T. (1933). Miocene primates from Kenya. *Zoology: Journal of the Linnaean Society, London*, **38**, 437–64.
Howard, J. C. (1988). How old is a polymorphism? *Nature*, **332**, 588–90.
Howell, F. C. & Coppens, Y. (1976). An overview of Hominidae from the Omo succession, Ethiopia. In *Earliest Man and Environments in the Lake Rudolf Basin*, ed. Y. Coppens, F. C. Howell, G. Isasc & R. Leakey, pp. 522–32. Chicago: University of Chicago Press.
Howell, F. C. (1951). The place of Neanderthal in human evolution. *American Journal of Physical Anthropology*, **9**, 379–416.
Howell, F. C. (1952). Pleistocene glacial geology and the evolution of 'classic Neandertal' man. *Southwest Journal of Anthropology*, **8**, 377–410.
Howell, F. C. (1957). Pleistocene glacial geology and the evolution of 'classical Neanderthal' man. *Quarterly Review of Biology*, **32**, 330–47.
Howell, F. C. (1993). Thoughts on the study and interpretation of the human fossil record. In *Contemporary Issues in Human Evolution*, ed. W. E. Meikle, F. C. Howell & N. G. Jablonski, pp. 1–45. Memoir 21. San Francisco: California Academy of Sciences.
Howell, F. C., Haessaerts, P. & de Heinzelin, J. (1987). Depositional environments, archeological occurrences, and hominids from Members E and F of the Shungura Formation (Omo basin, Ethiopia). *Journal of Human Evolution*, **16**, 665–700.
Howells, W. W. (1973). *Cranial Variation in Man: A Study by Multivariate Analysis of Patterns of Difference Among Recent Populations*. Papers of the Peabody Museum, Archaeology and Ethnology, vol. 67. Cambridge, MA: Harvard University Press.
Howells, W. W. (1980). Homo erectus – who, when and where: a survey. *Yearbook of Physical Anthropology*, **23**, 1–23.
Hrdlička, A. (1929). *The Neanderthal Phase of Man*. Washington, DC: Government Printing Office.
Hublin, J.-J. (1993). Recent human evolution in northwestern Africa. In *The*

Origin of Modern Humans and the Impact of Chronometric Dating, ed. M. J. Aitken, C. B. Stringer & P. A. Mellars, pp. 118–31. Princeton: Princeton University Press.

Hublin, J. & Tillier, A. M. (eds.) (1992) *Aux origines d'Homo sapiens.* Paris: Presses Universitaires de France.

Hublin, J. J., Barroso, C., Medina, P., Fontugne, M. & Reyss, J.-L. (1995). The Mousterian site of Zafarraya (Andalucia, Spain): dating and implications on the Paleolithic peopling processes of western Europe. *Comptes-Rendus de l'Académie des Science de Paris*, **321**, 931–7.

Hudson, A. (1988). *The Premature Reformation: Wycliffite Texts and Lollard History.* Oxford: Clarendon Press.

Huffman, M. (1996). In *Social Learning in Animals: The Roots of Culture*, ed. C. M. Heyes & B. G. Galef, pp. 267–89. London: Academic Press.

Hughes, A. L. (1993). Contrasting evolutionary rates in the duplicate chaperonin genes of *Mycobacterium tuberculosis* and *M. leprae. Molecular Biology and Evolution*, **10**, 1343–59.

Hughes, A. L. & Nei, M. (1988). Nucleotide substitution at major histocompatibility loci reveals overdominant selection. *Nature*, **335**, 167–70.

Hughes, A. L. & Nei, M. (1989). Nuclear substitution at major histocompatibility class II loci: evidence for overdominant selection. *Proceedings of the National Academy of Sciences, USA*, **86**, 958–62.

Hull, D. L. (1964). The effect of essentialism on taxonomy – two thousand years of stasis (I). *The British Journal for the Philosophy of Science*, **16**, 314–26.

Hull, D. L. (1965). The effect of essentialism on taxonomy – two thousand years of stasis (II). *The British Journal for the Philosophy of Science*, **17**, 1–18.

Hulse, F. T. (1957). Exogamie et héterosis. *Archives Suisses d'Anthropologie Général*, **22**, 103–25. (Translated into English with a comment by G. W. Lasker as: Exogamy and heterosis. *Yearbook of Physical Anthropology*, **9**, 240–57.)

Hulse, F. T. (1957). Some factors influencing the relative proportions of human racial stocks. *Cold Spring Harbor Symposia on Quantitative Biology*, **22**, 33–45.

Hummert, J. R. & van Gerven, D. P. (1983). Skeletal growth in a Medieval population from Sudanese Nubia. *American Journal of Physical Anthropology*, **60**, 471–8.

Hunt, K. & Vitzthum, V. (1986). Dental metric assessment of the Omo fossils: implications for the phylogenetic position of *Australopithecus africanus. American Journal of Physical Anthropology*, **71**, 141–56.

Hurford, A. J. (1986). Application of the fission-track method to young sediments: principles, methodology and examples. In *Dating Young Sediments*, eds. A. J. Hurford, E. Jager & J. A. M. Ten Cate, pp. 199–233. Bangkok: CCOP Technical Secretariat.

Hürzeler, J. (1954). Zur systematischen Stellung von *Oreopithecus.* Naturforschenden Gesellschaft in Basel, Verhandlungen, **65**, 88–95.

Huxley, J. (1939a). Clines: an auxiliary method in taxonomy. *Bijdragen tot de Dierkunde*, **27**, 491–520.

Huxley, J. (1939b). A discussion on 'subspecies and varieties'. *Proceedings of the Linnaean Society London*, **151**, 105–14.

Huxley, J. S. (1942). *Evolution, the Modern Synthesis.* London: Allen and Unwin.

Huxley, L. (1901). *Life and Letters of Thomas Henry Huxley.* New York: Appleton and Company.

Huxley, T. H. (1864). Further remarks upon the human remains from the Neanderthal. *Natural History Review*, **4**, 429–46.

Huxley, T. H. (1893). *Man's Place in Nature and Other Essays.* In *Collected Essays*, (1893–1894), 9 vols. London: Macmillan.

Imanishi, K. (1957). Identification: A process of enculturation in the subhuman society of *Macaca fuscata. Primates*, **1**, 1–29.

Irvine, W. (1959). *Apes, Angels, and Victorians.* New York: Meridian Books.

Ivanovsky, A. (1925). Die anthropometrischen Veränderungen russischer Volker unter dem Einfluss der Hungersnot. *Archiv für Anthropologie*, **20**,1.

Iwamoto, M. & Hasegawa, Y. (1972). Two macaque fossil teeth from the Japanese Pleistocene. *Primates*, **13**, 77–81.

Jablonski, N. G. & Chaplin, G. (2000). The evolution of human skin coloration. *Journal of Human Evolution.* (In press.)

Janczewski, D. N., Goldman, D. & O'Brien, S. J. (1990). Molecular genetic divergence of Orang Utan (*Pongo pygmaeus*) subspecies based on isozyme and two-dimensional gel electrophoresis. *Journal of Heredity*, **81**, 375–87.

Jauch, A., Weinberg, J., Stanyon, R., Arnold, N., Tofanelli, S., Ishida, T. & Cremer, T. (1992). Reconstruction of genomic rearrangements in great apes and gibbons by chromosome painting. *Proceedings of the National Academy of Sciences, USA*, **89**, 8611–15.

Jelinek, A. (1994). Hominids, energy, environment, and behavior in the Late Pleistocene. In *Origins of Anatomically Modern Humans*, ed. M. H. Nitecki & D. V. Nitecki, pp. 67–92. New York: Plenum.

Jensen, J. V. (1991). *Thomas Henry Huxley: Communicating for Science.* Newark: University of Delaware Press.

Jerison, H. J. (1973). *Evolution of the Brain and Intelligence.* New York: Academic Press.

Jerison, H. J. (1991). *Brain size and the Evolution of Mind.* New York: American Museum of Natural History.

Johanson, D. & Coppens, Y. (1976). A preliminary anatomical diagnosis of the first Plio/Pleistocene hominid discoveries in the Central Afar, Ethiopia. *American Journal of Physical Anthropology*, **45**, 217–34.

Johanson, D. & Edgar, B. (1996). *From Lucy to Language.* New York: Simon & Schuster.

Johanson, D. C., Lovejoy, O.C., Kimbel, W. H., White, T. D., Ward, S. C., Bush, M. E., Latimer, B. M. & Coppens, Y. (1982). Morphology of the partial hominid skeleton (A.L. 288–1) from the Hadar Formation, Ethiopia. *American Journal of Physical Anthropology*, **57**, 403–51.

Johanson, D. C., Masao, F. T, Eck, G. G., White, T. D., Walter, R. C., Kimbel, W. H., Asfaw, B., Manega, P., Ndessokia, P. & Suwa, G. (1987). New partial skeleton of *Homo habilis* from Olduvai Gorge, Tanzania. *Nature*, **327**, 205–9.

Johanson, D. & White, T. D. (1979). A systematic assessment of early African hominids. *Science*, **202**, 321–30.

Johanson, D., Taieb, M. & Coppens, Y. (1982). Pliocene hominids from the Hadar Formation, Ethiopia (1973–1977): Stratigraphic, chronologic, and paleoenvironmental contexts, with notes on hominid morphology and systematics. *American Journal of Physical Anthropology*, **57**, 373–402.

Johanson, D., White, T. D. & Coppens, Y. (1978). A new species of the genus *Australopithecus* (Primates: Hominidae) from the Pliocene of eastern Africa. *Kirtlandia*, **28**, 1–15.

Johnson, T. M., Hamilton, T. & Lowe, L. (1998). Multiple primary melanomas. *Journal of the American Academy of Dermatology*, **39**, 422–7.

Jolly, C. J. (1966). Introduction to the Cercopithecoidea, with notes on their use as laboratory animals. *Symposium of the Zoological of the Society London*, No. 17, pp. 427–57.

Jolly, C. J. (1978). *Early Hominids of Africa*. New York: St. Martin's Press.

Jolly, C. J. (1993). Species, subspecies and baboon systematics. In *Species, Species Concepts and Primate Evolution*, ed. W. H. Kimbel & L. B. Martin, pp. 67–107. New York: Plenum.

Jones, H. N., Priest, J. D., Hayes, W. C., Tichenor, C. C. & Nagel, D. A. (1977). Humeral hypertrophy in response to exercise. *Journal of Bone and Joint Surgery*, **59–A**, 204–8.

Jones, T. S. & Cave, A. J. E. (1960). Diet, longevity, and dental disease in the Sierra Leone chimpanzee. *Proceedings of the Zoological Society of London*, **135**, 147–54 (+4 plates).

Jungers, W. L. (1982). Lucy's limbs: skeletal allometry and locomotion in *Australopithecus afarensis*. *Nature*, **297**, 676–8.

Jungers, W. L. (1987). Body size and morphometric affinities of the appendicular skeleton in *Oreopithecus bambolii* (IGF11778). *Journal of Human Evolution*, **16**, 445–56.

Jungers, W. L. (1988). Lucy's length: stature reconstruction in *Australopithecus afarensis* (A.L. 288–1) with implications for other small-bodied hominids. *American Journal of Physical Anthropology*, **76**, 227–31.

Jungers, W. L. & Stern, J. T. (1983). Body proportions, skeletal allometry and locomotion in the Hadar hominids: a reply to Wolpoff. *Journal of Human Evolution*, **12**, 673–84.

Kappelman, J., Swisher, C., Fleagle, J., Yirga, S., Bown, T. & Feseha, M. (1996). Age of *Australopithecus afarensis* from Fejej, Ethiopia. *Journal of Human Evolution*, **30**, 139–46.

Keith, A. (1916). *The Antiquity of Man*. London: Williams and Norgate.

Keith, A. (1925a). *The Antiquity of Man*. Second edition. London: Williams and Norgate.

Keith, A. (1925b). The fossil anthropoid ape from Taungs. *Nature*, **115**, 234–5.

Keith, A. (1931). *New Discoveries Relating to the Antiquity of Man*. New York: W. W. Norton.

Kellogg, R. (1945). Macaques. In *Primate Malaria*, ed. S. D. Albemarle, pp. 115–134. Washington, DC: Office of Medical Information.

Kennedy, G. E. (1983). A morphometric and taxonomic assessment of a hominine femur from the Lower Member, Koobi Fora, Lake Turkana. *American Journal of Physical Anthropology*, **61**, 429–36.

Kennedy, G E. (1991). On the autapomorphic traits of *Homo erectus*. *Journal of Human Evolution*, **20**, 375–412.

Keynes, J. M. (1936). *The General Theory of Employment, Interest and Money*. New York: Harcourt, Brace.

Kiessling, E. & Eckhardt, R. B. (1990). Palatine fenestrae: windows on hominoid variation and its interpretation. *American Journal of PhysicalAnthropology*, **81**, 249.

Kimura, M. (1983). *The Neutral Theory of Evolution*. Cambridge: Cambridge University Press.

King, G. (1990). *The Dicynodonts: A Study in Palaeobiology*. London: Chapman and Hall.

King, J. L. & Jukes, T. H. (1969). Non-Darwinin evolution. *Science*, **164**, 788–98.

King, M. & Wilson, A. C. (1975). Evolution at two levels in humans and chimpanzees. *Science*, **188**, 107–16.

King, W. (1864). The reputed fossil man of the Neanderthal. *Quarterly Journal of Science*, **1**, 88–97.

Kingdon, J. (1971). *East African Mammals: An Atlas of Evolution in Africa*. New York: Academic Press.

Kish, L. (1965). *Survey Sampling*. New York: John Wiley.

Kitchener, A. C. (1999). Tiger distribution, phenotypic variation and conservation issues. In *Riding the Tiger*, ed. J. Seidensticker, S. Christie & P. Jackson, pp. 19–39. Cambridge: Cambridge University Press.

Kitcher, P. (1992). Species. In *The Units of Evolution: Essays on the Nature of Species*, ed. M. Ereshefsky, pp. 317–41. Cambridge, MA: MIT Press.

Klein, R. (1989). *The Human Career*. Chicago: University of Chicago Press.

Kohl-Larsen, L. (1940). Auf neuer Fahrt nach Njarasagraben. Deutsche Afrika-Expedition 1937–1939. *Umschau*, **44**, 228–32.

Korey, K. A. (1990). Deconstructing reconstruction: the OH 62 humerofemoral index. *American Journal of Physical Anthropology*, **83**, 25–33.

Kramer, A. (1986). Hominid-pongid distinctiveness in the Miocene-Pliocene fossil record: the Lothagam mandible. *American Journal of Physical Anthropology*, **70**, 457–73.

Kramer, A. (1993). Human taxonomic diversity in the Pleistocene: does *Homo erectus* represent mutiple hominid species? *American Journal of Physical Anthropology*, **91**, 161–71.

Kramer, A. & Konigsberg, L. W. (1999). Recognizing species diversity among large-bodied hominoids: a simulation test using missing data finite mixture analysis. *Journal of Human Evolution*, **36**, 409–21.

Krings, M., Stone, A., Schmitz, R. W., Krainitzki, H., Stoneking, M. & Pääbo, S. (1997). Neanderthal DNA sequences and the origin of modern humans. *Cell*, **90**, 19–30.

Kroeber, A. L. & Kuckhohn, C. (1963). *Culture: A Critical Review of Concepts and Definitions*. New York: Random House.

Krogman, W. M. (1969). Growth changes in skull, face, jaws, and teeth of the chimpanzee. In *The Chimpanzee*, ed. G. H. Bourne, pp. 104–64. Basel: Karger.

Kuman, K. (1994a). The archaeology of Sterkfontein – past and present. *Journal of Human Evolution*, **27**, 471–95.

Kuman, K. (1994b). The archaeology of Sterkfontein: preliminary findings on site formation and cultural change. *South African Journal of Science*, **90**, 215–19.

Kummer, H. (1971). *Primate Societies: Group Techniques of Ecological Adaptation.* New York: Aldine de Gruyter.

Kurtén, B. (1964). The evolution of the polar bear, *Ursus maritimus* Phipps. *Acta Zoologica Fennica,* **108**, 1–30.

Lahr, M. M. (1996). *The Evolution of Modern Human Diversity: A Study of Cranial Variation.* Cambridge: Cambridge University Press.

Lai, P. & Lovell, N. C. (1992). Skeletal markers of occupational stress in the fur trade: a case study from a Hudson's Bay Company fur trade post. *International Journal of Osteoarchaeology,* **2**, 221–34.

Lampl, M. & Johnston, F. E. (1996). Problems in the ageing of skeletal juveniles: perspectives from maturation assessments of living children. *American Journal of Physical Anthropology,* **101**, 345–55.

Landsteiner, K. & Miller, C., Jr. (1925). Serological studies on the blood of primates. II. The blood groups in anthropoid apes. *Journal of Experimental Medicine,* **42**, 853–62.

Lang, J. (1985). In *Praktische Anatomie,* V. I, Part 1A, ed. T. Lanz & W. Wachsmuth, pp. 222–3. Berlin: Springer Verlag.

Larsen, C. S. (1997). *Bioarchaeology.* Cambridge: Cambridge University Press.

Lartet, E. (1862). New researches respecting the co-existence of man with the great fossil mammals, regarded as characteristic of the latest geological period. *Natural History Review,* n.s. **2**, 53–71.

Lasker, G. W. (1952). Environmental growth factors and selective migration. *Human Biology,* **24**, 262–89.

Lasker, G. W. (1954). The question of physical selection of Mexican migrants in the USA. *Human Biology,* **26**, 52–58.

Lasker, G. W. (1969). Human biological adaptability. *Science,* **166**, 1480–6.

Le Gros Clark, W. E. (1967). *Man-Apes or Ape-Men?* New York: Holt, Rinehart & Winston.

Le Gros Clark, W. E. & Leakey, L. S. B. (1951). *The Miocene Hominoidea of East Africa.* Fossil Mammals of Africa, No. 1. London: British Museum (Natural History).

Leakey, L. S. B. (1959). A new fossil skull from Olduvai. *Nature,* **184**, 491–3.

Leakey, L. S. B. (1960). The affinities of the new Olduvai australopithecine (reply to J. T. Robinson). *Nature,* **186**, 458.

Leakey, L. S. B. (1967). *Olduvai Gorge 1951–1961: Fauna and Background.* Cambridge: Cambridge University Press.

Leakey, L. S. B., Tobias, P.V. & Napier, J. (1964). A new species of the genus *Homo* from Olduvai Gorge. *Nature,* **202**, 7–9.

Leakey, M. D. (1971). *Olduvai Gorge,* vol. 3. Cambridge: Cambridge University Press.

Leakey, M. D. & Harris, J. (1991). *Laetoli: A Pliocene Site in Northern Tanzania.* Oxford: Oxford University Press.

Leakey, M. D. & Hay, R. (1979). Pliocene footprints in the Laetoli beds at Laetoli, northern Tanzania. *Nature,* **278**, 317–28.

Leakey, M. G. (1988). Fossil evidence for the evolution of the guenons. In *A Primate Radiation: Evolutionary Biology of the African Guenons,* ed. A. Gautier-Hion, F. Bourlière, J.-P. Gautier & J. Kingdon, pp. 7–12. Cambridge: Cambridge University Press.

320   *Bibliography*

Leakey, M. G., Feibel, C. S., McDougall, I. & Walker, A. (1995). New four-million-year-old hominid species from Kanapoi and Allia Bay, Kenya. *Nature*, **376**, 565–71.

Leakey, M. G. & Leakey, R. E. F. (eds.) (1978). *Koobi Fora Research Project*. Oxford: Clarendon Press.

Leakey, R. E. F. (1973). Evidence for an advanced Plio-Pleistocene hominid from East Rudolf, Kenya. *Nature*, **242**, 447–50.

Leakey, R. E. F. (1976). New hominid fossils from the Koobi Fora formation in Northern Kenya. *Nature*, **261**, 574–76.

Leakey, R. E. F. & Lewin, R. (1992). *Origins Reconsidered*. New York: Doubleday.

Leakey, R. E. F. & Walker, A. (1989). Early *Homo erectus* from West Lake Turkana, Kenya. In *Hominidae: Proceedings of the 2nd International Congress of Human Paleontology*, ed. G. Giacobini, pp. 209–215. Milan: Jaca Book.

Lee-Thorpe, J. A. & van der Merwe, N. J. (1993). Stable carbon isotope studies of Swartkrans fossils. In *Swartkrans: A Cave's Chronicle of Early Man*, ed. C. K. Brain, pp. 251–64. Pretoria: Transvaal Museum.

Lee-Thorpe, J. A., van der Merwe, N. J., & Brain, C. K. (1994). Diet of *Australopithecus robustus* at Swartkrans from stable carbon isotope analysis. *Journal of Human Evolution*, **27**, 361–72.

Lernould, J. (1988). Classification and geographical distribution of guenons: a review. In *A Primate Radiation*, ed. A. Gautier-Hion, F. Bourlière & J. Gautier, pp. 54–78. Cambridge: Cambridge University Press.

Leroyer, C. (1987). Les gisements castelperroniens de Quinçay et de St. Césaire: quelques comparaisons préliminaires des études palynologiques. *Actes du IIIème Congrès des Sociétés Savants (Poitiers)*, pp. 125–34.

Leroyer, C. & Leroi-Gourhan, A. (1983). Problèmes de la chronologie: le Castelperronien et l'Aurignacien. *Bulletin de la Société Préhistorique Française*, **80**, 41–4.

Levine, P. (1942). On human anti-Rh sera and their importance in racial studies. *Science*, **96**, 452–3.

Levinton, J. (1983). Stasis in progress: the empirical basis of macroevolution. *Annual Review of Ecology and Systematics*, **14**, 103–37.

Levinton, J. (1988). *Genetics, Paleontology, and Macroevolution*. Cambridge: Cambridge University Press.

Lewin, R. (1994). Human origins: the challenge of Java's skulls. *New Scientist*, 7 May, 36–40.

Lewis, G. E. (1934). Preliminary notice of new man-like apes from India. *American Journal of Science*, **31**, 450–2.

Lewontin, R. C. (1972). The apportionment of human diversity. *Evolutionary Biology*, **6**, 381–98.

Lewontin, R. C. (1974). *The Genetic Basis of Evolutionary Change*. New York: Columbia University Press.

Lewontin, R. C. (1991). Twenty-five years ago in genetics: electrophoresis in the development of evolutionary genetics: milestone or millstone? *Genetics*, **128**, 657–62.

Li, W.-H. & Graur, D. (1991). *Fundamentals of Molecular Evolution*. Sunderland, MA: Sinauer.

Bibliography 321

Lindburg, D. G. (1980). *The Macaques.* New York: Van Nostrand Reinhold.

Linnaeus, C. (1736). *Fundamenta Botanica.* Amsterdam.

Lipscomb, D. L. (1992). Parsimony, homology, and the analysis of multistate characters. *Cladistics,* **8**, 45–65.

Littleton, J. (1999). Paleopathology of skeletal fluorosis. *American Journal of Physical Anthropology,* **109**, 465–83.

Livingstone, F. B. (1962). On the non-existence of human races. *Current Anthropology,* **3**, 279–81.

Livingstone, F. B. (1969). Polygenic models for the evolution of human skin color differences. *Human Biology,* **41**, 480–93.

Locke, R. (1999). The first human? *Discovering Archaeology,* **1**, 32–9.

Lovell, N. C. & Lai, P. (1994). Lifestyle and health of voyageurs in the Canadian fur trade. In *Strength and Diversity: A Reader in Physical Anthropology,* ed. A. Herring & L. Chan, pp. 327–43. Toronto: Canadian Scholar's Press.

Løvtrup, S. (1979). The evolutionary species: fact or fiction? *Systematic Zoology,* **28**, 386–92.

Lubbock, J. (1864). Cave-men. *Natural History Review,* new series **4**, 407–28.

Lyell, C. (1830–1833). *Principles of Geology.* London: John Murray.

Lyell, C. (1863). *The Geological Evidence of the Antiquity of Man.* London.

Macdonald, J. R. (1972). Are the data worth owning? *Science,* **176**, 1377.

Mai, L. L. (1983). A model of chromosome evolution and its bearing on cladogenesis in the Hominoidea. In *New Interpretations of Ape and Human Ancestry,* ed. R. L. Ciochon & R. S. Corrucini, pp. 87–114. New York: Plenum Press.

Madre-Dupouy, M. (1992). *L'Enfant du Roc de Marsal.* Paris: Centre National de la Recherche Scientifique.

Malina, R., Buschang, P. H., Aronson, W. L. & Selby, A. (1982). Childhood growth status of eventual migrants and sedentes in a rural Zapotec community. *Human Biology,* **54**, 709–16.

Mann, A. (1975). *Some Paleodemographic Aspects of the South African Australopithecines.* Philadelphia: University of Pennsylvania Publications in Anthropology.

Mann, A., Lampl, M. & Monge, J. (1990). Patterns of ontogeny in human evolution: evidence from dental development. *Yearbook of Physical Anthropology,* **33**, 111–50.

Maples, W. R. & McKern, T. W. (1967). A preliminary report on classification of the Kenya baboon. In *The Baboon in Medical Research,* vol. 2, ed. H. Vagtborg, pp. 13–22. San Antonio: University of Texas Press.

Markarjan, D. S., Isakov, E. P. & Kondakov, G. I. (1974). Intergeneric hybrids of the lower (42–chromosome) monkey species of the Sukhumi monkey colony. *Journal of Human Evolution,* **3**, 247–55.

Marks, J. & Lyles, R. B. (1994). Rethinking genes. *Evolutionary Anthropology,* **3**, 139–46.

Marks, J. T. (1993). Molecular anthropology in retrospect and prospect. In *Contemporary Issues in Human Evolution,* ed. W. E. Meikle, F. C. Howell & N. G. Jablonski, pp. 167–86. Memoir 21. San Francisco: California Academy of Sciences.

Marks, J. T. (1997). Systematics in anthropology: conceptual issues in modern human origins research. In *Conceptual Issues in Modern Human Origins Research*, eds. G. A. Clark & C.M. Willermet, pp. 11–27. New York: Aldine de Gruyter.

Marshall, I. & Zohar, D. (1997). *Who's Afraid of Schrödinger's Cat?* New York: William Morrow.

Martin, H. (1923). *Interproximal Grooving*. L'Homme Fossile de la Quina. Paris: Dión.

Martin, R. B. & Burr, D. B. (1989). *Structure, Function, and Adaptation of Compact Bone*. New York: Raven Press.

Martin, R. D. & MacLarnon, A. M. (1988). Quantitative comparisons of the skull and teeth in guenons. In *A Primate Radiation: Evolutionary Biology of the African Guenons*, ed. A. Gautier-Hion, F. Bourlière, J.-P.Gautier & J. Kingdon, pp. 160–83. Cambridge: Cambridge University Press.

Martin D. L., Goodman, A. H. & Armelagos, G. J. (1985). Skeletal pathologies as indicators of quality of diet. In *The Analysis of Prehistoric Diets*, ed. R. I. Gilbert, Jr. & J. H. Mielke, pp. 227–79. Orlando: Academic Press.

Masao, F. T. (1992). The Middle Stone Age with reference to Tanzania. In *Continuity or Replacement? Controversies in* Homo sapiens *Evolution*, ed. G. Bräuer & F. H. Smith, pp. 99–109. Rotterdam: Balkema.

Mascie-Taylor, C. G. N. & Bogin, B. (1995). *Human Variability and Plasticity*. Cambridge: Cambridge University Press.

Mathers, K. & Henneberg, M. (1995). Were we ever that big? Gradual increase in hominid body size over time. *Homo*, **46**, 141–73.

Mathur, U., Datta, S. L. & Mathur, B. B. (1977). The effect of aminopterin-induced folic acid deficiency on spermatogenesis. *Fertility and Sterility*, **28**, 1356–60.

Maxson, L. R., Sarich, V. & Wilson, A. C. (1975). Continental drift and the use of albumin as an evolutionary clock. *Nature*, **255**, 397–400.

Maynard Smith, J. (1987). Evolution stays unpunctured. *Nature*, **330**, 516.

Mayr, E. (1950). Taxonomic categories in fossil hominids. *Cold Spring Harbor Symposia in Quantitative Biology*, **15**, 109–17.

Mayr, E. (1956). Geographical character gradients and climatic adaptation. *Evolution*, **10**, 105–8.

Mayr, E. (1961). Cause and effect in biology. *Science*, **134**, 1501–6.

Mayr, E. (1991). *One Long Argument*. Cambridge, MA: Harvard University Press.

Mayr, E. (1963). The taxonomic evaluation of fossil hominids. In *Classification and Human Evolution*, ed. S. Washburn, pp. 332–46. London: Methuen & Co.

Mayr, E. (1965). *Animal Species and Evolution*. Cambridge, MA: Belknap Press of Harvard University Press.

Mayr, E. (1970). *Populations, Species, and Evolution*. Cambridge, MA: Belknap Press of Harvard University Press.

Mayr, E. (1997). *This is Biology: The Science of the Living World*. Cambridge, MA: Belknap Press of Harvard University Press.

Mazess, R., Picon-Reategui, E., Thomas, R. B. & Little, M. A. (1968). Effects of alcohol and altitude on man during rest and work. *Aerospace Medicine*, **39**, 403–6.

McBurney, C. B. M. (1965). The Old Stone Age in Wales. In *Prehistoric and Early Wales*, ed. I. L. C. Foster & G. Daniels, pp. 17–34. London: Routledge and Kegan Paul.

McConnell, T. L., Talbot, W. S., McIndoe, R. A. & Wakeland, G. K. (1988). The origin of MHC class II gene polymorphism within the genus *Mus. Nature*, **332**, 651–4.

McGrew, W. C. (1998a). Behavioral diversity in populations of free-ranging chimpanzees in Africa: is it culture? *Human Evolution*, **13**, 209–20.

McGrew, W. C. (1998b). Culture in nonhuman primates? *Annual Review of Anthropology*, **27**, 301–28.

McHenry, H. (1992). How big were the early hominids? *Evolutionary Anthropology*, **1**,15–20.

McMurray, R. G. (1995). Effects of physical activity on bone. In *Calcium and Phosphorus in Health and Disease*, ed. J. J. B. Anderson & S. C. Garner, pp. 301–17. Boca Raton: CRC Press.

Mellars, P. (1996). *The Neanderthal Legacy*. Princeton: Princeton University Press.

Mellars, P. A. (1993). Archaeology and the population-dispersal hypothesis of modern human origins in Europe. In *The Origin of Modern Humans and the Impact of Chronometric Dating*, ed. M. J. Aitken, C. B. Stringer & P. A. Mellars, pp. 196–216. Princeton: Princeton University Press.

Mellars, P. A., Aitken, M. J. & Stringer, C. B. (1993). Outlining the problem. In *The Origin of Modern Humans and the Impact of Chronometric Dating*, ed. M. J. Aitken, C. B. Stringer & P. A. Mellars, pp. 3–11. Princeton: Princeton University Press.

Mellars, P. A. & Stringer, C. B. (eds) (1989). *The Human Revolution: Behavioural and Biological Perspectives on the Origins of Modern Humans*. Edinburgh: Edinburgh University Press.

Melnick, D. J., Hoelzer, G. A., Absher, R., & Ashley, M. V. (1993). mtDNA diversity in rhesus monkeys reveals overestimates of divergence time and paraphyly with neighboring species. *Molecular Biology and Evolution*, **10**, 282–95.

Mendel, G. (1866). Versuche über Pflanzen-Hybriden. *Verhandlungen des Naturforschenden Vereines, Abhandlungen, Brünn*, **4**, 3–47.

Mercati, M. (1717). *Metallotheca*. Rome: Salvioni.

Mercier, N., Valladas, H., Joron, J.-L., Reyss, J.-L., Lévèque, F. & Vandermeersch, B. (1991). Thermoluminescence dating of the late Neanderthal remains from Saint-Césaire. *Nature*, **351**, 737–9.

Merriwether, D. A., Clark, A. G., Ballinger, S. W., Schurr, T. G., Soodyall, H., Jenkins, T., Sherry, S. & Wallace, D. C. (1991). The structure of human mitochondrial DNA variation. *Journal of Molecular Evolution*, **33**, 543–55.

Michelson, A. A. (1905). *Light Waves and Their Uses*. Chicago: University of Chicago Press.

Miller, G. H., Beaumont, P. B., Jull, A. J. T & Johnson, B. (1993). Pleistocene geochronology and palaeothermy from protein diagenesis in ostrich egg-shells: implications for the evolution of modern humans. In *The Origin of Modern Humans and the Impact of Chronometric Dating*, ed. M. J. Aitken, C. B. Stringer & P. A. Mellars, pp. 49–68. Princeton: Princeton University Press.

Milton, K. & May, M. L. (1975). Body weight, diet and home range area in primates. *Nature*, **259**, 321–5.

Minns, R. (1996). Folic acid and neural tube defects. *Spinal Cord*, **34**, 460–5.

Mishler, B. D. & Donoghue, M. J. (1982). Species concepts: a case for pluralism. *Systematic Zoology*, **31**, 503–11.

Mitlo, C. (1986). Protocultural primate prototypes: phenotypic diversity and genetic continuity among macaque and baboon populations, and in early hominids. *American Journal of Physical Anthropology*, **69**, 241–2.

Miyamoto, M. M., Koop, B. F., Slightom, J. L., Goodman, M. & Tennant, M. R. (1988). Molecular systematics of higher primates: genealogical relations and classification. *Proceedings of the National Academy of Sciences, USA*, **85**, 7627–31.

Molleson, T. (1976). Remains of Pleistocene man in Paviland and Pontewydd Caves, Wales. *Trans. British Cave Research Assoc.*, **3**, 112–6.

Molleson, T. (1989). Seed preparation in the Mesolithic: the osteological evidence. *Antiquity*, **63**, 356–62.

Moore, G. W., Goodman, M., & Barnabas, J. (1973). An iterative approach from the standpoint of the additive hypothesis to the dendrogram problem posed by molecular data sets. *Journal of Theoretical Biology*, **38**, 423–57.

Morant, G. M. (1927). Studies of paleolithic man. II. A biometric study of neanderthaloid skulls and of their relationship to modern social type. *Annals of Eugenics* II (Parts III and IV), 378–80 (Plates I–XI).

Morgan, T. H. (1916). *A Critique of the Theory of Evolution*. Princeton: Princeton University Press.

Morin, P. A., Moore, J. J., Chakraborty, R., Jin, L., Goodall, J. & Woodruff, D. S. (1994). Kin selection, social structure, gene flow, and the evolution of chimpanzees. *Science*, **265**, 1193–201.

Morrell, V. (1994). Did early humans reach Siberia 500,000 years ago? *Science*, 263, 611–2.

Movius, H. (1944). Early man and Pleistocene stratigraphy in southern and eastern Asia. *Papers of the Peabody Museum*, **19**, 1–125.

Movius, H. (1948). The Lower Paleolithic cultures of southern and eastern Asia. *Transactions of the American Philosophical Society*, **97**, 383–421.

Movius, H. (1949). Lower Paleolithic archaeology in southern and eastern Asia. *Studies in Physical Anthropology*, **1**, 17–81.

Movius, H. (1955). Paleolithic archaeology in southern and eastern Asia, exclusive of India. *Cahiers d'Histoire Mondiale*, **2**, 257–82.

Moyà-Solà, S. & Köhler, M. (1993). Recent discoveries of *Dryopithecus* shed new light on evolution of great apes. *Nature*, **365**, 543–5.

Moyà-Solà, S. & Köhler, M. (1995). New partial cranium of *Dryopithecus* Lartet, 1863 (Hominoidea, Primates) from the Upper Miocene of Can Llobateres, Barcelona, Spain. *Journal of Human Evolution*, **28**, 101–39.

Moyà-Solà, S. & Köhler, M. (1996). A *Dryopithecus* skeleton and the origins of great-ape locomotion. *Nature*, **379**, 156–159.

Muller, H. J. (1918). Genetic variability, twin hybrids and constant hybrids, in a case of balanced lethal factors. *Genetics*, **2**, 471.

Nagel, U. (1973). Social organization in a baboon hybrid zone. In *Proceedings of the Third International Congress of Primatology*, vol. 3, ed. J. Biegert & W.

Leutenegger, pp. 48–57. Basel: Karger.

Nakajima, H., Tanaka, T., Nigi, H. & Prychodko, W. (1970). Human-type ABO, MN and Lewis blood groups & Inv factors in several species of macaques. *Primates*, **11**, 243–53.

Napier, J. & Napier, P. (1967). *A Handbook of Living Primates*. New York: Academic Press.

Napier, J. R. & Davis, P. R. (1959). *The Fore-Limb Skeleton and Associated Remains of* Proconsul africanus. London: British Museum (Natural History).

Neer, R. M. (1975). The evolutionary significance of vitamin D, skin pigment, and ultraviolet light. *American Journal of Physical Anthropology*, **43**, 409–16.

Nei, M. & Roychoudhury, A. K. (1974). Genetic relationship and evolution of human races. *American Journal of Human Genetics*, **26**, 421–43.

Nei, M. (1993). Evolutionary relationships of human populations on a global scale. *Molecular Biology and Evolution*, **10**, 927.

Nilsson-Ehle, H. (1909). Kreuzungsuntersuchungen an Hafer und Weizen. *Lunds Universitets Årsskrift*, new series, Section 2, vol. 5 (122 pages); Section 2, vol. 7 (82 pages).

Nissen, H. W. (1942). Studies of infant chimpanzees. *Science*, **95**, 159–161.

Nissen, H. W. & Riessen, A. H. (1945). The deciduous dentition of the chimpanzee. *Growth*, **9**, 265–74.

Nissen, H. W. & Riessen, A. H. (1949a). Onset of ossification in the epiphyses and short bones of the extremities in chimpanzee. *Growth*, **13**, 45–70.

Nissen, H. W. & Riessen, A. H. (1949b). Retardation in onset of ossification in chimpanzee related to various environmental and physiological factors. *Anatomical Record*, **105**, 665–75.

Nissen, H. W. & Riessen, A. H. (1964). The eruption of the permanent dentition of chimpanzee. *American Journal of Physical Anthropology*, **22**, 285–94.

Nitecki, M. H. & Nitecki, D. V. (eds) (1994). *Origins of Anatomically Modern Humans*. New York: Plenum.

Nordenskiöld, E. (1927). *The History of Biology*. New York: Knopf.

North, F. J. (1942). Paviland Cave, the 'Red Lady', the deluge and William Buckland. *Annals of Science*, **5**, 91–128.

Nuttall, G. H. F. (1904). *Blood Immunity and Blood Relationships*. Cambridge: Cambridge University Press.

O'Brien, S. J., Wildt, D. E., Goldman, D., Merril, C. R. & Bush, M. (1983). The cheetah is depauperate in genetic variation. *Science*, **221**, 459–62.

O'Brien, S. J., Nash, W. G., Wildt, D. E., Bush, M. E. & Benveniste, R. E. (1985). A molecular solution to the riddle of the giant panda's phylogeny. *Nature*, **317**, 140–4.

O'Brien, S. J., Wildt, D. E., Bush, M. E., Caro, T. M., Fitzgibbon, C., Aggunday, I. &Leakey, R. E. (1987a). East African cheetahs: evidence for two population bottlenecks? *Proceedings of the National Academy of Sciences, USA*, **84**, 508–11.

O'Brien, S. J., Collier, G. E., Benveniste, R. E., Nash, W. G., Newman, A. K., Simonson, J. M., Eichelberger, M. A., Seals, U. S., Bush, M. & Wildt, D. E. (1987b). Setting the molecular clock in Felidae: the great cats, *Panthera*. In *Tigers of the World: the Biology, Biopolitics, Management and Conservation of an Endangered Species*, ed. R. L. Tilson & U. S. Seal, pp. 10–27. Park Ridge: Noyes Publications.

O'Brien, S. J., Martenson, J. S., Packer, C., Herbst, L., de Vos, V., Joslin, P., Wildt, D. E. & Bush, M. (1987c). Biochemical genetic variation in geographic-isolates of African and Asiatic lions. *National Geographic Research*, **3**, 351–60.

Oakley, K. P. & Campbell, B. G. (1977). *Catalogue of Fossil Hominids* (Part I: Africa; Part II: Europe, with T. Molleson; Part III: Americas, Asia, Australia). 2nd edn. London: British Museum (Natural History).

Oakley, K. P. (1964). The problem of man's antiquity. An historical survey. *Bulletin of the British Museum (Natural History), Geology*, **9**(5), 83–155.

Ohno, S. (1970). *Evolution by Gene Duplication*. Berlin: Springer-Verlag.

Oliver, E. & Kitchen, H. (1968). Hemoglobins of adult *Macaca speciosa*: an amino acid interchange (alpha15gly → asp). *Biochemical and Biophysical Research Communications*, **31**, 749–54.

Olson, T. R. (1978). Hominid phylogenetics and the existence of *Homo* in Member 1 of the Swartkrans Formation, South Africa. *Journal of Human Evolution*, **7**, 159–78.

Olson, T. R. (1985a). Cranial morphology and systematics of the Hadar Formation, Ethiopia and its significance in early human evolution and taxonomy. In *Ancestors: the Hard Evidence*, ed. E. Delson, pp. 99–128. New York: Alan R. Liss.

Olson, T. R. (1985b). Taxonomic affinities of the immature hominid crania from Hadar and Taung. *Nature*, **316**, 539–40.

Omoto, K., Harada, S., Tanaka, T., Nigi, H. & Prychodko, W. (1970). Distribution of the electrophoretic variants of serum $alpha_1$–antitrypsin in six species of the macaques. *Primates*, **11**, 215–28.

Oppenheim, S. (1907). Die suturen des menschlichen Schädels in ihrer-anthropologischen Beeutung. *Correspondent Blatt der Anthropologische Gesellschaft*, **38**, 128–35.

Orban, R. (1988). Hominid remains, an up-date: Italy. *Bulletin de la Société Royale Belge d'Anthropologie et Préhistoire*, Supplement No. 1.

Ossenberg, N. S. (1970). The influence of artificial cranial deformation on discontinuous morphological traits. *American Journal of Physical Anthropology*, **33**, 357–72.

Owen, R. C. (1984). The Americas: the case against an Ice-Age human population. In *The Origins of Modern Humans*, ed. F. H. Smith & F. Spencer, pp. 517–63. New York: Alan R. Liss.

Owsley, D. W. (1991). Temporal variation in femoral cortical thickness of North American Plains Indians. In *Human Paleopathology: Current Synthese and Future Options*, ed. D. J. Ortner & A. C. Aaufderheide, pp. 105–10. Washington: Smithsonian Press.

Panganiban, G. (1997). *Proceedings of the National Academy of Sciences, USA*, **94**, 5162–6.

Paradis, J. G. (1978). *T. H. Huxley: Man's Place in Nature*. Lincoln: University of Nebraska Press.

Pares, J. M. & Perez-Gonzalez, A. (1995). Paleomagnetic age for hominid fossils at Atapuerca archaeological site, Spain. *Science*, **269**, 830–2.

Park, E. A. & Richter, C. P. (1953). Transverse lines in bone: the mechanism of their development. *Bulletin of the Johns Hopkins Hospital*, **93**, 364–88.

Partridge, T. (1978). Re-appraisal of lithostratigraphy of Sterkfontein hominid site. *Nature*, **275**, 282.

Partridge, T. (1986). Paleoecology of the Pliocene and lower Pleistocene hominids of southern Africa: how good is the chronological and paleoenvironmental evidence? *South African Journal of Science*, **82**, 80–3.

Patterson, B. & Howells, W. (1967). Hominid humeral fragment from early Pleistocene of northwestern Kenya. *Science*, **156**, 64–6.

Patterson, B., Behrensmeyer, A. & Sill, W. (1970). Geology and fauna of a new Pliocene locality in north-western Kenya. *Nature*, **226**, 918–21.

Patterson, C. (1981). Significance of fossils in determining evolutionary relationships. *Annual Review of Ecology and Systematics*, **12**, 195–223.

Pearson, K. (1894). Contributions to the mathematical theory of evolution. *Philosophical Transactions of the Royal Society, A*, **185**, 70–110.

Pease, C. N. (1962). Focal retardation and arrestment of bones due to vitamin A intoxication. *Journal of the American Medical Association*, **182**, 980–985.

Pease, M. (1933). *Eugenics Society Papers*. Eug./C. 209. London: Contemporary Medical Archives Centre, Wellcome Institute for the History of Medicine.

Pease, M. S. (1930). Review of *Das Prinzip geographischer Rassenkreise und das Problem der Artbildung* by Bernhard Rensch. *Eugenics Review*, **21**, 287–8.

Pelaez, F. (1982). Greeting movements among adult males in a colony of baboons: *Papio hamadryas, P. cynocephalus* and their hybrids. *Primates*, **23**, 233–44.

Pengelly, W. (1869). The literature of Kent's Cavern. *Transactions of the Devonshire Association* (Plymouth), **3**, 191–482.

Pennisi, E. (1996). Evolutionary and systematic biologists converge. *Science*, **273**, 181–2.

Pennock, D. S. & Dimmick, W. W. (1997). A critique of the evolutionarily significant unit as a defintion for 'distinct population segments' under the US Endangered Species Act. *Conservatism Biology* **11**, 611–19.

Pennycuick, C. J. (1995). *Newton Rules Biology*. New York: Oxford University Press.

Philips-Conroy, J. E., Jolly, C. J. & Brett, F. L. (1991). The characteristics of hamadryas-like male baboons living in anubis baboon troops in the Awash hybrid zone, Ethiopia. *American Journal of Physical Anthropology*, **86**, 353–68.

Pickford, M. (1988). The evolution of intelligence: a palaeontological perspective. In *Intelligence and Evolutionary Biology*, ed. H. J. Jerison & I. L. Jerison, pp. 175–98. New York: Springer-Verlag.

Pickford, M., Johanson, D., Lovejoy, C., White, T. & Aronson, J. (1983). A hominoid humeral fragment from the Pliocene of Kenya. *American Journal of Physical Anthropology*, **60**, 337–46.

Pilbeam, D. R. (1969). Tertiary Pongidae of East Africa: evolutionary relationships and taxonomy. *Peabody Museum Natural History Bulletin*, **31**, 1–185.

Pilbeam, D. R. (1982). New hominoid skull material from the Miocene of Pakistan. *Nature*, **295**, 232–4.

Pilbeam, D. R., Rose, M.D., Barry, J. C. & Ibrahim Shah, S. M. (1990). New *Sivapithecus* humeri from Pakistan and the relationship of *Sivapithecus* and *Pongo*. *Nature*, **348**, 237–9.

Pittendrigh, C. (1958). Adaptation, natural selection, and behavior. In *Behavior and Evolution*, ed. A. Roe & G. G. Simpson, pp. 390–416. New Haven: Yale University Press.

Platt, B. S. & Stewart, R. J. C. (1962). Transverse trabeculae and osteoporosis in bones in experimental protein-calorie deficiency. *British Journal of Nutrition*, **16**, 483–95.

Pocock, R. I. (1921). The systematic value of the glans penis in macaque monkeys. *Annals and Magazine of Natural History*, **9**, 224–9.

Pocock, R. I. (1925). The external characters of the catarrhine monkeys and apes. *Proceedings of the Zoological Society, London*, 1479–1579.

Pope, G. (1983). Evidence on the age of the Asian Hominidae. *Proceedings of the National Academy of Sciences, USA*, **80**, 4988–92.

Pope, G. (1988). Recent advances in Far Eastern paleoanthropology. *Annual Review of Anthropology*, **17**, 43–77.

Pope, G. (1997). Paleoanthropological research traditions in the Far East. In *Conceptual Issues in Human Origins Research*, ed. G. A. Clark & C. M.Willermet, pp. 269–82. New York: Aldine de Gruyter.

Pope, G. & Cronin, J. (1984). The Asian Hominidae. *Journal of Human Evolution*, **13**, 377–96.

Pope, G. & Keates, S. G. (1994). The evolution of human cognition and cultural capacity: a view from the Far East. In *Integrative Paths to the Past*, ed. R. S. Corrucini & R. L. Ciochon, pp. 531–67. Englewood Cliffs: Prentice-Hall.

Post, P. W., Szabo, G. & Keeling, M. E. (1975). A quantitative and morphological study of the pigmentary system of the chimpanzee with light and electron microscope. *American Journal of Physical Anthropology*, **43**, 393–408.

Prestwich, J. (1859). On the occurrence of flint-implements, associated with the remains of animals of extinct species in beds of a late geological period, in France at Amiens and Abbeville, and in England at Hoxne. *Proceedings Royal Society (London)*, **10**, 50–9.

Pritchard, D. J. (1986). *Foundations of Developmental Genetics*. London: Taylor & Francis.

Pritchard, D. J. (1995). Plasticity in early development. In *Human Variation and Plasticity*, ed. C. G. N. Mascie-Taylor & B. Bogin, pp. 18–45. Cambridge: Cambridge University Press.

Protsch, R. (1981a). The Kohl-Larsen Eyasi and Garusi hominid finds in Tanzania and their relation to *Homo erectus*. In *Homo Erectus: Papers in Honor of Davidson Black*, ed. B. A. Sigmon & J. S. Cybulsi, pp. 217–26. Toronto: University of Toronto Press.

Protsch, R. (1981b). *Die Archäologischen und Anthropologischen Ergebnisse der Kohl-Larsen-Expeditionen in Nord-Tanzania 1933–1939*. Tübingen: Verlag Archaeologica Venatoria, Institut für Urgeschichte der Universität Tübingen.

Protsch von Zieten, R. R. & Eckhardt, R. B. (1988). The Frankfurt *Pan troglodyter verus* collection: description and research agenda. *Laboratory*

Primate Newsletter, **27**, 13–15.

Provine, W. B. (1971). *The Origins of Theoretical Population Genetics*. Chicago: University of Chicago Press.

Prychodko, W., Goodman, M., Singal, B. M., Weiss, M. L., Ishimoto, G. & Tanaka, T. (1971). Starch-gel electrophoretic variants of erythrocyte 6–phosphogluconate dehydrogenase in Asian macaques. *Primates*, **12**, 175–82.

Puech, P.-F., Cianfarani, F. & Roth, H. (1986). Reconstruction of the maxillary dental arcade of Garusi Hominid 1. *Journal of Human Evolution*, **15**, 325–32.

Punett, R. C. (1915). *Mimicry in Butterflies*. Cambridge: Cambridge University Press.

Purvis, A. & Harvey, P. H. (1997). The right size for a mammal. *Nature*, **386**, 332–3.

Pycraft, W. P. (1925a). On the recognition of post-Mousterian man and the need for superseding the Frankfort base-line. *Man*, No. 105, 169–73.

Pycraft, W. P. (1925b). On the recognition of post-Mousterian man: and the need for superseding the Frankfort base-line. *Man*, No. 117, 189–94.

Quatrefages, A. de & Hamy, E. T. (1882). *Crania Ethnica: Les crânes des races humaines. I: Races humaines fossiles*. Paris: Baillière.

Quiatt, D. & Reynolds, V. (1993). *Primate Behaviour*. Cambridge: Cambridge University Press.

Quierroz, L. (1996). Loss of body hair, bipedality and thermoregulation. Comments on recent papers in the *Journal of Human Evolution*. *Journal of Human Evolution*, **30**, 357–66.

Radosevich, S. C., Retallack, G. J. & Taieb, M. (1992). Reassessment of the paleoenvironment and preservation of hominid fossils from Hadar, Ethiopia. *American Journal of Physical Anthropology*, **87**, 779–81.

Rak, Y. (1983). *The Australopithecine Face*. New York: Academic Press.

Rak, Y., Kimbel, W. H. & Hovers, E. (1994). A Neanderthal infant from Amud Cave, Israel. *Journal of Human Evolution* **26**, 313–24.

Ramström, M. (1921). Der Java-Trinil Fund. *Upsala Läkareförenings förhandlingar*, **26** (parts 5,6).

Rensch, B. (1929). *Das Prinzip geographischer Rassenkreise und das Problem der Artbildung*. Berlin: Bornträger.

Rightmire, G. P. (1981). Patterns in the evolution of *Homo erectus*. *Paleobiology*, 7, 241–6.

Rightmire, G. P. (1984). *Homo sapiens* in Sub-Saharan Africa. In *The Origins of Modern Humans*, ed. F. H. Smith & F. Spencer, pp. 295–325. New York: Alan R. Liss.

Rightmire, G. P. (1986). Species recognition and *Homo erectus*. *Journal of Human Evolution*, **15**, 823–6.

Rightmire, G. P. (1990). *The Evolution of* Homo erectus: *Comparative Anatomical Studies of an Extinct Human Species*. Cambridge: Cambridge University Press.

Rightmire, G. P. (1998). Evidence from facial morphology for similarity of Asian and African representatives of *Homo erectus*. *American Journal of Physical Anthropology*, **106**, 61–85.

Roberts, D. F. (1952). Basal metabolism, race, and climate. *Journal of the Royal Anthropological Institute*, **82**, 169–83.

Roberts, D. F. (1953). Body weight, race, and climate. *American Journal of Physical Anthropology*, **11**, 553–8.

Roberts, D. F. (1995). The pervasiveness of plasticity. In *Human Variability and Plasticity*, ed. C. G. N. Mascie-Taylor & B. Bogin, pp. 1–17. Cambridge: Cambridge University Press.

Roberts, D. F. (1977). Human pigmentation: its geographical and racial distribution and biological significance. *Journal of the Society for Cosmic Chemists*, **28**, 329–42.

Roberts, D. F. (1978). *Climate and Human Variability*, 2nd edn. Menlo Park: Cummings.

Roberts, M. B. (1994). How old is 'Boxgrove man'? *Nature*, **371**, 751.

Roberts, M. B., Stringer, C.B. & Parfitt, S. A. (1994). A hominid tibia from middle Pleistocene sediments at Boxgrove, UK. *Nature*, **369**, 311–13.

Robins, A. H. (1991). *Biological Perspectives on Human Pigmentation*. Cambridge. Cambridge University Press.

Robinson, J. T. (1954). The genera and species of the Australopithecinae. *American Journal of Physical Anthropology*, **12**, 181–9.

Robinson, J. T. (1956). *The Dentition of the Australopithecinae*. Pretoria: Transvaal Museum Memoir.

Robinson, J. T. (1960). The affinities of the new Olduvai australopithecine. *Nature*, **186**, 456–8.

Robinson, J. T. (1963). Adaptive radiation in the australopithecines and the origin of man. In *African Ecology and Human Evolution*, ed. F. C. Howell & F. Bourlière, pp. 385–416. Chicago: Aldine de Gruyter.

Rodahl, K. & Moore, T. (1943). The vitamin A content and toxicity of bear and seal liver. *Biochemical Journal*, **37**, 166–8.

Roebroeks, W. (1994). Updating the earliest occupation of Europe. *Current Anthropology*, **35**, 301–5.

Rose, M. D. (1994). Quadrupedalism in some Miocene catarrhines *Journal of Human Evolution*, **26**, 387–412.

Rowe, T. (1988). Definition, diagnosis, and origin of Mammalia. *Journal of Vertebrate Paleontology*, **8**, 241–64.

Rowe, T. (1991). Paleobiology: homage to Rudyard Kipling. *Systematic Zoology*, **40**, 244–5.

Rubinstein, S. L. (1983). Details: the source of power. *The Writer*, **96**, 15, 16 and 47.

Rudwick, M. J. S. (1985). *The Meaning of Fossils*. Chicago: University of Chicago Press.

Ruff, C. B. (1984). Allometry between length and cross-sectional dimensions of the femur and tibia in *Homo sapiens sapiens*. *American Journal of Physical Anthropology*, **65**, 347–58.

Ruff, C. B. (1988). Climate, body size and body shape in hominid evolution. *Journal of Human Evolution*, **21**, 81–105.

Ruff, C. B. (1991). Climate, body size and body shape in hominid evolution. *Journal of Human Evolution*, **21**, 81–105.

Ruff, C. B. (1994). Morphological adaptation to climate in modern and fossil hominids. *Yearbook of Physical Anthropology*, **37**, 65–107.

Ruff, C. B. & Hayes, W. C. (1982). Subperiosteal expansion and cortical remodeling of the human femur and tibia with aging. *Science*, **217**, 945–8.

Ruff, C. B. & Hayes, W. C. (1983). Cross-sectional geometry of Pecos Pueblo femora and tibiae – a biomechanical investigation: II. Sex, age, and size differences. *American Journal of Physical Anthropology*, **60**, 383–400.

Ruff, C. B. & Walker, A. (1993). Body size and body shape. In *The Nariokotome Homo erectus Skeleton*, ed. R. E. Leakey & A. Walker, pp. 234–63. Cambridge: Harvard University Press.

Ruff, C. B., Walker, A. & Teaford, M. F. (1989). *Journal of Human Evolution*, **18**, 515–36.

Rupke, N. A. (1983). *The Great Chain of History: William Buckland and the English School of Geology*. Oxford: Clarendon Press.

Ruse, M. D. (1994). Quadrupedalism in some Miocene catarrhines. *Journal of Human Evolution*, **26**, 387–412.

Ruvulo, M. E. (1988). Genetic evolution in the African guenons. In *A Primate Radiation: Evolutionary Biology of the African Guenons*, ed. A. Gautier-Hion, F. Bourlière, J.-P. Gautier & J. Kingdon, pp. 127–39. Cambridge: Cambridge University Press.

Ruvulo, M. (1997). Molecular phylogeny of the hominoids: inferences from multiple independent DNA sequence data sets. *Molecular Biology and Evolution*, **14**, 248–65.

Ruvulo, M., Disotell, T. R., Allard, M. W., Brown, W. & Honeycutt, R. L. (1991). Resolution of the African hominoid trichotomy by use of a mitochondrial gene sequence. *Proceedings of the National Academy of Sciences, USA*, **88**, 1570–74.

Samuels, A. & Altman, J. (1986). Immigration of a male *Papio anubis* into a troop of *Papio cynocephalus* baboons and evidence for an *anubis-cynocephalus* hybrid zone in Amboseli, Kenya. *International Journal of Primatology*, **7**, 131–3.

Sanders, W. J. & Bodenbender, B. E. Morphometric analysis of lumbar vertebra UMP 67–28: implications for spinal function and phylogeny of the Miocene Moroto hominoid. *Journal of Human Evolution*, **26**, 203–38.

Sarich, V. M. & Cronin, J. E. (1976). Molecular systematics of the Primates. In *Molecular Anthropology*, ed. M. Goodman & R. E. Taschian, pp. 141–70. New York: Plenum.

Sarich, V. M. & Wilson, A. C. (1967). Immunological time scale for human evolution. *Science*, **158**, 1200–3.

Schaaffhausen, H. (1858). Zur Kentnis der ältesten Rassenschädel. *Archiv der Anatomie und Physiologie*, **25**, 453–78.

Schaafsma, G., van Beresteyn, E. C. H., Raymakers, J. A. & Duursma, S. A. (1987). Nutritional aspects of osteoporosis. In *Nutrition and the Quality of Life*, ed. G. H. Bourne, pp. 121–59. World Review of Nutrition and Dietetics, No. 49, 121–59.

Scheffrahn, W., de Ruiter, J. R. & van Hooff, J. A. R. A. M. (1996). In *Evolution and Ecology of Macaque Societies*, ed. J. E. Fa & D. G. Lindburg, pp. 20–42. Cambridge: Cambridge University Press.

Schell, L. M. (1995). Human biological adaptability with special emphasis on plasticity: history, development and problems for future research. In *Human Variation and Plasticity*, ed. C. G. N. Mascie-Taylor & B. Bogin, pp. 213–37. Cambridge: Cambridge University Press.

Scheuchzer, J. J. (1709). *Herbarium Diluvianum*. Tiguri: Literis Davidis Gessneri.

Scheuchzer, J. J. (1726). *Homo Diluvii testis.* Tiguri: Burgklin.

Schick, K. D. (1994). The Movius line reconsidered. In *Integrative Paths to the Past,* ed. R. S. Corrucini & R. L. Ciochon, pp. 569–96. Englewood Cliffs, NJ: Prentice-Hall.

Schmager, J. (1972). Cytotaxonomy and geographical distribution of the Papinae. *Journal of Human Evolution,* **1,** 477–85.

Schmerling, P. C. (1833). *Recherches sur les ossements fossiles découvertes dans les cavernes de la province de Liège.* 2 vols. Liège: P-J. Collardin.

Schmidt-Nielson, K. (1984). *Scaling: Why is Animal Size so Important?* Cambridge: Cambridge University Press.

Schnider, B. (1990). The last Pleiniglacial in the Paris Basin (22,500–17,000 BP). In *The World at 18,000 BP: High Latitudes,* ed. O. Soffer & C. S. Gamble, pp. 41–53. London: Unwin Hyman.

Scholander, P. F. (1955). Evolution of climatic adaptation in homeotherms. *Evolution,* **9,** 15–26.

Scholander, P. F. (1956). Climatic rules. *Evolution,* **10,** 339–40.

Schour, I. (1936). The neonatal line in the enamel and dentine of the human deciduous teeth and the first permanent molar. *Journal of the American Dental Association,* **23,** 1946–55.

Schultz, A. H. (1924). Growth studies on primates bearing upon man's evolution. *American Journal of Physical Anthropology,* **7,** 149–64.

Schultz, A. H. (1956a). Postembryonic age changes. *Primatologia,* **1,** 887–964.

Schultz, A. H. (1956b). The occurrence and frequency of pathological and teratological conditions and of twinning among nonhuman primates. *Primatologia,* **1,** 965–1014. Basel: Karger.

Schwalbe, G. (1899). Studien über *Pithecanthropus erectus. Zeitschrift für Morphologie und Anthropologie,* **1,** 16–240.

Schwarcz, H. P. (1993). Uranium-series dating and the origin of modern man. In *The Origin of Modern Humans and the Impact of Chronometric Dating,* ed. M. J. Aitken, C. B. Stringer & P. A. Mellars, pp. 12–26. Princeton: Princeton University Press.

Schwartz, G. T. (2000). Taxonomic and functional aspects of enamel thickness distribution in extant large-bodied hominoids. *American Journal of Physical Anthropology,* **111,** 221–44.

Schwartz, J. H. (1983). Palastrine fenestrae, the orangutan and hominid evolution. *Primates,* **24,** 231–40.

Schwartz, J. H. (1984a). Hominid evolution: a review and a reassessment. *Current Anthropology,* **25,** 655–72.

Schwartz, J. H. (1984b). On the evolutionary relationships of man and orangutans. *Nature,* **308,** 501–5.

Schwartz, J. H. (1988). History, morphology, paleontology, and evolution. In *Orang-utan Biology,* ed. J. Schwartz, pp. 69–85. Oxford: Oxford University Press.

Schwartz, J. H. & Tattersall, I. (1996). Significance of some previously unrecognized apomorphies in the nasal region of *Homo neanderthalensis. Proceedings of the National Academy of Sciences, USA,* **93,** 10852–4.

Scott, G. R. & Turner, II, C. G. (1997). *The Anthropology of Modern Human Teeth: Dental Morphology and Its Variation in Recent Human Populations.*

Cambridge: Cambridge University Press.

Semaw, S., Renne, P., Harris, J. W. K., Feibel, C. S., Bernor, R. L., Fesseha, F. & Mowbray, K. (1997). 2.5-million-year-old stone tools from Gona, Ethiopia. *Nature*, **385**, 333–6.

Senut, B. & Tardieu, C. (1985). Functional aspects of the Plio-Pleistocene hominid limb bones: implications for taxonomy and phylogeny. In *Ancestors: The Hard Evidence*, ed. E. Delson, pp. 193–201. New York: Alan R. Liss.

Seymour, W. (1995). *Battles in Britain*. London: Sidgwick & Jackson.

Shapiro, H. S. (1939). *Migration and Environment*. New York: Oxford University Press.

Shea, B. T. (1981). Relative growth of the limbs and trunk in the African apes. *American Journal of Physical Anthropology*, **56**, 179–201.

Shea, B. T., Leigh, S. R., & Groves, C. P. (1993). Multivariate craniometric variation in chimpanzees. In *Species, Species Concepts, and Primate Evolution*, ed. W. H. Kimbel & L. W. Martin, pp. 265–96. New York: Plenum.

Shearman, D. J. C. (1978). Vitamin A and Sir Douglas Mawson. *British Medical Journal*, **1**, 283–5.

Sheldon, P. (1987). Parallel gradualistic evolution of Ordovician trilobites. *Nature*, **330**, 561–3.

Sillen, A. (1992). Strontium-calcium ratios (Sr/Ca) of *Australopithecus robustus* and associated fauna from Swartkrans. *Journal of Human Evolution*, **23**, 495–516.

Sillen, A., Hall, G. & Armstrong, R. (1995). Strontium/calcium ratios (Sr/Ca) and strontium isotopic ratios (^{87}Sr/^{86}Sr) of *Australopithecus robustus* and *Homo* sp. from Swartkrans. *Journal of Human Evolution*, **28**, 277–85.

Simpson, G. G. (1963). The meaning of taxonomic statements. In *Classification and Human Evolution*, ed. S. L. Washburn, pp. 1–31. Chicago: Aldine de Gruyter.

Skinner, M. (1991). Bee brood consumption: an alternative explanation for hypervitaminosis A in KNM-ER 1808 (*Homo erectus*) from Koobi Fora, Kenya. *Journal of Human Evolution*, **20**, 493–503.

Smith, F. H. (1984). Fossil hominids from the Upper Pleistocene of Central Europe and the origin of modern humans. In *The Origins of Modern Humans*, F. H. Smith & F. Spencer, pp. 137–210. New York: Alan R. Liss.

Smith, F. H. (1993). Models and realities in modern human origins. In *The Origin of Modern Humans and the Impact of Chronometric Dating*, ed. M. J. Aitken, C. B. Stringer & P. A. Mellars, pp. 234–48. Princeton: Princeton University Press.

Smith, F. H. & Spencer, F. (eds.) (1984). *The Origins of Modern Humans*. New York: Alan R. Liss.

Smith, R. W. & Walker, R. R. (1964). Femoral expansion in aging women: implications for osteoporosis and fractures, *Science*, **145**, 156–7.

Smith, G. E. (1925). The fossil anthropoid ape from Taung. *Nature*, **115**, 235.

Soleki, R. (1971). *Shanidar: The First Flower People*. New York: Knopf.

Soloway, R. A. (1990). *Demography and Degeneration*. Chapel Hill: University of North Carolina Press.

Soriano, M. (1970). The fluoric origin of the bone lesion in the *Pithecanthropus erectus* femur. *American Journal of Physical Anthropology*, **32**, 49–58.

Spencer, F. (1984). The neandertals and their evolutionary significance: a brief historical survey. In *The Origins of Modern Humans*, ed. F. H. Smith & F. Spencer, pp. 1–49. New York: Alan R. Liss.

Spillaert, R., Vikingsson, G., Arnason, U., Palsdottir, A., Sigurjonsson, J. & Arnason, A. (1991). Species hybridization between a female blue whale (*Balaenoptera musculus*) and a male fin whale (*B. physalus*): molecular and morphological documentation. *Journal of Heredity*, **82**, 269–274.

Spoor, C. F., Zonnefeld, F. & Wood, B. (1994). Early hominid labyrinthine morphology and its possible implications for the evolution of human bipedal locomotion. *Nature*, **369**, 645–8.

Spuhler, J. N. (1959). *The Evolution of Man's Capacity for Culture*. Ann Arbor: University of Michigan Press.

Stanley, S. M. (1975). A theory of evolution above the species level. *Proceedings of the National Academy of Sciences, USA*, **72**, 646–50.

Stanley, S. M. (1979). *Macroevolution: Pattern and Process*. San Francisco: W. H. Freeman.

Stanley, S. M. (1981). *The New Evolutionary Timetable*. New York: Basic Books.

Stanley, S. M. Macroevolution and the fossil record. *Evolution*, **36**, 460–73.

Stanyon, R. (1992). How polymorphisms and homoplasy can be informative about the evolution and phylogeny of humans and apes. In *Topics in Primatology*, vol. 1, ed. T. Nishida, W. C. McGrew, P. Marler, M. Pickford & F. B. M. de Waal, pp. 423–39. Tokyo: University of Tokyo Press.

Stanyon, R. & Chiarelli, B. (1991). Human origins: a brief summary of biomolecular and paleontological data. In *Symposium on the Evolution of Terrestrial Vertebrates*, ed. G. Ghiara *et al.*, pp. 371–84. Modena: Mucchi.

Stanyon, R., Fantini, A., Camperio-Ciani, A., Chiarelli, B. & Ardito, G. (1988). Banded karyotypes of 20 Papionini species reveal no necessary correlation with speciation. *American Journal of Primatology*, **16**, 3–17.

Stern, J. & Sussman, R. (1983). The locomotor anatomy of *Australopithecus afarensis*. *American Journal of Physical Anthropology*, **60**, 279–317.

Stevens, P. F. (1980). Evolutionary polarity of character states. *Annual Review of Ecology and Systematics*, **11**, 333–58.

Stewart, R. J. C. & Platt, B. S. (1958). Arrested growth lines in the bones of pigs on low-protein diets. *Proceedings of the Nutrition Society*, **17**, v–vi.

Stini, W. A. (1990). 'Osteoporosis': etiologies, prevention and treatment. *Yearbook of Physical Anthropology*, **33**, 151–94.

Stini, W. A. (1995). Osteoporosis in biocultural perspective. *Annual Review of Anthropology*, **24**, 397–421.

Stiassny, M. L. J. & Meyer, A. 1999. Cichlids of the Rift lakes. *Scientific American*, **280**, 64–9.

Stoneking, M. (1997). Recent African origin of human mitochondrial DNA: review of the evidence and current status of the hypothesis. In *Progress in Population Genetics and Human Evolution*, ed. P. Donnelly & S. Tavaré, pp. 1–13. New York: Springer Verlag.

Stringer, C. B. (1986). The credibility of *Homo habilis*. In *Major Topics in Primate and Human Evolution*, ed. B. Wood, L. Martin & P. Andrews, pp. 266–94. Cambridge: Cambridge University Press.

Stringer, C. B. (1993). Current issues in modern human origins. In *Contemporary Issues in Human Evolution*, ed. W. E. Meikle, F. C. Howell & N. G. Jablonski, pp. 116–34. Memoir 21. San Francisco: California Academy of Sciences.

Stringer, C. B. (1993). Reconstructing recent human evolution. In *The Origin of Modern Humans and the Impact of Chronometric Dating*, ed. M. J. Aitken, C. B. Stringer & P. A. Mellars, pp. 179–95. Princeton: Princeton University Press.

Stringer, C. B. & Andrews, P. (1988). Genetic and fossil evidence for the origin of modern humans. *Science*, **239**, 1263–8.

Stringer, C. B. & Gamble, C. (1993). *In Search of the Neanderthals*. London: Thames and Hudson.

Stringer, C. B. & Grün, R. (1991). Time for the last Neanderthals. *Nature*, **351**, 701–2.

Stringer, C. B., Hublin, J. J. & Vandermeersch, B. (1984). The origin of anatomically modern humans in Western Europe. In *The Origins of Modern Humans*, ed. F. H. Smith & F. Spencer, pp. 51–135. New York: Alan R. Liss.

Struhsaker, T. T. (1967). Auditory communication in vervet monkeys. In *Social Communications Among Primates*, ed. S. A. Altmann, pp. 281–324. Chicago: University of Chicago Press.

Strydom, N. B. & Wyndham, C. H. (1963). Natural state of heat acclimatization of different ethnic groups. *Federation Proceedings*, **22**, 801–9.

Sturtevant, A. H. (1918). *An Analysis of the Effects of Selection*. Carnegie Institution of Washington, Publication No. 264. Washington, DC: Carnegie Institution.

Sugawara, K. (1979). Sociological study of a wild group of hybrid baboons between *Papio anubis* and *Papio hamadryas* in the Awash Valley, Ethiopia. *Primates*, **20**, 21–56.

Susman, R. (1988). Hand of *Paranthropus robustus* from Member 1, Swartkrans: fossil evidence for tool behavior. *Science*, **240**, 781–4.

Susman, R. (1989). New hominid fossils from the Swartkrans Formation (1979–1986 Excavations): postcranial specimens. *American Journal of Physical Anthropology*, **79**, 451–74.

Susman, R. (1993). Hominid postcranial remains from Swartkrans. In *Swartkrans: A Cave's Chronicle of Early Man*, ed. C. K. Brain, pp. 117–36. Pretoria: Transvaal Museum.

Susman, R. & Brain, T. (1988). New first metatarsal (SKX5017) from Swartkrans and the gait of *Paranthropus robustus*. *American Journal of Physical Anthropology*, **77**, 7–15.

Susman, R. L. & Stern, J. T., Jr. (1982). Functional morphology of *Homo habilis*. *Science*, **217**, 931–4.

Susman, R., Stern, J. & Jungers, W. (1994). Arboreality and bipedality in the Hadar hominids. *Folia Primatologica*, **43**, 113–56.

Sutton, W. S. (1903). The chromosomes in heredity. *Biological Bulletin*, **4**, 231–51.

Suwa, G. (1988). Evolution of the 'robust' australopithecines in the Omo succession: evidence from mandibular premolar morphology. In *Evolutionary History of the 'Robust' Australopithecines*, ed. F. E. Grine, pp. 199–222. New York: Aldine de Gruyter.

Swisher, C. C., Curtis, G. H., Jacob, T., Getty, A. G. & Widlasmoro, A. Suprijo (1994). Age of the earliest known hominids in Java, Indonesia. *Science*, **263**, 1118–21.

Takahata, N. (1990). A simple genealogical structure of strongly balanced allelic lines and trans-specific evolution of polymorphism. *Proceedings of the National Academy of Sciences, USA*, **87**, 2419–23.

Takahata, N., Satta, Y. & Klein, J. (1988). In *Progress in Immunology*, vol. VIII, ed. J. Gergely, pp. 153–8. Berlin: Springer Verlag.

Tanner, J. M., Hayashi, T., Preece, M.A. & Cameron, N. (1982). Increase in length of leg relative to trunk in Japanese children and adults from 1957 to 1977: Comparison with British and with Japanese Americans. *Annals of Human Biology*, **9**, 411–23.

Tanner, J. M., Wilson, M. E. & Rudman, C. G. (1990). Pubertal growth spurt in the female rhesus monkey: relation to menarche and skeletal maturation. *American Journal of Human Biology*, **2**, 101–6.

Tashian, R. E., Goodman, M., Headings, V. E., DeSimone, J. & Ward, R. H. (1971). Genetic variation and evolution in the red cell carbonic anhydrase isozymes of macaque monkeys. *Biochemical Genetics*, **5**, 183–200.

Tattersall, I. (1986). Species recognition in human paleontology. *Journal of Human Evolution*, **15**, 165–75.

Tattersall, I. (1989a). Commentaries. In *Evolutionary Biology at the Crossroads*, ed. M. K. Hecht, pp. 139–41. Flushing: Queens College Press.

Tattersall, I. (1989b). The roles of ecological and behavioral observation in species recognition among primates. *Human Evolution*, **4**, 117–24.

Tattersall, I. (1990). What was the human revolution? *Journal of Human Evolution*, **19**, 77–83.

Tattersall, I. (1992). Species concepts and species identification in human evolution. *Journal of Human Evolution*, **22**, 341–9.

Tattersall, I. (1993). *The Human Odyssey: Four Million Years of Human Evolution*. New York: Prentice Hall.

Tattersall, I. (1995). *The Fossil Trail: How We Know What We Think We Know About Human Evolution*. New York: Oxford University Press.

Tattersall, I. (1998). *Becoming Human: Evolution and Human Uniqueness*. New York: Harcourt and Brace.

Tattersall, I., Delson, E. & Van Couvering, J. (1988). *Encyclopedia of Human Evolution and Prehistory*. Chicago: St. James Press.

Teaford, M. F. (1991). Dental microwear: what can it tell us about diet and dental function? In *Advances in Dental Anthropology*, ed. M. A. Kelly & C. S. Larsen, pp. 342–56. New York: Wiley-Liss.

Teaford, M. F. & Lytle, J. D. (1996). Diet-induced changes in rates of human tooth microwear: as case study involving stone-ground maize. *American Journal of Physical Anthropology*, **100**, 143–7.

Teleki, G. (1973). The omnivorous chimpanzee. *Scientific American*, **228**, 32–42.

Templeton, A. R. (1992). Genetic architecture of speciation. In *Mechanisms of Speciation*, ed. C. Barigozzi, pp. 105–21. New York: Alan R. Liss.

Templeton, A. R. (1993). The 'Eve' hypothesis: a genetic critique and reanalysis. *American Anthropologist*, **95**, 51–72.

Templeton, A. R. (1998). Human races: a genetic and evolutionary perspective. *American Anthropologist*, **100**, 632–50.

Thackeray, J. (1995). Do strontium/calcium ratios in early Pleistocene hominids from Swartkrans reflect physiological differences in males and females? *Journal of Human Evolution*, **29**, 401–4.

Thenius, E. (1953). Zur Analyse des Gebisses des Eisbären, *Ursus (Thalarctos) maritimus* Phipps, 1774. *Säugertierkundliche Mitteilungen*, **1**, 1–7.

Thieme, H. (1997). Lower Paleolithic hunting spears from Germany. *Nature*, **385**, 807–10.

Thoday, J. M. (1965). Geneticism and environmentalism. In *Biological Aspects of Social Problems*, ed. J. E. Meade & A. S. Parkes, pp. 92–108. Edinburgh: Oliver and Boyd.

Thoma, A. (1958). Métissage ou Transformation? Essai sur les hommes fossiles de Palestine. *L'Anthropologie*, **61**, 469–502.

Tobias, P. V. (1967). *Olduvai Gorge*, vol. 2. *The Cranium and Maxillary Dentition of* Australopithecus (Zinjanthropus) boisei. Cambridge: Cambridge University Press.

Tobias, P. V. (1971). *The Brain in Hominid Evolution*. New York: Columbia University Press.

Tobias, P. V. (1973). Implications of the new age estimates of the early South African hominids. *Nature*, **246**, 79–83.

Tobias, P. V. (1985a). The former Taung cave system in the light of contemporary reports and its bearing on the skull's provenance: early deterrents to the acceptance of *Australopithecus*. In *Hominid Evolution: Past, Present and Future*, ed. P. V. Tobias, pp. 25–40. New York: Alan R. Liss.

Tobias, P. V. (1985b). Single characters and the total morphological pattern redefined: the sorting effected by a selection of morphological features of early hominids. In *Ancestors: The Hard Evidence*, ed. E. Delson, pp. 94–101. New York: Alan R. Liss.

Tobias, P. V. (1991). *The Skulls, Endocasts and Teeth of* Homo habilis. *Olduvai Gorge*, vol. 4. Cambridge: Cambridge University Press.

Tobias, P. V. & Baker, B. (1994). Palaeo-anthropology in South Africa. *South African Journal of Science*, **90**, 203–4.

Tobias, P. V. & Falk, D. (1988). Evidence for a dual pattern of cranial venous sinuses on the endocranial cast of Taung (*Australopithecus africanus*). *American Journal of Physical Anthropology*, **76**, 309–12.

Tobias, P. V. & von Koenigswald, G. H. R. (1964). Comparison between the Olduvai hominines and those of Java and some implications for hominid-phylogeny. *Nature*, **204**, 515–8.

Tompkins, R. L. (1996). Relative dental development of Upper Pleistocene hominids compared to human population variation. *American Journal of Physical Anthropology*, **99**, 103–18.

Trinkaus, E. (1975). Squatting among the Neanderthals: a problem in the behavioral interpretation of skeletal morphology. *Journal of Archaeological Science*, **2**, 327–51.

Trinkaus, E. (ed.) (1989). *The Emergence of Modern Humans: Biocultural Adaptations in the Later Pleistocene*. Cambridge: Cambridge University Press.

Trinkaus, E. (1981). Neanderthal limb proportions and cold adaptation. In *Aspects of Human Evolution*, ed. C. B. Stringer, pp. 187–224. London: Taylor and Francis.

Trinkaus, E. (1983). *The Shanidar Neandertals*. New York: Academic Press.

Trinkaus, E. (1984). Western Asia. In *The Origins of Modern Humans*, ed. F. H. Smith & F. Spencer, pp. 251–93. New York: Alan R. Liss.

Trinkaus, E. & Shipman, P. (1993). *The Neanderthals: Solving the Puzzle of Human Origins*. London: Thames and Hudson.

Turleau, C., de Grouchy, J., Chavin-Colin, F., Mortelmans, J. & van den Bergh, W. (1975). Inversion péricentrique du 3, homozygote héterozygote, et translation centromérique du 12 dans une famille d'orangs-outangs. Implications évolutives. *Annals of Genetics*, **18**, 227–33.

Turner, W. (1864a). On human crania allied in anatomical characters to the Engis and Neanderthal skulls. *Quarterly Journal of Science*, **2**, 250–8.

Turner, W. (1864b). Additional notes on the Neanderthal skull. *Quarterly Journal of Science*, **2**, 758–62.

Turner, C. G., II, Nichol, C. R. & Scott, G. R. (1991). Scoring procedures for key morphological traits of the permanent dentition: The Arizona State University Dental Anthropology System. In *Advances in Dental Anthropology*, ed. M. A. Kelley & C. S. Larsen, pp. 13–31. New York: Wiley-Liss.

Tuttle, R. (1981). Evolution of hominid bipedalism and prehensile capabilities. *Philosophical Transactions of the Royal Society of London (Biology)*, **292**, 89–94.

Tuttle, R. (1985). Ape footprints and Laetoli impressions: a response to the SUNY claims. In *Hominid Evolution: Past, Present and Future*, ed. P. V. Tobias, pp. 129–34. New York: Alan R. Liss.

Tuttle, R. (1987). Kinesiological inferences and evolutionary implications from Laetoli bipedal trails G-1, G-2/3 and A. In *Laetoli, a Pliocene Site in Northern Tanzania*, ed. J. M. Harris & M. D. Leakey, pp. 503–23. Oxford: Clarendon Press.

Tuttle, R., Webb, D. & Tuttle, N. (1991). Laetoli footprint trails and the evolution of hominid bipedalism. In *Origine(s) de la bipédie chez les hominides*, ed. Y. Coppens & B. Senut, pp. 187–98. Paris: CNRS.

Ubelaker, D. H. (1979). Skeletal evidence for kneeling in prehistoric Ecuador. *American Journal of Physical Anthropology*, **51**, 679–86.

Valéry, P. (1895). *Introduction à la méthode de Léonard de Vinci*. Paris: Libraire de la Nouvelle revue.

van Herwerden, M. A. (1925). 'Species' and 'Variety.' *Eugenics Review*, **17**, 49–50.

Vigilant, L. M., Stoneking, M., Harpending, H., Hawkes, K. & Wilson, A. C. (1991). African populations and the evolution of human mitochondrial DNA. *Science*, **253**, 1503–7.

Vondra, C. F., Johnson, G. D., Bower, B. E. & Behrensmeyer, A. K. (1971). Preliminary stratigraphical studies of the East Rudolf Basin, Kenya. *Nature*, **231**, 245–8.

Vrba, E. (1981). The Kromdraai australopithecine site revisited in 1980: recent investigation and results. *Annals of the Transvaal Museum*, **33**, 17–60.

Vrba, E. (1985). Ecological and adaptive changes associated with early hominid evolution. In *Ancestors: The Hard Evidence*, ed. E. Delson, pp. 63–71. New York: Alan R. Liss.

Waddington, C. H. (1942). Canalization of development and the inheritance of acquired characters. *Nature*, **150**, 563–5.

Waddington, C. H. (1953a). Genetic assimilation of an acquired character. *Evolution*, **7**, 118–26.

Waddington, C. H. (1953b). The 'Baldwin effect,' genetic assimilation' and 'homeostasis.' *Evolution*, **7**, 386–7.

Waddington, C. H. (1957). *The Strategy of the Genes*. London: Allen and Unwin.

Waddington, C. H. (1966). *Principles of Development and Differentiation*. New York: Macmillan.

Wade, P. T., Skinner, A. F., Barnicot, N. A. & Huehns, E. R. (1970). Duplication of the hemoglobin alpha-chain locus in *Macaca irus*. In *Protides of the Biological Fluids, Proceedings of the 17th Colloquium, Bruges, 1989*, ed. H. Peeters. New York: Pergamon.

Walcher, G. (1905). Ueber die Einstehung von Brachy- und Dolichocephalie durch willkürliche Beeinflussung des kindlichen Schädels. *Zentralblatt für Gynäkologie*, **29**, 193–6.

Walcher, G. (1911). Weitere Erfahrung in der willkürlichen Beeinflussung der Form des kindlichen Schädels. *Muenchener Medizinische Wochenschrift*, **3**, 134–7.

Walker, A. & Leakey, R., eds. (1993). *The Nariokotome* Homo erectus *Skeleton*. Cambridge: Harvard University Press.

Walker, A., Zimmerman, M. R. & Leakey, R. E. F. (1982). A possible case of hypervitaminosis A in *Homo erectus*. *Nature*, **296**, 248–50.

Walter, R. C. (1994). Age of Lucy and the first family: single-crystal 40Ar/39/Ar dating on the Denen Dora and lower Kada Hadar Members of the Hadar Formation, Ethiopia. *Geology*, **22**, 6–10.

Walter, R. C. & Aronson, J. L. (1993). Age and source of the Sidi Hakoma Tuff, Hadar Formation, Ethiopia. *Journal of Human Evolution*, **25**, 229–40.

Walimbe, S. R. & Gambhir, P. B. (1994). *Long Bone Growth in Infants and Children: Assessment of Nutritional Status. Monograph Series on Biological Anthropology, II*. Mangalore: Mujumdar Publications.

Walter, R. C., Manega, P. C., Hay, R. L., Drake, R. E. & Curtis, G. H. (1991). Laser-fusion 40Ar/39Ar dating of Bed I, Olduvai Gorge, Tanzania. *Nature*, **354**, 145–9.

Wanpo, H., Ciochon, R., Yunnin, G., Larick, R., Qiren, F., Schwarcz, H., Yonge, C., deVos, J. & Rink, W. (1995). Early *Homo* and associated artifacts from Asia. *Nature*, **378**, 275–8.

Ward, C. V., Walker, A., Teaford, M. F. & Odhiambo, I. (1993). Partial skeleton of *Proconsul africanus* from Mfangano Island, Kenya. *American Journal of Physical Anthropology*, **90**, 77–111.

Ward, R. & Stringer, C. (1997). A molecular handle on the neanderthals. *Nature*, **388**, 225–6.

Ward, S. & Hill, A. (1987). Pliocene hominid partial mandible from Tabarin, Baringo, Kenya. *American Journal of Physical Anthropology*, **72**, 21–38.

Washburn, S. L. (1951). The new physical anthropology. *Transactions of the New York Academy of Sciences*, **13**, 298–304.

Watson, R. C. (1973). Bone growth and physical activity in young males. In *International Conference on Bone Mineral Measurement*, ed., R. B. Mazess, pp. 380–6. US Department of Health, Education & Welfare Publication Number (NIH) 75–683. Washington, DC: US Government Printing Office.

Watts, E. S. (1986). Skeletal development. In *Comparative Primate Biology*, vol. 3, ed. W. R. Dukelow & J. Erwin, pp. 415–39. New York: Alan R. Liss.

Watts, E. S. & Gavan, J. A. (1982). Postnatal growth of nonhuman primates: the problem of the adolescent spurt. *Human Biology*, **54**, 53–70.

Wayne, R. K., Van Valkenburgh, B. & O'Brien, S. J. (1991). Molecular distance and divergence time in carnivores and primates. *Molecular Biology and Evolution*, **8**, 297–329.

Wegner, G. (1874). Ueber das normale und pathologische Wachstum der Röhrenknocken. Eine kritische Untersuchung auf experimenteller und casuisticher Grundlage. *Archiv für pathologische Anatomie und Physiologie und für klinische Medicin*, **61**, 44–76.

Weidenreich, F. (1936). Sinanthropus pekinensis and its position in the line of human evolution. *Peking Natural History Bulletin*, **10**, 281–90.

Weidenreich, F. (1937). The dentition of *Sinanthropus pekinensis*: a comparative odontography of the hominids. *Palaeontologia Sinica*, new series D, **I**, 1–180,plates 1–121.

Weidenreich, F. (1938). The classification of fossil hominids and their relations to each other with special reference to *Sinanthropus pekinensis*. *Congrès international des Sciences anthropologiques et ethnologiques, 2ième Session, Copenhague 1938. Bulletin of the Geological Society of China*, **19**, 107–10.

Weidenreich, F. (1947). The trend of human evolution. *Evolution*, **1**, 221–36.

Weinberg, W. (1908). Ueber den Nachreis der Vererbung beim Menschen. *Jahreshefte des Vereins für Vaterländische Naturkunde in Württemburg*, **64**, 368–82.

Weinberg, W. (1909a). Ueber Vererbungsgesetze beim Menschen. 1. Allgemeiner Teil. *Zeitschrift für Induktive Abstammungs- und Vererbungslehre*, **1**, 377–92; 440–60.

Weinberg, W. (1909b). Ueber Vererbungsgesetze beim Menschen. 2. Spezieller Teil. *Zeitschrift für Induktive Abstammungs- und Vererbungslehre*, **2**, 276–330.

Weinberg, W. (1910). Weitere Beiträge zur Theorie der Vererbung. *Archiv für Rassen- und Gesellschafts-Biologie*, **7**, 35–49, 169–73.

Weiner, A. S. & Moor-Jankowski, J. (1971). Blood groups of non-human primates and their relationship to the blood groups of man. In *Comparative Genetics in Monkeys, Apes and Man*, ed. A. B. Chiarelli, pp. 71–95. London: Academic Press.

Weiner, J. S. (1954). Nose shape and climate. *American Journal of Physical Anthropology*, **12**, 1–4.

Weiss, M. L. & Goodman, M. (1972). Frequency and maintenance of genetic-variability in natural populations of *Macaca fascicularis*. *Journal of Human Evolution*, **1**, 41–8.

Weiss, M. L., Goodman, M., Prychodko, W., Moore, G. W. & Tanaka, T. (1972). An analysis of macaque systematics using gene frequency data. *Journal of Human Evolution*, **2**, 213–26.

Weiss, M. L., Goodman, M., Pryodchko, W. & Tanaka, T. (1971). Species and geographic distribution patterns of the macaque prealbumin polymorphism. *Primates*, **1**, 75–80.

Wheeler, P. E. (1996). The environmental context of functional hair loss in hominids (a reply to Amaral, 1996). *Journal of Human Evolution*, **30**, 357–66.

White, T. D. (1981). Primitive hominid canine from Tanzania. *Science*, **213**, 348–9.

White, T. D. (1986). *Australopithecus afarensis* and the Lothagam mandible. *Anthropos*, **23**, 79–90.

White, T. D. (1988). The comparative biology of 'robust' australopithecines: clues from context. In *Evolutionary History of the 'Robust' Australopithecines*, ed. F. E. Grine, pp. 449–84. New York: Aldine de Gruyter.

White, T. D., Johanson, D. & Kimbel, W. (1981). *Australopithecus africanus*: its phyletic position reconsidered. *South African Journal of Science*, **77**, 445–70.

White, T. D. & Suwa, G. (1987). Hominid footprints at Laetoli: facts and interpretations. *American Journal of Physical Anthropology*, **72**, 485–514.

White, T. D., Suwa, G. & Asfaw, B. (1994). *Australopithecus ramidus*, a new species of early hominid from Aramis, Ethiopia. *Nature*, **371**, 306–12.

White, T. D., Suwa, G. & Asfaw, B. (1995). Corrigendum: *Australopithecus ramidus*, a new species of early hominid from Aramis, Ethiopia. *Nature*, **375**, 88.

Whiten, A., Goodall, J., McGrew, W. C., Nishida, T., Wrangham, R. W. & Boesch, C. (1999). Cultures in chimpanzees. *Nature*, **399**, 682–5.

Whiten, A. & Ham, R. (1992). On the nature of imitation in the animal kingdom: reappraisal of a century of research. *Advances in the Study of Behavior*, **21**, 239–83.

Whittaker, D. K. & Richards, D. (1978). Scanning electron microscopy of the neonatal line in human enamel. *Archives of Oral Biology*, **23**, 45–50.

Wiley, E. O. (1981). *Phylogenetics: The Theory and Practice of Phylogenetic Systematics*. New York: John Wiley and Sons.

Wilkins, A. S. (1986). *Genetic Analysis of Animal Development*. New York: John Wiley and Sons.

Willermet, C. M. & Clark, G. A. (1995). Paradigm crisis in modern human origins research. *Journal of Human Evolution*, **29**, 487–90.

Williams, B. J. (1973). *Evolution and Human Origins*. New York: Harper and Row.

Williams, L. E. (1983). Sociality among captive hybrid macaques. *Behavioural Processes*, **8**, 177–87.

Williamson, P. (1985). Evidence for Plio-Pleistocene rainforest expansion in east Africa. *Nature*, **315**, 487–9.

Winter, F. L. (1929) Continuous selection for composition in corn. *Journal of Agricultural Research*, **39**, 451–75.

Wilson, A. C., Sarich, V. & Maxson, L. R. (1974). The importance of gene rearrangement in evolution: evidence from studies on rates of chromosomal, protein, and anatomic evolution. *Proceedings of the National Academy of Sciences, USA*, **71**, 3028–30.

WoldeGabriel, G., White, T. D., Suwa, G., Renne, P., de Heinzelin, J., Hart, W. K. & Heiken, G. (1994). Ecological and temporal placement of early Pliocene hominids at Aramis, Ethiopia. *Nature*, **371**, 330–3.

Wolfe, L. (1981). The reproductive history of a hybrid female. *Primates*, **22**, 131–4.

Wolff, J. (1892). *The Law of Bone Remodelling*. (Translation by P. Maquet & R. Furlong.) Berlin: Springer Verlag.

Wolpoff, M. H. (1971). *Metric Trends in Hominid Dental Evolution*. Cleveland: Case Western University Press.

Wolpoff, M. H. (1978). Analogies and interpretations in paleoanthropology. In *Early Hominids of Africa*, ed. C. Jolly, pp. 461–503. New York: St. Martin's Press.

Wolpoff, M. H. (1983). Lucy's little legs. *Journal of Human Evolution*, **12**, 443–53.

Wolpoff, M. H. (1984). Evolution in *Homo erectus*: the question of stasis. *Paleobiology*, **10**, 389–406.

Wolpoff, M. H. & Caspari, R. (1997). What does it mean to be modern? In *Conceptual Issues in Modern Human Origins Research*, ed. G. A. Clark & C.M. Willermet, pp. 11–27. New York: Aldine de Gruyter.

Wolpoff, M. H., Thorne, A. G., Jelinek, J. & Yinyun, Z. (1994). The case for sinking *Homo erectus*: 100 years of *Pithecanthropus* is enough! *Courier Forschungs-Institut Senckenberg*, **171**, 341–61.

Wolpoff, M., Thorne, A. G., Smith, F. H, Frayer, D. W. & Pope, G. G. (1994). Multiregional evolution: a world-wide source for modern human populations. In *Origins of Anatomically Modern Humans*, ed. M. Nitecki & D. Nitecki, pp. 175–99. New York: Plenum.

Wolpoff, M., Zhi, W. X. & Thorne, A. G. (1984). Modern *Homo sapiens* origins: a general theory of hominid evolution involving the fossil evidence from East Asia. In *The Origins of Modern Humans*, ed. F. H. Smith & F. Spencer, pp. 441–83. New York: Alan R. Liss.

Woo, J. K. (1964). Mandible of *Sinanthropus lantianensis*. *Current Anthropology*, **5**, 98–101.

Woo, J. K. (1966). The skull of Lantian man. *Current Anthropology*, **7**, 83–6.

Wood, B. (1987). Who is the 'real' *Homo habilis*? *Nature*, **327**, 187–8.

Wood, B. (1992). Early hominid species and speciation. *Journal of Human Evolution*, **22**, 351–65.

Wood, B. (1993). Early *Homo*: how many species? In *Species, Species Concepts, and Primate Evolution*, ed. W. H. Kimbel & L. B. Martin, pp. 485–522. New York: Plenum.

Wood, B. (1994). The oldest hominid yet. *Nature*, **371**, 280–1.

Wood, B. (1996). Hominid paleobiology: have studies of comparative development come of age? *American Journal of Physical Anthropology*, **99**, 9–15.

Wood, B. & Chamberlain, A. T. (1986). *Australopithecus*: grade or clade? In *Major Topics in Primate and Human Evolution*, ed. B. Wood, L. Martin & P. Andrews, pp. 220–48. Cambridge: Cambridge University Press.

Wood, B. & Collard, M. (1999). The human genus. *Science*, **284**, 65–71.

Wood, B., Wood, C. & Konigsberg, L. (1994). *Paranthropus boisei*: an example of evolutionary stasis? *American Journal of Physical Anthropology*, **95**, 117–36.

Woodward, A. S. (1925). The fossil anthropoid ape from Taungs. *Nature*, **115**, 235.

Wrangham, R. (1975). The behavioural ecology of chimpanzees in Gombe National Park, Tanzania. Ph.D. Dissertation, Cambridge University.

Wright, S. (1931). Evolution in Mendelian populations. *Genetics*, **16**, 97–159.

Wright, S. (1930). The genetical theory of natural selection. A review. *Journal of Heredity*, **21**, 349–56.

Xu, X. & Arnason, U. (1996). A complete sequence of the mitochondrial genome of the western lowland gorilla. *Molecular Biology and Evolution*, **13**, 691–8.

Ya-Ping, Z. & Li-Ming, S. (1993). Phylogenetic relationships of macaques as inferred from restriction endonuclease analysis of mitochondrial DNA. *Folia Primatologica*, **60**, 7–17.

Zischler, H., Geisert, H., von Haeseler, A. & Pääbo, S. (1995). A nuclear 'fossil' of the mitochondrial D-loop and the origin of modern humans. *Nature*, **378**, 489–92.

Zollikofer, C. P. E., Ponce de Leon, M.S., Martin, R. D. & Stucki, P. (1995). Neanderthal computer skulls. *Nature*, **375**, 283–5.

Zubrow, E. (1989). The demographic modelling of Neanderthal extinction. In *The Human Revolution*, ed. P. Mellars & C. Stringer, pp. 212–31. Edinburgh: Edinburgh University Press.

Zuckerman, S. (1933). *Sinanthropus* and other fossil men. *The Eugenics Review*, **24**, 273–84.

Zullo, S., Sieu, L. L., Slighton, J. L., Hadler, H. I. & Eisenstadt, J. (1991). mtDNA insertions into nuclear genome. *Journal of Molecular Biology*, **221**, 1223–35.

Index